W9-AQF-191

George T. Wolf

St. Charles College

January 22, 1947

HUMAN HISTORY

Human History

By G. ELLIOT SMITH

M.A., M.D., Litt.D., D.Sc., F.R.S.

University of London

NEW YORK

W·W·NORTON & COMPANY, INC.

PUBLISHERS

PRINTED IN THE UNITED STATES OF AMERICA
FOR THE PUBLISHERS BY THE VAIL-BALLOU PRESS

Dedicated

TO

WILLIAM JAMES PERRY

AS A TRIBUTE OF ADMIRATION OF HIS
VISION AND COURAGE

ACKNOWLEDGMENTS

In addition to expressing his indebtedness to Dr. W. J. Perry for much of the information and many of the leading ideas in this book, the writer also has to acknowledge valuable help of various kinds from many others; in particular, Mrs. John Rogers, Jr., of New York, and Professor S. H. Hooke, for reading the proofs; Miss Nina W. Davis and Mr. L. T. Morton for preparing the manuscript; Miss Dorothy Davison, Mr. A. K. Maxwell, and Mr. F. Melville for illustrations; and Mr. D. C. Crawford for collecting data relating to Hellenic culture. He begs to thank the Cambridge University Press, the Oxford University Press, and Messrs. Methuen & Co. for permission to borrow illustrations from books published by them.

TABLE OF CONTENTS

viii   TABLE OF CONTENTS

LIST OF ILLUSTRATIONS

PREFACE

By discovering a New World, Christopher Columbus compelled European statesmen and philosophers to think of mankind in terms of the world as a whole. Many attempts have been made during the last four centuries to give expression to this idea in a universal history of mankind.

From the time of the Renaissance of learning, however, there has been a tendency to distinguish between, or perhaps it would be more accurate to say a reluctance to assimilate, the Study of Man and the Study of Nature. The latter used to be called Natural Philosophy and Natural History, now known collectively as Science, in contradistinction to the Humanities, which treat of the history of Man and his activities in thought and action. The various attempts that have been made in the past to merge these two departments of knowledge into a unified discipline—what has been called a science of history—have failed to attain complete success. From the time of Descartes it has been assumed that the principle of the scientific method was to define "laws of nature," and attempts have been made to draw mankind, with all its lawless disregard of rules and regulations, into the ambit of this misleading generalisation. Amidst the conflict between these two opposing tendencies, both highly charged with potential sources of error, a clear vision of the wider Humanity has in large measure escaped both schools of philosophers. Hence there is the need for a new synthesis.

The student of mankind working in the frontier that separates—unfortunately the word is the appropriate one—Natural History from the Humanities is made to realise how the subject of his studies suffers from the conflicting allegiance. It would be a great gain if the benefits of the two disciplines could be merged in a Greater Humanity, which might be called Human History, Adequate recognition might be given to the biological implications of the fact that Man is a living creature as well as to the consideration that he differs profoundly from all other living creatures in being human, and as such swayed by the influence of his own ex-

xiii

perience, which is personal and individual, even though it is
shaped largely by the traditions of his community. For the two
influences profoundly affect the expression of Man's distinctively
human qualities. The animal appetites and instincts that demand
satisfaction are in some measure controlled by Man's fuller insight
into the meaning, and foresight into the consequences, of his actions.
The possession of speech makes it possible for him to acquire something of other men's, and their predecessors', interpretations of their
personal experience, and so to cultivate traditions and devise symbolic expressions of his feelings and ideas, which come more and
more to dominate his behaviour and hamper his freedom of thought
and action.

It is no mere academic pretence to insist upon the need for a
Human History to expound this broader conception of the Study
of Mankind. The fuller understanding of human thought and behaviour is the most vital consideration for all men and women.
It is the only thing that really matters for human beings in general.

But, it may be asked, what more can the cooperation of Biology
and the Humanities do to interpret human thought and action
than is being done at present by the two disciplines independently?
This book is an attempt to answer the question. It has been written
in a scientific laboratory where the principal device for the Study
of Mankind is the process of dissection, which may seem very remote from the interpretation of the behaviour of living men and
women. There is, however, an intimate relationship between
Anatomy and Human History.

So far as the development of a systematic study of the human
body is concerned, the Ptolemaic school at Alexandria, founded
by the disciples of Aristotle three centuries before Christ, represents
the beginning of the story. In the Museum, which was the essential achievement of that school, the discipline of true science was
developed and organized. This Egyptian city gave the world its
greatest heritage, the scientific method. This decisive advance in the
history of civilisation extended to all sciences. It was the triumph
of the inductive method based upon observation.

The special force of these observations is revealed more clearly if
we push the enquiry to the dawn of civilisation, more than

thirty centuries before Aristotle. Then it becomes clear that the Study of Mankind (and in particular the phenomena of life and death) was indeed the sole aim of all science and art.

The structure of the human body only becomes really intelligible when one investigates not merely the functional significance of the various structural arrangements, but also the history of the processes whereby they attained their present structure and proportions. The study of Biology is in this sense essentially a discipline of History, what our predecessors called Natural History, as we in our generation call it Evolution. But if the true Study of Mankind is Man, it involves a good deal more than the mere examination of the dead corpse or the study of the actions of the heart, lungs, brain or any other individual system or part of the living body. Its chief aim should be the study of the actions of the organism as a whole, the behaviour of living men and women in all its puzzling manifestations. Moreover it should include something more than behaviour in the sense of such actions as can be observed and recorded. The thoughts and feelings that provide the motives for men's behaviour are the things that matter most.

In attempting to formulate the need for a wider vision of mankind to embrace the whole range of human actions and aspirations it is interesting to recall how fundamental a part the study of human anatomy played in more recent centuries. In the renaissance of science, the recognition of the importance of direct observation of Nature rather than what ancient Greek philosophers had written nearly two thousand years before, was inaugurated by the Belgian anatomist Vesalius, whose *De Fabrica Corporis* was published in 1543, the year which also witnessed the issue of the volume that established for all time the fame of Copernicus, and represents the beginning of our modern conception of the universe.

Throughout Man's career the study of the human body has always played a conspicuous part in shaping the advancement of learning. Nor was the decisive part played by the study of mankind merely vague and general, the method of the man in the street who cannot help puzzling over the behaviour of his fellows. The specific activities of the embalmer who preserved the bodies of the dead were in large measure responsible for giving civilisation its distinctive character. The man who dissected the human body for the practical purpose of preventing it from suffering corruption had a much more ambitious aim than the mere preservation of a corpse. Musing deeply on the problems of life and death, he persuaded himself that in making a mummy he was actually prolonging the existence of the body so that it might be reanimated as a living being. Hence around the mummy were created, not only many of the essential arts and crafts (architecture, stone and wood-working, sculpture and painting, the drama, dancing and music) that represent the scaffolding of civilisation, but also the deepest aspirations of the human spirit, the motives which have influenced the thoughts and actions of countless millions of human beings throughout the whole history of civilisation.

The farther back we go in time the more definitely and exclusively anthropocentric all enquiries into natural phenomena become. There is no innate curiosity in mankind to study the forces of nature; but such things as seem directly to affect his own welfare have always appealed to Man's interests. Man did not at first study physics, astronomy, zoology and botany simply for the intellectual joy of discovery, but so as to benefit himself in some more exact and tangible way than by a reputation for wisdom. In particular attention was paid to the problems of life and death, the solution of which might enable him to safeguard his own existence and avert the risks of death. For example, celestial phenomena at first interested Man because the moon seemed to control the physiological periodicity of women and the life-giving functions. The sky, therefore, was believed to regulate and measure the duration of life, as it did the year, the month and the day. It was studied for the purpose of controlling human destiny. It can be shown that in a similar way all Man's early nature studies were self-centered, and in the last resort were related to the expressions of life in his own body —the heart, the liver, the kidneys, the breath, the blood, the moisture, and the odour of life—the safeguarding of which was the underlying motive of all early speculation and belief.

Several millennia before Man systematically studied anatomy he was building up the fabric of civilisation under the influence of doctrines based upon his ideas of the functions of the heart and blood, the breath and moisture, the placenta and the hypothetical "life-substance." It would, in fact, not be an exaggeration to claim

that civilisation was evolved out of man's endeavours to understand the constitution of his own body and to preserve the life that
animated it.

All learning was at first focussed on the preservation of life. As
the Greeks expressed it many centuries later, the healer was a
naturalist (physician, from the Greek word meaning Nature)—one
who studied the forces of Nature to safeguard life. Throughout the
ages the essential doctrines of philosophy centred around the anatomical facts of the structure of the heart and brain, as the means
of interpreting thought and behaviour.

But it is not the aim of this book simply to study the dead past
of man and his strivings except as a means of interpreting the living
present.

Within recent years many treatises have been written to make
readily accessible to the general reader the evidence relating to the
ancestry and evolution of Man, the industries and the artistic
achievements of primitive Man, the dazzling achievements of the
early civilisations of Egypt, Sumer, Crete, Elam, India, China,
Indo-China, Java, Mexico and Peru, not to mention the wealth of
information relating to the legacy of Greece and the early history
of Europe. It is not the aim of this book to attempt to summarize
the details of such evidence. Its purpose is to search for the deep
motives that have shaped Man's career, and to call attention to the
vital factors in human thought and behaviour which have been
ignored by most writers.

Special attention will be devoted to the study of the tyranny of
tradition. This suggests the need for new emphasis on the fact of
the continuity of culture both in time and space. Most of the things
we are doing today are being done because someone, hundreds or
even thousands of years ago, in some more or less distant part of
the world, started the fashion, often for reasons of a different nature
from those which shape our own actions today when we, in defiance
of the usual connotation of the word fashion, continue doing these
things. The principle of continuity, which is the foundation of the
theories of geology and biology, as enunciated respectively by Sir
Charles Lyell and Charles Darwin, urgently needs to be rehabil-
itated and reapplied in the Study of Mankind, where it should play
an even more extensive and significant part than in these Nat-

ural Sciences. For Man's conscious activities make the principle of continuity and the historical method which expounds it the chief instruments for achieving a full and true interpretation of the data of Human History.

In the first section of the book a large amount of space has been devoted to the consideration of the evidence that goes to establish the truth of the fact that Natural Man did, and still does, exist—totally devoid of any of the customs, beliefs, arts and crafts, social and political organisation of civilisation—and that originally such primitive men were decent, generous and peaceful. Such deep-rooted scepticism has been expressed both in ancient and modern times concerning the reality of such a Golden Age as the ancient poets and philosophers depicted that an exceptionally free quotation from original sources has been made in the hope of overcoming the obstinate refusal of most modern people to examine the evidence.

The establishment of the truth of the fact that originally Man was utterly devoid of culture and was nevertheless "the gentle and noble savage" must obviously provide the foundation upon which to erect the story of how mankind acquired culture and with it social unrest, dangerous practices and methods of cruelty.

For the first thirty centuries of its career civilisation was concerned with the building up of the State System and establishing more or less complete subjection of individual men and women to its tyranny. Then in the sixth century B.C. the Ionians opened a new chapter in Human History by removing the shackles. They showed that men were free to think and act without such restraints. Men could enjoy the benefits of civilisation without being crushed by it.

In the attempt to interpret the true character of primitive Man and the critical phases of Human History which led to the creation of civilisation, Dr. W. J. Perry's brilliant researches have shown the way. Much of the material dealing with this important section, as well as with many other parts, of the book Dr. Perry has placed at the author's disposal.

It is a pleasure to dedicate the work to him as a tribute to his insight and genius, and as a token of admiration of the courage with which he has pursued his researches undismayed by persistent misrepresentation.

G. ELLIOT SMITH.

HUMAN HISTORY

CHAPTER I

INTRODUCTION

THE Study of Mankind is the whole time occupation of all human beings. At every moment of our lives we are occupied with our own thoughts and feelings as they affect our behaviour, and especially our attitude towards other men and women, whose actions are matters of constant interest and importance. Hence we feel an irresistible curiosity concerning their sentiments and especially their attitude towards ourselves. For our own welfare may be vitally affected, as our behaviour is profoundly influenced, by the feelings and actions of those other human beings who come within the range of our social activities.

A man may disclaim the imputation of being his "brother's keeper," but the vital interests of both are mutually affected by the behaviour of each. For, as St. Paul expressed the idea, if with a different meaning, "none of us liveth unto himself." Under the conditions of civilised life men can display real humanity only in so far as they are social, for in society alone can their distinctive qualities attain their proper development and their fullest expression. In immeasurably greater degree than any other living creature Man is dependent upon his fellows for knowledge of the way to live.

Other animals may follow their fellows, as sheep do, or learn by imitating their actions, as kittens and, in ampler measure, young monkeys acquire skill under the tuition of their mothers and other members of their families. Man's unique powers of visual discrimination, however, confer upon him an immeasurably greater understanding of what he sees than ever the most clear-sighted ape possesses. His vastly greater powers of manual dexterity and enhanced ability to acquire skill and to imitate his fellows imposes upon him the unavoidable need of the guidance of others. The complexity of the skill they themselves have attained gives him all the more to learn. Hence the human child is far more dependent on his fellows

3

than any other living creature for the knowledge of what to do and how to do it. But above all, his unique power of articulate speech provide him with the means of assimilating part of the accumulated knowledge of his social group, and, what is often even more significant in affecting his thoughts and behaviour, of assimilating the manner of interpreting their experience which is traditional among his associates. Every human being is thus subjected to the more or less rigid conventions of his society, which tend to hamper his freedom of thought by providing him with stereotyped ideas and manners, which in most cases profoundly affect his behaviour and his attitude towards the world. Hence it is obviously impossible to interpret his actions unless we know the history of his social setting. As Comte expressed it a century ago: "No conception can be understood except through its history." In other words, the principle of continuity and the diffusion of culture are the essential instruments for explaining Man's behaviour.

From the very nature of his distinctively human attributes, Man experiences a difficulty in seeing clearly the things that most closely affect himself and his own welfare. It is not merely the emotional factor of his personal feelings that affects his judgment, but also the influence, and in particular the beliefs, of the people amidst whom he lives his life. He is apt to see the world with the eyes of his society rather than to look for himself and really see his own personality.

Hence it is not wholly surprising to find that the study of human nature, which, from the nature of things, is the chief occupation of all mankind, is the thing about which most people know least. Obviously we should know and understand human nature better than anything else in the whole universe. Yet from the very familiarity with the springs of their thoughts and actions the judgment of most men is biased.

Throughout the ages philosophers have repeatedly marvelled at the paradoxical fact that of all things under the sun we know least of those which are our chief and almost exclusive interest. In 1754 Rousseau expressed the opinion that: "The most useful and least advanced of all human knowledge seems to me to be that of man himself." After nearly two centuries this statement is still true.

Hence the task seems worth attempting of discussing the nature of Man and his achievements, and in particular the wider aspects of Human History that play so tremendous a part in shaping the ideas and the behaviour of every member of a civilised society, and in affecting the welfare of mankind and the happiness of every individual.

If in this book undue attention seems to be paid to the consideration of the obvious and perhaps utterly banal it is because they are the most vital interests of every man. These things need emphasising because mere familiarity has induced most human beings to ignore them. We should not be deterred from saying the obvious when it is precisely the obvious that needs saying.

Perhaps it will enable the reader to get a clearer idea of the purpose of this book if some of the more important of these self-obvious propositions are enumerated before we attempt to discuss their wider implications.

The Life Quest

The fact that Man is a living creature involves the consideration that he is an organism, all parts of which (as well as every activity of his mind) are constantly active for the preservation of the life that is the essence of his being. The heart, the lungs and the other organs are ever working automatically to preserve the vital activities. Scores of special organs are constantly active in promoting and regulating the processes of growth and metabolism to maintain the highest efficiency of the organism and protect it from the risk of extinction. The human nervous system is the most marvellous instrument ever devised: its outstanding function is concerned with safeguarding the body from dangers that would imperil the very existence of life. But it does more than this: it confers upon the individual the ability to be aware of the danger, and the emotion of anxiety, to feel pain when injured, and to learn from experience how consciously to avert risks to life. It is therefore not surprising that ever since Man first acquired the ability to examine the conditions of his existence his chief occupation has always been the conscious search for the means of safeguarding his own life.

Delving into the remotely distant history of mankind we cannot fail to be impressed by the persistence with which throughout the whole of their career our ancestors have been constantly seeking for elixirs of life to safeguard their existence. Misled by the symbolisms of form and colour, and misunderstanding the essential factors involved in the natural phenomena of birth and death and in the defensive and offensive acts of wild animals, primitive Man imagined he had rational grounds for attributing to blood and shells, to the teeth and claws of dangerous animals, to the mere form of life-giving women and the colour of the life-blood, some magical quality to preserve and restore youth to ageing men and women, to prolong the days of active life to the living and restore to the dead life that had been lost. In other words the elixirs these men of old were seeking, and imagined they had found, were objects that would protect their lives from all the assaults, not merely of time, but also of circumstance, that would bring what we now call "good luck" in all the events of their lives, and prolong their existence after what we know as death. Most of the amulets, even of modern times, the lucky trinkets, the averters of the "Evil Eye," the practices and devices for securing happy results in love and sport, in curing bodily ills or mental distress, in securing material prosperity, such as good harvests, or attaining immortality, are survivals of the ancient and persistent striving after those objects which our early forefathers called collectively "Givers of Life."

The never-ending pursuit of this elusive aim was responsible for the creation of civilisation with most of its arts and crafts, its essential customs and beliefs. Architecture, which began with the invention of tombs and temples, involving the crafts of the carpenter and stone-mason, the artist and the sculptor, was devised to effect the extension of existence of the dead, which was regarded as essential for the attainment of the immortality which conferred divine rank. The ceremonies of incense-burning and the pouring of libations, the arts of dancing and the drama, were all intended to help the dead to regain life and all the vital activities of living people.

The earliest literature that has come down from antiquity, the Egyptian Pyramid Texts, as well as the later writings known as the Coffin Texts of the Middle Kingdom and the so-called Book of the Dead of the New Empire, are wholly concerned with the problem of how to attain new life.

But the same motive is the inspiration of all other ancient writings, whether they come from Babylonia, India or China. Among other peoples the religious rituals, the mythology that interprets the meaning of these ceremonies and the folklore, are concerned primarily with the problems of securing and maintaining life. As Dr. W. J. Perry has so clearly shown in his *Gods and Men,* the religion of primitive peoples is wholly concerned with the Givers of Life and with the Story of Creation, the dramatic representation of which is the ritual means of attaining the continuation of the benefits Creation itself conferred—in other words Life and New Life.

The essence of the teaching of Lao Tze in China was the idea of Tao, which gives the name to the religion Taoism. Its founder referred to it as a mysterious something that protected the living from death, conferred upon the actually dead the renewal of life which made them divine, rejuvenated the aged—it was in fact "life," the elixir of life. As the mystery of creation was repeated at the birth of a new human being, so did the Tao create new life when the suppliant gave unquestioning submission to its workings. The central conception of Taoism is the idea of life as a mysterious force that can work all such marvels as the mediaeval Christian theologian attributed to Providence.

Similarly the central idea in the belief of the Arabs of Morocco is known by them as *baraka,* which, according to Professor Edward Westermarck, is "a mysterious wonder-working force which is looked upon as a blessing from God." It is a life-giving power possessed in especial degree by "holy men" or "saints"; also by certain sacred places; by certain animals; by certain mountains, rocks, stones, springs, trees; and by certain vegetables, fruits and herbs. Even certain names, such as Mohammed, also have this luck-bringing magic, which is essentially the power of conferring life and protection, in other words, prosperity. In the *Expository Times* of May, 1928, Professor Maurice A. Canney has called attention to the fact that this same conception of life-giving and life-protecting (and the identical word) is found again and again in the Hebrew Scriptures. For example, from *Psalm* 133 Professor Canney quotes the phrase: "Like Hermon-dew which flows down upon the mountains of Zion: for there Yahveh commanded the *berakah* —life for ever," and again in *Psalm* 145: "I will exalt thee, my God, the King, and will ascribe *berakah* to thy name for ever and ever." Such ideas are widespread among all the peoples of Western Asia, and can be referred back to the most remote times.

In the Sumerian account of the Deluge the ark is called "She that preserves life." The whole story is really a record of the magical means for renewing youth and staving off the onset of old age and death.

In the Old Testament Jehovah is described as "One who causes to live and makes alive again" (I Samuel, 11, 6) and elsewhere as "the fountain of life." According to Professor Canney the Hebrew phrase usually translated "God save the King" means literally "long life to the King," "grant him a new lease of life." The Greek word *Soter,* which was applied to many gods and kings, is applied in the New Testament to Jesus and usually translated Saviour. But Professor Canney has pointed out that the real meaning of the word is "Giver of Life." In every religion the Deity is regarded primarily as the Giver of Life, the Creator who confers life on mankind. The chief concern of religion is to secure life and in some cases resurrection, in the sense of restoring to life or continuing life.

Under the conditions of modern civilisation it is the constant aim of most men to earn sufficient money to obtain food and security and to acquire the innumerable gadgets which the traditions of our own society have taught us to regard as necessary or desirable. But however artificial and arbitrary such a mode of existence may be, the underlying motives—the preservation of life and the full satisfaction of our appetites and our craving for power —are common to all living creatures.

When in the beginning men learned to contemplate the daily risks to which their own lives were exposed, and began to probe into the mystery of life itself, they were actuated by the desire to protect themselves from the dangers that surrounded them.

The experience of killing animals in self-protection or for food, and of witnessing the effects of injuries upon their fellows, impressed upon our early ancestors the vital importance of blood. The use of red ochre in the graves of the earliest representatives of our species is explained by the survival of such colour symbolism in later ages and even in our own times. The pictures of the heart and the indications of its vital significance tell the same story,

which seems to be corroborated again by such practices as the muti-
lation of the fingers and a variety of other forms of blood-offering.
These ancient customs are further illuminated by the widespread
beliefs concerning the symbolism of blood which are found in the
written records and the folk lore of every people. We can study the
ideas underlying the blood-covenant and the belief that blood is
the elixir of life, the material out of which the new life of a child
was fashioned in its mother's womb, in virtue of which what we,
in defiance of the teaching of modern science, still call a blood-
relationship is claimed. With all these survivals of old traditions
we can discover the probable meaning of much that at first sight
seems strange in the beliefs and practices of primitive men.

They learned to appreciate the fact that the loss of blood produced a state of unconsciousness, which they seem to have explained
by assuming that blood was mind. The red fluid was identified
with consciousness, memory and thought, all of which disappeared
when much of it escaped from the body. Hence, they seem to have
argued, blood is the mind-stuff, the material vehicle of experience.
By transfusion from one individual to another, and so physically
mixing their blood, a community of knowledge might be established. It was the material of sympathy.

As the loss of blood could produce a state of sleep-like unconsciousness, which might pass into what we know as death, men
in early times assumed that blood was also the life-stuff. Hence
they considered it a reasonable inference that by offerings of actual blood, such as might be obtained by gashing themselves, chop-
ping off a finger, by piercing their ears, lips or tongues, or by
such operations as circumcision, the existence of the sick or even
the dead might be prolonged.

The earliest conception of a god was a preeminent human being who had died and required to be reanimated by mortals in
order to attain the immortality which was the distinctive attribute
of his divinity. One of the varied ways of reanimating the deity
was to make offerings of blood. (Figure 1) The mutilations inflicted
by the suppliant on himself are often described by ethnologists
as acts of worship. But the original motive was very different
from the idea we associate with worship. The offering of blood
was made for the strictly practical purpose of providing the dead

Figure 1—An ancient Mexican picture of men performing three kinds of Life-Giving Ceremonies before a priest impersonating the Sun-God (after Mrs. Zelia Nuttall). Two are piercing their ears to make a blood-offering; others are burning incense and blowing shell trumpets.

god with vitality so that he might be restored to life and be able to listen to the suppliant's appeal for help. The principle of the theory underlying the act is that a mortal by his own sacrifice assists the god to recover his divine life, and in return the god will give supernatural help to the whole community. These later elaborations help us the better to understand the ideas underlying the vastly more ancient practices we are trying to interpret. It was believed that the reinforcement of vitality could be effected not only by blood itself, but also by substitutes. If men or women wore blood-like substances such as carnelian, or painted themselves with red ochre, they were supposed to be adding to their natural supply of vital substance, and so protecting themselves against the risk of losing their lives. Moreover, if red ochre was packed around the bodies of the dead, as the earliest known members of our species (*Homo sapiens*) were in the habit of doing, such a pro-

Figure 2—Palaeolithic artist's drawing of a mammoth showing the heart (the earliest known picture of the heart of any animal) and two bisons each with an arrow pointing towards the position of the heart.

cedure was believed to promote the prolongation of their existence. As additional corroboration of this interpretation of the evidence, attention may be called to the fact that the artists of the Upper Palaeolithic epoch recognised that the heart was the most vulnerable part of a living creature.

Ever since men began to puzzle over the problems of life and death, they formulated a belief in the life-giving properties of certain natural objects which they afterwards called "Givers of Life." To us it may seem incredible that anyone ever really believed a piece of carnelian could protect a living person against danger to his life, or red ochre could confer a prolongation of existence upon a corpse. Yet many of those sophisticated people who scoff at such childishness still pay homage to the same ideas when they accept the symbolism of holly-berries or believe and act upon the old fable expressed by the phrase "a red rag to a bull."

People who for the first time in the history of the world were beginning to grope for some explanation of the bewildering phenomena of nature accepted as a self-evident proposition the fact that the red fluid in our bodies was life; not in the symbolical sense, but in the most literal and concrete way, which the Old Testament writer intended when he referred to the blood of a human being as "the life thereof." Is it surprising that the most obtrusive character of the fluid, its redness, was regarded as the essence of its virtues? Once this premiss is admitted it was not wholly illogical, in the absence of any more exact knowledge, to assume that any red substance is also life-giving by virtue of the property which was believed to be the "life" in blood. However puerile such ideas may seem to us it is important not to forget how dominating an influence symbolism, both of speech and action, plays in the lives of all human beings, and that the quality of this mental device for interpreting and applying experience obviously depends on the range of knowledge and experience expressed in the symbols.

If blood was one of the earliest substances to which the reputation of being an elixir of life was credited, it was not the only one. Blood was at first regarded not merely as "life," but also as "new life," the material out of which a child was formed in its mother's womb, and given the qualities of a living being by being made of the life-substance itself. Since human life comes into being at birth, women are clearly Givers of Life, and the instruments whereby blood could be fashioned into "new life."

From the earliest human records of members of our own species, the magic of motherhood found expression in the making of models of women as elixirs of life, amulets to protect the living and prolong existence after death. At the same time cowrie shells were adopted as special symbols of the birth-promoting and life-giving powers. Hence it is common to find in association with skeletons of our earliest predecessors not only red ochre but also shells (cowries and others) and female figurines. A model of a cowrie may be so fashioned as to become a grotesque caricature of a woman. Reference has already been made to the ancient belief that the new life of a child was formed of the mother's blood. As the *Book of Wisdom* expresses it: "All men have one entrance into life." "In the womb of my mother was I moulded into flesh in the time of ten months, being compacted in blood and the seed of man." The cowrie was originally the symbol of the "one entrance into life," a belief that is still widespread among both uncultured and cultured peoples. This explains its reputation for magic, which has played so large a part in the economic history of the world. But even in the early days of the known history of our ancestors the same cowrie-resemblance seems to have been detected in the part of the female form from the waist to the knees. Many of the early figurines found in palaeolithic sites in Europe and in the remains of the earliest civilisations of the Ancient East, represent this part of the body realistically, whereas the rest—head, arms, thorax and legs below the knees—is merely

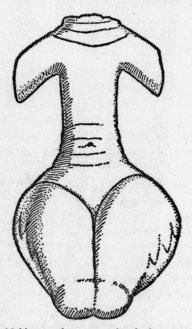

Figure 3—Ancient Nubian amulet representing both a woman and a cowrie shell.
(From the writer's chapter in *Art and Civilization*, Oxford, 1928.)

suggested on a smaller scale and very roughly shaped (Figure 3). This resemblance of part of the body to a cowrie shell made it possible for some ingenious palaeolithic modeller to express the magic of both motherhood and the shell combined in one amulet.

These two examples of symbolism, blood and shells, are merely examples of a process which permeated every aspect of primitive culture. Throughout Man's career the instinctive processes for the attainment of self-preservation shaped his conscious striving. In

particular primitive religion was inspired by the constant search
for Givers of Life wherewith to safeguard Man's existence.

The contents of the early graves, the walls of ancient Egyptian
temples, the pages of ancient manuscripts and the traditions that
have survived among people in all parts of the world are eloquent
of the prominence and persistence of the Life Quest. In ancient
Egypt temples and writings the *ankh* (so-called "key of life") is
found everywhere. The ancient writings, pictures and sculptures
are inspired by the same motive—they represent the ever-insistent
craving for the protection of existence and the preservation of youth.
All the ritual ceremonies are centred upon the king as the Giver of
Life to his people.

Figure 4—A necklace worn by one of the most ancient representatives of *Homo
sapiens* found at Mentone. The magical objects consist of shells, teeth and the
vertebrae of fish.

Not merely in Ancient Egypt, however, but in all civilised countries and in all religions, ancient and modern, the story of creation is so sacred and widespread, not from any interest on the part
of early man in history or tradition for its own sake, but because
the creation-ritual is the dramatic reenactment of the giving of life
to mankind. As such it is the most potent form of protection.

Hence in a book on Human History it is essential to insist upon
the fundamental significance of this biological factor as the essential motive of most human activities. In virtue of the fact that
Man is a living creature his constant preoccupation is to save his
own life. In his effort to do this he all unwittingly created civilisation.

The importance of the Life Quest has been emphasised in the
preceding pages, not only because it is the dominant motive in all

human thought and behaviour, but also because it has been ignored by most writers who have discussed the primitive customs and beliefs, where its influence is most obtrusive and where the neglect to invoke it necessarily implies a failure in interpretation and exposition. Though the sacred literature of all countries, as well as their mythology and folklore, persistently make the search for life or the elixir of life, whether it is called "salvation" or "good luck," the essential motive of human behaviour, students of history and ethnology with equal persistence ignore it. Critical examination of writings dealing with the Study of Mankind, and especially those relating to archaeology and mythology, leaves us in no doubt as to the reason for the strange omission of the most potent creative influence in human thought and action. The word "fertility" has become such an obsession that many writers are constantly using it when it is wholly inappropriate and often nonsensical. For example it has become almost a stereotyped automatism of language to refer to deities as fertility gods or goddesses instead of defining them correctly as Givers of Life. When the word "life" is substituted for "fertility" the whole significance of the interpretation is transformed. What men crave is life, not fecundity. Though the normal human being desires offspring and in primitive communities the failure to procreate children is an adequate reason for divorce, men do not often pray for fertility. Abraham is reported to have done so: also Henry VIII. But it is neither a universal human wish, nor, when it is present, does it affect the individual except on rare occasions. The sort of fertility in which deities play a part is that of crops and herds: but that is solely to provide life-giving sustenance for human beings. The gods as creators of mankind are regarded as the source of Man's life and their chief purpose in primitive religion is to preserve and safeguard the life they have created. The gods are Givers of Life and not fertility-mongers.

Even in the frankly phallic deities—such as the Hindu Siva or the bull- and ram-forms of deities in Egypt, Greece, India and elsewhere—the symbolism is not intended primarily, as is often supposed, to express fertility or sexual licence, but life-giving. Even the stories of the Holy Grail in Mediaeval Europe and the linga-yoni symbols in Hinduism, in which the emphasis seems to be so unmistakably sexual, are really intended to express salvation in the sense of the creation of life. Whatever interpretations subsequently came to be given to these legends and symbols, they were definitely not intended at first to relate merely to the satisfaction of a natural appetite or the procreation of children.

Within recent years, more particularly under the influence of the teaching of Professor Sigmund Freud, it has become the fashion to scent sex in all human behaviour. No one is likely to deny that the call of sex is imperious, and when its free manifestations are repressed as they are under the social circumstances of civilisation, they are apt to diffuse their emotional tone over a wide range of thought and action. But the instinct of sex, even when its influence overflows the normal bounds of its natural functions, does not play the same kind of rôle as the more fundamental and continuously active instinct of self-preservation does.

In affairs of sex Man rightly or wrongly is fully convinced of his competence to shape his own behaviour. But in the matter of preserving life he is dealing with a problem of infinite complexity and mystery, which he cannot for a moment evade and in respect to which he needs all the help he can obtain. The search for a sexual mate is a more direct and concrete adventure than the pursuit of that elusive will-o'-the-wisp we call life, which means the safeguarding of our very existence. Obstacles in the satisfaction of the former may drive the victim to sublimate his feelings in poetry. The striving to achieve the ever-present and essential Life Quest is religion.

The Distinctive Attributes of Man

If the most urgent need in the Study of Mankind is to give adequate recognition to the too much neglected fact that Man shares the Life Quest with all other living creatures, it is equally important not to ignore the attributes of his humanity which distinguish him from the rest of the animal creation. The behaviour of all other animals is determined mainly by physiological changes in their bodies and the influence of their environment. While Man also is subject to such influences and impelled by similar appetites and instincts, his behaviour is dominated by the effects of his own personal experience and his reactions, not merely to his environment, but in particular to what Professor Graham Wallas calls the social heritage, the accumulated knowledge and traditions of the society in which he lives.

Man's distinctive powers of vision confer upon him the ability, which is not enjoyed by any other living creature, of really seeing the world and understanding in some measure what is happening around him. He is the only animal capable of studying himself, not merely of exploring his body by sight and touch, but also of critically examining his feelings and aspirations and getting some idea of the part he himself is playing in the wonderful world his new vision has revealed to his understanding mind. The attainment of muscular skill and dexterity has enabled him not merely to achieve an endless series of directly useful actions and manipulations, but also to add enormously to his knowledge of the nature of things and by experimentation to acquire some understanding of the forces acting in the world. In these ways Man is preeminently a creature who has to learn from his personal experience by seeing and doing. Hence the knowledge gained is individual and distinctive. No man's experience is completely identical with another's for his innate qualities and the fortuitous events prevent standardisation. Every man's outlook on life and his behaviour are determined by his own experience. In this respect he differs from all other living creatures in that the knowledge and experience each human being acquires can control and override those physiological dispositions which, in the case of other creatures, regulate behaviour.

The range of Man's ability to learn is vastly extended by the acquisition of speech, which enables him to share other men's knowledge and in particular their varied interpretations of their own experience. Speech confers upon mankind also the means of accumulating such speculations and transmitting them from generation to generation to form traditions of thought and behaviour, which makes it possible for men to accept ready-made ideas and customs and become subject to an ever-increasing tyranny of convention. Moreover, as Robert Louis Stevenson expressed it, "Language is but a poor bull's eye lantern wherewith to show off the vast cathedral of the world." Every word we speak, and in even greater degree, every sentence, involves a complete symbolism and varying shades of meaning determined by the emotions and the personal experience of the speaker. Words cannot convey anything more than a very imperfect expression of what the speaker really feels and thinks, even when he is trying to express his true sentiments with calm deliberation and without exaggeration. But no other human being can be so sympathetically attuned to appreciate the exact meaning the speaker is trying to express. His emotional tone and his experience are different and the words, even when apt and appropriate, have a connotation that cannot be identical.

Hence while Man is so largely dependent upon his fellows for the information conveyed by speech it is important to recognise that the very imperfections of the means of communication tend to emphasise the individuality of what each person acquires from the common store of the community's knowledge. It is not merely a question of his ability and competence, but also of his experience, and in very special degree his unreasonable emotional experience, which colours the symbolism of spoken language and confers upon what he hears a meaning and an appeal to his interests which is distinctive and personal. No human being, however docile and plastic, is a puppet dancing to any tune that may be called. His actions cannot be made to conform to any general rule or law of Nature. He is a law unto himself. His innate qualities and their reaction to his individual experience confer upon his thoughts and behaviour a character that is as distinctive as his face, which enables any observer to recognise him as an individual and distinguish him from other human beings.

Every one is aware of the truth of this. We identify our acquaintances and label them by acoustic symbols which we call their names. In seeing and naming any individual we automatically associate with him certain acts or thoughts, something distinctive of his personality, which evokes a definite sentiment in the observer, admiration or disapproval, affection or resentment—feelings that are not necessarily due wholly to the intrinsic qualities of the individual, but in part to our previous experience of his actions and our present estimate of his attitude towards ourselves.

These obvious experiences of everyday life ought to make us aware that the social behaviour of any community is not a process that can be defined by any law of Nature, seeing that it depends upon the complex and unpredictable reactions of a number of individuals to fortuitous circumstances which to each of them convey a different meaning and have varied implications.

The conditions of human existence, even without the social complications of civilisation, are so different from those of other living creatures as to afford some measure of justification for the mediaeval practice of distinguishing the affairs of Man from those of Nature. The significance of these distinctively human attributes cannot be exaggerated. If then it is so obviously impossible to bring Man's varied waywardness within the scope of any law of nature, there can be no warrant for assuming that similar circumstances will evoke an identical or even truly similar reaction in any two human beings. The nature of the response must obviously be determined by what the particular individual has experienced, and in particular the social environment in which his personality was moulded.

As every human being is dependent on his fellows for the knowledge of speech and for the customs and ideas he learns or adopts, it is obvious that his normal and inevitable mode of behaviour necessarily involves participation in the diffusion of culture. He can no more avoid accepting and adapting to his own mental make-up some part of the rich cultural harvest exposed for him to choose from than he can live without food. Nor can he help adding to the general heritage his own modest contribution. Normal human behaviour is explicable only when the historical antecedents of each individual and his society are given due consideration. For diffusion of culture in time and space—the principle of continuity and the geographical linking of the culture of the world—is the fundamental factor in shaping human thought and action.

It is of the utmost importance to get these patent considerations clearly impressed upon our minds. Obvious as is the truth that every human being at every moment of his life is participating in the process, it is the fashion at the moment either to deny the reality of diffusion altogether or so to restrict the range of its influence as to make it an altogether insignificant factor in the history of civilisation. Hence it becomes necessary once more to emphasise St. Paul's saying that "none of us liveth unto himself." Without the help of our fellows the satisfaction of the innate impulse to speak could not be realised, and the deprivation of this distinctively human power would be the denial of our birthright as human beings. But the acquisition of speech involves sharing in the community's symbolism and becoming a part of the stream of continuity that shapes the traditions, to whose tyranny we have to submit.

One of the strange ironies of the attainment of human rank is that the acquisition of speech, which opens to Man almost unlimited opportunities for extending the range of his knowledge, at the same time provides him with the means for evading the effort of independent thought. For it offers him ready-made conventions of speech as well as of customs and ideas. The vast majority of mankind thus accept without question the guidance of tradition, and by sheer inertia lose the ability to observe or interpret evidence in any sense other than the conventional one that has been instilled into them by tradition.

Every one who has ever called attention to facts or inferences from them that came into conflict with fashionable doctrines must have been made to realise how little influence the experience of the scientific developments of the last three centuries has had upon men's readiness to make even the simplest observation or to admit the truth of the most obvious principles. Most men, even without being consciously dishonest or wilfully stupid, seem to be unable to examine heterodox views with understanding and impartiality.

Some months after the publication of his *Origin of Species* Charles Darwin modestly blamed himself rather than admit that his colleagues were stupid. In a letter to a colleague he confessed:—

"I am beginning to despair of ever making the majority understand my notions. . . . I must be a very bad explainer. . . . Several reviews and several letters have shown me too clearly how little I am understood. . . . I can only hope by reiterated explanations finally to make the matter clearer."

The inertia of tradition and the lack of courage to defy it when new evidence fails to conform to it seem to be potent to blind all except the ablest and most fearless of men to the most patent facts. Those who pretend that similar circumstances can determine the development of similar customs and beliefs ignore the common lack of human inventiveness and the obstacles created by stupidity and cowardice. Under conditions of civilisation courage is the rarest of human virtues.

Individual workers such as Copernicus, Vesalius and Galileo initiated great advances of knowledge by refusing to be fettered by tradition and by adopting the principle of appealing to nature. But their efforts produced little immediate effect upon the general attitude of their contemporaries towards the methods of acquiring knowledge. Yet they were slowly undermining the authority of Aristotle, Galen and Ptolemy, which was the real obstacle in the path of progress. When Galileo called attention to the spots on the sun his chief critic objected that he had searched the writings of Aristotle and could discover no reference to the matter. Therefore Galileo's senses or his glasses must be deceiving him.

This crushing domination of ancient authority was ultimately broken neither by observation nor by experiment, but by certain speculations of Descartes, which have since been shown to be fallacious. It is a curious phenomenon that Descartes and Francis Bacon, the value of whose writings as scientific documents is in large measure negligible, should have been able for the first time to secure acceptance for the consideration that the statements of those in authority, whether ancient or modern, were not enough to establish their truth. Both Bacon (1561–1626) and Descartes (1596–1650) were able to secure the attention of the public, and to persuade the general body of learned men, that truth could be attained only by observation and experiment. Although this is precisely what Descartes and Bacon were not doing, they were able to achieve a vast revolution in science and scholarship, a service which is none the less noteworthy if we recognise the ironical circumstance that one of the first effects of the adoption of their advocacy was to discredit their own speculations.

Nevertheless the world is reluctant to abandon theories, and the teaching of Descartes was no exception to this rule. It took a long time to secure a general adoption of the Newtonian discipline, even with the stinging whip of a Voltaire to arouse men to face facts. It is, however, to the credit of England that before his death Newton had the satisfaction of witnessing his own country's full acceptance of his teaching and the repudiation of

Descartes. In fact confidence in Newton threatened to confer upon him the reputation of being an "authority" and so to perpetuate the risks which Bacon and Descartes had so recently exorcised. The progress of mathematics in England was in fact hampered for a time by a belated devotion to Newton's theory of fluxions when great strides were being made on the Continent by Leibnitz's differential calculus.

Twenty-five years after the publication of *The Origin of Species* Huxley called special attention to the danger to the advancement of learning from the worship of authority, especially when it is buttressed by great achievements. Most men are prone to conform to fashionable ideas and to mimic and borrow rather than make observations and puzzle out their own interpretations of evidence. Darwin's great work opened the way for an understanding of Man's real status in the world. By establishing the fact of human descent it settled once for all the age-long dispute whether Man was really a part of the natural order of things. By this achievement he transformed our whole outlook upon nature and our own place in it, and inaugurated a new era of enquiry. He achieved in ample measure what the historian Lecky claimed for the great Humanists of the seventeenth century: "destroying the old prejudices, dispelling illusions, rearranging the various parts of our knowledge, and altering the whole scope and character of our sympathies."

Realising the risk to which learning was exposed by the very magnitude of Darwin's achievement—and remembering the centuries of obscurantism which a blind devotion to Aristotle, Ptolemy and Galen had inflicted upon learning—Huxley made an impressive plea for the exercise of constant vigilance in the pursuit of scientific truth. History, he said, warns us that it is the customary fate of new truths to begin as heresies and end as superstitions. There was a danger lest a new generation should accept the main doctrine of *The Origin of Species* with as little reflection, and it may be as little justification, as so many of his contemporaries years before rejected it. So dire a consummation, he declared, must be prevented by unflinching criticism of science, for the scientific spirit is of more value than its produce, and truths irrationally held may be more harmful than rejected errors.

The consideration of the evolutionary factors that conferred upon Man his distinctive attributes of mind is a matter of such fundamental importance as to make it desirable to return to the discussion of the facts involved.

The Human Brain

Man is distinguished from all other living creatures by the quality and the range of his intellect, and on the physical side by the nature of the brain which confers upon him this mental pre-eminence. Obviously these considerations cannot be ignored in any attempt to interpret Human History, which is the expression of Man's distinctive abilities. Hence it becomes a matter of direct relevance to the business with which we are concerned in this book to consider certain features of the human brain that confer upon Man his title to humanity. The correct assessment of these qualities is possible only by comparing the human brain with the non-human brain which most nearly resembles it, that of the gorilla. Moreover as the attainment of its exceptional powers was acquired by a process of evolution the true significance of the human attributes can only be appreciated by examining the history of their development. This subject has been considered more fully in the writer's little book on *The Evolution of Man,* but certain of the conclusions may be repeated here in more general terms and emphasised to bring out the fundamental factor in the evolution of Man's brain.

The human brain is an instrument so constituted as to impose upon its possessor the vital necessity of cultivating a knowledge of the world and his fellow men. Its outstanding feature is the provision it makes for learning. The very imperfection of the instinctive tendencies it can automatically provoke makes it incumbent on every individual to learn how to live and to acquire the knowledge to do so from his own personal experience and by imitating, or learning from, his fellow men. Hence the qualities of the human brain distinguish Man from all other living creatures by imposing upon him the need to build up rules of life and conduct which are individual and distinctive and not conformable to any general laws of Nature.

The enjoyment of the conspicuously human qualities of experience obviously depends largely on special powers of vision, touch and hearing—as well, of course, as taste and smell, with which many other animals are at least as well equipped as we are. The possession of an exceptional aptitude for the cultivation of a high degree of muscular skill, such as we call dexterity, is an essential factor both in the attainment and in the expression of these qualities. But the fundamental element in Man's intellectual eminence

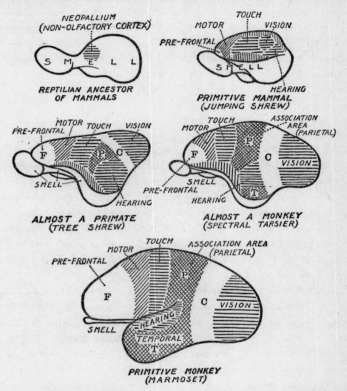

Figure 5—A series of diagrams to suggest the origin of the neopallium in the ancestors of mammals; the rapid development of this cortical area in mammals as touch, vision, hearing, as well as control of skilled movements, attain an increasing significance; the growing cultivation of vision which leads to the emergence of the Primates; the increased reliance on vision which brings about an enhancement of skill in movement (and a marked expansion of the motor territory) and of tactile and auditory discrimination. The diagrams of the brains of the two shrews are based on Professor W. E. Le Gros Clark's and of the Tarsier in Professor H. H. Woollard's Studies.

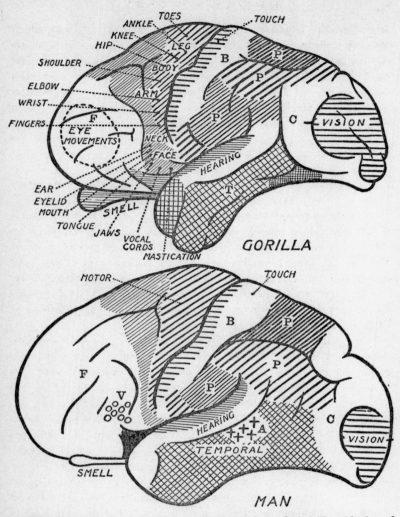

Figure 6—Comparison of the left cerebral hemisphere of a gorilla with that of an exceptionally small and primitive human brain. Every structure in the latter is represented in the former: but there is an enormous increase in the parietal (P), prefrontal (F) and temporal areas in Man. On the fringe of the territory concerned with the awareness of sound there is an area (marked with crosses at A) concerned with the higher function of appreciation of the symbolism of sound expressed in speech, and (at V) in the territory specially concerned with the process of learning and regulating muscular skill is an area that plays a part in the enunciation of articulate language.

is the unique character of his powers of vision, the qualities we know by the peculiarly significant words:—insight, foresight and the wider vision, not forgetting the slang expression "the glad eye." The distinctive powers of the human brain confer upon Man the ability to see the world and what is happening in it with an appreciation of the meaning of visual experience denied to all other living creatures. The comprehension of what he sees, the discrimination of form, colour, texture and of spatial relations, the identification of other individuals and the ability to read in their gestures and facial expressions something of their thoughts and intentions—all these things involve comparison with past experiences of things seen or felt or of actions accomplished. Apes are probably just as well equipped as we are to see, but they lack the fuller cerebral equipment to interpret the meaning of what they see. They cannot acquire the vast store of complex memories which we have at our command to compare and interpret the fuller significance of visual experience. The gorilla, for example, has just as large a cortical receptive area for vision as we have, but its parietal association area for recording experience is diminutive by comparison with ours (Figure 6).

Every human activity involves the principle of continuity, the dependence of our present state of consciousness on our personal experience in the past. The human brain is endowed with the aptitude for making this possible by its almost unlimited powers of recording sensory experience and feelings.

Sight enables us to find our way about and to know the scenes of our daily life, the hills and dales, the trees and sky, and the varied aspects of nature and all the kaleidoscopic changes of light and darkness, of brightness and shadow, the colours and shapes of the objects that come within our field of vision, the appreciation of distance and perspective, of size and solidity, of substance and shadow. By vision we learn to recognise our fellows and to distinguish them from one another, to identify their personal traits of features, colour and movement, to read in their gestures and the subtle changes in their expressions something of their feelings and intentions, and especially their attitude towards ourselves. The eyes, however, are not merely the instruments whereby we gain all this knowledge: in addition they are the most delicate recorders of our own thoughts and emotions. Almost instinctively we watch the eyes of our fellows. From their direction we can learn something of the objects upon which their gaze and attention are fixed and the quality of their interest. The most infinitesimal changes in the eyes and eyelids record emotional states which our wonderfully delicate sense of visual discrimination enables us to detect and interpret, however subtle the changes may be.

Visual discrimination itself could not have attained so high a pitch of efficiency if its development had not been intimately associated with the increase of muscular skill. For the cultivation of skill not only gives the sense of sight a biological usefulness, so to

Figure 7—The posture of a chimpanzee standing upright to suggest by contrast what Man has acquired by attaining the erect attitude.

speak, to justify and promote its evolution, but such powers of visual discrimination could not have been attained without exceptional precision and coordination of the movements of the eyes themselves. As the powers of vision increase they acquire a fuller influence over the animal's posture. The cerebral cortex acquires a direct control over the muscular actions concerned in maintaining the balance of the body, previously automatically controlled by lower parts of the brain, and with this the regulation of the habitual posture becomes a voluntary and consciously regulated action. The attainment of skill depends in large measure upon the cultivation of this voluntary control. By frequent repetition and the elimination of clumsiness and slowness, precise actions and responses attain an automatism which enables the individual to concentrate his attention on the changing circumstances—as the pace and flight of a tennis ball—and use his acquired automatisms of postural regulation and skill in movement to effect his purpose.

Skill in lawn tennis, for example, depends on a great deal more than being able to use the muscles of the arm to hit a ball with a racquet. The visual judgment of the direction and pace of the ball and the estimation of the power and direction of the stroke are obviously essential: but equally so are the quick movements and the correct posture of the whole body and the rapid performance of those acquired automatisms of arm movements that have been attained by long training.

Vision conferred on Man· the upright attitude and with it a tremendous enhancement of the ability to acquire skill. By doing so its instruments, the eyes, not only acquired a more advantageous position by being raised higher from the ground and so acquiring a wider range than the crouching attitude of the ape permitted, but the hands were freed to take fuller advantage of their rapidly increasing skill. Man's fleetness of foot and his agility were among the results.

The evolution of vision also was responsible for conferring upon the sense of touch a tremendous increase in delicacy and discrimination. When, under the guidance of sight, the hands became amazingly adaptable and skillful, they also became special organs of tactile discrimination, and this added enormously to the significance of visual experience by helping in the process of acquiring an appreciation of size, form and texture of objects in the outside world. By this cooperation of touch and sight a human being is able to acquire a fuller knowledge of the things he handles. In virtue of these powers he can explore and study his own body. The sense of curiosity, which was created when the awakening sense of vision first revealed to the startled gaze of Man's ancestors the wonders of the world in which they lived, was the chief factor in stimulating them to handle things and so incidentally to cultivate both muscular skill in manipulation and tactile discrimination.

The way in which these growing needs were met by the development of the cerebral cortex—the neopallium—as vision gradually became enhanced in importance in Man's ancestors, is graphically displayed in the series of diagrams (Figure 5). Such a degree of progressive change in the enhancement of the influence of vision was only possible in those animals whose limbs had not been subjected to precocious specialisation. The forelimbs of the horse, the cat, the bat and the porpoise, for example, had been variously modified to serve special functions. Fuller cultivation of vision in these animals would have lacked an adequate biological usefulness as the limbs were too specialised by particular purposes to respond to the new possibilities of skilled use.

But none of these vast powers could be attained until the brain had acquired the ability to record experience so that visual and tactile impressions could be interpreted by comparison with previous experience of objects seen and felt. High degrees of muscular skill could be acquired only by prolonged practice and attention to the causes of failure in the past. Man acquired the ability to accumulate knowledge and to interpret the meaning of experience by comparison with memories of the feelings and sensations he had previously enjoyed. Obviously continuity of experience is an essential quality of human behaviour. Man can interpret his present reaction to the world and to the society in which he lives, and shape his actions to meet the needs of the moment, only if he has the criteria for comparison and the skill acquired by long training to display the appropriate reactions. Thus the distinctively human character necessarily involves the continuity of experience. The historical method of study is therefore essential for the interpretation of human thought and conduct.

The evolution of speech enormously emphasised the significance of Man's dependence on his social environment and past history. The comprehension of the meaning of things and actions witnessed prepared the way for the development of speech—which involves the identification of objects in the outside world for which acoustic labels were invented to form nouns; actions for which verbs were devised; and the development of a high degree of

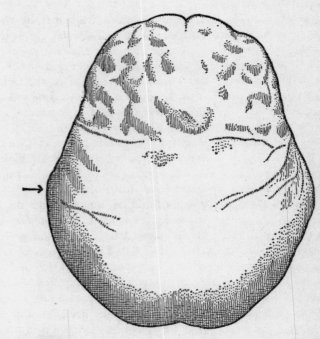

Figure 8—The upper aspect of a cast of the braincase of the earliest and most primitive member of the Human Family (*Pithecanthropus*) to show the obtrusive development of an area (see the arrow) corresponding to that (Figure 6, A) associated with the symbolism of spoken language in modern man.

motor skill to emit the sounds. Nor could speech and music be created and appreciated until hearing had been enriched with a fuller meaning than is implied in the mere understanding of emotional cries or responding to them by merely instinctive responses or imitations of cries that have been heard.

A mould of the braincase of the earliest and most primitive member of the Human Family at present known to us (*Pithecanthropus,* Figure 8) reveals a very conspicuous and precocious expansion of an area precisely corresponding in position to the part of modern Man's brain which is concerned with the appreciation of spoken language. The only inference is that speech is as old as Man himself. The acquisition of articulate language conferred the rank of humanity upon a simian ancestor. The powerful instrument of speech completely transformed Man's mode of behaviour. It made him dependent on his fellows for knowledge and subjected him to the influence of their erroneous interpretations of their experience. Man has the seeing eye, the understanding ear and the skillful hands to shape his own destiny.

It is important to get a clear idea of what is involved in the vast increase in Man's intellectual abilities when he sees, hears and feels. The instrument that confers upon Man his intellectual supremacy is the part of the cerebral cortex known as the neopallium, which attains an important functional significance only in mammals. It is essentially the ultimate destination of those impulses from the eyes, skin and ears which enable us to understand what we see, hear and feel, to associate the three kinds of sensory experience so that we can appreciate the various properties of an object which appeals to one or more of three senses and to compare our present impressions with similar or contrasted incidents in the past.

We have an objective demonstration of these processes of evolution in the comparison of the various phases in the development of the brain (Figures 5 and 6). The increase of the significance of vision is followed by an enhancement of the ability to perform skilled movements. This involves an increase in tactile and auditory discrimination: and the gradual emergence and expansion of the parietal association area (Figures 5 and 6, P) affords concrete evidence of the growing importance of coordinating the knowledge acquired by sight, touch and hearing, and recording the results of such fuller appreciation of the various properties of any object studied by sight, touch or hearing or by any combination of them. The size of the area· C is in a sense the measure of the richness and the intimacy of the connections of the visual cortex with the rest of the cortex.

The enormous size of the parietal area in the human brain demonstrates the dependence of Man upon memories of past experience and the part such memories play in his judgments of the present.

The neopallium was evolved from a primitive cortical instrument not concerned with any of these functions. The cerebral cortex was originally the receptor for impulses of smell and taste and the means whereby an animal could detect the presence of objects in the outside world to satisfy its imperative appetites, alimentary and· sexual, as well as appreciate sources of possible danger and be impelled to life-saving activity. With the assumption of its more exalted rôle as the organ of intelligence, and in particular of visual, tactile and auditory discrimination and skill in movement, it is not wholly exempt from the influence of its former functions. An odour can suddenly suffuse our consciousness with memories, highly charged with emotional tone, not merely of such experiences as appeal to the sense of smell, but with visual and auditory recollections of scenes and incidents of the past, with the feelings and emotions associated with them. Moreover, quite apart from the part played by olfactory experience in the satisfaction of the appetites, the affective side of sensation is an important element in our mental life. The pleasantness or unpleasantness of our sensory experience is obviously a vital factor. Whether or not we pay attention to an experience and allow it to influence our behaviour depends upon whether it attracts us by appealing to our interest or repels us by its unpleasantness or offensiveness. The highest manifestations of intelligence are provoked by such affective considerations. We are apt to ignore things that make no affective appeal to our feelings or our understanding. For example, the essential factors in human behaviour discussed in the preceding pages are all so familiar that most philosophers ignore them. The emotion of successful intellectual work, the achievement of some difficult task, and the circumventing of danger, provoke the joy of success and provide an incentive for further effort.

Thus the purely intellectual and the essentially affective and emotional aspects of experience are intimately bound up one with the other. In the social life of mankind the two elements are inextricably blended in every activity. Hence it comes about that all human beings are "swayed primarily by their feelings." "Seeing the light is something more than a purely mental process" (Herbert Farjeon). Vision requires a mind that is ready to see and is interested in seeing. This implies in plain language the sweeping away of all the obscuring clouds which are created by traditional views and tend to distract attention from the sensory experience of the moment and the fuller meaning experience confers upon it.

These considerations are of cardinal importance in the study of human conduct, not merely of interpreting the processes involved in the diffusion of culture among relatively uncultured peoples, but also in explaining the reasons why some elements of culture are accepted and others rejected. It also throws light upon the curious results of the assimilation and transformation of borrowed elements of culture by cultured as well as uncultured peoples.

No element of culture is ever diffused without change. Not only does the receiver fail to understand another man's ideas in precisely the same way as the giver interprets them, but he picks and chooses and perhaps only adopts certain elements of the culture that appeal to him and can be fitted into his own scheme of things and refashioned in accordance with his own mental make-up. Even the most superficial study of the everyday behaviour of human beings will reveal the fact that cultural diffusion is always going on, but each individual picks and chooses, misunderstands and re-creates the borrowed culture, before assimilating it and fashioning it according to his own desires. But such modifications do not destroy the fact of diffusion. When some ancient prospectors searching in Australia for gold inoculated the aboriginal people with their views about death and the practice of mummification, the natives afterwards took no interest in the gold that was lying about in their country but adopted the practice of embalming the dead and the ritual of Osirian initiation associated with it. The fact that these people neglected the practice which appeals most to us and adopted the useless and uninteresting custom does not imply an absence of diffusion. When the Greeks adopted the Egyptian legend of the god's enemies being converted into creatures of his enemy Set (meaning "stone" or "desert"), and by misunderstanding the story transformed it into a myth of petrifaction as the vengeance of the gods, the incidents were profoundly altered: but this does not destroy the fact that the story was diffused.

So far in this chapter we have been considering the perfectly obvious implications of the fact that Man is a living creature endowed with special aptitudes and modes of behaviour which are distinctive of his humanity.

The Scientific Study of Man

It is essential to refer once more to the historical circumstances that were responsible for obscuring issues of which no human being should be ignorant. Many attempts have been made during the last four centuries to bring the Study of Mankind under a stricter discipline of scientific method. But by a strange irony they have produced profound misunderstanding.

In 1566 Jean Bodin introduced a new theory of universal history which for the first time, according to Professor Bury, was based upon anthropological considerations. He was probably the first writer to take into consideration questions of climate and geography and to recognise frankly that history depends largely upon the will of men. Many facts played a part in preparing the way for this new movement. The work of the great pioneers in science was gradually "restoring a confidence in human reason" (Lecky). The idea that the Greek philosophers' authority was the sole guide to the interpretation of knowledge and experience was being questioned. The factor that played the greatest part in giving knowledge a new orientation was the discovery of the New World, which not only confirmed the opinion of those astronomers who had been claiming that the world was spherical, but also brought to the knowledge of Europeans vast territories and peoples until then unknown, whose existence had been quite unsuspected. Widespread curiosity was aroused and interest was stimulated by the surprising discovery of the genial qualities of these newly discovered peoples, who, in spite of the fact that they had not shared in the benefits of modern civilisation, were truthful, honest and well-behaved. How profound an influence these astounding discoveries made is revealed in the literature of the sixteenth, seventeenth and eighteenth centuries, when Man was put in the centre of the picture. In fact it would not be an exaggeration to claim that the first real conception of a universal history and the possible influence of natural conditions, geographical and climatic, was the direct result to the great maritime exploits. These extended the knowledge of the world and stimulated men's curiosity about the people who were living in regions far removed from Europe. In the course of the discussion of this new information a number of conflicting views emerged more than three centuries ago which still remain matters of dispute in the study of mankind to-day. Perhaps it will serve to clarify the controversial issues which justify the attempt to write a book on Human History at the present time, if we consider some of the points which were raised in the early days of the first serious study of this question.

Bodin's attempt to bring the history of Man into close connection with the rest of the universe was perhaps not altogether alien to the theories of astrology which had been gradually developing during the forty centuries or so before his time. In accordance with these ideas the destiny of Mankind was controlled by celestial events and in this sense Man was a part of the universe.

In the subsequent century when the interpretation of physical phenomena was being brought under the discipline of exact science, the tendency revealed itself of discriminating between Nature and Man. The views of the astrologers may perhaps have helped to strengthen the dogma of the theologians that there was an omnipotent Providence watching over Man's destiny. Hence human affairs were exempted from the operation of the laws of Nature, and the device crept into learning of separating Science from the Humanities.

It was inevitable, however, that the growth of Science should lead to the invasion of the domain of the Humanities. The strictly inductive method of basing any interpretation of the meaning of things and events in the natural world on the facts of observation was being adopted more and more widely. The attempt to apply the same method to Man was responsible for introducing disastrous elements of confusion, which have persisted until the present day. At the end of the seventeenth century Descartes laid it down as the aim of science to discover natural laws into conformity with which all the evidence had to be brought, and Fontenelle applied this doctrine to the affairs of Man. In the eighteenth century Newton insisted upon the necessity of formulating theories to interpret the established facts rather than trying to force them into the scheme of imaginary "laws of Nature." Descartes established the foundation of modern scientific method when he insisted upon the invariability of the laws of nature and so liberated the study of natural phenomena from the disturbing influence of theories of supernatural interference. But in the process of demonstrating this cardinal principle he also planted the seeds of new errors by forgetting that Man is a law unto himself. The distinctive feature of mankind, however, is that Man's thoughts and actions are profoundly influenced by his personal experience which is individual. Descartes's neglect of the essential qualities of Man has led to infinite confusion, which has not yet been eliminated, although three centuries have elapsed since his *Discourse on Method* was published.

It was necessary to break the tyranny of Greek and Roman authority so as to liberate the minds of men from such strange vagaries as were displayed, for example, by Galileo's critics who refused to admit that they saw spots on the sun because they could find no reference to such an observation in the writings of Aristotle. But Descartes went too far in his denial of our indebtedness to the Greeks. His failure to recognise the validity of historical continuity rendered it impossible for him to interpret human knowledge and the fact of progress.

In his famous treatise on *Primitive Culture* Sir Edward Tylor in 1871 gave luminous expression to the principles that should inform any attempt to interpret the behaviour of men under conditions of civilisation. "The notion of the continuity of civilisation is no barren philosophical principle, but is at once made practical by the consideration that they who wish to understand their own lives ought to know the stages through which their opinions and habits have become what they are." "History, taken as our guide in explaining the different stages of civilisation, offers a theory based on actual experience. This is a development-theory, in which both advance and relapse have their acknowledged places. But so far as history is to be our criterion, progression is primary and degradation secondary; culture must be gained before it can be lost. Moreover, in striking a balance between the effects of forward and backward movement in civilisation, it must be borne in mind how powerfully the diffusion of culture acts in preserving the results of progress from the attacks of degeneration. A progressive movement in culture spreads, and becomes independent of the fate of its originators."

Mediaeval scholars who put the Greeks and Romans upon a pedestal of infallibility had of necessity to admit in explanation of the fallibility of later generations that a process of degeneration must have taken place. The Cartesian doctrine which attempted to prick the bubble of classical omnipotence so as to prepare the way for the idea of Progress encouraged men to deny or unduly to minimise the process of degradation, which is an ever-present tendency in all human affairs. But for three centuries this question of degeneration has been a constant source of confusion and misunderstanding, especially when it became charged with theological emotion by drawing into its ambit the dogma of the Fall of Man. Readers of the late Professor Bury's brilliant book, *The Idea of Progress,* will find a very graphic account of the obstacles that have been put in the way of clear thinking by the continued quarrelling over the patent fact of degeneration. Civilisation is such an artificial and complicated product that it requires active thought and striving to preserve and develop it. Without such intensive human efforts degeneration rapidly supervenes, as many centuries ago happened in Egypt and Babylonia, Cambodia and Central America. It is not merely fortuitous that the dominant theories of ethnology to-day, which are essentially Cartesian, should lay undue emphasis on supposed natural laws of human thought and behaviour; and at the same time refuse to give due consideration to the patent facts of continuity and degeneration, and to the need for the historical method to elucidate their influence.

The real causes underlying all this confusion are a failure to recognise (a) the principle enunciated by Newton that the laws of Nature can only be determined inductively by taking into consideration all the observed facts and (b) that the working of the human mind cannot be explained by laying down laws of Nature, since the personal experience of each individual modifies the nature of his reaction to any set of circumstances. For the interpretation of human thought and behaviour the historical method is essential. The enthusiastic reformers who in the seventeenth century set out to apply scientific methods to the study of mankind overlooked the fact that they were discussing human beings and not puppets controlled solely by the forces of Nature. The irony of this situation would be amusing if it were not so tragic that the results of three centuries of devoted research should have been lost to the men who in the intensity of their enthusiasm for science lost their common sense.

Even when in 1750 Turgot uttered a warning and called men's attention to the fallacy of their methods they paid no heed. He contrasted the operation of the laws of Nature with the behaviour of Man:

"The phenomena of nature, subjected as they are to constant laws, are enclosed in a circle of revolutions that remain the same for ever! . . . The succession of men, on the contrary, offers from age to age a spectacle of continual variations. Reason, freedom, the passions, are incessantly producing new events. All epochs are fastened together by a sequence of causes and effects, linking the condition of the world to all the conditions that have gone before it. The gradually multiplied signs of speech and writing, giving men an instrument for making sure of the continued possession of their ideas, as well as of imparting them to others, have formed out of the knowledge of each individual a common treasure, which generation transmits to generation, as an inheritance constantly augmented by the discoveries of each age; and the human race, observed from its first beginning, seems in the eyes of the philosopher to be one vast whole, which, like each individual in it, has its infancy and its growth."

This translation was made by Lord Morley, who declared that it was "among the most pregnant, as it was among the most original, in the history of literature, and reveals in an outline, standing clear against the light, a thought which revolutionised old methods of viewing and describing the course of human affairs, and contained the germs of a new and most fruitful philosophy of society." It is the aim of this book once more to revive Turgot's fruitful philosophy.

Reference has already been made to the fact that in 1566 Bodin introduced the consideration of the influence of climate and geographical conditions upon mankind. This attempt to bring human destiny under the control of the terrestrial forces of Nature was the first step in a movement that has gained momentum during the three and a half centuries since Bodin set the ball of confusion rolling. It has wrought incalculable havoc with sober thinking and seriously interfered with the clear view of the factors that have shaped Man's destiny. Even to-day references to climate and geographical environment are given almost a mystical significance by some writers. Volumes have been written about the effects of desiccation on the history of civilisation without the slightest attempt to determine whether in fact regions that are now deserts were not also desiccated long before civilisation was introduced. The mere use of the words "grasslands" and "highlands" is supposed to imply some inevitable process of mechanically working development leading to inevitable results in shaping human qualities and behaviour. The considerations set forth in the preceding pages are fatal to such mysticism. But the influence of such devices of argument, to which many Humanists still resort under the mistaken idea that they are introducing methods of Science into History, is so destructive of clear thinking that attention must be specifically called to the fallacy underlying it. It is a very remarkable phenomenon that some of the most extreme critics of the historical methods are the professed historians themselves. They use the fashionable word "evolution" in apparent ignorance of the fact that evolution is a historical process, which involves a recognition of continuity and cataclysmic alterations in conditions to provoke change.

Fortunately some of the leading historians are active in appealing for the adoption of the historical method in the study of history. In a recent number of the *The National Review* (February, 1929) Sir Charles Oman calls attention to the patent fact that history is cataclysmic. The career of mankind has not been the inevitable result of the action of natural causes, but has in large measure been shaped by accidents and catastrophes, by the actions of dominating personalities who have deliberately provoked great movements, peaceful and warlike, which have shaped the destiny of the world.

Sir Charles Oman makes a vigorous protest against the fundamental fallacy involved in the modern speculations of old Bodin's misguided followers. It expresses so admirably one of the main propositions in the argument of this book that his exact words may profitably be quoted here:—"Two generations have now passed since the blessed word 'Evolution' was invented, and was applied as a universal panacea for all the problems of the Universe —historical no less than physical or metaphysical. By this I mean that a whole school of historians have set forth the thesis that history is a continuous logical process, a series of inevitable results following on well-marshalled tables of causes." He argues that if an aeroplane were to drop from the sky and kill him, "the result is not an example of necessary evolution, but an accident, and to me personally a catastrophe. And I hold this view against all the historians who want to turn history into a continuous and mechanical panorama of logical causes and inevitable results."

It is essential to get this point, obvious as it is, clearly established. The great events in Human History were provoked by individual human beings exercising their wills to change the direction of human thought and action or by natural catastrophes forcing men of insight to embark on new enterprises.

Reference has been already made to the influence of Christopher Columbus's discovery of the New World in opening a new era of Human History. The interference with the Asiatic trade provoked by the irruption of the Turks into Europe created the need for a new route to the Indies. According to Sir Charles Oman America would have been colonised by the Norse inhabitants of Greenland if the Black Death in 1350 had not completely destroyed these people who were in touch with the American coast. Hence it was left for the Spaniards and Portuguese to profit by the adventure across the Atlantic.

These historical incidents provided the predisposing circumstances for the momentous event which revolutionised knowledge as well as commerce. But it was the vision and persistence of Columbus that effected the transformation.

The course of civilisation has been determined by a series of men of insight and courage, pioneers who, like Osiris, invented such cardinal institutions as agriculture and induced their community to adopt them; or who, like Thales and Gautama, destroyed hampering conditions and enabled the human mind to escape from superstitions and see clearly; or by soldiers like Alexander and Napoleon, who fashioned empires in the roughshod adventure of wars, which spread their disturbing influences far and wide; or by great inventors who transformed conditions of life and industry and brought the whole world into intimate communication.

CHAPTER II

THE WANDERINGS OF MAN AND HIS RELATIONS

NO one who looks at a monkey can fail to be struck by its likeness to Man. The resemblance is not so much one of form and proportion as of the position and movements of the eyes and the use the animal makes of its hands. In the folk-lore and beliefs of many peoples living in the countries where monkeys or their allies occur, stories are told of their relationship to or identity with mankind. This is particularly the case with those apes which have always been called by the significant title "man-like" or anthropoid. The anatomy of the apes reveals an even closer likeness to human structure than the external appearance.

Hence it is not a matter of surprise that when zoologists attempted to classify animals and grade their status the monkeys were associated with Man in the same natural Order, which was called Primates. This includes not only the apes and monkeys, but also a number of small and more primitive creatures often called "Half Apes" or Prosimiae, but more generally known as the lemurs. There is one group of primitive members of the Order, which, though nearly resembling both the lemurs and monkeys, differs so much from both as to belong to a special category or Sub-Order, which is distinguished as the Tarsioidea. There is now only one Tarsioid genus still living. It is represented by the quaint little creature known as the spectral tarsier (*Tarsius spectrum*) which is found in Borneo, Billiton, Banka, and the Philippines.

Many millions of years ago, in the epoch which geologists distinguish as the Eocene, other Tarsioids were living in places as far apart as the South of France and the United States of America (Wyoming and its neighbourhood). The fossil remains of these creatures belong to a variety of genera differing in greater or less degree from *Tarsius*. Of these the most ancient and primitive are the American forms. These fossils are found in association with still more primitive (Lemuroid) members of the Order Primates, as well as tree shrews, animals presenting many points of resemblance to lemurs, but not yet admitted by most zoologists to full membership of that Order. Hence the possibility arises that Wyoming or some neighbouring place in North America may be the birthplace of the Order of Mammals from which millions

Figure 9—The Spectral Tarsier. (From the author's *The Evolution of Man*. Oxford University Press.)

of years afterwards, and in some distant part of the world, Man was destined to emerge. It is not certain that America was really the place where in the Cretaceous or early Eocene epoch one of the tree shrews became transformed into the parent of the Primates. All that we know is that the earliest fossil remains of the Order were found in Wyoming in association with those of the animals from which the Primates were undoubtedly derived. But as the members of the same three groups are still living in the Malay Archipelago there is the possibility that the Primates may have been evolved in Borneo, or somewhere else in the Asiatic region, and wandered to America by means of a trans-Pacific land bridge at, or even before, the beginning of the Tertiary Period of the geologists.

It is generally agreed that France was not the birthplace of the Primates. The Lemuroids and Tarsioids whose fossilised remains have been discovered in the late Eocene beds in France are cited as evidence that in the middle Eocene period primitive members of the Primates crossed the Atlantic from America by a land bridge.

Additional corroboration is provided for this hypothesis by the fact that in 1911 there were found in the Egyptian Fayum the most ancient fossil remains of monkeys yet recovered. It is not supposed that these monkeys were evolved in Egypt, or indeed in the Old World. The fact that the most primitive living monkeys are found only in South America seems to be susceptible of only one explanation. When the Lemuroids and Tarsioids crossed the Atlantic bridge to reach the Old World they must have been accompanied (or soon followed) by very primitive monkeys whose modified descendants are the Oligocene fossils found in Egypt. Some of the earlier original stock remained in America and found a permanent asylum in South America, where they still survive as the Platyrhine monkeys.

From Africa the small primitive anthropoid apes wandered east and their descendants seem to have found in India an environment congenial to their needs. For in the Siwalik Mountains, among the foothills of the Himalayas, a variety of large fossil anthropoid apes have been found in beds of the Miocene period.

In the course of their wanderings the Primates thus encircled the world. Their journeys necessarily occupied a vast span of years because they were obviously not deliberately planned but were such migrations as every kind of living creature was led by force of circumstances to undertake. In the case of creatures such as lemurs or monkeys the existence of trees and a warm climate were essential. Hence the range of their wanderings was strictly limited at any one time by the natural distribution of suitable forests in genial climates.

Probably before the end of the Eocene Period diminutive man-like apes had come into existence. For the fossil remains of *Propliopithecus,* the earliest known anthropoid, were found in 1911 in the Egyptian Fayum in beds of Early Oligocene Age, i. e. immediately after the Eocene.

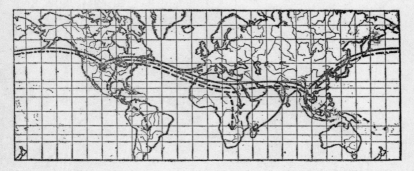

Figure 10—An attempt to indicate the routes taken by a variety of monkeys, Lemuroids and Tarsioids to encircle the world, possibly starting from North America.

In the next geological Epoch, the Miocene, millions of years later, many large anthropoids had come into being in India and from there had wandered east and west to the extreme limits of the continental land mass—as far as Borneo (then in unbroken continuity with Asia) in the East, and in the West as far as the Atlantic littoral, both in Europe and Africa. In the East the gibbons and orang-utans still live in the area their ancestors thus invaded in the Miocene, but they became extinct in India itself. During the Miocene period relatives of the gibbon also wandered west to Europe as far as France, accompanied by a large ape (as big as the chimpanzee) which is known as *Dryopithecus.* It is of special interest because it presents evidence of nearer kinship to Man than any existing ape. Both of the apes that reached Europe became extinct during the Pliocene Period, the geological age that followed the Miocene. But at the time *Pliopithecus* (the Miocene gibbon) and *Dryopithecus* wandered in Europe, probably from India, they were accompanied on their western journey as far as Arabia by some of their kindred who made their way into Africa, where their descendants survive to this day as the chimpanzees and gorillas. Just as the interesting manlike ape *Dryopithecus* lived in Europe in the Miocene and Pliocene, so also in Africa, at an unknown time but in all probability the Pliocene, did an ape about the same size as *Dryopithecus* and the chimpanzee, which Professor Raymond A. Dart has called *Australopithecus*. Its fossilised skull was found at Taungs in Bechuanaland in 1924. This specimen is of exceptional interest and importance not only because the skull is more nearly complete than any other known fossil of an anthropoid ape but also because it presents a closer affinity to Man even than *Dryopithecus*.

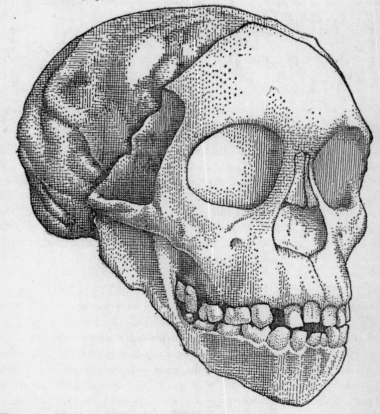

Figure 11—The fossil skull of *Australopithecus* found at Taungs in Bechuanaland.
(From the writer's *The Evolution of Man,* Oxford.)

It is interesting and probably not without significance that when the large anthropoids left their homeland and roamed far afield, the forms most nearly akin to Man wandered west, where to-day in Africa the two apes that resemble Man most nearly in structure, function and habits are still living. More than fifty-eight

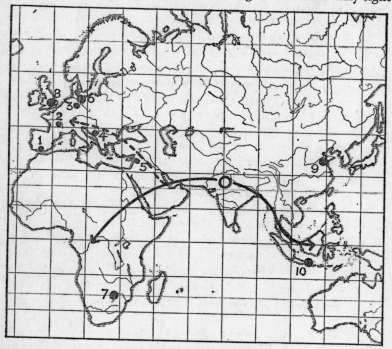

Figure 12—The wanderings of the Giant Anthropoids from India (O), the orangutan to Borneo; the chimpanzee, gorilla and *Australopithecus* to Africa; the now extinct ape *Dryopithecus* to Europe. The geographical distribution of the extinct genera of the Human Family is indicated by the numbers 10 (*Pithecanthropus*), 9 (*Sinanthropus*), 8 (*Eoanthropus*, Piltdown man), 7 (Rhodesian man), and 6 (Heidelberg man), and the extinct species, Neanderthal man, by the numbers 1 to 5.

years ago these facts led Darwin to suggest that Africa may have been the original home of the Human Family, a point of view that receives further corroboration from discoveries made since Darwin's time. When in 1891 the skull cap of an extremely ancient man was found in Java—so much akin to the ape in type that many writers maintained, as some still do, that it (*Pithecanthropus*) was not human but simian, it was assumed that Darwin was wrong in suggesting Africa as the cradle of mankind. Java, or at any rate Eastern Asia, was claimed as the place where Man evolved. The recent discovery in China of fossil remains of another very early and primitive member of the Human Family, which Professor Davidson Black has named *Sinopithecus,* has revived this old theory.

But while these two contrasted genera of early men were living in the Extreme East the (roughly contemporaneous) genus *Eoanthropus* was roaming the Far West, as its fossil remains found at Piltdown in England prove. Hence it is certain that at the commencement of the Pliocene period a variety of caricatures of men had already roamed across the whole breadth of the Old World. But the only apes that reveal a really close affinity with the Human Family were restricted, so far as our evidence goes, to the region from India toward the west. Hence it seems probable that the cradle of the Human Family lies somewhere between the Himalayas and the Heart of Africa.

For unknown thousands of years primitive types of men roamed far and wide in the more genial parts of Asia, Europe and Africa. Only the merest fragments have so far been recovered of the sharply contrasted early genera, *Pithecanthropus* in Java, *Sinanthropus* in China, *Eoanthropus* in England, *Palaeanthropus* (or *Homo heidelbergensis*) in Germany, and possibly also a member of the same genus in the *Homo* (*Palaeanthropus*) *rhodesiensis* from South Africa.

The acquisition of human qualities no doubt made it possible for Man to roam about the earth more rapidly than any of his predecessors had done, because he was able to adapt his behaviour to varying conditions and in the light of his fuller understanding to evade difficulties and circumvent dangers. During the time of his nomadic existence primitive Man used his high powers of discrimination and aptitude for learning to cultivate a marvellous skill in tracking which involved surprising powers of exact observation and logical inference. The biological usefulness of his alert brain and manual dexterity was displayed in the cunning of eye and hand which enabled him to be more than a match for any other living creature. He was able to survive in a greater variety of climates and environments than any other animal and to wander rapidly to the ends of the earth.

After many experimental types of the Human Family had occupied the world for thousands of years the genus *Homo* emerged and in course of time gave birth to many species.

Eventually one of these species attained exceptional skill and intelligence and so acquired the cunning and wit to surpass all its fellows and eventually to supplant them completely. The outstand-

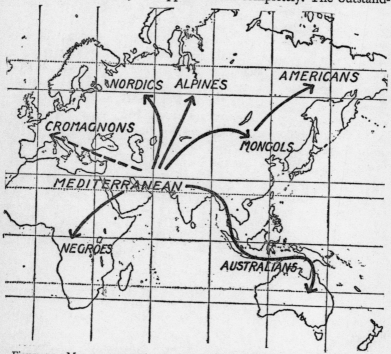

Figure 13—Map to suggest the directions of the wanderings of the various races into which the species *Homo sapiens* became subdivided to reach the areas in which they ultimately found a home.

ing distinction of *Homo sapiens* is the possession of small and amazingly adaptable hands endowed with the aptitude, in virtue of the high development of the frontal region of the brain, to attain a perfection of skill which made them the special instruments of Man's destiny.

Adequate information is lacking to enable us to decide where *Homo sapiens* was evolved from some more primitive species of the genus. But the considerations graphically expressed in the map (Figure 13) suggest the possibility that Southwestern Asia or Northeastern Africa may be the cradle of the species to which all living men belong.

Fifty centuries ago the members of the Mediterranean Race occupied the area which originally may have been the home of the species *sapiens,* from which at a much earlier period a series of varieties of the species (collectively labelled "Cro-Magnons" in the map, although Cro-Magnon Man is merely one of a number of fairly well defined groups) wandered west into Europe. The ancestors of the Australians (who are known to have occupied the region from India to the East) wandered along the Southern Asiatic littoral towards the region where they are now found in greatest abundance. The forebears of the Negroes probably wandered in a southwesterly direction to the heart of Africa. The original areas of distribution of the three other distinctively modified groups, which we call the Nordic, Alpine and Mongol races, are, so far as the evidence now available permits us to determine, such as to suggest that their respective ancestors must have wandered from the original home of the species towards the heart of Asia. The area of characterisation of the Mongols was probably in the Far East. Some of the primitive Mongols, possibly intermingled with certain proto-Alpine elements, wandered across the Behring Strait into America. But when this happened there is no evidence upon which to base any decision.

Until the year 1848 no human remains had been recovered that did not belong to the same species as ourselves and all other human beings now living on the earth. Since then, however, a sufficient number of fossil remains—most of them tantalisingly fragmentary —of extinct types have been found, to establish the fact that the Human Family is of vast antiquity. We lack the knowledge to measure the time in years. About 4000 B.C. men first began to build up the civilisation which we enjoy to-day. The fossil remains of Man establish the fact that even at the commencement of the period which the geologists distinguish as the Pleistocene, or quite early in that period, three widely different genera of the Human

Family were already in existence and dwelling as far apart as Java, England and Northern China. Obviously the common parent of the Ape-Man of Java (*Pithecanthropus*), the Dawn-Man of Piltdown (*Eoanthropus*) and the *Sinanthropus* of China must be far more ancient than his divergent descendants. Not only must we allow them time to wander to the uttermost limits, east and west,

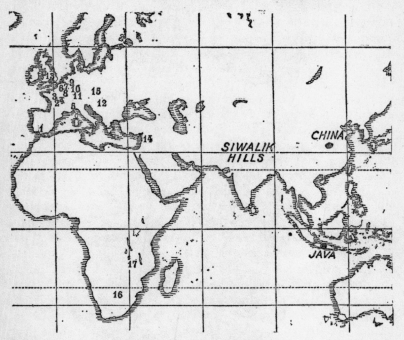

Figure 14—A map to emphasise the facts that bear upon the as yet insoluble problem of the place of origin of the Human Family. From the Miocene home of the Giant Anthropoids in the Siwalik Hills the ancestors of Man left no trace of their wanderings in Pliocene times while they were assuming human rank. When the curtain is rung up again in Pleistocene times divergently modified primitive types of the Human Family are revealed in Java, China, England (13), Germany (9), and Rhodesia (17). Subsequently, many thousands of years later, Neanderthal Man roamed through Europe (1 to 8 and 10 to 12) and Western Asia (14), and varieties of *Homo sapiens* occupied the Transvaal (16), Java and Australia.

of the great continental land mass, which somewhere or other must contain the cradle of mankind; but a vastly greater span of years must be allowed for the development of the profound contrasts revealed by the comparison of the Ape-Man of Java with

his more man-like contemporary in England. The various estimates of the length of the Pleistocene period which have been

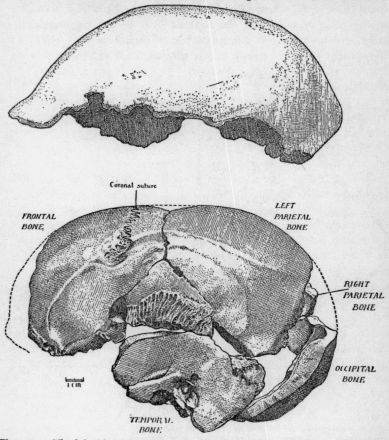

Figure 15—The left side of the braincase of *Pithecanthropus* (above) compared with
that of *Eoanthropus* (below).

made by geologists in recent years vary from a quarter of a million to five million years. The range of earlier conjecture even
transcends this vast discrepancy. But if we admit that mankind
is certainly much older than the Pleistocene—seeing that the earliest man, the remote ancestor of the three earlier genera, must have
been alive during the Pliocene period—a million years at least

must be allowed for the career of mankind on the earth. It would probably be nearer the truth to say several millions. But even if the minimum figure of one million years is adopted that is more than adequate to bring out the contrast to the mere six thousand years of civilisation.

By comparison the history of civilisation is merely a thing of yesterday and to-day. Nevertheless in studying Human History it is important never to forget that man was wandering up and down the earth for countless thousands of years, pushing his way into every accessible part of it, and coming under the influence of every variety of climate and environment. Yet he did not attempt to create a system of civilisation or anything that could be called culture. Obviously, therefore, speculations based on the supposed influence of climate and geographical environment leave something to be explained. During all these aeons of time he was content to do without houses or clothes, as indeed some of his descendants do to this day. Apart from the making of a few rude implements he devised no crafts. He created no social organisation other than the family grouping he inherited from his simian ancestry. Nor did he develop any customs or beliefs to hamper his freedom or restrain his actions. He was content to remain the genial and happy child of Nature without attempting to do any of the manifold things that we include in the practice of civilisation.

In any attempt to interpret human nature and explain human thought and behaviour it is essential not to forget Natural Man and his innate honesty and decency.

The scope of this book is so wide that the question will naturally suggest itself whether the attempt to cope with so tremendous a task is not merely courting failure. By making the effort to estimate the significance of Man's structure and the factors that control his thinking and actions there emerges a clearer view of the real nature of Man. Interpreting the evidence that throws light on the circumstances which brought the Human Family into existence, the essential limitations of Man's capabilities are more easily assessed. Studying the behaviour of primitive people with the illumination afforded by biological considerations, we can pry into the motives that determined the creation of civilisation. In so doing we get a clearer conception of human nature itself than we could gain merely by studying the behaviour of our fellow men without this vision of primitive Man in all his nakedness.

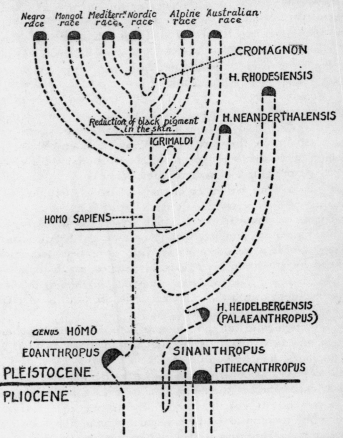

Figure 16—Scheme to suggest the possible relationships in time, and affinities of the genera, species, and races of the Human Family. The places assigned to the Cro-Magnon and Grimaldi races are wholly tentative.

For the fact seems to emerge quite clearly and definitely from our enquiries that, so far as we are able to interpret the actions of people in remote antiquity, the motives are essentially identical with those that determine our own. As the circumstances of these people were much simpler than those of the present time, it is easier to recognise the springs of their activities than those of Modern Man under the complex conditions of civilisation. By taking this wide view of Man's career the real aim is to simplify the problem which awaits solution. It is a matter of getting a view of the whole field of enquiry and appreciating the fundamental factors that have played a part in the development of the Human Family and in the building up of civilisation.

Figure 17—A restoration of Neanderthal Man (Dorothy Davison, *Our Prehistoric Ancestors*, Methuen).

Using the term in a strictly biological sense, all peoples living on the earth are members of one and the same species. The Negro, as even a child can see, differs profoundly from the Chinaman, and the European from both. Nevertheless we are bound to admit that all belong to the same zoological species. It is divided into a number of races, but there is no agreement among anthropologists as to the number. For simplicity of treatment we may agree to admit six easily distinguishable groups—the Australian, Negro,

Mongol, Mediterranean, Alpine and Nordic. The aboriginal Australian is the most primitive of existing peoples. He is to be regarded as the survivor of one of the lowest forms of the species *Homo sapiens*. The Negro comes next, but he is not nearly so primitive as the Australian and in some respects is highly specialised.

In the process of evolution of the races of mankind there was a progressive loss of pigmentation, only the Australian and the Negro races retaining the colour that in all probability was at first common to all mankind.

Until the middle of last century no human beings were known who did not belong to one of these existing peoples. A skull discovered in 1856 in the Neanderthal Cave near Düsseldorf became a subject of violent discussion for many years. Most competent anatomists now admit that the Neanderthal skull is the representative of an extinct species of the Human Family, quite distinct from *Homo sapiens*. It conforms to the same type as the fossil skull found at Gibraltar in 1848, which remained undescribed until the interest awakened by the Neanderthal discovery eventually opened men's eyes to its importance. But when first found there was some doubt as to the significance of the Neanderthal skull. Some suggested that it was not human at all; others that it was definitely

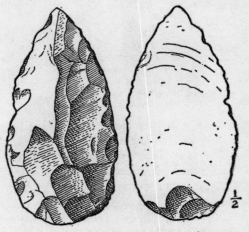

Figure 18—A flint implement of Mousterian type.

pathological. It is a great flat skull with enormous prominent eye-brow ridges, very different from the skull of an ordinary human being. These opinions were held until 1887, when two other skulls of precisely the same type in every respect were found in Belgium at Spy, near Liége. This convinced most people that the Neander-thal skull was not a pathological specimen but belonged to a repre-sentative of a species of the Human Family now extinct. Since that time a large number of specimens of the same type have been found in Western Europe, including Gibraltar (where Miss Dorothy Garrod found a second skull), Yugoslavia and Palestine.

The fossils found at Spy in 1887 were associated with a particu-lar type of flint implement, with which archaeologists had been familiar for many years. Such artifacts were originally recognised at Le Moustier, in the Dordogne: hence they are distinguished by the name Mousterian. The association of a distinct type of mankind with a definite phase of culture and a number of extinct animals, such as cave bears, mammoths, etc., confirmed the impression that Neanderthal Man was of vast antiquity in comparison with *Homo*

STEPPE HORSE.
NEANDERTHAL MAN.   IBEX.   CAVE-LION.
CAVE-LEOPARD.   MUSK OX.
CAVE-BEAR.   MAMMOTH.   RED DEER.   REINDEER.
WOLVERENE.   ARCTIC FOX.   ARCTIC HARE.
ARCTIC PTARMIGAN.   LEMMINGS.   WOOLLY RHINOCEROS.

Figure 19—Animals living in the Mousterian Period (Dorothy Davison, *Our Prehistoric Ancestors*, Methuen).

sapiens in Europe. In 1923 the announcement was made of the discovery of a skull of this type in Palestine. A large number of fragments of the same type had, however, already been found in Croatia, so that this discovery of the Galilee Man was not altogether surprising.

Neanderthal Man is now revealed as an uncouth creature with an enormous flattened head, very prominent eyebrow ridges and a coarse face. The trunk is short and thick, the robust limbs are short and thick-set: the broad and stooping shoulders lead by a curve to the forwardly projected head set on an abnormally thick neck. The hands are large and coarse and lack the delicate play between thumb and fingers which is found in *Homo sapiens*. The large brain is singularly defective in the frontal region. It is clear that

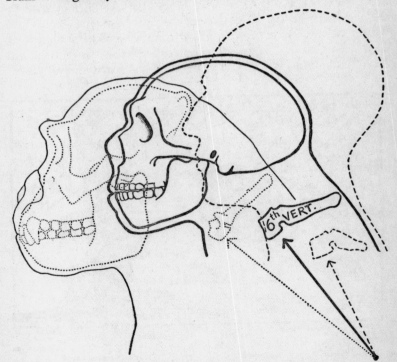

Figure 20—The contrast between the poise of the head in Neanderthal Man (centre) and Modern Man (right) and the gorilla (left).

Neanderthal Man's limbs and brain were incapable of performing those delicately skilled movements that are the special prerogative of *Homo sapiens* and the chief means whereby the latter has learned by experiment to understand the world around him, and to acquire the high powers of discrimination that enabled him to compete successfully with the brutal strength of the Neanderthal species.

The Neanderthal men, with their characteristic Mousterian culture, suddenly disappeared from Europe, and were replaced by immigrants belonging to our own species, who brought with them to Europe the germs of the phase of culture known as Aurignacian. The newcomers were members of the Cro-Magnon race, a very tall people with large dolichocephalic skulls and relatively broad faces. They probably entered Europe from the South, because their settlements are found chiefly near the Mediterranean coastline, in northern Africa, Sicily, Italy, southern France and Spain. The coming of this superior race of highly intelligent men is revealed also by the sudden improvement in the technique of the flint-work and the appearance, especially in the caves of southern France, of mural decorations exhibiting new powers of artistic observation and skill in depicting the animals which these people hunted. There is revealed for the first time the genius and the aesthetic feeling of members of our own race. At a later period the members of another race (also dolichocephalic, but with much narrower and more harmonic face than the Cro-Magnon people) began to make their way into Europe from the East, probably by way of Poland and Moravia, Hungary and Bavaria, thence into France. These people are often known as the Brünn race and their culture as Solutrean. The skeletons are found deeply imbedded in loess along with the bones of the woolly mammoth, woolly rhinoceros, giant deer, reindeer, etc. Their culture is distinguished by the wonderful skill in flaking flint implements. Although it lasted only a short time in Europe and never extended as far as Spain or the Mediterranean area, this method of stone-working spread far and wide, to Egypt, Australia and America, and in the latter two countries persisted until the present time.

After the Solutrean came the Magdalenian phase of culture, which marked the culmination of the skill and achievement of Man before agriculture. This new development was not derived from the Solutrean art, but was brought into Europe and replaced the latter. It lacked the superb skill of the Solutrean flint-workers, but was characterised by a high degree of ability in painting and sculpture.

Now in many respects Neanderthal Man resembles the aboriginal Australian—so much so, in fact, that certain anthropologists at one time were inclined to regard the Australian as a survivor of the species. But, primitive as he is in structure, the Australian conforms in essential features to the type that is distinctive of the species *sapiens*. The probable explanation of the likeness lies in the fact that the Australian has retained some of the primitive features which *Homo sapiens* had when his ancestors first became differentiated from Neanderthal Man.

Since the discovery of Neanderthal Man, remains of other members of the Human Family have been found which have compelled anthropologists to create still further species for their reception. Others have been discovered so much more ancient and different in type that new genera distinct from Homo have been made. In 1922 a skull was found at the Broken Hill Mine in Rhodesia for

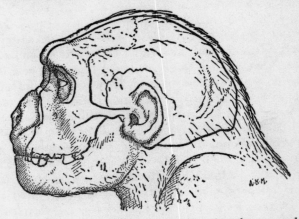

Figure 21—The outline of the Rhodesian skull with the soft parts modelled after the gorilla.

the reception of which the new species *rhodesiensis* was created by Sir Arthur Smith Woodward. Although the actual specimen re-

covered seems to be comparatively recent it may represent the survival of an extremely ancient type.

In 1908 a jaw was found near Heidelberg, which belongs to a
man of far greater antiquity than Neanderthal Man. The Rhodesian and Heidelberg skulls have often been put in association with

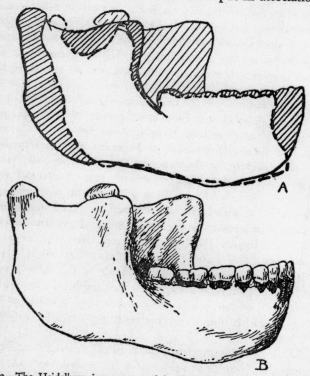

Figure 22—The Heidelberg jaw, compared in the upper diagram with the jaw of
Modern Man (Dorothy Davison, *Our Prehistoric Ancestors*, Methuen).

each other, the reason being that the Heidelberg jaw nearly fits
and harmonises with the Rhodesian skull, of which the jaw has not
been recovered. Their correlation, however, is but a tentative suggestion. The jaw of Heidelberg Man differs so profoundly from the
two known species of the genus *Homo* as to raise the possibility that
this very ancient inhabitant of Germany, and possibly also the man
of Rhodesia, may belong to a distinct genus which has tentatively

received the distinctive name *Palaeanthropus.* At present, however, four distinct species of the genus *Homo—Homo sapiens,* Neanderthal Man, Heidelberg Man and Rhodesian Man—are generally recognised. Below *Homo* come the representatives of the Human Family which cannot be put into this genus. There is the Piltdown skull found in Sussex in 1912, for the reception of which the genus Eoanthropus was created by Sir Arthur Smith Woodward. In 1891 a skull-cap was found near Java which is much more primitive. The discoverer of this fossil, Professor Dubois, named it *Pithecanthropus erectus* and assigned this newly defined genus to the geological period known as the Pliocene. Most geologists, however, now agree in placing it at the beginning of the Pleistocene. It is not yet possible to establish any exact synchronism between the geological horizons of Europe and Eastern Asia: but so far as we can judge at present the Dawn-Man of Piltdown and the Ape-Man of Java, vastly different as they are in physical type and distant in habitat, were living approximately at the same epoch. But whether that was one million or five million years ago no one can say. The whole aspect of this problem has received new and significant illumination by the recent discovery in China of yet another extinct genus of the Human Family, of approximately the same age as *Pithecanthropus* and *Eoanthropus.* Professor Davidson Black has given the name *Sinanthropus pekingensis* to this newly revealed relative, which, in spite of its nearer geographical propinquity to the Javanese Ape-Man, much more nearly approximates in type to the Dawn-Man of Britain. Nevertheless it is generically distinct from both.

The finding of the Piltdown skull illustrates the fortuitous circumstances that have been responsible for the recovery of the few scraps of extinct men we possess. In 1911, or perhaps earlier, the late Mr. Charles Dawson, a lawyer practising at Lewes in Sussex, who for many years had been in the habit of collecting fossils, was attending in his professional capacity a land court at Barkham Manor. When he was approaching the court, he noticed that the road was being mended with flint, and throughout the sitting his thoughts kept puzzling over the problem why flint was being used when, so he believed, there was none to be had nearer than five miles away from the spot, in which case the expenses of cartage would have been almost as great as the price of proper road metal. Hence, as soon as the court rose, he went to make enquiries of the workmen, who informed him that the flint was obtained from a small patch of gravel alongside the road, which was not shown on the official geological map. He told the workmen to look out for fossils, and for many months visited the place from time to time to see if anything had come to light. One day he found that the workmen had dug out a piece of fossilised bone, which they mistook for a coconut. They had been throwing stones at it, and had broken it into three pieces. Mr. Dawson was struck by the thickness of the bone, which obviously was part of a human skull, and, remembering the Heidelberg jaw, thought he had found the skull belonging to that species. In the course of further digging he found some other fragments—a piece of the occipital bone and a bit of the other side of the skull.

In the summer of 1912 he took the fragments to the British Museum and showed them to Dr. (afterwards Sir Arthur) Smith Woodward, suggesting that they might belong to a man of the Heidelberg type. Smith Woodward returned with him to Piltdown to resume excavations. They unearthed a remarkable jaw of a type generically distinct from the Mauer jaw. Its outstanding peculiarity was that it had a shelf extending horizontally backward towards the tongue like that found in the ape's jaw at the junction of the two halves. As the jaw was found close to the skull Sir Arthur Smith Woodward assumed that the two belonged to the same individual. But no sooner had the account of the discovery been published than a violent controversy arose, which lasted for many years, and even now is not wholly assuaged. Some anatomists said that the jaw was obviously that of a chimpanzee and could not be associated with the human skull. But Sir Arthur Smith Woodward took the view that it was improbable that a hitherto unknown type of human skull without a jaw should be found in association with the jaw of a hitherto unknown type of chimpanzee without a skull. Even to this day, however, some anthropologists (for instance, Professor E. Werth of Berlin, *Der fossile Mensch,* 1928, and Professor Boule of Paris, *Les Hommes Fossiles,* 1923) regard this jaw as belonging to a new type of ape. Possibly the original account of the skull may have been responsible for some misunderstanding. When

Sir Arthur Smith Woodward said that it was undoubtedly human in type, he did not mean to suggest that it belonged to *Homo sapiens*—merely that it was an undoubted representative of the Human Family. Foreign anthropologists, seeing that the skull did not possess the huge eyebrow ridges such as they assumed to be always present in early types such as Neanderthal Man, wrongly assumed that it was essentially modern in type. In reality, while the jaw and braincase reveal unmistakable evidence of their human

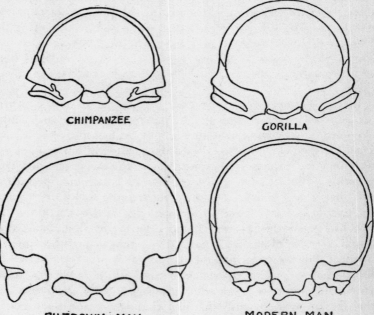

Figure 23—Cross-sections of skulls of a chimpanzee, a gorilla, Piltdown Man and Modern Man—all at the situation of the ear-holes—to afford a graphic demonstration (which requires no technical knowledge for its appreciation) of the simian build of the Piltdown skull.

status, both display features unknown in any other human remains which are found in the apes.

The anatomical features leave us in doubt as to the way in which the fragments should be put together to reconstruct the braincase (see Figure 15, p. 52). The Piltdown skull when properly reconstructed is found to possess strongly marked simian peculiarities. In respect of these features it harmonises completely with the jaw, the simian form of which has not only been admitted, but also exaggerated by most writers.

While many anthropologists were still persisting in doubting whether the skull and jaw should be associated, there was found about two miles away another tooth of the same type as those in the original jaw in association with two fragments (frontal and occipital) of a braincase of the same type as the original fossils. Hence there is no longer a reason for attaching any significance to criticisms that have been made by anthropologists not acquainted at first hand with all the evidence now available.

In conclusion Professor Davidson Black's researches in China have not yet received the recognition their vast significance demands. The discovery of *Sinanthropus* is not merely a question of the recovery of yet one more long-lost cousin of generic rank. It is of even greater interest to know that there was living in the extreme East in Early Pleistocene times a primitive type of man differing profoundly from *Pithecanthropus* and *Eoanthropus,* but approaching in structure much more nearly to its geographically distant cousin than to its Javanese contemporary. In spite of the generic distinction the old man of China presents an association of simian resemblances in its jaw with unquestionably human characters in teeth and skull that affords most significant corroboration for the view that the remains found at Piltdown represent parts of one individual—a very primitive man.

CHAPTER III

THE INDUSTRIES OF PRIMITIVE MEN

ALTHOUGH the actual bony remains of any of the extinct species of Man were unknown before 1848, when the skull now included in the species *neanderthalensis* was discovered at Gibraltar by Lieutenant Flint, their handiwork—the rough implements of stone made by these men—had been the subject of much discussion before then.

Dr. Blinkenberg has written a treatise devoted to the discussion of *The Thunderweapon in Religion and Folk-lore*. For many centuries superstitious men and women regarded stone implements as thunderbolts and treasured them as objects endowed with a sacred power of protection. Even before the close of the sixteenth century, however, Michael Mercati claimed that the so-called "thunderstones" were implements made by early Man. But opinion was not ripe for such a novel view and as, for some unknown reason, his book was not published until the seventeenth century, long after his death, he was denied the opportunity of defending his views against the stereotyped idea, which in the course of centuries had become so firmly set as a convention as to be impregnable to reason and argument. Thus when other men of insight attempted to defend Mercati's reasoning they were met by such statements as that of the learned Tollius, who in 1649 informed a credulous world that the chipped and polished stones found in the earth were "generated in the sky by a fulgurous exhalation conglobed in a cloud by the circumposed humour." Such was the state of learning in the seventeenth century that this fatuous verbiage was potent to interfere with the advancement of knowledge.

As long ago as the year 1690 a flint implement, made long before Neanderthal Man came into being, was found along with a mammoth's tooth in the course of excavations in Gray's Inn Lane

in London. What is more important, it was not thrown away.
Though described in the Sloan Catalogue, and exposed to public
view in the British Museum ever since the foundation of that institution, no serious notice was taken of it until 1859, when Sir A. W.

Figure 24—Flint implement of Chellean type found in London in 1690.

Franks recognised that it fell into the same category of extremely
ancient implements as M. Boucher de Perthes, the distinguished
French pioneer, had discovered in the ancient river gravels of the
Somme Valley. Many other implements associated with the bones
of extinct mammals and men were found before 1847, when M.

Boucher de Perthes published an account of these rude flint implements. He claimed that these weapons had been fashioned by men who were contemporaries of the mammoth in France and Britain.

To the student of history the persistent courage required of Boucher de Perthes to persuade even learned men to admit the significance of perfectly obvious and unmistakable facts of observation is full of interest as a revelation of the obstinate stupidity a false theory of knowledge can generate. Yet for more than a century the way was being prepared by repeated discussions for the eventful emergence of the light of truth.

The finding of the implement in Gray's Inn Lane failed to convince the believers in the thunderbolt theory of the error of regarding such stories as tangible witnesses of "the wrath of heaven." In 1723, however, M. Jussieu reopened the serious discussion of the subject in the French Academy with an address on *The Origin and Uses of Thunderstones.* In this important communication he demonstrated that travellers had brought back to France from various parts of the world stone implements that were essentially identical with the objects Europeans were calling thunderstones. A year later the Jesuit priest, Père Lafitau, strengthened the implication in Jussieu's argument by showing that not only the stone implements, but also the customs of the native peoples who made such implements, resembled those of the early inhabitants of Europe. But the claim that Man was more ancient than the span of years assigned to him by tradition was dangerous ground for speculation. For another century as one clear minded man after another, Montesquieu, Mahudel, Buffon, Boué and others, repeated such observations and drew the only logical inference, they were assailed and their views suppressed by the voice of orthodox opinion.

When in 1800 Mr. John Frere reported to the Society of Antiquaries in London his discovery at Hoxne of implements made by Man at a very remote geological epoch, he was unable to make any impression upon the commonly accepted opinions. Even twenty years later the eminent geologist Dr. Buckland, of Oxford, when forced to admit that the implements of the type we now call palaeolithic were made by Man, claimed that as they were associated with the remains of extinct animals they afforded proof of Noah's Deluge! M. Cuvier, the French leader of Zoological Science, denied the geological age of the remains!

In 1825 Father McEnery, a Roman Catholic priest, made im-

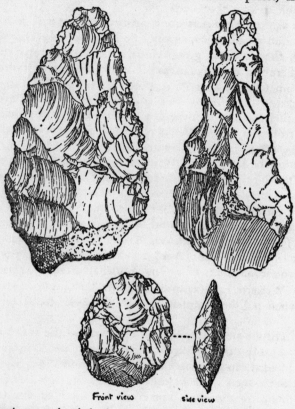

Front view   Side view

Figure 25—An example of the large roughly chipped flint implements known as Chellean (Dorothy Davison, *Our Prehistoric Ancestors*, Methuen).

portant discoveries of human bones and implements in association with extinct animals at Kent's Cavern, near Torquay, and faithfully interpreted their true significance. But his manuscript remained unpublished for thirty years, until after his death. By that time the fight for the recognition of the patent facts had been begun by M. Boucher de Perthes, who courageously persisted in it until complete victory was gained. It was only after many years of the most strenuous opposition and in the face of the bitterest ridicule that M. Boucher de Perthes obtained recognition for his claim, for which earlier pioneers after more than two centuries of conflict had been unable to gain acceptance.

In course of time the flint implements were classified: and in 1869 they were arranged by M. Gabriel de Mortillet in a chronological sequence, the different groups of which were named from the places where the representatives of each were first found and defined—from Chelles, near Paris; Saint-Acheul, at Amiens; and Le Moustier, near the Vézère—just as those of the Upper Palaeolithic received their distinctive titles from the grotto of Aurignac, from Solutré, from the rock-shelter of La Madeleine, and from the cavern of Mas-d'Azil in Ariège. However, the so-called Azilian period, named after the latter place, is probably nothing else than the first stage of the Neolithic phase of culture, and the beginning of agriculture.

After Edouard Lartet had laid the foundations of the classification of the stone implements Sir John Lubbock (afterward Lord Avebury) in his book *Prehistoric Times* (1865) suggested the use of the term "Palaeolithic Age" to distinguish the period when rough stone implements (the *pierre taillée* of French writers) were made in Western Europe, and the term "Neolithic Age" for the period when polished implements (*de la pierre polie*) were fashioned.

These terms were suggested at a time when little was known of the early history of Man except such evidence as his stone implements provided, and for half a century they served a very useful purpose. Since then a great deal of information has been acquired of the remains of the actual makers of such implements and their achievements other than mere flint-knapping. As the result of this fuller knowledge it is coming to be recognised that the use of the terms "Palaeolithic Age" and "Neolithic Age" is fruitful of misunderstanding. If these expressions were used merely with reference to the stone implements themselves and to the area of Western Europe, they would be misleading, though perhaps not so seriously as they are now. But even if the confusing chronological implication and the obvious disadvantage of defining stages of culture by one class of local evidence alone be put upon one side, there is the still more fundamental objection that the great cultural break in Western Europe itself (and even in its flint work) did not fall between the so-called Palaeolithic and Neolithic Ages, but between the earlier and the later phases of the Palaeolithic itself.

There is a much closer kinship between the flint work of the so-called Upper Palaeolithic and that of the Neolithic Ages than there is between the former and that of the Lower Palaeolithic Period.

Not only so, but a whole series of other industries of the Upper Palaeolithic Period, new methods of stone work, modelling, painting and other kinds of artistic work, reveal the modern spirit of Man in a manner that is unknown in the Lower Palaeolithic. But what is more important still, men of the modern type, undoubted members of our own species, *Homo sapiens*, came upon the scene at the commencement of the Upper Palaeolithic, the Aurignacian Period, and replaced *Homo neanderthalensis* of the Mousterian phase of culture (Lower Palaeolithic).

Thus the new spirit of Man and men of the modern type are revealed in the Upper Palaeolithic Period. This *Neanthropic phase* begins in the Aurignacian Period and includes all the subsequent epochs of Man's history. (When this term was first introduced by the writer in 1916 it was spelt "Neoanthropic," but the omission of the "o" makes the word less bizarre.)

The term "Palaeolithic" has become so ambiguous and misleading that it would make for clearness and accuracy if it were wholly discarded. The varied types of mankind who lived in the so-called "Lower Palaeolithic Age" have their own distinctive names, *Pithecanthropus, Eoanthropus, Sinanthropus, Homo heidelbergensis, Homo neanderthalensis* and *Homo rhodesiensis*, as also have the different categories of implements, Chellean, Acheulean and Mousterian. All these extinct types of mankind and their various cultures might be known collectively as "Palaeanthropic." It must not be supposed, however, that, except in the case of Neanderthal Man who made Mousterian implements, there is any close relationship between the human varieties and the two industries. In other parts of the world stone implements of Chellean, Acheulean, Mousterian and other types are made by members of the species *sapiens*. Hence it must not be assumed that there is any necessary connection between a particular type of implement and a species or race of mankind. It is clear that the forerunners of various races and communities of men of modern type have adopted methods of flint-knapping from peoples that have long been extinct. Somewhere in the domain of early Man certain members of the species *sapiens* must have been in cultural relationship with the makers of the Mousterian implements. Otherwise the former could not have acquired the Mousterian technique, which certain primitive men are still using.

Much of the ambiguity that results from the application of the term "Palaeolithic" to the Neanthropic phases of culture, Aurignacian, Solutrean and Magdalenian, is avoided by French writers, who often speak of these three periods as the Reindeer Epoch. The confusion that is introduced into the consideration of these problems, especially by English writers, is nowhere revealed so emphatically as in the discussion of the question whether or not "Palaeolithic Man" is still in existence. Such references are intended, as a rule, to mean only men of the Reindeer Epoch, i. e. people of the same species as modern men; but many writers, not excluding even scientific men, often become confused and interpret the term "Palaeolithic" as a reference to Neanderthal Man, concerning the reality of whose extinction there is no doubt.

In the early history of the Human Family primitive Man probably put to immediate use his newly acquired skill in manipulation, and fashioned implements of stones and sticks to meet his immediate needs. For many ages he roughly shaped pebbles of flint or other hard material to meet his immediate needs and then threw them away as the Australian aboriginal frequently does at the present time. It is obviously a matter of extreme difficulty to recognise many of these roughly chipped and ephemeral artifacts as really implements worked by human hands. Controversies have been going on for years on the subject of these crudely chipped implements, so-called "Eoliths." They deal with an issue upon the general truth of which everyone must be agreed—that man made rough implements long before he made those more unmistakably fashioned implements which we know as Chellean and Acheulean. But while admitting the general truth of the fact that this went on for vast periods of time, it is almost impossible in many cases to be certain that a particular piece of flint is an Eolith, for we can to-day witness aboriginal Australians making crude instruments which might not be identified as artifacts if we had not happened to see them being made and used.

The earliest type of unmistakable implement which everyone recognises as a definitely shaped tool is distinguished by the name "Chellean" (Figures 24 and 25). Before that time cruder implements of the type known as "Pre-Chellean" were being made in England, France and Spain. But constantly at the beginning of the Third Glacial Epoch we find in these countries, in localised areas, large numbers of flints chipped in a way different from anything produced by nature; chipped implements not only having a definite type of flaking, but displaying a symmetry which is not found in Nature. These implements are used to define a very remote phase in the Old Stone Age. In her book *Our Prehistoric Ancestors* Miss Dorothy Davison has given such an excellent account of the stone work that her drawings and descriptions have been used to make this point clear.

The earliest division of the Old Stone Age is called the Chellean, from Chelles on the Somme, not far from Paris, where many of the big, rough flints typical of this period are found.

Miss Davison gives a very graphic picture of the Chellean flint-maker: "We can imagine the old flint-knapper wandering along the river banks, selecting well-shaped nodules of flint, and taking them back to his "workshop" to chip. There he squatted in his favourite spot between the two heaps of flint flakes, the result of hours of hard work on many tools and weapons. Taking up his hammer-stone (a round hard stone) he carefully knocked round the edges of his flint, the chips flying onto the heaps by his knees. The other side of the flint was chipped in the same way; and by the time he had finished, about two-thirds of the circumference of the stone resembled a knife-edge, of which, no doubt, he was very proud. Seen sideways, this edge had a wavy outline, for the workman had not yet sufficient control over his material to enable him to obtain a clean, straight, cutting edge. The other lower third of the stone was often left round and smooth for the hand to grasp. It would not be easy to hold such a large stone firmly if it were rough and jagged all over."

Typical Chellean shapes are shown in Figures 24 and 25. The oval flint is a scraper and is crude and blunt in the extreme; it must have been used by Chellean Man for cutting up meat and scraping skins.

The scraper of this period can be distinguished from that of the next (the Acheulean) by its edge—it is always a straight line in contrast to the double curve so characteristic of the more recent implement. "The heavy, pear-shaped axe is common in most Chellean stations. It is always large—from 4½ to 12 inches long—clumsy, thick, and unevenly chipped, so that the cutting edge is more or less a zigzag. A similar tool is the borer, except that it is longer and narrower. It is rarely found in later times. The flint-worker was always careful to choose stones which were roughly the shape of the tool he wished to make, for he was not capable of cutting out the shape he desired from any piece of flint. All he could do was to chip the surface in a rather haphazard fashion until a very rudely sharpened edge was produced."

During this time there was little specialisation of tools—all had to do many kinds of work, and their weight and size would make it impossible for an active hunter, roaming far over the country, to carry a great number with him.

Chellean Man seems to have lived in the open, having no need of caves to shelter him from the cold winds. He is only known to have lived in a few of the countries of Europe. There are a number of stations in France, England, Spain and Portugal and a few in Belgium and Italy. The flints from all these places are so similar that there can be little doubt that the method of chipping originated in one spot, where a pioneer invented it. Thence the fashion spread abroad until eventually it was diffused over a wide area.

The fact that so few stations are known may be due to the small number of men who settled in Europe, or to the wandering life they led, since they never settled long enough in one place to leave any trace behind them. The origin of these people is quite unknown, but the route by which they came to Europe can at least be surmised. As there are no stations in Central or Eastern Europe it is not likely that they came along the Danube valley; and, as there is only one trace of them in North Italy, they can hardly have crossed from Africa by the Sicilian land-bridge. There remains, however, the Gibraltar route, and this is probably the one they used, passing up through Spain to France and across the fertile valley where the English Channel now is to England. Their search evidently was for flint, and the finest hunting grounds were only attractive if flint was to be found near them.

There is no sharp division between the Acheulean method of flint-chipping and the Chellean from which the former was de-

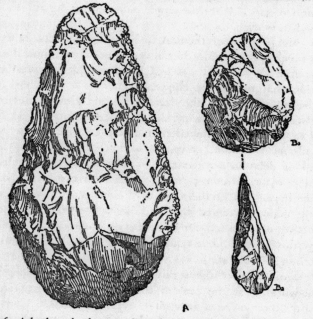

Figure 26—Acheulean implements (Dorothy Davison, *Our Prehistoric Ancestors,* Methuen).

rived. The Acheulean implements reveal a great advance in the skill of the flint-knapper, which was probably due, at any rate in part, to the immigration into Europe of skilled workmen. The wider diffusion of flint-working corroborates the view that new people were arriving: the population was increasing and spreading into new regions. The Acheulean technique spread into places, such as Germany, Austria and Russia, where Chellean implements have not been found, and there is evidence of a wide extension in

Italy. The new method represents a great advance in skill. It was not now considered sufficient merely to chip a pebble of suitable size and shape so as to give it sharp edges. The Acheulean craftsman would take a nodule of flint and skillfully work its whole surface until he had given it a form of perfect symmetry: then he would carefully retouch the edges so as to give them sharp double curves in strong contrast to the blunt, zigzag edges of Chellean tools. This improved cutting edge made the great weight of earlier flints unnecessary. Hence the implements decreased in size as they increased in efficiency.

The chief interest of these Acheulean implements, however, is not so much the fact that they reveal a definite technical advance when compared with the earlier Chellean implements as the consideration that men were chipping flints daily for thousands of years before they made the relatively slight change necessary to attain such greater efficiency. In the face of this evidence who would be rash enough to claim that the new technique was the inevitable result of some process of so-called Evolution?

The long delay in discovering the Acheulean technique is both a testimony to the extreme rarity of the inventive spirit in Man and evidence in support of the view that some one individual of outstanding genius invented the method, which was spread abroad and meticulously copied for countless thousands of years. Then a new genius arose and invented the technique known to us as Mousterian (Figure 18, p. 56).

The significance of the survival of these very ancient methods of flint-working at the present time—hundreds of thousands of years after their original invention—will be discussed later in this chapter. Obviously the issues raised by this amazing phenomenon —not merely the length of time during which the implements have been used, but even more the fact that the technical knowledge must have been handed down from peoples of different species and even genera to men of our own species—are of fundamental importance in estimating the ways of Man in the earliest phases of Human History.

Miss Dorothy Davison gives a vivid account of the conditions under which Acheulean Man lived in Europe: "When Acheulean flint-working was first introduced the climate was still warm and rather damp, but gradually it grew colder and drier. High easterly winds swept over the country, bringing clouds of dust, which settled in thick layers over large parts of Europe. These dust layers are known as "loess" and in the "lower loess" Acheulean flints are found. This shows that these hardy people must have been living in the open in spite of the bitter east winds. The southern mammoth and hippopotamus could not endure it, and left Europe for ever. The climate must have varied in different localities, as it does to-day; for while in some regions traces of Acheulean life are found with the remains of the warm animals of the Interglacial times, in others they are associated with the woolly-coated animals, who came south as the glaciers advanced.

"The increasing cold must have tried these roaming hunters severely. So far as we know, Man up to this time was without the knowledge of fire; for in the Acheulean strata are the ashes of the first hearths, and in the next period they are quite common.

"Fire made such a vast difference to the life of Man that the question of how he first learned to use it is of great interest and fascination. There are many theories and native legends, and many primitive ways of producing fire, and it is possible that in different parts of the world fire was obtained by different methods. Long before Man learnt to produce fire he had conquered his fear of it, and used it. There are peoples living to-day, such as the Andamanese, who have fires but have no idea how to make a new one. Their fires are never allowed to die out, and when the people move from place to place smouldering wood is carried with them."

Long after the procession of experimental types of mankind, Piltdown Man, Heidelberg Man, Neanderthal Man, and perhaps it may in the future be necessary to add to the list the Lloyd's Man of London, had passed by, there came into Europe men of our own species, Grimaldi Man and Cro-Magnon Man and other types, living in the Reindeer Period, which is now commonly known by the confusing name "Upper Palaeolithic."

The men of the Lower Palaeolithic used in succession implements of the types we have already considered, Pre-Chellean, Chellean, Acheulean and Mousterian. With the coming of men of our own species the Neanthropic chapter of Human History begins. The first phase of this "Reindeer Period" is now distingushed as

Aurignacian, the second phase as Solutrean and the last definite phase (before the Neolithic) as Magdalenian.

There are many indications that the phases of culture of the

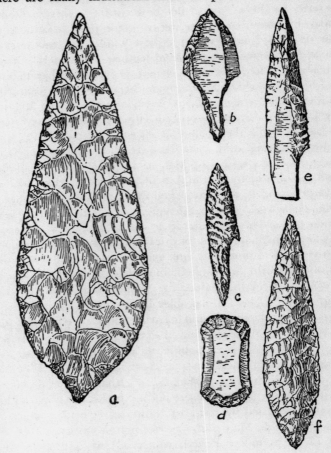

Figure 27—Solutrean flint implements (Dorothy Davison, *Our Prehistoric Ancestors*, Methuen, 1926).

Reindeer Period in Europe which are distinguished respectively by the terms Aurignacian, Solutrean, and Magdalenian, cannot be regarded, although so many writers tacitly, and probably erroneously, make the assumption, as epochs in the history of mankind as a whole. Even in Europe itself there are definite limitations to the application of these terms. It is now generally admitted that the Solutrean and Magdalenian industries did not make their way into Italy, Southern Spain, and the greater part of the Mediterranean area. Hence these regions remained in the Aurignacian phase, while Western and Central Europe were passing successively through the Solutrean and Magdalenian stages of culture. Thus the Mediterranean lands as a whole passed directly from the Aurignacian stage to the Neolithic, or to its inaugural phases, now known as Azilian and Tardenoisian.

These facts serve to emphasise the confusion involved in the use of the word "Age." They also reveal how devoid of foundation is the mis-named "evolutionary" theory that claims all these phases of culture as so many natural stages through which every people must inevitably pass. The fact that the greater part of the Mediterranean area seems to have escaped typical Solutrean and Magdalenian stages becomes all the more significant when it is recalled that the industries which attained such a remarkable pitch of excellence in Predynastic Egypt were essentially Solutrean in character.

The Solutrean industry is generally believed to have made its way into Europe from the neighbourhood of the Black Sea. After a short time it was driven out of Europe again by the Magdalenian culture, which shows no affinity to the Solutrean, but is apparently related to the Aurignacian culture. Although the Solutrean methods of stone work endured only for a very brief period in the West, they spread in other directions to the uttermost parts of the earth, to South Africa, Australia, and America, where they have persisted with remarkable constancy until the present day and have attained a pitch of excellence which is exceeded only by that of Predynastic Egypt, nearly sixty centuries ago.

Wherever the home of this industry may have been, it is quite clear that it must have been the source of the inspiration of Egypt's early industry.

Remembering the fact that the climate of Europe, which in the "Reindeer Epoch" had been very cold, became more genial toward the end of the Magdalenian, and in fact settled down to the sort of conditions that have prevailed ever since, it is important

to bear in mind that there was also a great change of climate in
Egypt not long before the settlement of the Predynastic people in
the valley of the Nile (circa 4000 B.C.). No doubt the people who
dwelt in the forests, which until then existed east of the Nile, were
making implements of Solutrean type. Egypt and East and South
Africa probably acquired this industry from the same source. It
is equally probable that in the Neolithic implements of Europe is
revealed still further evidence of the influence indirectly exerted
by the Solutrean industry, not locally in Europe, but in some other
region where the new development was in more or less intimate
relationship with the phase represented in Predynastic Egypt.

The terms "Neolithic Age" and "Neolithic phase of culture"
cannot be used without ambiguity except with reference to Western
Europe. But if the adjective Neolithic be interpreted as defining
a particular method of chipping and polishing stone, it can legi-
timately be used in the wider sense in which so many writers erroneously employ the phrases to which I have just objected.

It must be remembered that the term "Neolithic Age" is usually
interpreted (for example, by Déchelette) as meaning a definite
period in history when men first began (a) to shape their stone
weapons by polishing them, without, however, giving up the
practice of chipping; (b) to domesticate animals; (c) to cultivate
cereals and fruit trees; (d) to erect megalithic monuments; (e) to
make pottery; (f) to weave linen; and (g) to give definite evidence
of religious beliefs and a funerary cult.

Now it is generally recognised that, except in some parts of
Europe, megalithic monuments are found in association with the
"Ages of Metal," Copper, Bronze, or Iron, in different areas. Hence
their inclusion within the Neolithic culture-complex is only valid
in the case of Western Europe. This implies that the latter part
of the so-called Neolithic "Age" there is at least as late as the
Bronze Age in the East, i.e. after 2000 B.C. Nor are the domestication of animals and the practice of agriculture necessarily connected with the manufacture of flint implements of Neolithic type.
In fact, polished stones are found in use among many peoples who
have no domesticated animals, except the dog, and do not cultivate cereals. In other words, the Neolithic culture in Europe is
compounded of a number of ingredients that are found in other

parts of the world dissociated the one from the other, and each of them linked on to other culture-complexes which belong to totally different "Ages" in Europe.

The term "Neolithic," therefore, cannot be used without confusion for a phase of culture anywhere else than in Western Europe; and even there it is likely to lead to grave misunderstanding. Most writers so exaggerate its antiquity as to obscure the fact that the Neolithic phase in the West did not begin until many hundreds—probably thousands—of years *after* metals had been in use in those Eastern lands, from which Western European Neolithic population received its inspiration and its cultural capital. The Neolithic Period was brought to an end by the introduction of the use of the alloy of copper and tin which inaugurated the Age of Bronze. As this did not happen in the Eastern Mediterranean until about 2000 B.C. it is clear that in the West the close of the Neolithic phase must be more recent than this.

Writing in the seventeenth century Olaus Wormius called attention to the close resemblance between the polished stone implements now called Neolithic and some of those made of metal, and seriously discussed the hypothesis whether the former (then commonly regarded as thunderstones, *cerauniae*) might not be simply petrified metal tools or fossils! The resemblance is beyond question. Its true significance is now for the first time coming to be recognised. The so-called Neolithic implements are really imitations of metal tools by people who appreciated the greater efficiency of copper implements but lacked the skill and experience to cast in metal. The earliest polished stone implements were in fact imitations of copper axes. The Long Barrows made by the Neolithic people in England were planned on a model not common in the East until the time (2000 B.C.) of the Middle Kingdom in Egypt. Hence the Neolithic Period cannot be older than, if indeed as remote as, 2000 B.C., if allowance be made for the diffusion to Western Europe.

The evidence that compels us to adopt these conclusions. is set forth in the author's essay on "The Evolution of the Rock-Cut Tomb and the Dolmen" in the *Essays and Studies presented to William Ridgeway* (1913) and more cogently in Dr. W. J. Perry's chapter on "The First Civilisation of England" in Marvin's *Eng-*

land and the World (1925) and in Mr. H. J. Massingham's *Down-land Man* (1926).

The only other attempt to fix the date of the Neolithic phase of culture strictly on the basis of the established facts was made by the late Mr. Clement Reid. In his book *Submerged Forests* (Cambridge, 1913) he suggested 3000 B.C. as the approximate date of commencement, and a thousand years as the duration, of the Neolithic phase in England. Though both these estimates—and Mr. Reid too modestly pretended that his calculations were little more than guesswork—are very considerably smaller than the figures that most archaeologists give, they must be reduced still further. There are no reasons for believing that the Neolithic phase began in England before 2000 B.C., if indeed it was so early; nor is there anything to suggest that it lasted longer than two or three centuries. In Italy metals occur in so-called Neolithic burials. It is hardly likely that it took the Neolithic people in the West more than two centuries to learn to cast metals! The correction of the widespread miscalculation of the duration and remoteness of the Neolithic phase is a matter of fundamental importance. The whole perspective of early Man's achievements in Europe has been distorted by chronological exaggerations of the grossest kind. Many of the estimates of age for prehistoric times as a whole have been based upon the dates and duration of the Neolithic phase and the false assumption that every people passed through such a phase before the introduction of the use of metals. Moreover the use of the term Neolithic for a phase of culture (and even more for a period of time) with reference to any region other than Britain and Western Europe is not only meaningless and unjustifiable, but also confusing and misleading.

With reference to the claim that the Neolithic culture of England was derived indirectly from the earlier copper-using civilisation of Egypt in the second millennium Dr. Nils O. Holst has given valuable corroboration and support in the *Geographical Magazine* (1925):

"I consider that it can be shown, and indeed already has been shown, that Egypt, which during the 'pluvial period' was a 'promised land,' was also a centre of civilisation for the whole of Europe right from the earliest Palaeolithic period time down to almost the close of the Stone Age, and in general sent its civilisation into Europe by the roads along the south and west of the Mediterranean. Clearly this was still so after the kitchen-midden time (Early Neolithic), as shown by the distribution of Megalithic monuments—the dolmens and the long barrows or chambered barrows."

During the last half century there has been much discussion as to whether or not there was a hiatus between the so-called "Palaeolithic" and "Neolithic" Ages. But if the whole of the evidence now available be viewed in proper perspective it is clear that this question has loomed so large mainly because Lubbock's terminology was responsible for magnifying into a vast revolution what is really a relatively insignificant incident in Human History. The real revolution occurred in Europe at a much earlier period represented by the replacement of Mousterian by Aurignacian culture, when the more nimble-witted *Homo sapiens* replaced the inferior type of *Homo neanderthalensis,* whose mere brute-strength was not sufficient to protect him from extinction. In the later stages of the so-called "Palaeolithic Age" there were many movements of varied peoples in Europe presenting in greater or less degree affinities to the populations of the so-called "Neolithic Age," both in physical structure and in their industries; whereas they were succeeded by another series of peoples, some or all of which are included by various authorities in the "Neolithic Age," although they have not yet acquired many, or indeed most, of the arts that are regarded as distinctive of Neolithic culture. Thus the much-discussed "hiatus" disappears. If the Neolithic and later phases of the whole of the so-called "Upper Palaeolithic Epoch" are linked together so as to include the whole of the history of *Homo sapiens* in a Neanthropic Age, it will then be possible to examine the great events of the history of our own type of mankind without the prejudice and bias the misleading terminology is apt to create.

From the time of the advent in Europe of men of the species *sapiens,* bringing with them from the East the germs of the culture called Aurignacian, there has been a series of waves of immigrants reaching Western Europe by the most varied routes, and introducing from time to time new elements of culture. The study of the history of this early civilisation of Europe reveals the phenomena of decadence and replacement of arts and industries which, though the merest commonplaces of more recent history, have been a never-ending source of difficulty to many who have discussed the Reindeer Epoch in Europe. It has been clearly demonstrated in the case of ancient Egypt that, with the development of the art of making stone vases, there was a pronounced falling-off in the potter's skill, and with the introduction of the use of metals an equally marked decadence in the working of flint. No doubt this was due partly to the fact that the most skilled artists and artisans devoted themselves to the new crafts. Their patrons wanted the more fashionable and more durable objects. The same principle is witnessed at every stage of the early history of Europe. In the Magdalenian phase, during which a multitude of new arts came into being, and the skill of the fresco-painter and modeller attained to a pitch of excellence far surpassing that of his predecessors, there was a most pronounced decadence in the workmanship of the flint-knapper, who in the Solutrean phase had become so deft an artist (see Figure 27). So again in the Neolithic phase, when the crafts of the potter, the agriculturist, the weaver, and the cattle-breeder were first introduced, there seemed no longer to be any demand for high art, nor indeed any evidence that there was any of the feeling which prompted the masterpieces of the Magdalenian painters.

These fluctuations of skill and interest must not be attributed wholly to the reasons suggested by the Egyptian analogies. In Western Europe, not only did the centre of interest change from time to time, but also the people themselves. In Magdalenian times new immigrants came in with their own interests to cultivate. They had no reasons for acquiring those arts in which their Solutrean predecessors were preeminent. So again in the Neolithic Age a succession of new waves of population intruded from time to time, each bringing some new contribution to the growing civilisation, some newest fashion upon which the attention of the community would for a season be concentrated. Thus the early history of Europe becomes intelligible if we bear in mind the usual behaviour of human beings.

This is one more illustration of the fact that the spirit of Man is the same in every age, and that much of the difficulty in interpreting the "Stone Age" disappears if it be remembered that changes were brought about then in much the same way as they are effected in modern times in our civilisation.

There is no evidence to justify the supposition that Man was evolved in Europe. Moreover, in the opinion of most serious investigators, all the known early types of Man, those of Piltdown, Heidelberg, Neanderthal, Lloyd's and Cro-Magnon, and the various peoples who intruded into Europe until the Neolithic phase of industry came into existence, were immigrants who had acquired in some place other than Europe their distinctive features and the germs of such culture as they displayed. In other words, there is nothing to suggest that the evolution of one type from another occurred in Europe. Although most scholars do not hesitate to accept this conclusion when the question is put to them categorically, nevertheless few writers wholly rid themselves of the bias or the tacit assumption that the successive series of races and industries revealed in Europe represent an orderly procession of so-called "evolutionary" changes. It is of the utmost importance deliberately to set aside this assumption, which in the past has been so fruitful of ambiguity and confusion.

The profound contrast between the physical characters and technical achievements of the Neanderthal and Neanthropic peoples, and the sudden appearance of the latter in Europe, justify the conclusion that the newcomers were not evolved there from their predecessors. The two species represent divergent offshoots from the common stock of the genus *Homo,* which respectively acquired their distinctive features and their initial cultural equipment beyond the limits of Europe.

It must not be supposed that, when the ancestors of the peoples whose remains have been found at Cro-Magnon, the Grimaldi caves, Combe Capelle, etc., came into existence and wandered west into Europe, they were the only representatives of the species *sapiens* then alive. It is not only probable, but quite certain, that long before then many other varieties must also have been budded off the common stem of our species and scattered in other directions. For there is a large series of other types, some of them definitely more primitive than the men of Cro-Magnon, which never came into Europe. Others again did not reach Europe until the commencement of the Neolithic phase of culture had developed. The ancestors of the aboriginal Australians, while conforming in certain essential respects to the type of modern Man and being unquestionably members of the species *sapiens,* also present a number of primitive structural features that suggest affinities with the species *neanderthalensis.* These facts can be explained only by the assumption of the early origin of the Australian from the original members of the species *sapiens.* At a time when the species *neanderthalensis* and *sapiens* had recently become specialised along their distinctive lines (see Figure 16), no doubt both retained a good many features in common that were also shared by the parent stock from which both had sprung. In course of time many members of both phyla became profoundly modified. The great expansion and specialisation of the brain of Neanderthal Man, and the far-reaching transformations in the structure of most members of the species *sapiens,* afford ample evidence of this. But the retention of so many primitive features in association with Neanderthaloid characters as the aboriginal Australian presents can only mean that in that race is revealed the persistence of the earliest features of the species *sapiens,* with certain relatively unimportant specialisations which have since been acquired.

The hypothesis which is involved in the application of the unfortunate term "Caucasian" to the Australians shows a lamentable lack of perspective on the part of those anthropologists who use this expression. This is not intended to refer to the colloquial use of the term Caucasian in America to distinguish people of the European ancestry from those of Negro blood. The persistence of such usage, which to the scientific anthropologist is anathema, is due, no doubt, to the fact that citizens of the United States, and especially those who are born there, naturally object to calling themselves "European." But in a scientific discussion of race this colloquial convenience should not be allowed to become a source of confusion. When the easterly migration of the most primitive representatives of our own species began is quite unknown. The discovery at Talgai, in Queensland, of the fossilised remains of a human skull reveals the fact that the earliest known Australian, who possibly reached the island continent when the great extinct Marsupials were still living, presents the distinctive traits of the modern Australian, in association with even more primitive features in the teeth and jaws. It is also true that fossilised dog's teeth have been found in geological strata of similar age. But the fact that he was probably accompanied by his dogs suggests that his easterly migration set out from Asia approximately at the same time as the beginning of the Predynastic period in Egypt—say 4000 B.C.—for the earliest Egyptians had already domesticated the dog and come to regard it is a friend, for they buried dogs in human cemeteries. Of course the movement may have begun long before this: but the fact that the domestication of the dog in Europe is not known before the time of the Danish kitchen-middens suggests that 4000 B.C. may be near the date of the first adoption of the dog as the friend of Man. If the practice of mutilating the hands and recording impressions of them upon rocks was introduced by the earliest immigrants—which of course there is no warrant for assuming—it is important to remember that this curious procedure was brought to Europe by its earliest colonists of the species *sapiens,* the men of the Aurignacian phase of culture. Elsewhere in this volume the problem of the possible relationship between Early European culture and that of Australia has been discussed.

The fossil skull discovered in 1913 at Boskop in the Transvaal is an example of another diversely specialised, but probably much later, branch of the species *sapiens,* which wandered as far as South Africa. It is much more nearly akin to the European Cro-Magnon type than the Australians are, but it also presents certain features (not those, however, to which reference was made in the case of the Australians) distantly reminiscent of the Neanderthal Race.

When and how the diversely specialised Negro and Mongolian races came into existence will be discussed in the next chapter.

Two of the races of which the modern population of Europe is compounded—the olive-skinned Race of the Mediterranean area and the western littoral, and the blond Race of the Baltic—reveal evidence perhaps suggestive of affinity with the earlier Neanthropic series of waves of immigrants, more especially those of the Magdalenian phase, although there are no grounds for assuming that they were derived from the latter. They probably originated further

Figure 28—The earliest evidence of domestication of the dog. Dog buried in the same way as human beings in an early Predynastic cemetery in upper Egypt, c. 4000 B.C.

east and began to filter into Europe at the time when the Magdalenian art was at its height.

But the third of the principal components of Europe's population—the broad-headed race commonly called Alpine—certainly arrived later, and came from a more distant area of characterisation, the centre of which was probably somewhere in the area

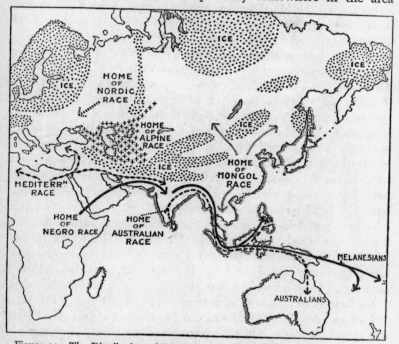

Figure 29—The Distribution of Ice during the Glacial Period when the ancestors of the Nordic, Alpine and Mongol Races became segregated. The areas of characterisation of the Nordic, Alpine, Mongol and Negro Races have been tentatively suggested, as well as the assumed early movements of the Australian, Negro and Mediterranean Races.

between the Caspian Sea and the Altai. This race differs more obtrusively from the Cro-Magnon people than the brown and the blond races do. In some respects, such for example as the form of the skull, it is highly specialised. In other respects, such as the robustness of build, the prominence of the eye-brow ridges, and the abundant development of hair, it is more primitive. It certainly acquired its distinctive characters in some domain that for a long period was shut off from contact with the territories of the other white-skinned races (in Western Asia, Europe, and North Africa), to which no doubt it is distantly akin, and those of the yellow race further east, from which it is more widely differentiated. The unlocking of these areas of characterisation by the great thaw during the Magdalenian Age in Europe probably opened the way for the great movements of the Human Family that closely followed this momentous event.

Little is known of the early history of Man in America. Fossilised human remains have been found in Florida and elsewhere, but as they were associated with pottery, which even in Western Europe (near to the home of its invention about 4000 B.C.) is unknown before the Neolithic phase of culture, i.e., about 1500 B.C., no great age can be assigned to them. So far as his physical structure is concerned the American Indian reveals evidence of distant kinship with the Mongolian race. But there are many points of difference. In any case there is a remarkable similiarity to, and probably a racial identity with, certain people who still survive near the head waters of the Yenesei in Siberia and elsewhere in Northeastern Asia. Presumably these represent outlying and less highly specialised members of the Mongolian race, who have survived as persistent witnesses of the source of the main element in the composite stock of the original American population. When it is recalled that before the first immigration into America there must have been profound intermingling of early types of the Mongolian and Alpine (Turki) races in Northeastern Asia (see Figure 13) it seems more than probable that the earliest inhabitants of America must have included a not inconsiderable element of Alpine origin.

Beyond the limits of Europe practically nothing is known of the early history of the Human Family, except a few hints as to its ancestry, and such information as the finding of flint implements provides. But the lack of direct evidence ought not tacitly to be assumed to mean that the great events which must have been happening in Asia, Africa, and, later, in America, can be left wholly out of account. The mere fact that such diversely specialised races exist and have each of them wandered in certain definite directions must be given due weight in discussing primitive Human History. That all these races belong to the species *sapiens* is presumptive evidence that the disposal of the members of this species, which, as has been seen, was unknown in Europe before the Aurignacian phase of culture, was relatively recent in the geological sense. The validity of such chronological inferences is strengthened when it is realised that the methods of flint-working of practically every race conform essentially to the same types as those which are revealed in Europe. Such arguments acquire still further cogency when it is realised that in South Africa, Australia and America, methods of flint-working which appeared in Europe in succession, and with very long intervals of time between the different phases, may be found associated with one another in the same deposit. In other words, some movement of population must have begun after the introduction of the most recent of the series of industries thus represented, and as it advanced other more ancient methods that had lagged behind in more backward areas were added to the equipment of the wanderers, so that a collection of methods distinctive of widely different periods in the respective homes of their invention may simultaneously have been introduced into some new region.

It must not be assumed that the Aurignacian culture was necessarily invented by the same people who introduced it into Europe and whose remains are associated with it there; nor, if on the other hand proof should some day be forthcoming that such people as we label Cro-Magnon were responsible for this great progress in civilisation, should we expect to find this physical type invariably associated with it elsewhere. For any culture can be transmitted to an alien people, even when it has not been adopted by many branches of the race which was responsible for its invention, just as gas-illumination, oil-lamps, and even candles are still in current use by the people who invented the electric light, which has been widely adopted by many foreign peoples. This elementary consideration is so often ignored that it is necessary thus to emphasize it, because it is essential for any proper understanding of the history of civilisation.

If, for the moment, we assume that the distinctive elements of the Aurignacian industry were invented by people of the Cro-

Magnon type—who of course are known to be associated with that particular phase of culture—such an assumption implies that the Cro-Magnon people originally—i.e. before their most significant inventions were made—were using implements of another type, not necessarily Mousterian, though possibly akin to it. For there is no necessary inevitable connection between race and culture. The Japanese make steam-engines and build battleships although they had no share in the invention of these devices of Western civilisation. When the new inventions were made no doubt the history of their adoption was essentially identical with that of every similar occurrence since the world began.

In the early history of the gropings after new knowledge and skill in arts and crafts human nature was probably not very different from what it is to-day. When, after countless thousands of years' experience of the use of stones as implements, some man of clearer insight learned to appreciate the fact that an edge could be given to the stone by deliberately chipping it in a particular way, no doubt he was regarded as a foolish visionary, whose pretensions were resented by his staider and duller companions. Perhaps he was even reproved with the Palaeolithic argument that his predecessors found unchipped stones good enough for them, and it was therefore supremely foolish to attempt to supersede methods that experience had shown to be so thoroughly efficient. However, in course of time, the momentous invention was adopted: but although there are scores of ways of chipping a stone implement, the one original method was meticulously followed for many centuries to the exclusion of all others. Not only so, but it became stereotyped and adopted far and wide as one people after another learned the technique of this particular method.

After this process had been going on for many centuries some new genius arose, who invented a new technique. Although no Samuel Smiles has put on record the history of the difficulties he had to overcome before he could persuade his generation to adopt a slightly different method of chipping flint, there can be no reasonable doubt that his experience was similar to Galileo's, Watt's, and Lister's. He had to fight against the forces of cultivated prejudice and inherent stupidity. In time, however, the new technique became the fashion; and in the course of centuries it slowly percolated to the ends of the earth. So, age after age, new methods of flint-working were successively devised, and, persisting among living men in various localities, or buried in the soil in many parts of the world, they have left indelible records of these earliest migrations of culture. These facts afford perhaps the most amazing illustration of the rarity of true inventive genius and the thraldom of a definite routine for doing things. It took hundreds of thousands of years before some pioneer discovered the mode of chipping stone which we distinguish as Chellean and countless centuries during which unnumbered thousands of craftsmen in widespread parts of the world were meticulously imitating the Chellean technique before someone discovered the relatively slight change required to fashion the more efficient Acheulean implement. The fact that these arbitrary methods were devised at such distant intervals and became so widely adopted affords the most illuminating commentary on human behaviour, the rarity of real inventiveness, the slavery of fashion and the reality of the diffusion of culture.

The influence of the fashionable doctrines of ethnology, however, has made itself felt among archaeologists, certain of whom refuse to accept the clear demonstration of cultural diffusion provided by flint implements, emphatic and decisive though it is.

It is admitted that flint implements made in accordance with a distinctive method, say Chellean, may be found in places as far apart as France, South Africa, India and America. The details of the arbitrary technique may be so closely identical that all of these implements, collected from the ends of the earth, might have been made by the same workman. Yet many writers are still willing to believe that this result has been achieved by the blind operation of some process of independent development wrongly called evolution. They pretend that these identities of technique afford evidence, not of the diffusion abroad of an arbitrary procedure from the centre of its invention, but of the perfection and precision of the mysterious "psychic unity" that leads men independently the one of the other to arrive at the same destination.

In the report published in the *Revue Anthropologique* (January, 1917) of a course of lectures on the origin and method of making of the chief types of stone weapons and implements, Professor L. Capitan discusses these problems with all the authority of his wide knowledge and experience. It is a remarkable. circumstance, he says, that in whatever part of the world Chellean and Acheulean implements are found, they invariably present the same form, whether they came from the banks of the Thames or from the Cape of Good Hope, or such intervening regions as Tunis or Egypt, Timbuctoo or Somaliland, or from the banks of the Delaware or from India. Their general shape is so definite and presents such an individuality that one is tempted to regard them, not as sporadic creations of the human intellect working simultaneously and independently in different parts of the world, but rather as a tradition handed down from one place to another.

But what other interpretation of the facts is credible? The implements in question were in Europe the handiwork of the predecessors of *Homo sapiens*. The first immigrants, say into America, were members of the species *sapiens* living at a time long after implements of Chellean type were made in Europe and Asia by some very primitive type of men, belonging to a different species or even genus. We have the most definite evidence that such distinctive techniques of stone-chipping survived in some places, when the newer devices which we distinguish as Acheulean, Mousterian, Aurignacian et cetera, in succession displaced them in the more progressive centres. Many communities of *Homo sapiens* continued to use these antiquated devices of their extinct predecessors, and there is every reason for believing that the earliest immigrants into America took with them implements of Chellean and Acheulean types. Is it credible that, after carrying with them in their migrations weapons of these or later types, they should, on arriving at their destination, have thrown them away, repressed all memory of them, and then immediately have set to work again and invented the same arbitrary forms they had just discarded, proceeding to devise an identical technique? Surely no serious enquirer can admit the possibility of such fantastic happenings! The reality of the ancient migrations of culture of which these implements provide such clear and unimpeachable evidence cannot be denied by anyone capable of estimating the value of established facts.

Yet Dr. Capitan does show signs of weakening. For, after referring to the extension of the use of such implements in time (from the beginning of the Chellean to the middle Aurignacian) as well as in geographical range, he expresses the opinion that "It is very probable that this evolution, which is apparent in Europe, and especially in France, must have followed a similar course throughout the world." But if each type of implement was spread abroad from the centre where it was invented, can one speak of a series of these types in some outlying area as evidence of local evolution? If a wax match were found in the heart of Africa, or on one of the upper reaches of the Amazon, far away from any settled community of European people, no one would be foolish enough to claim it as evidence of local evolution, even if any record of a white man having been there or of the way in which the match reached the spot was completely lacking. Why then does the ethnologist refuse to apply the same reasoning to the case of the flint implements? Why, moreover, does he regard those of us who attach some importance to such historical resemblances as hazardous dogmatists? Surely common sense and common experience count for something in matters that after all are interpretations of the expressions of the human nature common to all of us. In many places several forms of implements that made their appearance in Europe successively at long intervals seem to have been introduced elsewhere simultaneously and many centuries after their use in Europe had been completely abandoned. This affords clear evidence, not simply of the diffusion of culture, but also of a mixture of several cultural elements that became collected in one spot.

Leaving the Palaeanthropic peoples and passing to the Neanthropic group, Dr. Capitan says that in the technology of the implements, the transformations introduced into Europe by the Aurignacian people were radical.

There was in fact the great break between the men and the industries of the now extinct species and the advent of our own species and its distinctive innovations. The latter are displayed especially in two features, first, the invention of the technique that made it possible to obtain long, narrow, and fine blades, and secondly, the utilisation of bone, horn and ivory, which had been almost completely ignored by Neanderthal men and their predecessors.

In his memoir Dr. Capitan tells us further that, just as the Acheulean technique was spread abroad throughout the world, so also was that of the Solutrean period, which is all the more remarkable in that this phase of culture lasted only a very brief time in Europe. Yet elsewhere in outlying places in the world it was not only adopted, but in some cases has persisted even to the present time, as, for example, among the aboriginal people of Central Australia, who still make exquisite implements of Solutrean type from broken soda-water bottles and telegraph insulators. In the next chapter attention will be called to other remarkable coincidences between the material culture of the aboriginal Australians and the Solutrean practices in Europe. Reference has already been made to the Australians' adoption of the Aurignacian practice of making impressions of mutilated red hands upon rocks and the walls of caves. These facts illustrate not only the worldwide diffusion of early culture but also its unity. The sacrificial knife with which the Aztecs used to cut into the bodies of their human victims for the purpose of tearing out the heart was a Solutrean blade.

In the middle of the fourth millennium B. C. the Egyptians manufactured admirable implements of this kind (the most beautiful on record). In Japan, the United States, Australia and Africa, this industrial type was extremely widespread and is still used for ritual purposes. It has been claimed that the different methods of chipping flint implements form a natural series, passing from the crude to the more highly finished technique, and represent the stages through which the process of evolution would have passed independently among any people. But consideration of the actual facts lends no support to this view. Moreover it is at least as simple, if not definitely easier, to shape an implement by rubbing and polishing. Yet this was not attempted until many thousands of years after flint-knapping had been practised.

The problems arising out of these discussions have been further confused by the assumptions made by some writers that the finding of implements of some definite Palaeolithic type implies the existence of a Palaeolithic "Age" throughout the world. The fact that such implements are being made to-day in certain localities ought to be sufficient to put this matter in its right perspective. But there is the further fact to which reference has already been made, that in some places implements representing a series of cultural phases in Europe, which were separated the one from the other by vast intervals of time, may be found under circumstances which suggest that they were all manufactured at the same time. Illustrations of this are provided in South Africa, Australia and America.

No fact is more notorious than the reluctance on the part of any people to give up methods or ideas with which long usage has familiarised them. It has already been suggested that the Chellean inventor was probably regarded by his fellow men as a crazy visionary. No doubt he had to struggle against their ridicule and practical opposition before he was able to convince them that his method of chipping flint was a real advance upon their Eolithic crudities. And even when it was adopted it is highly probable, to judge from the history of other inventions which is known to us, that it spread abroad only with extreme slowness. In fact, although it was many centuries before some conspicuous genius discovered that there were other ways of chipping flint and invented the technique which we call Acheulean, it is not unlikely that the Chellean method had not yet reached the outlying parts of the world, when perhaps the Acheulean or even the Mousterian or Aurignacian methods had been successively adopted near the progressive centre of invention. Thus, if some great movement took place, such as that which led to the first peopling of South Africa or America, it is quite possible that wanderers from the centre, say at the time when polished stone implements (of Neolithic type) were coming into use, in passing outwards to the periphery, may have passed through a series of zones in which they might have found in succession the Magdalenian, Solutrean, Aurignacian, Mousterian, Acheulean, and Chellean methods as severally the latest fashions in stone-working; and, though themselves the pioneers of the Neolithic phase, they may have attracted to their wandering band representatives of these other zones who were accustomed to make use of more ancient procedures. Thus it was possible for people contemporaneous with the Neolithic phase in Europe to have introduced, say into America, an alien culture that was a jumble of a variety of earlier phases definitely associated with different times and places in the Old World.

Within the limits of our brief chapter upon so vast a subject as the history of Primitive Man it has been possible merely to glance at certain facets of the mass of problems presented for discussion. Fortunately many books, such as those of Déchelette, Sollas, Osborn, Boule, McCurdy, Dorothy Garrod, Burkitt and scores of others, are now available to give full information to the reader who is not familiar with the rich harvest of knowledge that has been garnered in this field of investigation during the last quarter of a century. But the aspect of the problems to which chief attention has been devoted here has been almost entirely neglected by most writers. In fact, Professor Sollas is almost the only one who has attempted to discuss the wider question of the relationship of the information derived from the early remains of Man in Europe to the world-wide history of the Human Family. His book *Ancient Hunters* gives an excellent survey of the results of the recent investigations, and it will be convenient to refer the reader to it for fuller information on most of the topics raised for discussion in this chapter.

Unlike most writers Professor Sollas has not been content merely to study the succession of races and industries that made their appearance in Europe, but he has endeavoured to discover whence they came and whither they went. In the course of such enquiries he has made use of the evidence afforded by peculiar and distinctive elements of culture in substantiation of the reality of these early movements of peoples and the diffusion of customs and beliefs.

The peculiar custom of mutilating the fingers and silhouetting upon the walls of caves the evidence of the damage so inflicted has preserved the record of one of the earliest examples of such a blazing of the pathways of diffusion of early culture. Concerning this custom of making impressions of mutilated hands Professor Sollas says:

"We have another instance of a singular practice which is common to a great number of peoples who are isolated, and have long been isolated, from one another by great distances and other geographical conditions.

"There is room, no doubt, for more than one explanation, but the simplest and most satisfactory would seem to be that which is based on the great antiquity of the custom, for . . . it was already in existence when the forefathers of these now widely separated races were probably in direct or indirect communication with one another. If, as may well be the case, they once occupied the old world, that cradle of the human race, and have since been dispersed to their existing homes, carrying their ancient customs with them, our problem would be solved."

In considering the fact that peoples so remote in space as the North American Indians, the Bushmen of South Africa, and the Aboriginal Australians "all possess the same curious custom of mutilating the fingers, it is scarcely likely that so strange a proceeding was evolved in response to the environment. The motives alleged are various, but probably the idea of sacrifice is the most fundamental. It would be not a little remarkable, however, if this idea found independent expression in the same extraordinary fashion in three several instances. I cannot help thinking that it is far more likely we have here a case of borrowing from a common source."

In view of the fact that this particular custom was already being practised in Europe at the time when men of the modern type first became known, there is a strong element of probability in Professor Sollas' view that when the different varieties of *Homo sapiens* radiated out from the common home (see Figure 13, p. 49) they may have carried this primitive custom with them. Yet this interpretation of the facts, which common sense proclaims as obviously true, is denied by the vast majority of students of mankind. This attitude of antagonism is not the result of a critical examination of the evidence or of rational argument, but rather of the refusal seriously to consider the bare possibility of the diffusion which so obviously must have taken place. Déchelette, for example, disposes of this fundamental issue simply by putting the question: "what prehistorian would be reckless enough to explain by a monogenist theory the red hands of the Australian caves and the red hands of the grottos in the Pyrenees?" But surely the observance of the same fantastic practice in Europe by the most primitive existing members of the species *sapiens* and in Australia by the earliest members of the same species (who originally must have been derived from the same source, seeing that they belong to the same species) cannot be disposed of merely by an impotent gesture! When the issue is clearly stated and critically examined there can be only one answer. Immigrants into Australia brought with them this practice which we associate with Aurignacian culture in Europe.

Against one link in Professor Sollas' chain of argument a protest must be made, because its weakness is more fully revealed when he applies it to cases in which it cannot support the strain put upon it. For example, in his discussion of the fantastic practice of totemism—the belief that the original ancestor of a group was born as one of a pair of twins, the other twin being the totem in the form of an animal, plant or inanimate object—he says: "When a custom is thus widely, but discontinuously, distributed we may conclude that it must be very ancient."

But the customs of using steam engines and wax matches, and in fact most elements of modern civilisation, are "widely, but discontinuously, distributed," yet many of them are known to be recent. Like most writers on such subjects Professor Sollas ignores or unduly minimises the influence of small bands of wanderers in spreading abroad customs and beliefs—a process which has been in operation ever since speech was invented. Totemism was not invented until many centuries after the primary dispersal of *Homo sapiens,* in fact, probably not before the third millennium B. C. Diffusion does not need the migration of a whole people, even though it is obvious that no transference of customs can occur unless some human being not only takes them to a new locality, but actively practises them in the new place until they are adopted.

Professor Sollas ignores the means by which rapid diffusion of practices has been taking place throughout the history of mankind. Hence he is not justified in assuming that "if it (totemism) originated once for all at a single centre . . . it must on any hypothesis have taken a long time to reach places so remote from one another as North America, Africa and Australia." On the contrary the fact can be demonstrated that totemism was practised in the neighbourhood of Northeastern Africa for many centuries before it spread far afield. Then it was suddenly diffused along definite routes to the ends of the earth.

How can any reasonable student disagree with Professor Sollas in his exposure of the fallacy underlying the modern ethnological dogma of the independent evolution of such arbitrary customs? "If it is difficult to conceive how such ideas as are involved in totemism originated at all, it is still more difficult to understand how they should have arisen repeatedly and have developed in much the same way among races evolving independently in different environments. It is at least simpler to suppose that all totemic beliefs have a common source . . . and may have since been carried by migrating races" (it would have been more exact if Professor Sollas had said by individuals or groups of wanderers by land and sea) "to remote parts of the world."

The issue raised in these quotations has of late years intruded itself into almost every branch of humanistic study, ethnology and archaeology, sociology and politics, psychology and educational theory. The divergence of opinion between the historical and the mis-named "evolutionary" school is fundamental. It extends as a deep chasm between the two possibilities in interpretation. The historical attitude is based upon the solid foundation of the known facts of history and human behaviour. When identities are found between complex and arbitrary customs and beliefs in different parts of the world, these are explained in accordance with the analogy of similar incidents of which the history is known. The American Indian's belief that a Dragon equipped with wings and deer's antlers is a power controlling water is assumed to have been derived from Asia, where the same complexly eccentric belief is entertained. Even though no official records have been preserved of the flight of this Asiatic wonder-beast across the Pacific Ocean, the historical school of ethnologists maintains that it got to America in very much the same way as the Spaniards' guns or the Englishmen's steam engines. In other words, the arbitrary nature of such beliefs or contrivances affords the most definite and conclusive evidence of contact and diffusion of culture in the past.

The other school, which, under the misapprehension that it is applying to ethnology and sociology the principles of biological evolution, has appropriated to itself the wholly misleading legend "evolutionary," starts out with the large demand that Man is endowed with extensive powers of originality (which, however, as we have just seen, are conspicuously lacking in mankind, considered as a whole). But these powers of invention are assumed to be guided into certain definite channels by some mysterious force, quite unknown to psychologists, which the ethnologists, following the lead of Dr. Adolf Bastian and Sir Edward Tylor, call "psychic unity." It is not psychic unity which we have been studying in this book, but some blind force, a sort of mechanically working destiny, which drives men to restrain their inventive genius in all directions but those which fall into the scheme of these idle speculations. But in these it leads mankind with the precision and definiteness of aim with which instinct guides the bee to build its honeycomb and to fill it with honey. Mankind in Europe had to wait countless thousands of years before the idea of making a Chellean implement occurred. Yet it is assumed that the same arbitrary event was exactly repeated long afterwards in South Africa, India and America! These "evolutionary" ethnologists indignantly protest if a critic insists that the working of their brand of "psychic unity" is indistinguishable from what the psychologist calls instinct. But if peoples upon opposite sides of the Pacific independently invent a winged Dragon with deer's horns to look after the weather, and provide this wonder-beast with an extensive repertory of identical and very fantastic tricks, how can this be explained except by postulating a highly specialised human instinct to dream Dragons? The only means of escape is to drop all such puerile speculation and admit the patent fact that the American Dragon came from Asia. There is hardly any element in the Pre-Columbian civilisations of America the source of inspiration of which cannot be identified, as the writer has explained in *Elephants and Ethnologists* (1924), and referred to its proper epoch and place in the history of the Old World.

Idle speculations such as these we have just been considering have sterilised a vast amount of laborious research during the last half-century, and prevented the reaping of the rich harvest of knowledge of ancient history awaiting those who refuse to be blinded by sophistry. Such views come into definite conflict with the historical method of interpretation, which implies continuity and the diffusion of culture. Sir Edward Tylor, who, more than any one writer was responsible for introducing into ethnology the doctrine of "psychic unity" and the erroneous use of the word "evolution," quotes with approval Comte's statement that "no conception can be understood except through its history." But he goes much further than this in his scathing exposure of what he calls the elaborate sophistry of those who neglect the historical method. In *Primitive Culture* (1871, Vol. I, pp. 18 and 19) he wrote: "to ingenious attempts at explaining by the light of reason things that want the light of history to show their meaning, much of the learned nonsense of the world has indeed been due." This occurs in the very book that was destined to obscure for a time the light of history! But he goes on to cite specific illustrations of the effects of such neglect in the writings of his contemporaries, and then adds the comment: "Such are the risks that philosophers run in detaching any phenomenon of civilisation from its hold on past events, to be simply disposed of by a guess at some plausible explanation." It is surely ironical to find these sane views in the very book that was mainly responsible for making this game of plausible guessing the fashionable method in ethnology for the past fifty years!

While frankly admitting that Western Asia and Egypt exerted some indirect influence upon Neolithic Europe M. Joseph Déchelette says:

"We should not subscribe to the intransigent doctrines of orientalists and archaeologists of Professor Sophus Müllers school . . . and explain all the similarities in industries and ethnography by assuming connections. It has been justly said that the use of such a method might claim an Egyptian origin for the civilisations of America and for all countries in the world."

This argument was all M. Déchelette adduced against the recognition of the Egyptian origin of the conception of constructing megalithic monuments. He does not seem to have realised that in referring to the American civilisation he was using a boomerang which would hit and demolish the foundations of his case. He proceeds:

"Walking through the galleries of an ethnological museum is enough to demonstrate that the initial phase of civilisation among every people of the world presents, if not a uniform appearance, at least an identity of fundamental features. Everywhere the same

industry corresponds to the same stage of culture. The more fully
the primitive civilisations are studied the more definitely the constant effects of determinism can be recognised as the factor which
shapes human achievements. What prehistorian would be bold
enough to explain by any theory of unity of origin the red hands
in Australian caves and the red hands in the grottos of the Pyrenees, the mummies of Peru and Egypt, the burial in jars in the
New World and the Iberian Peninsula, the attitude of the skeletons in prehistoric European and American graves, the superstitious cult of cup-marked stones found in the lands on the other
side of the Atlantic as well as in many parts of Europe and Asia?
Moreover, most of these analogies seem to present a criterion more
exact and more characteristic than the polishing of stone implements and the circular shape of a hut."

At the time (1911 and 1912) when M. Déchelette was putting
these questions as an argument by *reductio ad absurdum* the writer
was citing the same evidence for the purpose of demonstrating the
reality of the diffusion of culture, the mere possibility of which
M. Déchelette considered to be manifestly absurd. The writer's
little book *The Ancient Egyptians* was issued in 1911, six months
before M. Déchelette's great treatise. The argument was more
fully developed in *The Migrations of Early Culture* (1915).

It is commonly assumed that the earliest population of America
was derived from the Old World "during the Neolithic Age." For
example, Dr. Pliny E. Goddard wrote in his essay on "The Antiquity of Man in America" (*Natural History*, 1926, p. 257): "It
is said that they (immigrants into America) came during the Neolithic period. It is only in Western Europe that the successive
periods of stone art are known, and there the Neolithic is fairly
recent, later than the last great glaciation, presumably not more
than 25,000 years ago."

Earlier in this chapter reasons have been given for the view
that the so-called Neolithic period in Western Europe was not more
ancient than between 2000 and 1500 B.C. Why is it absurd to suggest that so distinctly Neolithic a practice as burial in the flexed
position is due to the Old World influence? The alternative assumption is that the original immigrants into America, who in
Asia may have been in the habit of burying their dead in the

flexed position, abandoned this custom, with all their stone weapons, as soon as they arrived in America, and then immediately set to work to devise precisely the same burial customs and methods of making implements as those which, according to the implication of M. Déchelette's hypothesis, they had just discarded. Surely such speculations are unworthy of serious consideration, revealing as they do a complete absence of any attempt really to examine the factors involved in statements so flippantly made.

Speculations on Dates

No phase of Human History can be dated before 3500 B.C.: but we are safe in assuming that civilisation began with the invention of agriculture about 4000 B.C.

It may have been a million years since *Pithecanthropus, Eoanthropus* and *Sinanthropus* roamed the earth.

The Chellean industry may have begun, at a rough guess, half a million years ago.

The Mousterian industry and Neanderthal Man may be fifty thousand years old.

The earliest human prototype of *Homo sapiens* (as revealed in The Lloyd's Skull) is at least as ancient. This London fossil is unique and vastly more ancient than any other remains of the species *sapiens*.

The Aurignacian phase of culture and the Grimaldi and Combe Capelle skeletons may not be more than (if indeed as much as) ten thousand years old.

The Neolithic phase of culture in Western Europe (*where alone the term can be used with cogency or intelligible meaning*) did not begin before 2000 B.C., or possibly even 1500 B.C.

Bronze was discovered in Western Asia about 2000 B.C. The Age of Bronze, which brought the Neolithic phase to a close, began in Western Europe about 1500 B.C., and in Britain and Scandinavia possibly not before 1000 B.C.

The twenty centuries which elapsed between the creation of civilisation in the Ancient East (4000 B.C.) and the beginning of the Neolithic phase in the West (2000 B.C.) represent in the latter a period characterised by the Solutrean and Magdalenian phases of culture, before the Neolithic Age began.

Nothing is known of the ages of the various races of Mankind. Human remains reveal racial traits as well defined fifty centuries ago as those of to-day.

(

CHAPTER IV

THE RACES OF MANKIND

EUROPE is occupied by three peoples of different origin—
the Mediterranean Race, dwelling mainly around the shores
of the Mediterranean and in the West; the Nordic Race,
mainly in the North of Europe, found in its greatest purity in
Scandinavia, and forming the main element in the population of
the British Isles; the Alpine Race, occupying the centre and western
area of Asia and forming a wedge of people thrust westward into
Europe. None of these races are restricted to Europe; and the only
justification for the continued use of the terms Alpine and Mediterranean is that they were originally invented with reference to
the peoples found respectively in the Alps and on the coasts of the
Mediterranean. The Mediterranean Race is found, however, not
only on the coast of the Middle Sea, European, African and Asiatic,
but down the Nile Valley, through East Africa as far as Somaliland, to Asia, in Arabia, Persia, India, Indo-China and the Malay
Archipelago, and forms a definite element in the population of
Polynesia. The Alpine Race is not only found in Central Europe,
but also forms the chief ingredient in the population of Western
and Central Asia.

The Mongolian Race is found mainly in Eastern Asia and the
Malay Archipelago and also forms the chief element in the aboriginal population of the New World. The Negro Race occupies
the whole of Africa south of the Sahara, and is found again in
a mixed and modified form in New Guinea and Melanesia. Later
we shall have to consider how these races became so widely spread
over the earth.

The Australian Race

The Australian Race is found in its greatest numbers and its
greatest purity in Australia. At one time it occupied the whole
of the continent, but has now been driven out of most of it by

British colonisation. The majority has taken refuge in the North-west, but considerable numbers are still living in Queensland. In Victoria they have entirely disappeared. In New South Wales the few that remain are found only in government reserves. People with the same physical characteristics are found in the South of India and in Ceylon, and, mixed with other races, in Northeastern India, especially in Chota Nagpur. Others, again, are found in Malaya, Sumatra, Celebes, Borneo, and some islands of the Philippines.

We have to consider what can be gathered of the history of the race from this distribution. But first we must deal with the question of the Tasmanians, who have now completely disappeared. They differed from the Australians; the hair, for instance, being curly instead of wavy or straight; so showing a closer approximation to the inhabitants of Melanesia than to the Australians. As to how they ever got into Tasmania we have absolutely no information. It is often claimed that the Tasmanians were in Australia before the Australians arrived there, but we have absolutely no evidence to justify such a statement.

There are reasons for believing that the aboriginal Australians of to-day are not pure in type. There is considerable contrast in type between the different groups. Those of the Northwest, for instance, are tall, while those that formerly dwelt in the South-east are small.

Figure 30 reveals in a crude way the general principles of what must have happened in the past history of their wanderings to Australia. People evidently moved from the jungle regions in Chota Nagpur eastward and southward through the Malay Peninsula. In early times the Malay Peninsula was continuous with Borneo and Java. Celebes, New Guinea and the neighbouring islands were joined to Australia. But there was always a break between Borneo and Celebes, which is now known as Wallace's Line. This is shown by the difference of fauna on each side of the strait. Hence, even if the mainland of Asia was then continuous east to Borneo and Java, and Australia was still joined to Papua and Celebes, there still remained the break between Borneo and Celebes to cross. The early wanderers must have used boats or rafts of some kind to cross Wallace's Line.

At the time when the earliest representatives of the species *Homo sapiens* became broken up into the groups that afterwards developed into different races, the conditions, not only of geography, but also of climate, were very different from what they are to-day (see Figure 29). In the Ice Age there was always a large region in Southern Asia, including some of the hottest parts of the world, which was always free from ice, and where conditions congenial to primitive Man prevailed. Men have always been free to wander along this great tropical belt, and the ancestors of the Negro and Australian Races probably moved backwards and forwards across this region unhindered.

But it was not until 1914 that a scrap of tangible evidence was obtained to shed a solitary beam of light on the ancient history of the Australian Race. A fossil of great interest was shown at the meeting of the British Association for the Advancement of Science at Sydney. The Talgai skull had been found thirty years before by a boundary rider working at a sheep station on the Darling Downs, and he had kept it as a' curiosity. The forecasts that appeared in the newspapers in anticipation of the meeting of the British Association in 1914 prompted the man in whose possession the fossil then was to send it to Sydney to be exhibited at the meeting. The skull was completely fossilised and broken into fragments. It was embedded in a solid mass of stone which it took several months of careful work to develop. The general form was like that of a modern Australian skull, but the lower part of the face was more prominent, and the palate enormous. The canine tooth was exceptionally large and prominent. The author's brother described it in the *Philosophical Transactions* of *The Royal Society* in 1918.

Most of the creeks in the region of the Darling Downs only contain water at certain seasons; for the rest of the year they are mere dried-out gulleys. In such a dry watercourse the skull was found, just at the line of separation between the top black soil and the underlying red-brown clay. No implements or animal remains were found with it to give us any idea of its age. But in the Darling Downs a good many fossil remains of gigantic Marsupials had been found on the red-brown clay. These animals are like enormous kangaroos, some of them as much as 14 feet high.

One of the interesting features of the discovery was that for some time it had been thought human remains might be found in

Australia because the fossilised bones of dogs had been discovered in Victoria and New South Wales. Now the dog is not indigenous to Australia, and it is difficult to conceive of a dog getting to Australia except with Man's help. Dogs and men must have crossed at least one stretch of water (Wallace's Line) to get there. These remains probably belonged to the ancestors of the dingoes which accompany the aboriginal Australian. As the domestication of the dog is unknown earlier than Predynastic times in Egypt (at most 4000 B. C.), and two millennia later in Europe, it is open to question whether the Talgai Man is likely to be more than four or five thousand years old.

A comparison of the outline of the skull with that of a modern Australian shows that the two conform in proportions and in type. The comparison is made somewhat difficult by the fact that the fossil skull belonged to a boy about 15 years of age who had not attained to adult proportions, especially in regard to the eyebrow ridges, which do not develop until several years later. Nevertheless we have sufficient evidence to show that we are dealing with a member of the Australian Race. The prominence of the jaw and the size of the teeth indicate that he was of a more primitive type than the modern aboriginal Australian.

The Australian shows primitive characteristics such as are rarely found in Modern Man. In many cases he is extraordinarily hairy, possibly a survival of the simian hairiness of body. In this he presents a marked contrast to the Negro with his slight development of hair. In the writings of anthropologists the most diverse views have been expressed as to the racial affinities of the aboriginal Australian. Half a century ago, when Huxley and others were claiming the characters of the hair as the surest criterion, the aboriginal Australian was assigned to the same race as the European. The curly hair of the Negro and the coarse, perfectly straight hair of the Mongol were contrasted with the European's elliptical hair, which is never completely straight and never curly like the Negro's. In those days no distinction was made between the different ingredients in the population of Europe. Mediterranean, Nordic and Alpine were classed together in the so-called "Caucasian" Race, in spite of their obvious differences in colour of skin, hair and eyes, in head-form and stature. The term "Caucasian" is still used and has become crystallised in the language. In many books of anthropology the statement is still being made that the aboriginal Australian is of Caucasian race. So far as hair is concerned, it is true that the Australian conforms to the European type, for both have retained the primitive wavy type of hair, in contrast to the Mongol and Negro, whose hair is highly specialised, and correspondingly different from the primitive type. The error involved in this identification of Australians with Europeans should be a warning against relying on any one feature as a test of race. In the determination of racial characters we must work upon as wide a basis as possible and take into consideration every factor. The skin of the Australian is black like the Negro's. The nose, again, is very primitive and flattened like that of the Negro. In every part of the bodily structure the Australian displays features that are more primitive than those of any other people. The Australian is in fact as far removed from the European as is possible within the same species.

Nevertheless there are reasons for believing that the Australians are profoundly mixed. The evidence in substantiation of this conclusion is not merely cultural, but is also revealed by the study of the living people. Mr. Northcote Thomas has called attention to the fact that Australia had been exposed to external influences, and in confirmation of this he refers especially to the fact that in the northern zone of the three into which he divides the continent. the language spoken is not Australian, but Papuan. He also points out the striking contrast between certain of the Queensland tribes and those of the rest of the continent, because the latter seem to have failed to devise anything that could be called a house, whereas the Queensland tribes learned hut-building from the people of New Guinea'. Other influences can be detected in the Northwest coast, where many practices suggestive of Timor and the Malay Archipelago are found. But the alien custom of mummifying the dead, and the complex system of totemism and the social organisation all afford unmistakable evidence of the influence of contact with more highly civilised peoples, from whom these diverse fragments of higher cultures have been borrowed.

The bodies of the people themselves reveal evidence of admixture. There are marked differences in physical characters, stature, head-form, hair, *et cetera,* in different parts of Australia suggestive of widespread admixture. The recent studies of varieties of human blood, as revealed by living tests, have provided the surprising result that in many aboriginal Australians the blood conforms in its reactions more nearly to that of Europeans than to other kinds of human blood. This may possibly be explained in the same way as the similarity of hair has been interpreted. But alternatively it may be the result of the ancient drift of culture and its bearers along the Southern Asiatic coasts. In this case Huxley's old comparison with the Egyptians and the more recent use of the term "Caucasian" for the Australians might not be so fantastic as they seem at first sight. Although the Australian has a high domed forehead that is apt to give one an exaggerated idea of the size of his brain, the actual capacity of the brain-case is small because it is so narrow. Some years ago when Professor Sollas was studying this question, he obtained an aboriginal Australian skull that was quite as flat as the Neanderthal skull. When the Australian skull was superimposed upon the Gibraltar skull the outlines agreed, as far as the Gibraltar extended, in a remarkable manner. At the time when Professor Sollas was making this comparison, he was using it to show that the aboriginal Australian was a survivor of the Neanderthal species, but since that time facts have come to light to show that the development of the front end of the brain, which is distinctive of *Homo sapiens,* is sufficiently marked in the Australian to make it certain that we are dealing with a member of the species *sapiens.*

The Australians are in many respects—such as their nomadic habits, their lack of agriculture, houses, clothes and settled communities—extremely primitive. Yet they have a highly specialised social organisation, with totemism and strangely complicated marriage regulations: some of them practise the difficult and wholly exotic custom of mummifying the dead.

The incongruity of this mixture of primitive and highly developed customs points to the influence of immigrants as the explanation of Australian totemism and social organisation and practice of mummification. Many practices found on the North-west coast and Bathurst Island afford clear evidence of influence from the Malay Archipelago and from the Timor region. In Northern Queensland, on the other hand, there is equally definite evidence of culture contact with the Torres Straits and New Guinea. Then again in the Southeast there is evidence of definite racial admixture with Tasmanians.

During the last twenty-five years the view has been widely adopted that the customs and beliefs of the Australians represent the earliest phase of human culture, and they have been repeatedly cited in works dealing with the history of human society, as an example of a really primitive institution uncontaminated by alien influences.

The case against such a misleading assumption was clearly put by the late Dr. W. H. R. Rivers in his contribution to the volume of Essays presented to the late Sir William Ridgeway on the occurrence of his 60th birthday in 1913, which shortly before his death Sir William gave the writer permission to quote:—

"In the many works in which the the Australian aborigine is held to have been the originator of human institutions, there is necessarily implied the idea that his culture is simple. If it could be shown that Australian culture is complex and contains many elements derived from without, perhaps in even ethnologically recent times, there must arise the most serious doubts whether we are justified in looking to it for material whereon to found theories of social origins. Certainly, such a procedure is wholly unjustifiable without a preliminary analysis of the complexity of its elements, and there can be little doubt that the result of this analysis would be to cut away the ground underlying many of the speculations concerning human institutions which have arisen out of the study of Australian culture.

"There are few parts of the world where there seems at first sight so much to support the idea of unity of culture. Rarely do we find so high a degree of uniformity of physical type over a large area [which, however, as has already been explained, is more apparent than real]; rarely such similarity of custom and of institution and apparently of the underlying ideas and beliefs. The differences, and highly significant differences, are there ready to be seen by those who look for them, but it is not unnatural that under the influence of the dominant idea of the unity of this culture, they have been overlooked, and that there are ethnologists prepared to acknowledge the complexity of human culture in general, who still hold firmly to the unity of that of the Australian aborigine."

Dr. Rivers had on several occasions called attention to features of Australian culture that suggest its complex character. The combination of two forms of social organisation which elsewhere are found apart and the nature of Australian mythology seem to indicate complexity. Few customs of mankind take so firm a hold of his imagination as his modes of disposing of the bodies of the dead. If, therefore, Australian culture has been isolated, and is the outcome of spontaneous growth through immense stretches of time, we should expect to find much uniformity in the disposal of the dead. It is difficult to see in the environment of the Australian anything which could have led him, unaided and untaught, to evolve a variety of funeral rites.

Yet nearly every one of the chief known methods of disposal of the dead is practised in Australia. We find burial in the extended and the contracted positions; we find preservations on platforms, on trees and in caverns. There is embalming, though of a simple kind, and, lastly, there is cremation.

On the assumption of the unity of Australian culture we have to suppose that this lowly people with their relative uniformity of social structure, of art and of material culture, have yet independently evolved the chief methods of disposing of the bodies of the dead which are found throughout the world. We know the Australians to be a people of far greater mental power and initiative than the extreme simplicity and crudeness of their material culture would suggest: but it is straining the doctrine of independent invention to the breaking-point to suppose that these people have been capable of such extensive and revolutionary changes in a department of culture where all the emotions and sentiments which influence mankind most deeply might be expected to have preserved unity and conformity to established custom.

Comparison of Australian modes of disposal of the dead with those of neighbouring Oceanic peoples makes it still more difficult to accept the independent origin of the Australian practices. In this comparison, we find not merely general resemblances, but those of detail which are still more useful indications of a common source. If the Melanesian and Polynesian modes of disposal of the dead belong to the cultures of peoples who have reached these regions from elsewhere, it should be found impossible to withhold assent to the proposition that there has been a similar introduction from without into the Australian continent.

Further, there is an aspect of the subject about which we can be confident. New funeral customs are not widely adopted as the result of the visits of strangers who come and go, nor can they possibly be due to visits of the Australians themselves elsewhere for trade or other purposes. People do not adopt new funeral rites merely because they see or hear of them elsewhere. If the funeral customs of Australia have been introduced from without, they have been the outcome of permanent settlements of strangers who lived and died in such close relations with those among whom they settled that the visitors were able to prescribe how their own bodies should be treated, and were so honoured, if not reverenced, that the customs they introduced have become established and time-honoured practices.

The problem before us is to reconcile this diverse influence from without with the relative uniformity of the physical type of the Australian people. The clue to the solution of this problem might be found in the introduction of the diverse funeral rites of Australia by relatively small bodies of immigrants who had so great an influence only through their possession of cultures, which seemed to those among whom they settled to be vastly superior to their own.

The area of the Australian continent is so large and the natural means of travel so scanty that if the introduced cultures were brought only by small bodies of immigrants, it is unlikely that these would themselves have been able to pass to the interior in any number. The introduced elements of culture would have been carried chiefly by means of secondary movements of the earlier inhabitants who had been influenced. Thus the relative uniformity of the physical features of the Australian would not be disturbed.

It is clear that the Australians have received practically every element of their culture from abroad in relatively recent times. Hence it is altogether misleading to assume that their social organisation, their customs and beliefs are primitive. The fact that the aboriginal population of Australia belongs to the most primitive race now living suggests the possibility of its very remote antiquity, though not necessarily in the island continent that is now its home. There is no doubt that it came from Asia and had to accomplish the long and hazardous journey from the Malay Peninsula. Australia· is separated from New Guinea by the Torres Strait (Figure 30, C) which is a hundred miles across, but has some scattered stepping-stones in the form of small islands, which are known to have been used in recent centuries as links between the two greater islands. On the Northwest three hundred miles of open sea (Figure 30, D) separate Australia from Timor (the gap between Timor-Laut and Melville Island is a hundred miles less). But before people can pass from Asia to New Guinea, Timor or Timor-Laut, they must cross many stretches of ocean. From the Malay Archipelago the Malacca Strait must be ferried to get to Sumatra and the Sunda Strait to get to Java. The wide expanse of the Java Sea and the Strait of Macas-

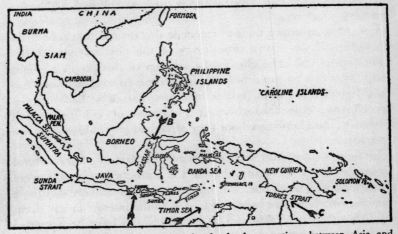

Figure 30—Map to show the gaps in the land connections between Asia and Australia—A and B indicate the site of Wallace's Line, the break between the Archaic continent of Asia and the former extension of the Australian continent.

sar (Figure 30, B) serves to isolate Borneo and Celebes respectively. A series of straits separate Java (Figure 30, A) from the string of islands, of which the largest are Bali, Lombok, Sumbawa and Flores, before Timor can be reached: or to the north the Molucca

Passage and the scattered islands of the Molucca group have to be crossed by the wanderer from Celebes to New Guinea. Even if it be assumed—and it is important not to forget that there are no valid grounds for such an assumption—that at the time when the earliest human immigration into Australia took place many of the now isolated islands may have been linked to Asia or to Australia by land bridges; it is certain that there was at least one sheet of open sea (Figure 30, A), the fifteen miles that separate Lombok from Bali (or alternatively, [Figure 30, B], the wider strait of Macassar between Borneo and Celebes), that had to be crossed. Hence the earliest men to reach Australia must have used some sort of boat to cross one of these breaches of continuity of the land connection with Asia. In all probability they made many sea journeys, such, for example, as the voyages from New Guinea across Torres Strait and perhaps from Timor across the Timor Sea.

It is surely irrelevant to assume that the aboriginal Tasmanians may have reached their island from Australia without the use of boats, i.e. before Bass Strait was formed. Their own predecessors must have crossed at least one sheet of water as wide as Bass Strait, in all probability scores of them, on their way to Australia. The absence of sea-going vessels amongst them can be explained only by a loss of the art of ship-building, such as Dr. Rivers (in 1912) has shown to have happened amongst some of the kindred peoples in Melanesia, and assumed to apply also to the case of the Tasmanians (W. H. R. Rivers, *Psychology and Ethnology*, 1926, p. 207). As their predecessors could not have got to Tasmania without traversing stretches of open sea in the Malay Archipelago, to which reference has just been made, if not also Bass Strait between Australia and Tasmania, the loss of the art of seafaring is not an assumption but a historical fact.

The aboriginal Australian belongs to a race that is sometimes called Predravidian, a term intended to emphasise the fact that certain jungle tribes of Southern India, the Kadir of the Anaimalai Hills, the Paniyan of Malabar, the Wynad and Nilgiris, the Irula and the Kurumba of the Nilgiris, scattered amongst the Dravidian peoples, conform to the same physical type as the Australians and obviously belong to the same race. Before we attempt to discuss the antiquity of the population of Australia it is clearly important to remember this most westerly relic of the same people. The Vedda of Ceylon, the Sakai of the Malay Peninsula and East Sumatra, the Toala of Celebes, and possibly also some of the people of Borneo, provide evidence in corroboration of the fact of the migration of the Australian race. As these people must have reached Australia by immigration from Asia, it is important to consider what is involved in the demonstration that they are found as far west as India, which brings us close to the place near the Caspian from which the earliest known distributions of the various races—Negro, Mediterranean, Alpine, Nordic and Mongol—radiate in different directions (Figure 13, p. 49). In the tentative working hypothesis suggested on a previous page the cradle of *Homo sapiens* was located somewhere between India and Northeastern Africa. Thus the tracing back of the most primitive of the living races to India is obviously a matter of special significance. The most ancient remains of *Homo sapiens* that have been recovered are the two skeletons of the so-called Grimaldi race found near Mentone, on the Italian frontier in the Riviera, the Combe Capelle skull found in France and the remarkable collection of skeletons discovered at Prdmost and Brno in Moravia by Professor Absolon, all belonging to the Aurignacian phase of culture. In addition there is the enigmatic fossil known as "The Lloyd's Skull" found in 1925 in the city of London, which is probably the earliest member of the species *sapiens* at present known. Elsewhere (in the writer's *Evolution of Man*) attention has been called to the points of resemblance—though it is not an identity—which most of these earliest members of the species *sapiens* present to the most primitive living race, the aboriginal Australian. The possibility was there suggested that this likeness was not merely fortuitous, but a concrete illustration of the fact that both are close to the original type of the species when it was first differentiated from *Homo neanderthalensis*.

The Prdmost skeletons found in Eastern Europe were associated with a large collection of cultural objects some of which present a close resemblance, not only in form but also in their decorative patterns, to the magical objects known to the Australians as *churinga*. This raises for discussion the possibility whether the proto-Australians, when they first began their easterly wanderings, may not have carried with them from some place between Moravia and India the cultural objects they seem to share with the earliest people of Eastern Europe who belong to the species *sapiens*. If this were so the Aurignacian phase of culture in Moravia may provide the clue to the date at which the Australoid people of India could have started on their long journey to Australia.

Having now sketched a hypothetical scheme (in accordance with the principle of continuity, which is the dominating principle of this book) to bring the Australian problem into the world-wide perspective of the history of the species *sapiens*, let us consider the concrete facts.

No human remains of great antiquity have yet been found in India: but amongst the earliest series found at Adittanullar (Madras Presidency) are Australoid types. Fossilised skulls of proto-Australians were found at Wadjak in Java by Professor Dubois.

Since 1857 many reports have been made of the finding in different parts of Australia of bones of the dingo (the dog of the aboriginal people) in alluvial deposits and cave breccias associated with the remains of extinct marsupials. The most important of such discoveries was that reported by Mr. Gerard Krefft in 1865. In the breccia of the Wellington Cave in New South Wales he found two dog's teeth associated with the remains of the extinct animals *Thylacoleo, Sarcophilus* and *Diprotodon;* and these identifications were afterwards confirmed by Mr. R. Etheridge, Jr. from the specimens in the Australian Museum at Sydney. For it must be obvious, as Mr. Etheridge fully appreciated in 1896, that the dog could not possibly have reached Australia without the help of Man. The presence of the dingo in association with *Thylacoleo* and *Diprotodon* implies that Man must have reached Australia before the giant marsupials became extinct. Hence there is no reason for doubting Krefft's early observations that in the breccia of the Wellington Cave he found the "fractured crown of a human molar tooth in the same matrix as *Diprotodon* and *Thylacoleo*."

In 1914 Sir Edgeworth David learned of the discovery, which had been made thirty years previously, of the fossilised human skull, which was picked up near Talgai in the Darling Downs (Queensland).

The state of mineralisation of the Talgai skull affords in itself no evidence of great antiquity, for, as Sir Edgeworth David has emphasised, the Dalrymple Creek, near Talgai Station, where it was found, deposits a considerable amount of carbonate of lime in a relatively short space of time. Nor does the presence of the extinct Marsupials as contemporaries necessarily imply a remote age. For the dogs that Man introduced may have played a decisive part in the extermination of these relatively small-brained creatures, who had never before had to cope with a real Carnivore. Moreover, the similar phase in Southern Europe, when Man lived as a contemporary with many large mammals that are now extinct, may not be more remote than five or six thousand years ago. For men of the same species as ourselves were depicting mammoths and other extinct animals in France and Spain a short time before the arrival of Neolithic men in Europe, i. e. about 2000 B. C. If so, it may be used as a standard of comparison in attempting to obtain some idea, necessarily not an exact estimate, of the date of Man's first intrusion into Australia. The only evidence that suggests a greater antiquity is the primitive character of the large jaw and teeth of the Talgai skull. Even in the home of civilisation and shipbuilding we have no certain knowledge of the use of any definite kind of canoe before six thousand years ago, if indeed we can push back the history much earlier than 3500 B. C. (when canoes presenting the same peculiarities of construction as those made by the Tasmanians first became known). This naturally arouses a feeling of doubt whether members of the most primitive race were already (at a period even as remote as this), not only building some sort of vessel capable of carrying them with their women and dogs, but also putting out into the open sea—say from Bali to Lombok. From what we know of the earliest history of sea-trafficking in the Mediterranean and Erythraean Sea the possibility that the original immigration into Australia or Tasmania was older than forty centuries seems hardly credible.

In the past vast assumptions have been made as to the antiquity of the aboriginal culture on the basis of its supposed primitiveness. But recent research, and in particular Dr. A. P. Elkin's critical analysis of the evidence afforded by initiation ceremonies, has made it abundantly clear that most of the rites and customs, the totemism and beliefs, as well as the material culture, have been introduced into Australia within the last thirty centuries by two distinct routes, one entering the continent from the direction of New Guinea, somewhere in the direction of Cape York Peninsula (Figure 30, C), and the other, probably coming from Timor, by way of the North-west coast (Figure 30, D).

The problem of the antiquity of the aboriginal population of Australia is complicated by the curious enigma of the now extinct people that formerly occupied the island of Tasmania to the south. Amongst anthropologists there is a wide divergence of opinion as to their origin and affinities. But there does not seem to be any real justification for denying the kinship of this black-skinned, "woolly-haired" people of medium height with the Papuans, who formed the basis of the Melanesian population of the Western Pacific. When and how they got to Tasmania we do not know: nor can we be certain that they got there before the Australians arrived in their island-continent. Their ancestors may possibly have reached Tasmania by sea at the same time as their kinsmen reached such islands as Fiji and New Caledonia. For the absence of sea-going canoes in Tasmania is to be explained, not as evidence that they did not once have such vessels, but that they have lost the arts of ship-building and navigation. It is certain that their predecessors must have had some sort of sea-going craft: otherwise it would have been impossible for them to have travelled from Asia to Tasmania, even if the journey was done at so remote a period—a most improbable possibility—that only the Bali-Lombok Strait (Figure 30, A) had to be crossed by water.

The late Sir William Turner, one of the most cautious of anatomists, examined with scrupulous thoroughness and critical discrimination all the evidence relating to the Tasmanian's place in nature, and established upon a sound morphological basis the conclusion that "the Tasmanian in his physical characters seemed to occupy a place intermediate to the Negrito and the Papuo-Melanesian, though more closely associated with the former" (*Transactions of the Royal Society of Edinburgh*, Vol. L, 1914, p. 343). In a previous memoir (*ibid.*, 1908, p. 394) he expressed the view that "the evidence seems to be in favour of the descent of the Tasmanians from a primitive (Negrito) stock, which migrated across Australia, rather than by the route of the Melanesian Oceanic islands lying to the north and east of the Australian continent."

The Negro Race

The Negro is a very primitive member of the Human Family, and yet in some respects is highly specialised. The average size of his brain is much smaller than that of the peoples of Europe and Asia. Moreover, anatomical peculiarities suggesting affinities with the apes are commoner than they are in most other peoples. But if we look at other features, we find that in respect of some of them (the hair, for example) the Negro is highly specialised. If the hair of a European is cut across, the section will be found to be elliptical, and, as the result of this flattening, it tends to become either wavy or curly. In the Negro the flattening is carried much further, so that the hair becomes almost ribbon-shaped. Instead of being merely wavy, it tends to become rolled up in tightly curled masses, commonly called "peppercorns." No other race has hair that is so flat or tightly curled. The hair of the Mongol, on the contrary, is almost circular in section, and is considerably coarser than that of any other race; it is quite straight, showing no tendency whatever to become wavy. The difference of hair is of use in discriminating between these races, but, as was mentioned in the last section, it is important not to rely upon the characters of the hair alone in the assessment of racial characters. If we compare human hair with that of the apes, we find that the hair of Europeans and aboriginal Australians is most like that of the gorilla and chimpanzee and is therefore nearest the primitive type. The Negro and the Mongol are highly specialised in different directions. The hair is one of the most distinctive features of the Negro, and perhaps more reliable than any other characteristic as a means of distinguishing him from the other races such as the Australian, who in skin colour and form of nose presents some analogy. In the Australian, however, there is a tendency for the size of the eyebrow ridges to become exaggerated, though not to the same degree as is displayed in most crania of Neanderthal Man. In the Negro the eyebrow ridges are singularly defective. They are, in fact, even less noticeable than in the European.

The bones of the Negro are also peculiarly specialised. They are more slender and denser than those of other races. Less robust in build, the limb bones depend for their strength upon their dense, ivory-like texture.

Although the Negro and the Australian are more primitive than any other living peoples, many features, in addition to those just mentioned, enable us to discriminate between them. I need refer to only one. The Negro is characterised by a singular lack of hair; the pure Negro very rarely has more than a few tufts of hair for a beard. The Australian sometimes has, not only a thick beard, but often a great development of hair on the body.

Both races have retained the dark skin pigment which probably was the heritage of all human beings. In the others the development of the colouring matter in the skin is hindered so that it appears as though it had passed through a sort of bleaching process. The difference of skin colour between the blond Nordic Race, the olive-brown Mediterraneans, and the so-called yellow races, the Mongols, has often led to the question, Why is it that when the skin is bleached, it assumes first of all a yellowish-brown colour? Newborn babies of apes and human beings have a pale skin: the pigment develops after birth. Babies of the aboriginal Australian first take on a yellow colour, rather like that of a Mongol, and then gradually assume their black colour. In the babies of Negroes, the skin is distinctly yellow at the time of birth. The yellowish-brown colour of races like the Mediterranean, the Bushman and the Mongol is due to a partial bleaching of the original black common to the African anthropoid apes and to the earliest members of the human family.

One or two other characteristics of the Negro must be mentioned. The shape of the nose, which is one of his most distinctive features and resembles that of the Australian, is very flat and the wings of the nostrils are broadly expanded. The extreme flatness is seen in certain branches of the Mongol Race, but these Asiatics lack the broadly outsplayed nostrils of the African and Australian races. The flattening of the nose in Australians, Negroes and Mongols probably represents the retention of a primitive trait which is still manifest in the human foetus of every race.

Another characteristic feature is the full fleshy lips. This is often referred to as a primitive feature, but in reality it is a sign of high specialisation distinctive of the Negro. The lips of the anthropoid apes are thin, not fleshy.

The muscles of the face in the Negro and Australian Races are not so highly differentiated as those of Europeans and are less apt to express fine shades of emotion than those of the other races of mankind. The Negro's facial suppleness is less varied and less subtle, and his robuster manifestations of mirth and sorrow less restrained.

Like other races of mankind, the Negro Race is subject to extreme variations in stature. In fact, the tallest and the shortest people in the world both belong to the Negro Race. These two extremes live in close proximity to one another. The extremely tall group, the Shilluks and Dinkas, live near the head waters of the Nile in the southern part of British Sudan. Not far away, in Equatorial Africa, dwells the group of Pygmies, whose average height is nearly two feet less than the Shilluk's. Both these groups are Negroes, with the typical hair, skin colour, full lips and other distinctive morphological characters. There are other groups of Negroes of intermediate statures.

The geographical distribution of the peoples revealing evidence of Negro blood raises for discussion a problem of far-reaching significance. The Negro population of the world was in ancient times broken up into two main groups, African and Melanesian, widely separated in the geographical sense. In trying to account for this distribution, we may leave on one side the movements of Negroes in modern times—as, for instance, the importation of tens of thousands of Negroes into Portugal in the sixteenth century, and the wholesale transportation from Africa to America, which continued until the nineteenth century, and has been responsible for the addition to the population of the New World of many millions of Africans and hybrids distributed in North, Central and South America as well as the Caribbean Islands.

The vast bulk of the Negro Race is to be found in Africa, where it occupies the tropical belt as far north as the Sahara, and spreads up the West coast almost as far as Morocco. In fact, Negro admixture is so evident amongst the Moroccan population itself that the word Moor is often used to suggest Negro influence, as we see in the name "Blackamoor." But we shall leave the peoples north of the

Sahara out of the question. In the South are those peculiarly primitive yet, in respect of certain features, highly specialised members of the Negro Race, the Bushmen and Hottentots. They have preserved a very primitive type of culture, and especially their art, which presents many points of analogy to the Upper Palaeolithic cave-paintings in Europe.

The other great mass of the Negro Race occupies New Guinea, and spreads right through Melanesia, the Bismarck Archipelago, the Solomon Islands, New Caledonia and Fiji, and even to Easter Island far out in Eastern Polynesia and the American coast. These Melanesian Negroes present the general characteristics of the African Negro, but in a form suggesting more or less admixture with other races. We thus have the race divided into two great groups, African and Oceanic. In the intervening area only comparatively small numbers of Negroid people are found. One of these is worthy of special attention—the people of the Andaman Islands. As in Africa, there also is amongst the Melanesian group a considerable number of small or only moderately tall people. Leaving out of account for the moment the exceptionally tall peoples of the Upper Nile, the Negro's height averages about 5 feet 6 inches. Then there are very small peoples, known in Africa as the Negrillos, in the East as Negritos. The members of the small African group are usually called Pygmies, but the term Negrito is the common appellation for the small Melanesians.

The question naturally arises as to the geographical situation of the original home of the Negro. Did the Negro acquire his distinctive traits in Africa and spread to the Far East (Figure 29, p. 89), or in the Far East and spread west? Or was his original home in some region between East Africa and Papua? We have little evidence with which to answer this conundrum beyond the fact that Africa contains the vast majority of Negroes at the present time, and that in Africa the Negro is found with relatively less evidence of extreme admixture than elsewhere. The distinctive features of the Negro Race are revealed in a much more obtrusive and constant form in Africa. These facts would suggest that Africa was their original home. If that is accepted, it must be assumed that in early times Negroes reached the Far East, i.e. Papua and Melanesia, after wandering along the Southern littoral of Asia.

There are clear signs of Negro mixture in Southern Persia, where the people show a marked contrast to those in Northern Persia. Again in India, although one great factor in the population is the presence of members of the Australian race called Predravidian, there are also traces of intermingling with the Negro Race, to which part of the darkness of skin colour so widely prevalent in India may be attributed.

Leaving aside this question for the moment, let us go back to consider the distribution of the Pygmy population. In Africa, in addition to the Bushmen and Hottentots, there are two groups of really Negroid Pygmies, one in Equatorial Africa and one in the Belgian Congo. They are the two smallest peoples in the world. These little folk dwell in great forests. They are extremely primitive, being quite devoid of any kind of culture. They are skilled in hunting, and they have no other arts or crafts; they wear no clothes; they build no houses; their needs are few, and their activities extremely limited in scope.

In the South we find another group of Pygmies, which presents a marked contrast to the Equatorial Negrillos. These are the Bushmen and the Hottentots. Their skin is not black, but yellow in colour, rather like that of a typical Mongol, but apart from skin colour they are truly Negro in type. Their hair is not only Negroid, but ultra-Negroid; in the Bushmen we see the "peppercorn" type of hair in its most extreme form—the head looks as if it had been shaved and peppercorns stuck on to it leaving spaces in between them. The nose is even flatter than that of the ordinary Negro. In fact, one could describe the Bushman as a diminutive Negro with all the characteristic features of the race carried to the extreme, with the exceptional distinction that the skin is bleached to yellow.

One peculiarity of the Bushman and Hottentot peoples must receive special mention because references to the condition known as steatopygy occupy so prominent a place in the discussions of the amulets made by the early members of the species *sapiens* in Europe, Northern Africa and Western Asia. In the women of the Bushman and Hottentot peoples enormous masses of fat develop in the region of the buttocks and hips, giving the form of the body a monstrous and often grotesque appearance. It differs from the condition that is frequently found in women of all races, in whom an unusual obesity produces a distortion of the whole body. The condition known as steatopygy is not due simply to obesity but to the localised deposition of large masses of fat in one region of the body. Moreover this condition is normal throughout the whole community, but is seen in its most obtrusive form in adult women.

The Hottentots resemble the Bushmen very closely, but they are slightly taller and are probably mixed with the ordinary Negro to some extent. They may even have intermingled slightly with members of the Mediterranean Race who spread down the East coast of Africa in early times.

Some authorities recognise a third group, the Korannas, who are found at the present time on the banks of the Orange River. They are said to have come there from the West within the last two centuries. They have a darker skin and generally show more signs of Negro affinity than the other two, but they are worthy of notice, because, unlike other Negro peoples, they show a tendency to develop prominent eyebrow ridges. It is possible that they intermingled with some more primitive race which existed in former times in Africa. Occasionally the Korannas present resemblances to the Australian Race, and so contrast remarkably with the other Negro peoples.

The Bushmen have been gradually pushed by the Bantu Negroes towards the South and particularly into the Kalahari Desert, where they exist to-day. This fact, together with their custom of painting pictures on the walls of caves, which show a remarkable likeness, both in subject matter and mode of treatment, to the Upper Palaeolithic paintings of Southern France and Spain, has led Professor Sollas to suggest that the Bushmen may at one time have been in contact with the peoples of France and Spain, and then have been pushed down south further and further until they got into the Kalahari Desert.

Many writers have claimed to have discovered evidence of the former existence of Bushmen in the Nile Valley. But there is no justification for such statements. In the Upper Palaeolithic phase of culture in Europe and amongst the peoples of the Mediterranean littoral the earliest manifestation of belief was the use of statuettes in the form of a gross caricature of the female form. Grotesque images of women with the distinctively maternal features much exaggerated were made. Many writers thought they could detect in these a resemblance to the figure of Bushman and Hottentot women. But, as was suggested in Chapter I (Figure 3), the form of these statuettes had nothing to do with race, but was associated with the ideas about the power of a female amulet to give life and protect those who used the image. The fact that these statuettes are found widespread in Europe, Egypt and Western Asia has led some anthropologists to claim that the Bushmen formerly existed in Europe, Egypt and elsewhere. But we really have no evidence, either on the physical or cultural side, to support such a theory. This claim is still being advanced by Professor Boule of Paris in support of the view that the skeletons in the Grimaldi caves are Negroid and once belonged to Bushmen-like people: but reasons have already been given in this chapter for the conclusion that the skeletons from the *Grottes des Enfants* did not belong to members of the Negro Race, but simply showed the retention of primitive features more nearly akin to those of the aboriginal Australians.

The Negro peoples of Africa are divided into two groups—one, the Sudanese Negroes, stretching across Equatorial Africa from the head waters of the Nile, to Nigeria and the Gold Coast; the other, known as the Bantu Negroes, occupying the region from the Great Lakes southward. The distinction is largely, but not wholly, linguistic. The people of the equatorial belt speak a language quite distinct from the Bantu language of the South. There is also a difference in the peoples themselves, which is partly due to the contrast in the process of intermingling with neighbouring races that has taken place in the two cases. For thousands of years there has been a steady traffic to and fro across Equatorial Africa of members of the Mediterranean Race (Hamites and Arabs). The result of these movements has been the introduction into the Negro population of considerable Hamitic and Semitic elements, as well as a variety of cultural influences. Every kind of intermingling has taken place between the original groups of Negro, Hamitic and Semitic peoples. Even across the Sahara, admixture of essentially the same character has taken place with peoples of the Mediter-ranean littoral. So that the character of the Nilotic Negro, itself highly variable, has been greatly modified by free mixture with these groups. Their language is a mixture of Negro, Hamitic and Semitic.

The people of the South have undergone another type of blending. The Mediterranean Race originally extended right up the Nile and the coast of East Africa to Somaliland and Equatorial Africa. At the head of the Blue Nile we find very warlike Hamitic people who have retained their Mediterranean characteristics with relatively slight admixture. It is possible this may have been the original home of the Mediterranean Race. In early ages, this warlike group intermingled with the neighbouring Negroes, to whom they gave leaders, teaching them the art of war. Gradually the Southern group of Negroes, the Bantus, became infected with warlike practices, in virtue of which they fought and conquered the whole of the South. We thus find two influences at work in Africa —intermingling in the Southern Bantu region with the warlike Hamitic group, and in the Northern Sudanese area the more peaceful penetration by peoples from the East and North in search of raw materials.

The Far Eastern group of Negroes in Papua and Melanesia is even more mixed than the African group. We do not find here the distinctive features of the African Negro in their most extreme form. It is probable that the Melanesians were intermingled with many other peoples during their easterly wanderings. In particular they became mixed with peoples of Australian and Mediterranean affinities. In the Solomon islands, and elsewhere in Melanesia, one frequently finds amongst the Negroids individuals who are almost indistinguishable from Australians. The two races not only intermingle in the islands, but probably mixed from time to time long before they reached Melanesia.

On Easter Island, in distant Eastern Polynesia, three quarters of the way across the Pacific, many individuals present a strongly Negroid appearance. There are suggestions also of Melanesian influence in New Zealand. It is possible that in the early stages of colonisation in the Pacific mariners of other races carried with them Negroes from Melanesia, so introducing the definitely Negroid element we find there to-day.

As in the case of the migrations of the Australian Race, so also with the Negroes: groups were left on various islands to blaze the trail of the ancient wanderers. There are Pygmy Negritos in the Andaman Islands and in various parts of the Malay Archipelago as far east as the Philippines and New Guinea to help us plot the easterly migration. The absence of Negroes of more normal stature in these places may be due to the fact that they have intermingled with people of other races to such a degree that their individuality has been lost.

Critically studying the achievements of the Negro race the same conclusion is forced upon us as the study of the aboriginal Australians has already revealed. Neither in Africa nor in Melanesia can any significant element of culture be attributed to Negro invention. Many of them, like the African pygmies and the Indonesian and Papuan pygmies, seem to be almost wholly devoid of any culture. As regards the other Negroes in Africa, who for more than forty centuries have been in contact with the pioneers of civilisation, the few arts and crafts that are scattered sporadically through the vast continent are all alien in origin. No more striking testimony is needed to emphasise the lack of enterprise and initiative in the Negro race.

Statements made by early European travellers in America suggest that Melanesians reached the Pacific coast of America, as we know they did Easter Island. The fact that they did reach Easter Island is presumptive evidence that a vastly greater number of them missed this islet and went on to America. Many writers have called attention to the somatic and linguistic evidence in support of this suggestion. Within recent years Professor Rivet of Paris has advanced strong arguments in corroboration of this surmise. In the third section of this book we shall return to the consideration of this matter.

The Mongol Race

In studying the Australian Race we saw that, although the bulk of it was living to-day in the island continent, scattered groups were to be found elsewhere, ranging westward as far as India; and it was suggested that early members of the race probably made their way to Australia from some region either in India or to the west of India. When we discussed the Negro we found that, although the race was spread in isolated groups as far East as New Guinea, Melanesia and beyond, it seemed probable that the race has assumed its characteristic features in or near Africa, and that it had wandered eastward along the Southern littoral of Asia through Southern Persia, India and Indo-China, to the Malay Archipelago and further east. It was suggested that these two peoples (Australians and Negroes) originated somewhere in the region between India and Africa. When we consider the other races we shall find that there are reasons for believing that the Alpine originated in Turkestan, the Mongol somewhat further east, and the Nordic somewhere in Eastern Europe west of the Urals (Figure 29). Thus they all converge towards Southwestern Asia, and it is likely that somewhere in this region was the original home of the species *sapiens*. None of our evidence is conclusive: but on the basis of the known distributions of the six fundamental races and what little is known of their past history the Southern littoral of Western Asia seems to be the most probable place (Figure 13).

In many books on anthropology the Mongol is confused with the Turki Race, whose home is in Central Asia, not far from the head waters of the Yenesei River. The profound difference between these two peoples cannot be too strongly emphasised; it would be difficult in fact to imagine two peoples more clearly differentiated one from the other. The features of the Turki people are prominent, in contradistinction to the extremely flat face of the Mongol Race. Their hair is wavy, and oval in section, as opposed to that of the Mongol, which is straight, and round in section. The Turki have full, flowing beards, and are, in fact, amongst the hairiest peoples of the earth, while the Mongol is characterised by a lack of hair. In these, and in many other characteristics, there is a marked contrast between the Mongols and Turki, who are really a highly specialised branch of the Alpine Race.

The references to the Mongols in most modern anthropological writings are marred by a serious confusion of race and culture. In ethnological discussions few people seem to be able to steer clear of such elements of confusion. Race and the culture of a race are two very different things. Any member of any race can adopt the culture of another people without undergoing any change in his physical characteristics. In the case of the Mongols, there is also much discussion as to where the Chinese got their culture. Did they create it themselves, or did they acquire it from some other people? Many writers, attributing the source of Chinese culture to Mesopotamia, proceed to confuse the peoples of the two countries (who are racially distinct), and assume that the Chinese people also came from Mesopotamia! It is a common pretence to recognise Mongol characteristics in early Sumerian statues, which conform to Mediterranean and Alpine types—the latter distinguished by the high-bridged nose, the heavy jaws, and the large, broad head—which reveal a contrast to the Mongol of as definite a character as it is possible to find.

The skulls found in the tumuli at Anau (in Turkestan) conform to the Mediterranean type. They belonged to people who came up from the South at a time definitely later than the early settlements in Mesopotamia. Instead of a movement south from Central Asia to Sumer, everything points to an immigration into Central Asia of colonists from Mesopotamia.

The intrinsic problems of the Mongol Race, quite apart from the confusions which obscure a clear vision of the question, are enormously complex and difficult. As in the case of the Negro Race, the physical characteristics of the different groups of the race reveal a great degree of variability. Only a relatively slight admixture with Hamitic and Semitic stock had been effected in the majority of the Negroes in Africa. In the case of the Mongol, however, factors of racial admixture have to be considered in every branch of the race. We find that the Mongol has come into contact, not only with one or two, but with a large series of different peoples.

It is difficult to say with certainty where the Mongol came into existence. The whole question is largely a matter of conjecture. The segregation of peoples in Asia was probably determined by the great ice barriers in the glacial epoch (Figure 29, p. 89). At that time, Tibet was entirely under the ice sheet, so that Professor Keane's theory of a Tibetan area of Mongol characterisation is obviously impossible. People of Alpine stock can be shown to have occupied the North of Asia as far as Mongolia, and a series of primitive peoples, Australoid, Negroid and Mediterranean, were making their way East along the Southern shores of Asia. Excluding, then, the parts of Asia that were under ice, and those parts which are known to have been occupied by other races, China itself, possibly the fertile area extending from the Hoang-Ho to the Yang-tze-kiang, would seem to be the most likely area of characterisation of the Mongol Race. In China, this group probably became separated from the other races of *Homo sapiens*. Living there in isolation for many centuries, they gradually assumed those characteristics which we associate to-day with the Mongol Race.

We have no exact information to justify these inferences. But so far as is known, the fertile area of China between the two great rivers was free from ice: it is not likely that it was uninhabited: no other people is known to have occupied it in early times: from what we know of the subsequent history of the Mongol Race this Chinese area of characterisation fits the facts more easily than any other. Before the introduction of agriculture (possibly about 2500 B.C.) the population was probably sparse and widely scattered.

It would be difficult to discover any other area in Asia in which, in the Ice Age, the Mongols could have become completely separated from the other races of mankind. The peculiar specialisation of their distinctive physical characteristics seem to suggest that the segregation must have been complete and of long duration.

Wherever the race acquired its distinctive features, it wandered far and wide as soon as climatic conditions permitted; North into Mongolia, Manchuria and Eastern Siberia, West into Turkestan and Tibet, and South into Yunnan and Burma and into what we now call Indo-China, the Malay Peninsula and the Malay Archipelago. Different groups had assumed distinctive characters so that Northern, Southern and Maritime Mongols became differentiated; and as the first and third of these subdivisions intermingled freely with other races their differences from the Southern Mongols (who exhibit the characteristic features of the race in their most extreme form) became further emphasised. To interpret the physical characters of the people we have to picture members of the Mongolian group wandering away from the centre (where the most intensive specialisation of racial characters was taking place) before the process of differentiation was far advanced, for on the fringe of the Mongolian domain one finds members of the race differing less emphatically from other races than, say, the Chinese do. But as this fringe extended its wanderings it came at length into contact with the expanding edges of other races, in particular the Alpine people in Central Asia, and the Indian and Indonesian people (both essentially Mediterranean in race) in the South.

It was probably an admixture of primitive Mongols with a small minority of primitive Alpines that at some time, the date of which we cannot even guess, crossed Bering Strait and provided America with its first human population, which in course of time multiplied and roamed until it colonised the whole of the Americas, North and South, as far as Tierra del Fuego. There are no valid reasons for refusing to admit that what these primitive immigrants did in early times without much in the way of equipment could be done, and was repeatedly done, by people in later ages when fuller knowledge and ampler and better facilities were available.

The Mongol Race is divided into a number of groups among which great contrasts of stature, features, and skin colour occur. But the most constant and easily recognisable characteristic is the hair. The coarse, perfectly straight hair, almost circular in section, clearly differentiates the Mongol from all other races. It is present in the aboriginal American, showing this people to be of Mongol stock. It is sometimes stated that the Mongol is distinctive in the colour of his skin, and we frequently find the term "Yellow Race." Many Mongols certainly have this yellow skin—especially the Chinese, who are the most highly specialised group of Mongol people —but when other branches of the race are taken into consideration, skin-colour is found to be a very variable feature. The Japanese, for instance, sometimes has a skin as white as the European, especially in those parts of the body which are protected by clothing from exposure to the sun. Further north, in Manchuria and Siberia, the people have a definitely brown skin. Skin colour is not a reliable test for discriminating members of the race from other peoples.

Most Mongols are broad-headed, but the nature of their broad-headedness differs from that of the Alpine Race, the skull not being flattened at the back, and there being no tendency for the eyebrow ridges to become prominent. The cheek-bones are broad, and pushed forward so as to give a peculiar flatness to the face. The nose is small and flattened, and very wide at the root; there is no groove between the root of the nose and the forehead, in which it differs from the nose of the Negro. The hair is singularly scanty; even on the head, the number of hairs is few, although the great coarseness of each separate hair gives a general appearance of thickness. The form of the eye is very distinctive in some Mongol peoples. In the eye of most human beings there is a triangular area at the corner by the nose, known as the inner canthus. In the Mongol the upper eyelid is often pulled down over the canthus so as to produce a fold extending on to the side of the nose. This is called the epicanthic fold. This gives a curious oblique slit-like appearance to the eye, although the position of the eye itself is in no way different from that of other human beings. This epicanthic fold is found in no other race, and not invariably, though frequently, in the Mongol.

As we have already seen, these and other distinctive features were gradually developed in this subdivision of *Homo sapiens,* after it had become segregated from the rest of mankind, probably in China. There, too, the skin underwent a partial bleaching process, losing its original black, and taking on a yellow tint. This yellow colour is an intermediate stage in the process of bleaching of the primitive black, which has been carried furthest in the Nordic Race.

In the course of the segregation, groups of Mongols from time to time wandered out from the area of characterisation, before the process of development had been completed. One finds, for instance, near the head of the Yenesei River, people who are obviously Mongols, but are far less specialised than the Chinaman. They differ in stature, in the form of the head, in the degree of flatness of the face; the nose is much less flattened and is rather like that of a typical Mediterranean. The occurrence of these, and other variations elsewhere can only be explained by the theory that before high specialisation had taken place, groups of Mongols had strayed away from the home of the race to the North, West and South. This probably took place soon after the melting of the great ice barriers (Figure 29), when Central Asia became free, and it was made possible for primitive members of the Mongol Race to come into contact there with primitive members of the Alpine, and even of the Nordic, Races (Figure 13).

One group, as we have seen, at some period of unknown date, wandered across the Bering Strait—or some land bridge—and so reached America. The American Indians are definitely Mongol, but they differ considerably from the Mongol as typified in the Chinese. The nose, for example, far from being flat and short, has a high, narrow bridge, and is of the type implied in the phrase "hawk-faced." There is also considerable variation in stature. The characteristics of the American Indian are not distinctive of the American Continent. In Central Siberia we find people who are almost indistinguishable from them. The American Indians are probably the descendants of one of the primitive groups of Mongols who went out of the area of characterisation before the development of the type had been completed. Intermingled with their definitely Mongol characteristics, their hair, skin colour and formation of the skeleton, we find widespread throughout America, long before contact with other peoples of the Old World was possible, many Alpine peculiarities, in particular the form of the jaw. The assumption forced upon us is that the people who immigrated into America were a mixture of primitive members of these two races, in whom the Mongol strain predominated. The statement is made in some books that the Indian is mixed with Nordic, but there is no justification for this.

The Mongol Race is found to-day in China, Manchuria, and Mongolia, spreading right up to the Arctic Tundra. Southwards they spread down from China into Indo-China, forming the main element of Cambodia, Siam and Burma, and to some extent in Assam. They extend right through the Malay Archipelago, Japan, Formosa and the Philippines. In Siberia the Mongol population is broken up by Alpine groups who have moved eastward through this area.

Owing to the confusion between Mongol and Turki, the statement is still made by many writers that the Asiatic peoples who immigrated into Europe during the Christian Era, such as the Hungarians and Magyars, were Mongols. These peoples were essentially Alpine, and came from Central Asia, where, it is true, they may have intermingled with Mongols, but were still definitely and predominantly Alpine. The Hungarians are entirely free from Mongol affinities, and it would be hard to find a people more European in type. Yet the statement still continues to be made that, because the ancestors of the Magyars came from Central Asia, the Hungarians are Mongols. Whatever mixture with Mongolian peoples may have taken place in Central Asia, that element was in large measure eliminated as the people moved towards the West.

The Mongol Race can be divided into three main groups. The Southern Mongols occupy China, Tibet, Indo-China, spreading into Assam and the southern slopes of the Himalayas in India. The Northern Mongols include the Manchurians, the Mongolians and the Tundra peoples. Similar groups are found in Szechuan and Eastern Siberia. The Northern Mongols differ from the Southerners in their greater stature, their darker skin-colour and less flattened faces. The nose is more prominent, having a far better bridge; and the cheek-bones do not show the extreme flatness. The type spread down the coast as far as Korea, where the tall, slenderly-built people present a marked contrast to their neighbours in China. The Mongols of the Malay Peninsula should perhaps be called the Proto-Malays, because the term Malay is now applied to the whole mixed population of the Archipelago. Or they might be termed the Maritime or Oceanic Mongols.

The third Mongol group, the Japanese, are an extremely mixed people. It is probable that the whole Japanese group of islands was originally occupied by a curious people known as the Ainu, who are not of Mongol Race. They are now restricted to Saghalin and the north of the Japanese group, but evidence that they originally occupied the whole group of islands is furnished by the fact that there are obvious traces of them to-day in the most Southern of the islands, Lu-chu. These people are undoubtedly members of the Alpine Race. They must have wandered to the Japanese islands in very early times, and become segregated there.

Probably the next people to invade Japan were tall Northern Mongols from Korea. These invaders pushed the Ainus progressively further and further north.

A third ingredient (in addition to Ainus and Mongols) was

added later when Indonesian people came in from the South.
These were probably descended from the so-called Indonesians,
the people who lived in the East Indies before the Malays intruded into the Archipelago. It is probable that in very early times
they had wandered along the Southern littoral of Asia, through
India, Indo-China, and the Malay Peninsula. In course of time
these people, who belong to the Mediterranean Race, became intermingled in the Malay Archipelago with Maritime Mongols, and
the two formed the chief element in that mixed race—the modern
Malay population.

But the people who had wandered East from the far West did
not abandon their roving there. Some of them moved on to Japan.
A considerable ingredient in the composition of the population of
Japan is formed by this Mediterranean element. Hence we find in
the inhabitants of the Japanese islands three main racial stocks:—
Ainus, Northern Mongols and Indonesians. They differ profoundly
from the Chinese, being racially quite distinct. The character of the
Japanese, apart from racial inheritance, was originally determined
by much the same sort of factors that moulded the character of the
British people, for both were of necessity a sea-faring people and a
mixture of continental immigrants with seamen from the South.

There are, however, some characteristics of the Japanese people
that we are hopelessly at a loss to explain. Take the question of
stature, for example. We have said that the Japanese are a mixture
of people from Korea and people from the South. Of these, the
former are exceptionally tall, the latter moderately tall. Yet the
Japanese are diminutive in size, and their legs, especially, are in-
explicably short and stumpy. Possibly a Malay element in the
Indonesian invaders may be partly responsible for this.

One of the most interesting problems of race is the unravelling
of the chequered history of the Malay Archipelago. This region is
doubly important from its bearing on the relationship to the peopling of Polynesia. The Mediterranean Race extended right up the
Nile Valley, through Arabia, India, Indo-China, to the Malay
Archipelago. In the course of their wanderings they became profoundly mixed with other racial strains.

When we come to consider the culture of the Mongol Race we
find among the various tribes every gradation of level from the

high state of civilisation of the Chinese down to the almost complete lack of anything that can be called culture in certain of the American tribes. There was clearly no racial impulse to build up a distinctive type of customs and beliefs, nor, in fact, an inevitable development of any culture at all. We shall see later on that, as in the case of the Australians and the Negroes, the development of civilisation amongst the Chinese was inspired by certain alien influences; and the shape it assumed was determined partly by the circumstances under which the Chinese were led to participate in the process, and partly by the abilities and opportunities of the Chinese themselves.

It is important at this stage to insist again on the consideration, ignored by so many modern writers, that the demonstration of the fact of the derivation of the foundation of Chinese civilisation from Elam and Sumer does not imply any close racial kinship between the peoples of Eastern and Southwestern Asia. Although in the very distant past the ancestors of all living people were sprung from one community, which may conceivably have dwelt in Mesopotamia, it would be a profound error to regard the population of Mesopotamia in the third millennium (i. e. the time when Chinese civilisation was probably born in the Shensi province) as Mongolian: and it would be almost equally mistaken to call the people of Shensi Mesopotamian, even if it be admitted as conceivable that a few Elamite prospectors might have got as far as China at that time.

These are questions that can be discussed more profitably after the other three races of mankind have been mentioned.

The Mediterranean Race

The Mediterranean Race occupies a territory that probably includes the original home of the species *sapiens*. The term "Mediterranean" was introduced more than thirty years ago by the Italian anthropologist, Professor Giuseppe Sergi. To him, more than anyone else, are we indebted for clearly differentiating this race from the other racial ingredients in the population of Europe. The race had been identified long before and was commonly known as "Iberic." His achievement was to call attention to the fact that it was far more widely spread through the world than had been realised before. When archaeologists first began to call attention to the difference between the men of the Old and New Stone Ages, it was recognised that the earliest inhabitants of Britain then known were a Neolithic people who were described as "Iberic" in race. This name was given to the people we now call Mediterranean, and was used because these people were believed to have come from Spain to Britain in very early times. The merit belongs to Sergi of pointing out that people of this type agree in the main with the original population found round the whole littoral of the Mediterranean, and preserved to-day in great purity in islands such as Corsica and Sardinia, and also in Southern Italy and in fact the greater part of the Mediterranean coast.

Collecting all the available evidence, he put forward the claim that this race occupied not only the shores of the Mediterranean, both North and South and the Levant, but also Northern and Eastern Africa and Western Europe, including the British Isles. We now know that long before them there were other primitive types living in Western Europe. Many hundreds of thousands of years ago men of the Piltdown type were living in Western Europe. Later came members of the Heidelberg and later still the Neanderthal types. Then or possibly even earlier came men of a curiously enigmatic type of which we know nothing except what we can learn from the fossil skull found at Lloyd's in the City of London in 1925. Then a series of primitive types of modern men found at Paviland in Wales, Kent's Hole in Devonshire and the Aveland Cave in Somerset prove that there were many dwellers in England long before the coming of the so-called Iberic people.

However, to return to Sergi's work, he found that the Mediterranean people extended up the Nile Valley, through Abyssinia and Somaliland to the Equator, and he made the suggestion that possibly the home of the race was in East Africa. Thus the term "Mediterranean" is not a very appropriate designation. The peoples of Arabia and many of the inhabitants of Palestine and Syria conform in all essential respects to the Mediterranean type. The earliest inhabitants of Mesopotamia, the Sumerians, were members of the Mediterranean Race. Further east, people of this race form the main element in Persia, mixed in the South with a Negroid and in the North with an Alpine strain. Still further east, in India, the predominant element in the teeming population is undoubtedly identical in type with the Mediterranean element in Europe and Africa. The skin colour of the Indian population, however, differs from that of the ordinary Mediterranean, owing in part to the fact that the original population of India was made up of Pre-dravidians or Proto-Australians, and probably in part to the stream of Negroes who passed through India when migrating from Africa towards Melanesia. The physical characteristics of the population of Southern India reveal a considerable amount of admixture with Australian and Negro strains, but nevertheless both in the ancient and modern people Mediterranean characteristics predominate. In the Northwest mixture with the Alpine Race has taken place, and in the Northeast with the Mongols—in fact, the hill tribes are mainly of Mongol stock, with some admixture of Mediterranean. The early population of Indo-China, the Malay Peninsula, and the Malay Archipelago was not Mongol but of the same racial type as the Mediterranean, possibly superimposed on earlier Australian and Negro immigrants. In the early centuries of the Christian Era, mar-iners from the Malay Archipelago ventured out into the Pacific and conveyed to the distant islands of that ocean their first set-tlers. Hence the Polynesian population consists of a mixture of races including Indonesian members of the Mediterranean Race, somewhat mixed with Alpine and later with Mongolian elements.

Many anthropologists have been puzzled by the fact that the population of Easter Island is more Melanesian than Polynesian. When one considers that the Melanesians were not such venture-some sailors as the Polynesians and probably only reached new islands when they were swept by the forces of nature out of their course, while the Polynesians built ships that would carry 250 to 300 people and could stay at sea for five months at a time, it seems probable that the presence of Melanesians in Eastern Polynesia must be due to the Polynesians. In the course of their navigations they probably recruited people from Melanesia from time to time, and so conveyed members of Melanesian stock as boats' crews to distant islands like Easter Island. This is the only feasible working hypothesis to explain this geographical distribution.

The Mediterranean Race is fair skinned, but is definitely

swarthier than the Nordic Race of Northern Europe or the Alpine Race of Central Asia. The skin colour is olive brown; the eyes dark with black irises. The stature is approximately the average of mankind, the men being about 5 ft. 5 in. and the women about 5 ft., and, unlike the other races so far discussed here, this race shows surprising uniformity of stature in whatever country it may be living. We find the same figures in the earliest inhabitants in the Nile Valley as in the Neolithic Englishman or the modern Welshman, Egyptian or Indian. We find the same uniformity in the other physical characteristics. The head is long and narrow, the proportion of the breadth of the skull to the length being on the average about 70 per cent. The shape of the head is distinctive. The eyebrow ridges are usually insignificant. The back of the head tends to become prominent, and the skull and the skeleton generally are characterised by a lack of robustness. The hair is always brown or black, and neither straight nor curly. As regards the development of the beard, most of the Mediterraneans have a small tuft of hair on the chin and little hair on the cheeks.

In their portraits of themselves the earliest Egyptians used to exaggerate this little chin tuft and eventually after inventing the art of shaving took to using an artificial beard to exaggerate this racial peculiarity.

People conforming to the Mediterranean type are still found in the British Isles, especially in South Wales, Cornwall and the islands along the West coast of Scotland, as well as in Ireland, particularly in Western Donegal and some of the islands off the coast of Connaught. The oval graceful face, black eyes and dark hair and chin tuft beard are seen as clearly in these people as in inhabitants of the Mediterranean area. The race is, in fact, characterised by such a singular uniformity that it is almost impossible to distinguish members of one area from those of another.

The early Neolithic inhabitants of Britain were not all of pure Mediterranean Race. After the melting of the great ice barrier in Turkestan, members of the Alpine Race were free to wander south, where they intermingled freely with the Mediterranean Race in the regions around the Black Sea and south of the Caspian. In particular Asia Minor and Syria were flooded with broad-headed men of Alpine Race. The invention of ships led to an even more considerable admixture with Alpine stock in the maritime populations in the Eastern Mediterranean and its islands, and eventually this process spread to the West as far as to the coast of Western Europe. Even in Britain the so-called Iberic immigrants in the Neolithic, and in particular the Bronze Ages, displayed increasingly pronounced evidences of admixture with Alpine stock, until in the Bronze Age the broad-headed people were so numerous as to have inspired the very misleading idea that the long-headed inhabitants of Britain were suddenly replaced by round-headed people.

The physical characteristics of the Mediterranean race are, on the whole, primitive. There is no distinctive specialisation of the hair, of the skeleton or of the architecture of the skull. The race retains far more of the primitive character than either the Nordic or the Alpine people do. In association with this, we find that it occupies what is assumed to be the original home of the species. Studying a series of different mammals belonging to any given natural Order it is found that those which wander away from their original home and become subjected to new environments and new conditions of life, new food to search for and new dangers to overcome, are more rapidly transformed than those which stay at home. This, of course, is not surprising since, when they are suddenly exposed to new circumstances, they must adapt themselves if they are to survive. In the same way, the Mediterranean Race, which seems to have remained in the original home of *Homo sapiens,* had less need to become specialised in diverse ways than perhaps any other existing members of the species. In making this suggestion, which obviously is tentative, it is important not to overlook the considerations that such stabilisation could only have been effected after the two black races, Australian and Negro, had become separated respectively on the East and Southwest of the cradle of the species before being pushed further towards Australia and Equatorial Africa by the expansion of the Mediterranean Race.

The tentative hypothesis just suggested seems to come into direct conflict with the evidence provided by such a race as the Mongols. It has already been suggested that China, being the only territory in Eastern Asia which, during the Glacial Epoch, was free from ice and not occupied by other peoples, must have been the area in which the race developed its peculiar physical characteristics, and that the less specialised branches of the race must have wandered out from the area of characterisation before the process of differentiation of type was complete.

We know more of the history of the Mediterranean Race than of any other people, because the earliest records that have come down from antiquity are Egyptian and Sumerian, and the most abundant and most illuminating archaeological data are provided by Egypt, Sumer, Elam, Crete, Syria, Palestine and Asia Minor, all of which were occupied by the Mediterranean Race with, except in the earliest phases, more or less Alpine admixture. When the claim for the superiority of the Nordic Race is advanced with uncritical enthusiasm, it is well to remember that the Mediterranean people were the inventors of our civilisation. Whether we consider Egypt, Babylonia or Syria as the home of civilisation, there is no room for doubt that the pioneers were of Mediterranean Race. The Nordic Race, which has played an obtrusive part in developing and spreading abroad civilisation during the last thirty centuries, did not take any part in the task of creating it. The foundations of civilisation were laid down for all time by members of the Mediterranean Race during the thirty centuries of arduous toil, in association with members of the Alpine Race, before any of the blond nomads of the North played any part whatever in the process.

Until the year 1894 nothing was known of the early history of Egypt prior to the building of the Pyramids, which began about 2800 B.C. But in that year a series of graves was discovered which proved not only to be earlier than the Pyramid builders, but to date back to before the First Dynasty. The First Dynasty came into existence when Upper and Lower Egypt were united and fused into one kingdom at a time that is commonly admitted as about 3400 B.C. The range of possible error is a single century more or less, making the possibilities 3500 to 3300 B.C. These figures are not accepted by all, but the majority of the leading Egyptologists agree that there is evidence to justify this date. The graves that can be proved to be earlier and are recognised as Predynastic, may be at least five or possibly as much as ten centuries earlier than 3500 B.C. Here we are justified in assuming the date 4000 (or possibly 4500 B.C.) for the earliest human events in the Nile Valley the age of which we can guess.

Within the last five years claims have been made for the existence of a still earlier phase of culture in Egypt, to which the name "Badarian" has been applied. It cannot be too emphatically impressed upon the reader that so far no evidence that lends any sort of justification for these claims has been forthcoming. It seems that the Badarian is an intrusive culture which probably came from Nubia at a more recent date than the earliest Predynastic phase in Egypt. Until about 3000 B.C. the population of Egypt was composed of members of the Mediterranean Race who were freer from admixture with other strains than almost any other known population. This people occupied not only Egypt but the Nile Valley up to the Sudan, where it was still free from Negro admixture. There were also people of Mediterranean stock dwelling in Abyssinia and Somaliland. If we turn to study the evidence from Crete, which was the centre of a high civilisation built up somewhere about 3000 B.C. (that is, after sea-going ships were invented to take people to the island—a condition obviously essential for the introduction of both population and culture), we find that here also the original inhabitants were Mediterranean and conformed in every respect to the Mediterraneans in Egypt.

Passing to Southern Mesopotamia, to the original inhabitants of Sumer, who were the predecessors of the Babylonians, we know less of these because the skeletons found here are rarer and less well preserved than in Egypt, where, in the dry desert sands, not only skeletons but complete bodies were found (preserved by a process of desiccation long before mummification had been introduced).

Very divergent opinions were expressed as to the racial affinities of these people. At the time (1911) when it was the fashion to pretend that the earliest inhabitants of Sumer came from the highlands of Turkestan and were "Turanian" or Mongol in race, the writer (*The Ancient Egyptians*), arguing from the few portrait statues that had survived, expressed the opinion that the people were Mediterranean in race. Numerous skeletons have been found in Sumerian graves during the last ten years. They afford a complete corroboration of this suggestion made in 1911.

Some of the Sumerian statues are obviously Mediterranean in type, having the narrow, oval face with no obtrusive features, whereas others reveal evidence of Alpine admixture. In other words there is the same sort of racial blending as was found contemporaneously, that is after the time of the Second Dynasty, in Egypt. Later on, some time after the Sumerian period, people of Alpine type (the variety of that race known as Armenoid), with the broad heads, prominent noses, and full beards, became much more numerous and in fact obtrusive. In Babylonian times sculptors began to represent their kings with great full beards and an extreme Armenoid type of countenance.

There is more confusion in books regarding the question of race in this area than in any other part of the world. One of the chief elements of confusion is the widespread assumption, repeatedly made in flagrant defiance of the patent facts, that all people in this region commonly called Semitic represent members of the same race. "Semitic" is a linguistic term and cannot be used as a racial designation. The Arabs are a Semitic people and belong to the Mediterranean Race: the Jews are a Semitic people and belong for the most part to the Alpine Race. The contrast in physical type clearly indicates this difference in race. The old assumption, so often disproved in the past, is constantly being repeated, even at the present, that, from time to time, the Arabs living in the deserts raided the settled communities in Palestine, Syria, Mesopotamia and Egypt, and adopted a settled mode of life, so becoming responsible for adding a Semitic element to the people. Unfortunately for this theory, the people who made their appearance after the Sumerian period were not Semitic Arabs, but Semitic people of Alpine Race (Northern Semites). A certain number of people speaking a Semitic language did no doubt come in from time to time and settle in the prosperous areas. But this action did not broaden their heads and lengthen their noses to give them such emphatically Armenoid traits! The Semites in Babylonia were Armenoids from Syria.

A study of these facts throws into relief the importance of the Mediterranean Race in the inauguration of civilisation. Civilisation had already assumed its distinctive features in Egypt, Sumer, Syria and Crete long before people of Alpine or Nordic Race had made their way into the area. It is claimed by several influential writers that the Negro and Mediterranean Races are specialised branches of the same stock. The Mediterranean people are primitive in type and occupy a territory adjoining the area of characterisation of the Negro. But the latter retain primitive features (such as skin colour) which the Mediterranean Race has lost, and acquire many distinctive specialisations which the former has not developed. The two races are quite distinct. The explanation of the confusion into which writers like Professor Ripley have fallen is to be sought elsewhere. The Hamites, members of the Mediterranean Race, dwelling in Nubia and East Africa, have for many generations intermingled with Negroes, so that their skin has assumed the black colour of the Negro Race. Whether there were Negroes in this area in the very early times we have been discussing it is impossible to say. It is probable that they lived in the tropical belt and did not come into contact with the Hamites until a relatively recent period. In studying the ancient remains in Nubia we find no trace of the Negro Race till the time of the building of the Pyramids, which is well into the third millennium. The Nubians to-day are almost uniformly black, but they rarely show the Negro type of hair or nose. The whole population has become permeated with Negro influence, but they still conform far more closely to the original Egyptian (Mediterranean) type than to the Negro.

Some of the people of the Nile Valley call themselves Arabs, and this has greatly misled many anthropologists: for most of them are Arabic only in language.

We have seen that there is the greatest uniformity in the Mediterranean Race: but it is not so great that one cannot tell the Arab from the Egyptian, the Egyptian from the Libyan, and all of them from the European representatives of the race. This is very slight admixture of Arab blood in the veins of the Egyptians, because when the Arabs conquered Egypt there was only a relatively slight immigration of Arabs. When the Egyptians were converted to Islam, they took to calling themselves Arabs to emphasise their Mohammedan orthodoxy. The Copts, who are considered the representatives of the pure Egyptian Race, are, taken as a whole, less like the ancient Egyptians than these so-called "Arabs." Occasionally, it is true, Copts may reveal the old Egyptian traits with amazing fidelity. But more often they show evidence of Alpine admixture. Being Christians, they have intermarried with people of the same religious faith as themselves from the neighbouring countries, with Syrians, Armenians, people of extreme Alpine type. Hence the so-called "Arabs" have retained the physical characters of pure Egyptians far more generally than the Christian Copts, who call themselves the descendants of the ancient Egyptians.

These are the essential facts concerning the Mediterranean Race. Certain other points will be dealt with when we come to the consideration of the Nordic Race and the relationship of these two before the great wedge of Alpine people came into Europe from the East and pushed the one to the South and the other to the North.

The Alpine Race

The Alpine Race is by no means confined to the Alpine region in Europe, nor does it show, as the name suggests, any special partiality for mountainous country. Several distinguished anthropologists have been misled by the symbolism of the name into speculating on the connection between an Alpine habitat and the broad-headedness of the Alpine Race! The vast majority of Alpines, however, are to be found, not in the mountainous regions, but in the great plains of Russia and Siberia.

As its name implies, this race is also found in certain highland areas in Europe—in Switzerland, and in other mountain regions, not necessarily Alpine in character, such as the central plateau of France, the low plateaux of Brittany, Bavaria, Savoy, and on the Eastern side of the Adriatic Sea. The population of the Balkans and Asia Minor is predominantly Alpine. But the race is found in greatest numbers in the Russian Plain, and these Alpines of the plain extend far into Asia, through Siberia and Turkestan. The Turki people are predominantly Alpine. In more limited numbers Alpines are found in certain places along the shores of the Indian Ocean, in India and Indonesia. Skulls from certain Pacific Islands and America establish the fact that the influence of admixture with people of Alpine type can be detected throughout the Pacific area, including the Western coast of both the Americas. This evidence must not be confused with the infiltration of Alpine people into America from Northeastern Asia by way of the Bering Strait and the Aleutian Islands. A group of relatively pure Alpines, the Hairy

Ainus, exist to-day in Northeastern Asia in the Northern Islands of the Japanese group.

Some years ago a German anthropologist, the late Professor von Luschan of Berlin, gave the name "Armenoid" to certain Alpine peoples found in greatest numbers and purity in Anatolia and Armenia. These people show the Alpine characteristics in their most accentuated form. Armenia, however, is by no means the area of the widest distribution of the Alpine type.

In considering the physical characteristics of the Alpine people, two main factors must constantly be kept in mind. Firstly, there is a marked contrast between this race and the other broad-headed race, the Mongol. Apart from the mere figures (cephalic index) stating the proportion of the breadth of the skull to its length, there is a marked contrast in form between the two. We have only to compare the flat face and nose of the Mongol, with the prominent nose, heavy jaw and projecting eyebrow ridges of the Alpine to realise how vastly dissimilar they are. And even in their common feature, their round-headedness, there is a fundamental difference. The Mongol's skull is low, and the broadness of the skull makes up for the lack of depth: the Alpine skull is high, and the broadness is associated with flattening at the back of the head. Hence we should not confuse the Turki with the Mongol Race, though there is often an admixture of Mongol blood in them. They are obviously and predominantly Alpine.

The second point to be borne in mind is that great differences occur within the group known as the Alpine Race. It is impossible to say whether these variations developed successively in one area of characterisation from which the Alpine moved out at various times; or whether they represent local modifications developed in certain areas after the people had left their area of characterisation. Stature is one of the most variable elements. One group living near the eastern shores of the Adriatic Sea, in the Balkan Peninsula, is so unusually tall that Dr. Deniker of Paris suggested making a separate race for their reception. He suggested the name "Dinaric" for it. But if this principle were recognised we should have to split up the Negro Race into half a dozen; for both the Shilluk and the Pygmies, the Bushman, the Melanesian and the Andamanese would have to be differentiated from the African Negroes of more ordinary stature.

In the Armenian, Alpine characteristics are found in their most extreme form. The head is high and broad, and flattened at the back: the nose is exceptionally large and prominent with a high narrow bridge, and there is a general heaviness in cast of countenance. The jaw of the Alpine is characteristic, both on account of its massiveness, which is in great contrast to the delicately-made Mediterranean jaw, as well as by reason of its form, its peculiarly high ramus. The orbits, also, are distinctive, being large, high and square in shape. The skeleton is extremely massive and robust in build. The stature is usually short, but, as we have already seen in the case of the "Dinaric" Alpines, it is subject to a wide range of variation. The Alpine shows a greater tendency to development of fat than any other race. Taken as a whole, they are the hairiest people still existing on the earth: in particular they generally show a very full development of beard.

The earliest evidence we have of members of the Alpine Race may possibly be the relatively broad-headed people who came into Europe from the East during the Upper Palaeolithic period, bringing with them the new and delicate technique in flint-work known as Solutrean (Figure 27, p. 78). But we are on more certain ground, both as regards the identification of race and the estimate of age, when we consider a group of Alpine people who began to percolate into Egypt during the Second Dynasty, and to form a very considerable element in the aristocracy of Lower Egypt during the Pyramid Age. That round-headed people were living in Syria at the beginning of the Dynastic period is shown by the portrait of a captive with definitely Armenoid characteristics depicted on an ivory from a First Dynasty tomb. Similar people began to come into Egypt itself at about 3000 B.C. The Predynastic Egyptians were little small-boned men of pure Mediterranean type. Among the Second Dynasty remains, however, certain skeletons show features of a different character. By no possibility could these traits be regarded as modifications of the Mediterranean type. The peculiarly high ramus of the jaw in itself was enough to show that this alien influence was Alpine. The head is loftier and flatter at the back, the cranial capacity is definitely greater, averaging 1500 c.c. while that of the Predynastic people averages only 1400 c.c. Another un-mistakable difference is revealed in the shape of the orbits. The orbits of the Mediterranean people are flattened and elliptical; the top of each orbit is relatively horizontal for some part of its length. In the Alpine the orbits are square, and show a dragging down-wards and outwards. This distinction in the shape of the orbits was very noticeable in the Giza remains of the "alien" type. Evi-dence of the existence of Armenoid people in Mesopotamia has also been found. Hence we may safely conclude that from about 3000 B.C. onwards there was a movement of Alpine people south-wards into Syria, Egypt and Mesopotamia.

Although the Alpine type was found in considerable numbers at Giza, it must be remembered that their coming into Egypt did not change the culture in any fundamental way. The general trend of development continued in the same way as before. Funerary architecture, for instance, was in no way modified, but continued to develop on the old lines until it reached its climax in the Great Pyramids of the Fourth Dynasty.

It will naturally be asked why the Alpine should have come into Egypt at this time. We know that at the time of the admixture the Egyptians were trafficking with, or rather exploiting, Syria for the purpose of obtaining timber, resins and other substances. Hence it is possible that it was in Syria the first contact between Alpine and Egyptian was made. But we know no more than this. The evidence we have shows us that similar movements of Alpine peoples were taking place on a larger scale into Mesopotamia and some time later also into India, to judge by the portrait statue re-cently found in Sind.

While there can be no doubt that these aliens in Egypt be-longed to the Alpine Race, yet their skulls are not of the very broad-headed type. Their cephalic index varies between 75 and 77, while an index of over 80 is not unusual in the Alpine Race. We must place them, therefore, among the "mesocephalic" peoples, rather than amongst the broad-headed. In other characteristics, however, they are too definitely Alpine to leave any room at all for doubt as to their race. Perhaps they were the earliest strain of Alpine people, in whom the extreme brachycephaly had not developed. They are the earliest known members of the Alpine

Race to be certainly identified. Possibly the process of specialisation had not yet been carried quite so far as it has in such relatively recent members of the race as the round-headed peoples of Europe in the Bronze Age, and the Modern Armenians and Turks.

The fact that there were movements into Egypt, Syria, Mesopotamia and India at some time in the third millennium B. C. suggests that the area of characterisation of the Alpine peoples was in some centrally placed area to the north of this region. In correlating these facts with the present distribution of the Alpine Race the conclusion is forced upon us that the area of characterisation of the Alpine people must have been somewhere in the neighbourhood of Turkestan. The conditions in the remote glacial epoch were such (Figure 29, p. 89) as to form a secluded area in which such specialisation might well have taken place. During the glacial epoch the plateaux of Armenia, Persia and Asia Minor were covered with ice sheets. At the same time a great inland sea, which has since disappeared, lay between the Aral and Caspian Seas, and there were, in all probability, either water or marsh and tundra conditions extending from the Caspian up towards the Arctic. Turkestan was thus effectively cut off on all sides. If we assume this to be the original home of the Alpine Race, no great difficulty presents itself in explaining the present geographical distribution of its members and what little is known of its early history.

In post-glacial times, Alpine peoples must have entered the highland zone to the south of Turkestan, from which, some time before the third millennium, the outward movements already mentioned took place. To the west, Alpine peoples moved along the plain to the south of the Ural Mountains, occupying the great lowland of Russia, while to the east they spread far into Northeastern Asia and probably added its contribution to the population of the New World.

When at a much later period in their history people of the Alpine Race moved into Europe they exerted a much more obtrusive cultural influence than they did elsewhere. In Egypt the newcomers found a culture far superior to their own to which they had nothing to add: the lines of development had already been laid down. When they went into Europe they brought with them a new and superior culture, the knowledge of the use of bronze, in virtue of which they were able to exert a far-reaching influence and inaugurate a new epoch. Still later, Alpine people developed a culture based on the working of iron; spreading westwards they again introduced a new culture into Western Europe, that of the Celts. Here we see the importance of making a clear distinction between race and culture. In one region, an immigrant people make no important change in the life of the area; in another people of the same race effect a fundamental change in virtue of the fact that their culture was superior to that of the indigenous population.

In later times new racial ingredients were added to the population of Southern Europe. Specially important were the Nordics, who, it is often, but probably quite erroneously supposed, were able to dominate and drive out of the plains large numbers of the Alpine population. According to this theory, the concentration of people of Alpine Race in the highlands is to be explained by the fact that the Nordics did not penetrate into the upland country. The highlands, reinforced with Alpine stock, have remained predominantly broad-headed to the present day. The Russian Plain, to which the Nordic came only in small numbers, has maintained its original Alpine population.

The members of the Alpine Race who made their way into India are "mesocephalic" in type, like those who came into Egypt in early times. The name "Maritime Armenoid" has been suggested for this class of Alpine because they played an obtrusive part in the great sea-adventures which began in the Eastern Mediterranean before 3000 B.C. Perhaps this may afford an explanation of the presence of isolated groups of this Alpine type in distant parts of the world, such as the Todas in Southern India, the Moriori in the Chatham Islands, and a definite Alpine strain elsewhere in Polynesia. The members of the Mediterranean Race who form the basis of the Indonesian and Polynesian populations are considerably mixed with the same type of Alpine, and to a lesser degree with Mongols and Melanesians. This fact becomes more interesting when we realise that in the population of Central America there are definite traces of Alpine influence. These do not occur very frequently, but they are unmistakably "Maritime Armenoid" in character. The conclusion we must draw from these facts is that in the drift of population from West to East along the Southern littoral of Asia and out into the Pacific Ocean there has been an appreciable Alpine element, which has left indelible traces in the physical characters of the people in India, the East Indies, Oceania and America.

The Nordic Race

We still have to consider the last of the six races—the Nordic. But before we discuss the race itself, there are several important points to be mentioned.

It is essential once more to protest against the use of the term "Caucasian," which is applied to the peoples of Europe and to some peoples in Asia who are akin to them. It was introduced more than a century ago by the earliest scientific anthropologist, Blumenbach. In 1811 he made the first serious attempt to classify the races of mankind. As he happened to have in his collection certain skulls from the Caucasus, which displayed a very definite contrast to the Mongolian and Negro types, he took these as the type of the inhabitants of Europe and called the race Caucasian. During the last twenty years it has come to be recognised by serious anthropologists how confusing and misleading is the use of this term. During recent years, however, there has been an attempt to revive it, as a useful if not strictly scientific expression. In America, where problems concerning the distinction of black and white people are, like the poor, "always with us," it has been found convenient to use the word Caucasian (in the sense of people of European extraction) to denote white people as opposed to Negroes. And as a large proportion of anthropological literature comes from America, it is not surprising that the term has been readopted by some of the less critical writers in England. But the use of the word, from a scientific point of view, promotes confusion. For, in speaking of a Caucasian Race, three peoples are included who present an obvious contrast to one another—a contrast, indeed, which is as definite if not so great in degree, as that between the white peoples and the Mongol, Negro and Australian Races. In the Alpine Race we find the broadest-headed people in the world; people of the Mediterranean Race are among the longest-headed still living. The Mediterranean Race is least well equipped with a hairy coat; the Alpine, taking the population as a whole, is the hairest race now living, even if occasionally an Australian aborigine may be still more hirsute. If we take one characteristic after another, we find the most profound contrasts between these peoples, so that to put them all together in one group is quite an impossible basis for any scientific classification of the races. There is another factor which has led to the revival of the term Caucasian—the realisation of the fact that intermingling has been going on in Europe between the three races for so many thousands of years as to make it almost impossible to get a pure type or to give a definite racial name to an individual. But this should not deter us from making an effort to define the definite racial traits and to assess the ingredients in any individual's constitution.

Another point that has a very direct bearing on the question of the Nordic is the controversy which came into prominence in the middle of the nineteenth century concerning the Aryan language. When it was realised that Sanskrit and the early language of the Persians belonged to the same group as Latin, Greek, Celtic and all the modern European languages, excepting only Basque, philologists fell into the mistake, which is still so rife among anthropologists, of confusing language and race. They began to speak of an Aryan Race as well as an Aryan language.

Although, for example, the Scandinavians, the Bavarians and the Spanish spoke varieties of the same language, it was recognised that this did not necessarily imply membership of the same race. We know in fact that the first group is predominantly Nordic, the second Alpine, and the third Mediterranean. A few individuals may suffice to bring about the adoption of a new language, as for example Arabic in Egypt, without any appreciable effect upon the racial constitution of the population as a whole.

To some extent this controversy concerns the early history and origin of the Nordic people. Although it is obvious that the speaking of a common language does not imply unity of race (take, for example, the English-speaking Negroes in America) yet it is equally obvious that a particular language must originally have been used by the members of a particular race.

For the past seventy years the question has been discussed as to which race first spoke the Indo-European language. The region of the Pamirs was assumed to be the home of the language, and it was thought that the original inhabitants of the region were members of the Alpine Race, although that term was not yet in use. This view is still very widely held. But in 1851 the English philologist Dr. Latham put forward the suggestion that the people who first spoke this language lived in Europe and not in Asia. The suggestion was hotly criticised—especially in Germany. One German scholar described it as "the language of a madman, which could only have come from an inhabitant of the land of cranks," by which he meant England. But within twenty years the idea had been eagerly adopted by German philologists, who began to exploit it with Chauvinistic enthusiasm. Germany was claimed to be the home of the Nordic Race and the Indo-European, or as it was called "Indo-Germanic" language, and the inspiration of what is best in European civilisation. Gobineau's old claim that the blond people of the north represent a superior type of mankind was revived and pushed to the most extravagant lengths, regardless of the fact that the great civilisations of antiquity were built up by representatives of the non-Nordic races, both the Egyptians and the Sumerians being of Mediterranean Race and what early admixture there was being Alpine.

The controversy about the original home of the Nordic Race has been very largely mixed up with the question of the original home of the Indo-European language. So far as we know, the earliest members of the Alpine Race probably spoke the language that was known in the nineteenth century as Turanian, and is now more correctly called Turki. This was the language of those Alpines who had made their way into Europe in historic times. The Mediterraneans spoke either Hamitic, in the West, or Semitic, in Arabia. So that no language is left for the original members of the Nordic Race, unless we assign to them the Indo-European language.

The original home of the Nordic people may tentatively be located somewhere in Russia, between Moscow and the Ural Mountains (Figure 29, p. 89). One reason for giving consent to the view put forward by philologists is the fact that at the glacial epoch this region was free from ice for a sufficient length of time to permit its population to have developed their own distinctive language during their segregation. Only when the ice melted could they have made their way across to the West, where they are found in greatest numbers to-day. After the ice melted they seem to have congregated round the shores of the Baltic, which thus became their second home. From one group of this people in all probability came the language spoken to-day practically all through Europe, which we call Indo-European.

Philologists have devoted an enormous amount of attention to the discussion of this language. They agree that the most primitive form of the language is neither Celtic nor Sanskrit, but Lithuanian, which is spoken on the shores of the Baltic. The preservation of original type is best shown in those people who have not wandered far from their original home. For example, people who have for many centuries accepted the folk-lore and superstitions in their own country will, when they emigrate to a country like Australia and find among their fellow-colonists stories that differ from their own, tend to lose them or modify them so profoundly that they are unrecognisable. So people who have wandered away from their original home and come under the influence of other languages will modify their speech more than those who were left behind. Both these arguments and such facts as we have concerning physical traits fit in well with the theory that the ancestors of the Nordic people became segregated in the region of Russia west of the Urals and then moved to the shores of the Baltic. It is more probable than not that they spoke the Indo-European language. This gives us a consistent working hypothesis, but it must be remembered that all this is very largely speculative. To discuss the question in more detail would involve us in a most difficult anthropological controversy, which at the present moment is insoluble from lack of data.

Let us now consider what is known of the early history of the Nordic people. The first definite evidence of people with fair hair, fair skin and blue eyes is given in certain pictures in an Egyptian temple of Seti the Great, built in the Nineteenth Dynasty, about 1300 B.C. In this temple at Abydos four varieties of mankind are represented. In addition to Egyptians there are Negroes from the South, and Syrians from the East, and fair-haired, blue-eyed people from Libya, the North coast of Africa. The Libyans present a striking contrast to all the others. We cannot say what people of this type were doing in Libya in the fourteenth century B.C. The pictures have another interest for us; they are the first definite anthropological records made by man, or rather the earliest that we know, to classify all the peoples the artist was acquainted with. The first evidence we have of the use of the Indo-European language is found in Syria and Asia Minor in the fourteenth century B.C. At about this time, we hear of a group of people called the Mitanni, who came into conflict with the Syrians and the people of Palestine and who spoke this language. In the course of excavations made during the past fifteen years, records have been found written in Hittite, and, as far as they can be deciphered, they appear to use the names of gods which were worshipped in India about a thousand years later. The date at which the language made its appearance in India is not known. The earliest literature of India goes back only to the eighth century B.C., but it is obvious that stories preserved in these Vedas are many centuries earlier, having survived as verbal traditions.

We have further evidence from Persia. The earliest literature from Persia (the Avesta) is written in the Indo-European language. This is much later than the Rig Veda of India, but the stories belong to the same cycle as the Indian ones. Hence it is probable that the people who made their way into India, and those who invaded Persia, were members of the same group.

Further evidence is to be found in the stories of Homer, which, although not put into writing until long after 1000 B.C., preserve the traditions of several centuries earlier. They tell of a fair-haired, blue-eyed group of people known as the Achaeans, who are thought to have come down into Greece from the North. This again confirms the impression that fair-haired immigrants made their entry, at about the same time as the Indo-European language, into Greece, North Africa, Asia Minor, and perhaps Persia and India.

We thus have several suggestions which, taken separately, are not very convincing, but, collectively, form an impressive whole, pointing to the possibility that in the middle of the second millennium people with fair hair, fair skin and blue eyes moved south from some place on the North of the Black Sea and the Caspian.

For more than half a million years a series of now extinct types of the Human Family were stray wanderers into Britain. But the earliest settled communities were members of the Mediterranean Race. These people introduced the practice of agriculture and the use of polished stone implements, at a period which most writers have put at about six thousand years ago or more. It is very doubtful, however, if they arrived before 2000 B.C., or indeed as early. Soon after the appearance of these members of the Mediterranean Race, and long before the close of the age of polished stone, Nordic people began to come into Britain from Northern Europe. The difference in the distinctive traits revealed in the skeletal remains is not easy to express in figures, as it depends less on actual measurements than on greater robustness of build. The Nordics are somewhat bigger in stature, and stronger in build, and they have rather more prominent eyebrow ridges. The form of the skull presents some analogy to the Mediterranean type. This similarity in type, so striking when the contrast to the Alpine Race is considered, has prompted some anthropologists to suggest that the Nordics are simply a group of the Mediterranean Race, who wandered into the North, and had their skins bleached by the colder climate! The story is not quite so simple as that; but there is undoubted evidence that the Nordic is far more nearly akin to the Mediterranean than to any other group of the human family.

It has been suggested that the remains of pre-Neolithic culture found at Maglemose a couple of decades ago represent the earliest traces of the Nordic Race. If we are right in assuming that the earliest dwellers on the shores of the Baltic were members of the Nordic Race, the makers of the Maglemose harpoons were more likely to have belonged to the Nordic than to any other race: but we have no evidence to prove it, for no scrap of human bone has been found in connection with the archaeological remains.

In the South of France, just north of the Spanish frontier, a peculiar type of culture was found, known as Azilian. Much discussion has taken place as to whether this Azilian culture should be included in the Upper Palaeolithic period, or whether it should be included in the Neolithic Age, or alternately whether it occupies a place intermediate between the two. It is obvious that when a new culture is introduced into a country, unless the whole population is replaced, it will at first form only a very insignificant addition to the arts and crafts that are already established. The old culture will continue to be predominant for some time. Hence it is more instructive to regard the Azilian culture as the first wave of the age of polished implements rather than as the surviving Palaeolithic. The new factor that distinguishes it is surely the Neolithic practices. This suggestion is strengthened by the fact that the Azilians introduced agriculture for the first time. Grains of barley are said to have been found in their burials, which suggests that they may have been cultivating this cereal. Reference is made to this matter here because the Azilian culture in the South is contemporaneous with the Maglemosian—both occurring at the inauguration of the Neolithic Age. Certain implements, small arrow-heads, are common to both, but in other respects they are very different. The harpoon is the favourite implement of the Maglemosians.

Remains of both types of industry, Azilian and Maglemosian, have been found in Scotland and in certain islands on the West coast, such as Colonsay. Although we have nothing to prove that the people who were responsible for the Maglemose culture were of Nordic Race, the evidence of the skeletons found in British graves' suggests that Nordics were in this region at the beginning of the Neolithic Age. They have formed perhaps the chief ingredient in the population in Britain ever since.

People of Nordic Race form the main element of the population of Scandinavia, and are found in large numbers in Germany, especially in Saxony, in Denmark, Holland and the British Isles. In France, the proportion is not so great: but blonds are well represented in Northern Italy, and in early times, about the fourteenth century B.C., members of this race reached North Africa and as Libyans attracted the attention of the artists of Seti I. If we accept the region west of the Urals as their original home, they must have moved eastward as well as south and west, for they form a large element of the population of Turkestan and Central Siberia. In early Chinese literature we read of people with "green eyes," who seem to have made a great impression on the Chinese. In the Pamirs and Hindu Kush, we find people with fair hair, blue eyes and pale complexion, who made a striking contrast with the bulk of the population. After the great barriers of ice and water which separated the homes of the Alpine and Nordic (Figure 29, p. 89) had disappeared there must have been a good deal of intermingling between the two races.

The question has been raised time and again, as to whether the Nordic people are the survivors of people of the Upper Palaeolithic period who, we have seen, occupied France, Spain and Britain, and differed so markedly from the modern inhabitants of these countries. The Cro-Magnon people were exceptionally tall and robustly built, and the possibility suggests itself whether they were ancestors of the Nordic Race, who were pushed north by the inrush of Mediterraneans. The Mediterranean people had the advantage as they were in possession of the early arts and crafts of civilisation invented in the Ancient East.

It is impossible completely to dismiss the view, which, however, has not found acceptance with anthropologists, that the Nordic and Cro-Magnon peoples may possibly belong to the same race. It is claimed that there are still survivors of the Cro-Magnon Race to be found in the Dordogne and in the Canary Isles. They have dark hair and dark eyes, so that it is unlikely they are related to the Nordics. This fact, however, does not wholly exclude the possibility of relationship, as the whole tendency of modern ideas on this subject is that the fair people have passed through a sort of bleaching process, in other words they are the descendants of people who were brunets. But the proportions of the limbs and the characters of the face differentiate these people from the Nordics.

One of the human beings of the Upper Palaeolithic is of special interest, the Magdelenian skeleton found at Chancelade. It differs profoundly from Cro-Magnon Man. The late Professor Testut of Lyons stated that it presented an amazing likeness to the modern Eskimo. This raised a number of extremely difficult problems, because the Eskimo is supposed to have a strong Mongol strain. Professor Testut made it clear that not only the skull but the whole skeleton showed striking resemblances. In the sixties of the last century, twenty years before the Chancelade skeleton was discovered, the late Sir William Boyd Dawkins claimed that the Eskimo people must have derived the few arts and crafts they possess, and especially their harpoons, from the people of the Upper Palaeolithic period. This suggests the possibility of a group of people being pushed up farther and farther north as the line of glaciation shifted and taking their arts and crafts with them.

The Basques, who live on the shores of the Bay of Biscay, partly in France and partly in Spain, raise difficult problems. These are in the main Mediterranean in type, short in stature, but having disharmonic skulls suggestive of some alien admixture. Their language is extraordinary, being quite unlike any other language in Europe. This has been claimed by some to represent the Hamitic tongue, a view that may be put aside. Others regard it as being akin to the language of the Finns and Hungarians. There is another possible view. If it be accepted that the people of Mediterranean Race brought their (Hamitic) language with them to Western Europe, that the Nordics brought the Indo-European language, which is spoken practically all through Europe to-day, and the Alpines a primitive form of the Turki speech, such as was spoken in their original homeland in Asia, what language is left for the Cro-Magnon peoples, before Celtic was introduced in the North and Hamitic in the South? Might we not assume that in the Basque tongue we may have evidence of the survival of an Upper Palaeolithic language? If, as I have already suggested, the Neolithic Period began in Western Europe only about 4000 years ago, would it not be surprising if no trace of the language spoken before this period had survived? Celtic has been preserved in the West, in Wales, Scotland and Ireland, as well as in certain parts of the continent, chiefly Brittany. We have to find a language for the predecessors of the Celtic-speaking peoples. May it not be Basque? This is put forward only as a tentative solution of one of the difficult problems of European history until further evidence is forthcoming.

In the course of the discussion of the Alpine and Nordic Races reference has been made to the lack of any evidence to suggest that they had any culture of their own apart from what they borrowed from the civilisation of the peoples of Mediterranean Race. The so-called Aryan culture, about which so much used to be heard thirty or forty years ago, is now believed by certain scholars—especially those who have critically examined and compared the earliest literature of Persia and Sumer—to have been derived from Mesopotamia.

Hence we arrive at the conclusion that the building up of civilisation of the world at large began amongst members of one race—and from them was diffused abroad.

CHAPTER V

PRIMITIVE MAN (I)

IN those remote times when certain human beings first abandoned nomadic habits and began to create the system of civilisation, they did not lose the memory of their former simple life when "men were not worn by toil, and war and disease were unknown." Even if they forgot the traditions of their own ancestors—a very unlikely possibility in the days before the invention of writing curtailed a reliance upon memory—the earliest pioneers of civilisation would learn from neighbouring peoples, who were still living as primitive nomads, to hold up the mirror to their own history.

Long afterwards the Greeks referred to the simple, happy life of primitive people as the "Golden Age." It was commonly assumed that the acceptance of the belief in this ideal life implied a degradation of mankind. For obviously the state in which the philosophers found men actually living implied a falling away from the high virtures of the Age of Gold.

During more than twenty centuries the story of the Age of Gold and the Theory of Degradation have been constant causes of misunderstanding and confusion, and to this day continue to be obstacles that interfere with a proper understanding of Human History.

In his book, *The Idea of Progress,* the late Professor J. B. Bury has given a brilliant picture of the profound influence of these contentious issues from the time of Plato down to our own times. After critically examining the historical evidence this usually clear-sighted scholar scouts the idea of the Golden Age as a mere myth on the part of the Greek poets and philosophers, and as something for which no historical basis can be found. Yet anthropologists have provided us with the most definite evidence that such a condition of affairs as the poets describe as the "Golden Age" did in fact exist. No amount of ridicule can possibly blind us to the true meaning of the overwhelming· mass of information which is now available in substantiation of this conclusion. Facts collected by many hundreds of travellers and serious students of Anthropology in Africa, Asia, America and elsewhere can no more be laughed out of court than Galileo's observation of the spots on the sun, or the rings of Saturn.

It is obviously a matter of fundamental importance to establish the truth concerning human nature. Hence, even at the risk of tedious repetition, a sufficient number of quotations from the actual observers of primitive conditions of human existence must be cited to convince the impartial reader of the evidence, whatever interpretation of it he may adopt.

In the development of the conflicting interpretations of Human History several more or less distinct factors played a part. For the belief in the Golden Age and Degradation was genetically associated with the theory of world-cycles and the idea of a culture-hero, and myths have in large measure obscured the essential truths in the traditions.

The most ancient story in the world is an account of the rejuvenation of an old king, Osiris, known in his solar manifestation as Re, who was the creator of civilisation. His subjects began to spread reports that he was growing old—a type of rumour to which an archaic King was particularly sensitive, as it was the practice to kill a ruler who was no longer able to perform the rituals of his office. Hence their gossip was regarded as a particularly heinous form of disloyalty. This was the wickedness which in later ages was the essential factor in calling them "degenerate"—what the theologians regard as "The Fall of Man." For this sin of idle chattering the king-god punished his subjects by destroying them. But if mankind was thus wholly destroyed some explanation was obviously needed of the continued presence of men upon the earth. They were clearly a new creation. There was a new "world-cycle" in which a new generation of men replaced those who formerly existed. Forgetting their disobedience the old historian identified them with the simple nomads and regarded the Age of Gold as the age of innocence.

The mythical accretions—and what W. S. Gilbert would call the "corroborative detail"—added to this story disguised the fact that it contained the germ of truth in the tradition of the genial qualities of primitive Man, of the fact that the first king brought this age of simplicity to an end when he created civilisation, and of the further consideration that degeneration is inevitable in all human culture unless men of insight and courage are continuously active in preventing it.

It is a curious circumstance that the discrediting of the old. theory of degeneration—concerning which scholars have been wrangling, as Professor Bury has shown, for more than twenty centuries—should have induced anthropologists in modern times to deny the fact of degeneration, in spite of the eloquent witnesses of its reality which the ruins of ancient glories in Egypt and Western Asia, Cambodia, Java and Central America, and the loss of useful arts provide, no less than the experience of our own forgetfulness of vital information.

Stories of the world-cycles, of which the first was said to be perfect, spread in ancient times throughout the world. They are found in Greek and Celtic mythology, in Indian and Chinese legends and in the folklore of the New World. Kwang-Tze, the follower of Lao-Tze (604–532 B.C.) in China, writing of the world-ages and the Taoist religion of his Master, said:

"In the age of perfect virtue men attached no value to wisdom. . . . They were upright and correct, without knowing that to be so was Righteousness: they loved one another, without knowing that to be so was Benevolence: they were honest and leal-hearted, without knowing that it was Loyalty; they fulfilled their engagements without knowing that to do so was Good Faith." After Fu-hi and other sovereigns disturbed the harmonies of heaven and earth, "the manners of the people, from being good and simple, became bad and mean."

Such stories can be found in the earliest traditions of most peoples and they preserve the true report of the original state of human society. A new realisation of this amazing truth was deeply impressed on men's minds at the beginning of the sixteenth century by the discovery of the New World; and during the seventeenth and eighteenth centuries new discoveries compelled scholars with growing insistence to pay attention to the facts of primitive life.

It is no exaggeration to claim that the constant reiteration of this experience was through three centuries the most potent stimulus in Humanitarian enquiry.

Sir Thomas More, Lord Chancellor of England, was born ten years before Christopher Columbus discovered the New World. Years afterwards, in 1516, when the imaginations of men were stirred by the stories of hitherto unknown lands of vast extent inhabited by "gentle savages," to use the phrase the poet Pope used to express a similar revelation two centuries afterwards, More wrote his *Utopia* to give expression to the profound revolution in ideas regarding social organisations, morals and politics created by the surprising discoveries. But the full extent of the influence of such discoveries in compelling men to hold up the mirror to themselves and examine with a new instrument of critical discrimination their social, moral and religious principles and practices has never been fully investigated. It is no exaggeration to claim that in discovering the New World the way was also being prepared for the revelation of the truth concerning human nature.

In 1517 Erasmus wrote a book which was later issued in English under the title "The Complaint of Peace." It is a violent diatribe against the horrors of war, of which he had constantly been hearing in his own country, harassed by long continued fighting. It is one of those unrestrained outbursts in which professed pacifists so often display the dangers to which peace is exposed by the intemperate utterances of its champions. Although he does not refer to the new geographical discoveries, it is unlikely that the intimate friend and associate of Sir Thomas More could have failed to be influenced in his views by the new vision expressed in the *Utopia* only a year before. How else can the language of his description of Natural Man be explained?

"From nature man receives a mild and gentle disposition, so prone to reciprocal benevolence that he delights to be loved for the pleasure of being loved, without any view to interest; and feels a satisfaction in doing good, without a wish or prospect of remuneration. This disposition to do disinterested good is natural to man, unless in a few instances, where, corrupted by depraved desires, which operate like the drugs of Circe's cup, the human being has degenerated to the brute. Hence even the common people, in the ordinary language of daily conversation, denominate whatever is connected with goodwill, humane; so that the word humanity no longer describes man's nature merely in a physical sense, but signifies human manners, or a behaviour worthy the nature of man, acting his proper part in civil society."

A long line of philosophers from the time of Sir Thomas More down to modern times have had glimpses of the truth: and several modern historians, such as Mr. E. J. Payne (*The Cambridge Modern History,* I, Renaissance, 1903, p. 56) and Professor Bury (*The Idea of Progress,* 1921) have referred to the profound effects of the new geography upon the renaissance of learning and upon political theory and practice.

If the Lord Chancellor's book had relatively little practical effect there can be no doubt that it was a most potent leaven among learned men. His picture of an imaginary Utopia compelled men to revise their social and political ideas. It was not inspired by Plato's *Republic,* but was rather the result of the thought-provoking revelation of a New World inhabited by "savages" who were not savage in the usual connotation of the word. Hence More was inspired to imagine "a state of society diametrically opposed to the aspect of contemporary Europe." His "romance" (to quote Mr. Payne) "lost its hold on public attention as soon as headstrong enthusiasts on the Continent endeavoured to realise some of its fundamental principles; but at a later date, through the founders of New Jersey and Pennsylvania, it had some ultimate effect on, as it took its motive from, the New World, which was beginning to stir human minds to their depths at the time when it was written."

Just as in England More was directly inspired by Columbus' achievement, so also in France Montaigne's habits of thought were profoundly influenced by the still more startling stories of the discoveries upon the mainland of North and South America.

Fifteen years before Dr. W. J. Perry ("The Peaceful Habits of Primitive Communities," in the *Hibbert Journal* for 1917) revived interest in the classical stories of the *Golden Age,* Mr. Payne expressed the opinions that may be quoted in his own words: "No close reader of Montaigne will dispute that the contemplation of the New World, in connection with the events which happened after its discovery, greatly contributed to give him that large grasp of things, that mental habit of charity and comprehensiveness, something of which passed from him to Bacon and to Shakspere, both diligent students of his writings." Montaigne was born in 1533, when Pizarro was overrunning Peru. "The facts of aboriginal American history and ethnology, narrated by the 'Conquistadores' and by other travellers, sank deep into his mind; and his knowledge of the New World was not mere book-learning. As a counsellor of Bordeaux, he often came in contact with merchants and seamen who were familiar with America; but his chief source of information was a man in his own service, who had lived ten or twelve years in Brazil, whom he describes as a plain ignorant fellow, but from whom he seems never to have been weary of learning at first hand. Before Colombo's voyage the savage or 'brute man' had been as little known in Europe, and was in fact as much of a myth as the unicorn or griffin. When Montaigne wrote, he had become as well known as the Moor, the Berber, or the Guinea negro, and the spectacle of a new transatlantic continent, scarcely less extensive than the aggregate of those Old World countries of which Europe possessed any definite knowledge, and peopled by men scarcely above the state of Nature, seized the French philosopher with a strange fascination. By its contrast with European life it suggested some startling reflections. What if civilisation, after all, were a morbid and unnatural growth? What if the condition of man in America were that for which the Creator designed him? What if those omnipotent powers, law and custom, as at present constituted, were impudent usurpers, destined one day to decline under the influence of right reason, and to give place, if not to the original rule of beneficent Nature, at least to something essentially very different from the systems which now passed under their names? Montaigne puts these questions very pointedly. In the Tupi-Guarani of Brazil, as described by one who had known them long and intimately, he recognised nothing of the character associated with the words 'barbarous' and 'savage.' They were rather a people permanently enjoying the fabled Golden Age of ancient poetry; strangers to the toils, diseases, social inequalities, vice, and trickeries which chiefly made up civilised life, dwelling together in vast common houses, though the institutions of the family were strictly preserved, and enjoying with little or no labour, and no fears for the future, all the reasonable commodities and advantages of human life, while knowing nothing of its superfluities; refined in their taste for poetry, specimens of which were recited to him by his domestic informant, and which appeared to him Anacreontic in their grace and beauty: and employed chiefly in the chase, the universal pleasure of the human race, even in the highest state of refinement."

These ideas were the potent ferment which when revived in the eighteenth century provoked revolution in political and social ideas and practices.

The exploits of Columbus, which excited so vast an influence upon Man's outlook, were themselves inspired in part by the interest in maritime adventure that had survived in the Mediterranean from ancient times and had been revived in Italy by the increasing activity of Venetian trafficking with the East. The irruption of the Turks into Europe, by interfering with the Oriental trade, compelled the people of Western Europe to seek new routes to the Indies. The discovery of America was thus one of the remote results of the capture of Constantinople by the Turks.

Columbus was also influenced by the writings of Friar Roger Bacon, the first systematic geographer, who lived two centuries before his time. Like Columbus and Montaigne, he was in the habit of collecting information directly from travellers. He was also stimulated to take an interest in the wider field of Science and the Humanities.

But as so often happens in the domain of the Humanities exact data often provoke a reaction that is the very antithesis of the meaning the man-in-the-street sees.

Among those who were profoundly influenced by the geographical discoveries in the sixteenth century was the Lord Chancellor, Francis Bacon. Mr. A. W. Benn has well said that "the desperate efforts of apologists to whitewash Bacon are apparently due to a very exaggerated estimate of his services to mankind." In his *History of Ethics*, the late Professor Henry Sidgwick speaks of "Bacon's great task of reforming scientific method," which "left morals on one side." However he quotes Bacon's saying: "It must be confessed that a great part of the law moral is of that perfection whereunto the light of nature cannot aspire"; for though this "light of nature" is "imprinted upon the spirit of man by an inward instinct, it is only sufficient to check the vice, not to inform the duty"—statements which corroborate Mr. Benn's judgment of his ability.

Bacon, however, was not an ethical philosopher. English Ethics began with Hobbes. The starting point of Hobbes's ethical speculation was the idea of the Law of Nature to which the sixteenth century had directed an unusual amount of attention.

Grotius expounded the principles of Natural Law as applicable to international relations. Natural Law is the essential nature of Man. Sidgwick makes the comment that "the language of the jurists clearly implied that a period of human history had existed prior to the institution of civil society, in which men were governed by the Law of Nature alone: it was known from Seneca that the Stoic Poseidonius had identified this period with the mythical Golden Age.

"Thus there had come to be established and current a conception of a state of nature, social in a sense, but not yet political, in which individuals or single families had lived side by side—under none other than such 'natural laws,' as those prohibiting mutual injury, and mutual interference with each other's use of the goods of the earth that were common to all, giving parents authority over their children, imposing on wives a vow of fidelity to their husbands, and obliging all to the observation of compacts freely entered into. This conception Grotius took, and gave it additional force and solidity by using the principles of this Natural Law for the determination of international rights and duties."

Commenting on the teaching of Hobbes, the founder of English Ethics (1640), Professor Sidgwick says:

"The state of Nature, in which men must be supposed to have existed before government was instituted, and into which they would relapse if it were abolished, is indeed a state free from all moral restraint; but it is therefore utterly miserable. It is a state in which, owing to well-founded mutual fear . . ." But it is unnecessary to quote any more. It is patent that Hobbes was turning the blind eye to all the established facts.

According to Hobbes, love of power is the very essence of human nature. A well-governed community such as Hobbes contemplated would be, as A. W. Benn has lucidly explained, "a machine for crushing the life out of society and transmitting the will of a single despot unresisted through its whole extent." He died before the great discoveries of Newton "turned away men's minds from the purely mechanical interpretation of energy." Hobbes rejected Aristotle's notion of sociability as an essentially human characteristic. His idea of the instinct of self-preservation was "an insatiable appetite for power, leading each individual to pursue his own aggrandisement at the cost of any loss or suffering of the rest." But as Benn remarks: "Modern researches have shown that there are very primitive societies where the assumed war of all against each other is unknown, predatory conflicts being a mark of more advanced civilisation, and the cause rather than the effect of anti-social impulses" (p. 26).

"Granting an original state of anarchy and internecine hostility there is, according to Hobbes, only one way out of it, which is a joint resolution of the whole community to surrender their rights of individual sovereignty into the hand of one man, who thenceforth becomes absolute ruler of the State, with authority to defend its citizens against mutual aggressions, and the whole community against attacks from a foreign Power. This agreement constitutes the famous Social Contract, of which so much was to be heard in the next century and a half."

Hobbes was confusing the effects of the tyranny of the State System with the original condition of mankind, and attributing to the latter the vices that were due to the creation of civilisation.

None of these, nor in fact most later philosophers, seem to appreciate the fact that Man is by nature good and unselfish and maintains these ethical virtues until the fear of aggression or injustice forces him to realise that he has to defend himself. Before the eighteenth century, except in the case of such writers as Erasmus and More, the appreciation of the facts of the innate good in Man was in large measure due to the survival of the classical stories of the Golden Age. Then philosophers began to realise that the facts concerning the actual behaviour of primitive peoples, which travellers from Eastern Asia and America were bringing to Europe, afforded a more definite corroboration.

During the succeeding centuries from time to time philosophers got glimpses of the truth concerning human nature. For example, in 1726 Butler claimed that: "The social affections are no less natural than the appetite and desires which tend more directly to self-preservation."

But more often men refuse to consider the evidence, which in an ever-widening stream has been increasing in volume for four centuries. By a strange irony those scholars who make it their business to discuss human nature are the worst offenders in ignoring the facts concerning it.

The evidence is so definite and abundant that it becomes a problem of psychological interest to discuss why men persist in denying the fact of Man's innate peacefulness. Each of us knows from his own experience that his fellows are on the whole kindly and well-intentioned. Most of the friction and the discords of our lives are obviously the result of such exasperations and conflicts as civilisation itself creates. Envy, malice and all uncharitableness usually have for the object of their expression some artificial aim, from the pursuit of which primitive Man is exempt.

But there are much more impressive reasons than these experiences of our daily lives, which by their very obviousness and banality are liable to be overlooked and forgotten, for treating the Utopias of the Golden Age as something more than poetic fictions or the fantasies of sentimental dreamers.

For more than four centuries travellers have been recording the fact that uncultured peoples in Africa, Asia and America—beyond the influence of modern civilisation—are truthful, unaggressive, hospitable, helpful and sympathetic to strangers in need, grateful, and plucky in fighting when they have to defend themselves. Indeed the leaders of European thought were so impressed by these facts in the sixteenth, seventeenth and eighteenth centuries that many of the greatest achievements in literature were directly inspired by the wonder of the new revelation of human nature, vouchsafed respectively by the voyages of Christopher Columbus and Pizarro. The great social and political reforms of the eighteenth century were due above all to the newly revealed anthropological evidence. The renaissance of philosophy, and in fact of learning as a whole, was likewise in large measure the direct result of the series of geographical discoveries and the surprising realisation of the geniality of hitherto unknown communities of Natural Men.

Yet it is still a common belief that the nobler qualities of mankind are a product of civilisation. No one questions the fact that there has been a refinement of manners and a tremendous increase in comfort and luxury in modern times: but it must not be forgotten that warfare and cruelty, injustice and brutality are equally the results of civilisation and are not natural modes of behaviour. All men will fight in defence of their lives and for the safeguarding of their families: but the causes that provoke such conflicts are the results of a departure from the original Arcadian manner of living.

In spite of repeated corroboration of these facts during more than four centuries there is still the most profound and widespread misunderstanding of human nature. In a debate in the House of Commons several years ago the leaders of all three Parties were in agreement on one point. Hence it is enough to quote *The Times'* report of the then Prime Minister's (Mr. Stanley Baldwin) statement, which equally expresses the sentiments of the speeches delivered by Mr. Ramsay Macdonald and Mr. Lloyd George:

"Very little, if anything, had been said about one of the greatest difficulties which they found in dealing with this question [the preservation of peace]. That was the fighting instinct which was a part of human nature, and he proposed to say a few words about that with a view to explaining how, in his view, they had to attempt to eradicate or at least to combat it so as to produce that will to peace without which all efforts by legislation, arbitration, rule, or otherwise must be vain. That fighting instinct in Man was the instinct of the tiger, and it dated from his creation, and was probably given to him to enable him to fight for the survival of his species, for the provision of space in which to bring up his race, and to provide food for it. They found through the ages that that instinct had had full play. They found it even among men whose political views could be classed as pacifist. That was the reason why they had often found in history that men of pacifist views advocated policies which must, if carried to their logical conclusion, end in war.

"He mentioned these innate characteristics of human nature to make them realise what difficulties were before them in carrying out a policy with which everyone in the House was in sympathy."

If Mr. Baldwin had made it clear that, although Man is innately peaceful, he was always ready to defend his life and if need be to fight to avert danger, no objections could be raised to his statement. But this cannot be said of the dangerous doctrine more recently expressed by Viscount Cecil of Chelwood. In the First Rickman Godlee Lecture on *The Co-operation of Nations* (delivered at University College, London, in 1927) he gave expression to these amazing views:

"Coincident with the growth of political ideas came the elaboration of social and economic institutions, and fighting became rarer. In purely barbarous tribes combat is endemic. The savage walks through the forest with his club or tomahawk as ready to slaughter his fellow-men as he is to kill any other animals. When he is organised in clans and tribes he no longer fights his fellow-clansmen or tribesmen, but still one of his chief occupations consists of raids and forays on other clans and tribes."

When such opinions are expressed by responsible statesmen no further excuse need be made for quoting at length from the records of travellers whose personal testimony presents so profound a contrast to Lord Cecil's imaginary picture of life among savages.

In face of these gloomy misunderstandings it is a relief to find President Coolidge proclaiming the true gospel of anthropology in his Armistice Address (November, 1928) where he claimed that "peace is coming to be more and more realised as the natural state of mankind." This chapter and the following one will provide the evidence in substantiation of this claim.

The Biological Factor in Decent Behaviour

Before proceeding to cite the observations of travellers on this issue let us consider the biological aspect of the problem.

Knowledge of the outside world is derived from our sensory experience. Our sense-organs and brain provide us with the means of appreciating two aspects of conscious experience. We touch an object, for example, and in the light of previous experience are able to estimate its size, its weight, its roughness or smoothness, its hardness or softness, and finally to distinguish it from other objects and perhaps even identify it as a particular object. This is the highly trained discriminative side of experience, which is made possible by a process of education involving the activity of the cerebral cortex. But there is another aspect of sensory experience—the mere awareness of sensations and the feeling of pleasure or the reverse. This affective side of experience is innate and is due to the activity of a part of the brain known as the thalamus. A new-born child can appreciate the pleasantness or unpleasantness of a stimulation, such as stroking the skin or the application of a certain degree of warmth: but it is only by experience that the child learns to recognise degrees of stimulation and by comparison to interpret them.

In the light of experience recorded in the cerebral cortex the latter is able (Figure 31, B) to control the affective activities of the thalamus, and so restrain too exuberant tendencies to pleasure or pain and the associated emotional states. The human will is able to shape conduct in defiance of discomfort and instinctive antipathies.

It must be obvious that the behaviour of any living creature is determined by its feelings of pleasure or aversion, and that discrimination comes into the process only as an influence that extends the range of choice by introducing the factor of past experience as well as the wider vision of the present circumstances, and controls the innate tendencies. Keen as is the competition of every living creature for the means of subsistence and the maintenance of its selfish interests, in other words the preservation of its life, animals are not naturally quarrelsome or vindictive. Every keeper of animals, and in particular everyone with experience of creatures living under natural conditions in the wild state, knows that even the most voracious carnivores do not attack other creatures except to satisfy their hunger, or to protect their own lives when attacked, or when they think they are in danger. As their range of understanding is limited great tact is essential in handling animals, so as not to give them the idea they are in danger. It is obviously a matter of vital importance, from the point of view of survival, both in wild animals and in men alike, not to be quarrelsome or vindictive. Observation of living creatures does in fact reveal a decency of behaviour as the normal condition.

The instinctive activities of the thalamus, upon which the feelings and sentiments are mainly dependent, naturally impel every living creature to conduct that is neither vicious nor violent. But any

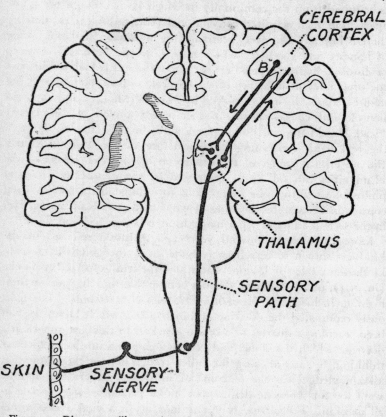

Figure 31—Diagram to illustrate how the skin is connected with the central nervous system. A sensory nerve passes into the spinal cord. A sensory path carries the effects of this impulse to the opposite side of the brain as far as the thalamus. Some of the impulses end in the thalamus and excite an awareness of sensation and appreciation of its affective qualities. Other impulses pass from the thalamus to the cortex (A) to provide the information for discrimination, which is acquired by experience, in some way recorded in the cerebral cortex. This discriminative activity of the cortex regulates and controls (B) the affective and emotional activities of the thalamus. (After Sir Henry Head, "Sensation and the Cerebral Cortex", *Brain*, 1918.)

creature can be trained to be vicious; and human beings, in virtue of the high development of their cerebral cortex, are more readily educable in this as in other respects than living creatures in general. Hence while Natural Man is "Nature's gentleman," under more complex social circumstances his conception of right and wrong is acquired from the community in which he is brought up. Quite apart from such acquired conventional (cortical) ideas of morality there is implanted in every human being an innate (thalamic) sense of honesty and goodness, which may, however, be readily warped or distorted by the personal experience of the individual, in virtue of the preponderant influence of the cortical control. The facts of human behaviour as it is displayed by Natural Man, no less than the neurological considerations so lucidly expounded by Sir Henry Head, should impress philosophers with the need for the study of the real truth concerning human nature as the basis of Ethics. But no critical reader of the discussion of this vital aspect of the Humanities can fail to be impressed by the depressing fact that philosophers seem to be more prone to indulgence in hair-splitting controversies over the meaning of what Plato and Kant wrote than in the serious study of what living human beings feel and think.

More than two thousand years ago Aristotle referred to the kindness shown to travellers as evidence of the goodwill of mankind. Many later philosophers admitted the truth of this. But Locke (in 1671), unlike Spinoza, did not believe that morality was natural in Man. In his *Essay Concerning Human Understanding* he vigorously repudiated the doctrine of Innate Ideas which Descartes had been teaching a quarter of a century earlier. In this just attack on a doctrine which has done, and is still doing, infinite harm to clear thinking, he was arguing for fuller recognition of the claim that all knowledge was the outcome of individual experience. But he went too far when he denied that moral principles were innate in all mankind. For obviously innate morality is a vital and essential quality. Locke's qualification of his attitude at times comes very near to a clear vision of the whole truth. Thus he writes:

"Nor will it be of much moment here to offer that very ready but not very material answer, viz. that the innate principles of morality may, by education and custom, and the general opinion of those among whom we converse, be darkened, and at last quite worn out of the minds of men."

In 1711 Clarke attacked Hobbes's egoistic interpretation of goodness as being inspired by self-preservation and pleasure on the ground that such ideas could only be justified if Man was an isolated being. But Man is a social animal and is dependent on his fellow men for the knowledge of how to live. His social affections are natural. Clarke might have added force to his argument if he had claimed that the social affections are not only innate, or as we might now say 'thalamic,' but essential for the maintenance of the family.

Butler assumed the existence of two inner authorities. We might adopt his view and express it in the phraseology of modern neurology. The intuitive natural impulse to decent behaviour is thalamic and is akin to animal behaviour. Conscience is the awareness of the innate natural impulse and the feeling that it should be obeyed. The conscious examination of motives and the discrimination between good and evil is cortical—it is reason. Every living creature is constantly active in self-preservation: but when Man consciously formulates the protection of his existence as an aim to strive after, culture is born. So with morals. Consciousness of the impulse to do right is what we call conscience.

Two years before the publication of Adam Smith's *Theory of Moral Sentiments,* Price, the English philosopher most nearly akin to Kant, published his *Review of the Chief Questions and Difficulties of Morals* (1757), in which he says: "There is not anything of which we have more undeniably an intuitive perception than that it is right to pursue and promote happiness for ourselves as for others." But, as Professor Sidgwick explains, he agrees with Butler that "gratitude, veracity, fulfilment of promises, and justice are obligatory, independently of their conduciveness to happiness."

Belief in what Professor Sidgwick called the "happy ignorance, simple virtues and transparent manners of uncultivated men" seems, however, to have been as distasteful to philosophers in the eighteenth century as it is at the present time. Even as early as 1739 Hume was protesting (in his *Treatise on Human Nature*) that justice, veracity and fidelity were all "artificial virtues" due to civilisation, and not belonging to Man in his "ruder and more natural condition." This disregard of information acquired by direct observation of Natural Man (which, it should not be forgotten, was responsible for starting this fire of controversy in the sixteenth century and, by adding fresh fuel, in the seventeenth and eighteenth, kept the conflagration going) illustrates the profound difference between the methods of science and philosophy. Hume was not at liberty to express such opinions seeing that there were facts, accessible to direct study, which were fatal to his opinions. Any theory of ethics that ignores the innate qualities of primitive men must necessarily come into conflict with the truth. For no interpretation of human character can possibly conform to the principles of scientific enquiry unless the justice, veracity and fidelity of natural men is admitted as a fact of observation, and any departure from such innate morality as the result of some specific interference, physical, psychical or social, with the natural process. In the seventeenth and eighteenth centuries many philosophers did seriously attempt to base their ethical theories on the observed facts. A century ago Dugald Stewart expressed the opinion that there is in the human mind, independently of calculations of utility, a natural and instinctive love of truth and the impulse to sincerity in men's mutual communications.

But unfortunately this fundamental consideration is not only ignored but often vigorously denied. Several leading scholars of the present generation have written large treatises on the evolution of morals, which not only ignore the consideration that decent behaviour is an innate human quality, but express profound amazement that Natural Man should display moral qualities! Nevertheless they brush aside this record as an irrelevant and curious eccentricity without realising that they are stultifying their argument by failing to recognise the fundamental principle of human behaviour.

The Food-Gatherers

The recognition of the fact that the practice of agriculture is the foundation of civilisation provides a criterion for the definition of what we understand by the much-abused word "primitive." In his treatise on *The Children of the Sun* (1923) Dr. W. J. Perry has applied the term "Food-Gatherers" to those simple nomads who have not adopted any devices, either of farming or cattle-breeding, for securing a more abundant and reliable supply of food. Those who practice agriculture and other methods for increasing the resources of animal and vegetable food he calls "Food-Producers."

The Food-Gatherers live mainly on the outskirts of the world, far from the great centres of civilisation. In some cases they occupy countries, such as Australia, that reveal little trace of a higher civilisation. Others dwell in territories which formerly were visited or are now in part occupied by peoples with a more or less advanced civilisation. Their distribution is very wide, for in addition to

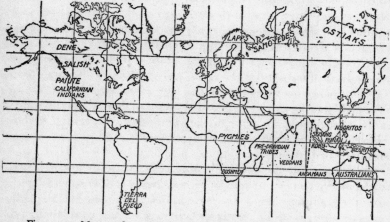

Figure 32—Map to show the general distribution of the Food-Gatherers.

Australia they are found in Africa, India, Malaya, Indonesia and America.

Although they breed animals to provide food and are not strictly speaking simply Food-Gatherers, it is convenient to refer to the lowly reindeer keepers of Northern Siberia and Europe in the discussion of primitive Man.

The primitive populations include the Pygmies of the Congo basin and adjoining regions, Bushmen of South Africa, Veddahs of Ceylon, Predravidian jungle tribes of Southern India, Semang of Malaya (Negrito), Sakai, Senoi, Jakun of Malaya (Australoid), Andaman Islanders, Kubu of Sumatra, Punan and allied tribes of Borneo, a food-gathering tribe of the Aru Islands (west of New-

Guinea), Negritos of the Philippines and of New Guinea, Australians, Tasmanians (now extinct) Eskimo, Dene of the Mackenzie Basin in Canada, the Salish of British Columbia, the Northern Ojibway, the Paiute of Nevada, Utah and Arizona, the Paviotso of Nevada, the indigenous peoples of California, the inhabitants of Tierra del Fuego, the Lapps, the Samoyedes and the Ostiaks.

An adequate account of the customs of these peoples would extend to the dimensions of a large treatise. If it is impracticable in this book to find room for such an exhaustive report, it is essential to provide a sufficiently large series of extracts from the writings of actual observers to establish the reality of the essential facts concerning the social grouping and general behaviour of primitive people. At the risk of tedious repetition this attempt must be made. The true interpretation of human nature is not possible without an understanding of the thoughts and conduct of Natural Man. The profound misunderstanding of the plain significance of the recorded facts depicting the geniality and morality of primitive men is the chief reason for most of the controversy concerning human nature. In many cases even those who have studied such people and recorded their observations in unequivocal terms are profoundly sceptical, if not of the statements they themselves have made, at any rate of their obvious implications and worldwide application. By setting out side by side a series of such records made by numerous observers in widely distant parts of the world with reference to peoples of varied races and the most profoundly contrasted environments, we can appreciate the fact that the essential geniality of mankind is universal. So long as he is free from the disturbing influence of civilisation the nomad is by nature a happy and well-behaved child, full of generous impulses and free from vice.

Montaigne in his *Essays* gives characteristically quaint expression to this new revelation of human nature. "Those who return from that new world, which of late hath beene discovered by the Spaniards, can witnesse unto us, how these nations being without magistrates or law, live more regularly and formally than we. . . . It was that, which a Roman Senatour said, that their predecessors had their breath stinking of garlicke, and their stomach perfumed with a good conscience: and contrary, the men of his times, outwardly smelt of nothing but sweet odours, but inwardly they stuncke of all vices."

Most of the food-gathering peoples have in the course of time adopted from their more civilised neighbours certain beliefs and practices. The Bushmen of South Africa make pottery with tubular handles. Pottery-making is not usually found among peoples of this stage of culture, and there is little doubt that, in this case, there has been borrowing from other peoples. Some of the exceptions to the general type of culture characteristic of Food-Gatherers as a whole will, on the other hand, be dealt with at length, for they are of great theoretical importance.

The behaviour of primitive people presents certain general features that can be regarded as the originally universal attributes of all mankind. They have, of course, no agriculture and no domesticated animals, except the dog in some cases. They do not build permanent houses, and at most make rough shelters. They would seem formerly to have gone about naked, as many of them still do. They were ignorant of pottery-making, and of metal-working. They have no social classes, and usually no organisation in clans or other similar social groupings. In fact, their condition can truly be defined as being practically devoid of social institutions. Many of them still live in this original way in natural family groups, such, for example, as are found among the gorillas and other anthropoid apes.

The African Pygmies

The Pygmies of the eastern part of the Congo basin in Africa (the Mambuti) may be taken as an example. Writing in 1922 Van den Bergh says: "Originally they had a free hand in this country and roamed about as they pleased, occupying a stretch of open land now and then, or retiring to the forest, as the spirit moved them. They resented the settlement of the Wanyari (a group of Negroes) in their territory to such an extent that even now they kill the Wanyari, whenever they feel so inclined, if intruders dare to invade the domains of the Pygmy forest. They do this by sniping, because they dare not fight their foe in the open, where they know that they would not be the equal of the Wanyari. They lie in wait for them in the forest, and from ambush it is an easy matter, comparatively, to land one of their poisoned arrows in the anatomy of their hated enemies." This account of their actions may seem to corroborate the popular conception of the behaviour of "savages" as people addicted to treachery and murder. Hence we must not overlook the consideration that the violence was provoked by other people intruding into their domains, and was inspired by the idea of safe-guarding their means of livelihood which, rightly or wrongly, they believed was being threatened.

At present, however, the Pygmies are not, as a race, quite so hostile to the Wanyari. They have taken their ejection philosophically for the last half century, and now they look upon the Wanyari not only as a race of conquerers, but almost as friends in general. But they do not soon forget a personal slight or injustice; hence occasional vendettas.

We are told by Van den Bergh that they do not attempt to build anything worthy of being called houses. They sometimes make shelters of twigs and leaves, but seem as contented without any such cover as with it. No mention is made of their social organisation, but writers (Christy, 1924, Schumacher, 1927, and others) on the Pygmies of the Ituri forest state that they have no chiefs, and that the basis of society is the family, taken in the wide sense of the term. "The strangest thing about them is that they are monogamous. What struck me [Van den Bergh] most forcibly was that they are not devoid of an ethical moral code. Indeed, the contrast of their ideas of morality with those of other African tribes is so great as to be astounding. It has for some time been a conviction with me that among most of the African tribes, especially those with which I have come into contact, there is almost a complete absence of morality. I was, to say the least, surprised to find the Mambuti imbued with such high moral instincts. Stealing is so far foreign to their habits that the Wanyari chiefs give them their goats and sheep to mind whenever a tribe lingers for any length of time in the same locality. This they do because they can rest more easily having their flocks in the hands of the Mambuti than in the hands of men of their own villages. Adultery seems to be almost unheard of among them. That they do not indulge in excesses we found out when they received tobacco and native banana beer from the chief. They drank of the beer in moderate quantities and they smoked of the tobacco very frugally.

"Their temperate habits were emphasised when we asked the leader of the little dwarfs to pose before us smoking with his pals. He did so, and at the second draft which he took at the pipe, which was as big as himself, he turned over and became fearfully sick, to such an extent that the perspiration gushed down his wrinkled little skin. He was counted out for the rest of the day. That experience also showed us another trait in their character—that they are very sympathetic with one another. As soon as the little man showed a sign of sickness his friends took him out of the sun and laid him in a shaded hut [a mere shelter] without walls, so that he was out of the sunshine and yet exposed to the open air. A little woman, who evidently was his wife, ran for water and plied him with plenty of it, both for drinking and bathing purposes. And when we came to the distribution of salt they took me down to the little invalid and motioned me not to forget the tiny smoker.

"Their manners are very gentle and they have a sense of delicacy. I am told also that they do not kill among themselves, and my information went so far as to state that the oldest Mambuti of the two villages with which I came in contact had never known of such an act being committed among themselves. It is true that a couple of Wanyari had become the victims of their poisoned arrows, but they were explained as cases of warfare rather than homicides, because they had intruded into the forest which the dwarfs consider their inviolable domain. In cases where one Mambuti had wounded another with a poisoned arrow they had always applied an antidote in the making of which they are experts.

"A very curious trait of the Mambuti is their courage in the hunting field. It sounds paradoxical that the smallest people known in the human family should have a special predilection in hunting down the largest type of animal life. . . . Having no cord or rope, they make their nets of vines and creepers in the form of very coarse and irregular meshes.

"They have large families. I saw one family of four children and spoke with a mother who had raised nine. They have great respect for their elders, and in this connection I noticed that a girl whom I pushed ahead to lead a dance withdrew, made a place for the oldest woman of the party, and took her own place near the rear of the line. The same rank was in order with the men, the oldest always in the lead, and when he fell out another grey-haired elder took his place. When we went to their forest home a young woods-man led the way, but he withdrew in favour of the oldest in the village, who led us on and found the intricate path which wound its way to their abode."

Schumacher, writing in 1927, says of the Kivu Pygmies that they show a great affection for their children. The old people are bound with the strongest ties of affection to their children and grand-children. Little children are punished simply by a slight tweaking of the ear.

In his book on *The Uganda Protectorate*, Sir Harry Johnston speaks of "their merry, impish ways; their little songs, their little dances; their mischievous pranks; unseen, spiteful vengeance; quick gratitude; and prompt return for kindness." Another writer (Stuhlman) describes them as naturally intelligent, but cunning, revengeful, and suspicious in character.

Comparison of these reports with those relating to other peoples in the following pages suggests the possibility that the words "cunning, revengeful and suspicious" may be due to misunderstanding on the part of the recorder. Unsophisticated people who must ever be on the alert to detect danger and resent injury necessarily display such qualities as an observer might misrepresent by the use of these three adjectives.

The Bushmen

The Bushmen of South Africa are a branch of the Negrito people, but differ in skin colour and in the peculiar disposition of fat on the buttocks known as steatopygy. There is evidence to sug-gest that in former times their domain extended much farther north than the present range of their distribution. They paint, or until recent times painted or engraved in caves or on rocks, pictures of the animals they hunted. They made pottery, often with tubular handles, reminiscent of that made more than fifty centuries ago by the Predynastic Egyptians. They had a stone industry similar to that practised in ancient times in North Africa, where it is distinguished by the term Capsian. They were pushed southward by the advancing Bantu-speaking peoples, and now are mostly confined to the Kalahari Desert. Soon after the Dutch colonised South Africa a war of extermination began. The first fight was in 1688. According to Dornan "Regular commandoes were formed to hunt them down. The men were shot as wild beasts, and the women and children carried off as slaves. The reason for this war to the knife was the cattle-stealing propensities of the Bushmen. As the Dutch occupied the land they drove away or slaughtered the game on which the Bushmen lived, and the latter took to looting the herds and flocks of the colonists. . . . There is good reason to believe that the Bushmen were not originally thieves, that where they had plenty of other food they usually left the stock of both Bantu and European alone, and it was only when they saw their means of existence destroyed that they took to looting and plunder."

Here again there is no evidence to suggest that the Bushman's conduct was essentially immoral. The act of cattle-stealing cannot be regarded as vicious in a people ignorant of the idea and the rights of private property. The live stock was to them potential food not altogether different in kind from the wild animals they were in the habit of hunting. To the Bushmen, who were accustomed to hunt any animal without restriction, the outrage committed by the Dutchmen in trespassing on their domain and so neglecting the traditional respect every group of natural men were accustomed to show to another's territory is the most heinous offence, which invariably provokes retribution. It is tantamount to the deprivation of the only means of sustenance.

The Bushmen have no tribal organisation and no paramount chiefs. "In face of danger the nearest clans or families combined to resist the foe, under the most courageous and capable leader, but as soon as the need of combination ceased, the alliance came to an end." Occasionally a strong man asserted his leadership, but he only kept it by force, and often lost it by a violent end.

Each group was constituted by blood relationship. It kept to its own hunting grounds, and bitterly resented the intrusion of others, either natives or Europeans. "Each little family goes its own way and the father is a despot as long as he can maintain his authority, that is so long as he is in the full possession of his physical powers, but once these show signs of decline he is soon displaced. Occasionally a man who has shown great prowess in hunting or war may remain at the head of the family for some time after he has retired from active participation in the chase, but sometimes even this does not last long. The Masatwas have such a struggle to maintain their existence, and to-day it is greater than ever, that they have no desire to be burdened with despots who cannot feed themselves. Fights between rivals for the possession of power in the family or clan were not infrequent in the old days and may occur even yet. Such ended in the victor either killing, or maiming, and driving out his opponent, who henceforth went off on his own, and nourished feelings of revenge, which he ever sought occasion to gratify. Sometimes he was able to carry out his desire, but his rival was usually too much on his guard, and too wary to be caught napping, realising only too well what his own fate would be if he were, and that his tenure of power depended upon his ability to maintain it. Yet in spite of the impatience of the Bushmen to all forms of authority they were not naturally cruel or vindictive to each other, and in times of stress a leader was implicitly obeyed, and in his turn expected such obedience."

Mr. Dornan, from whose writings the preceding paragraphs are quoted, also tells us that the communities of relatives are small, and usually did not number more than twenty. They have no permanent habitations, but used wind-screens, rock-shelters, caves or even holes in the ground. The Bushmen are mostly monogamous, but some are polygamous, particularly those living about the Shashi and Motloutsi rivers. "Feats of hunting are regarded as of great importance in procuring a wife. . . . The young man is most favoured who is the bravest or most successful hunter, but in any case ability to provide for a wife is an absolute necessity before marriage. The strongest and bravest man in a clan could and did take as many of the women and girls as his power enabled him to do. . . ."

The Bushmen formerly wore little or no clothing, sometimes going quite naked: even when adults adopted clothing the young boys continued to go nude until the age of puberty. "What little clothing they did wear was a skin thrown over the shoulders in cold weather, a fillet of skin around the head in the case of the men, in which they were accustomed to stick their arrow points, or a band of discs out of ostrich shells in the case of the women, who also wore a girdle of the same round the loins, or a small piece of skin with fringes in front, usually made from the hide of a springbok or the skin of a jackal. Sometimes the men had a narrow piece of skin threaded on a sinew and that went round the loins, the skin being passed between the legs and tied in front.

Mr. Dornan has some interesting remarks to make about the general behaviour of the Bushmen. "The Bushmen of the Kalahari are not cruel, certainly far less cruel than the Cape Bushmen, according to what we read and hear, and I have never come across any well authenticated statements of their atrocities upon the Bechuanas, or Matabele. With the Makaranga they get on very well, and these people do not speak of them with the contempt that the Bechuanas do." The cruel behaviour between the Bushmen and the Bantu was, as in the case of Bushman and European, due to the pressure exerted by the more highly civilised people upon the Bushmen, causing the Bushmen to thieve in order to live.

"One thing that has struck me about all Bushmen that I have known is their sense of loyalty and faithfulness to their friends and employers. It is an admirable trait in their character, and many who have employed them have borne this testimony. I have not seen anything to be afraid of in the Bushmen, or for that matter in any native people that I have had to do with in South Africa."

As regards affection he says: "It has been stated that the Bushmen are wanting in feelings of affection towards one another. I have often heard the statement made that mothers are cruel to their children, somtimes destroying them if they prove too great a burden. This is not borne out by what I have seen. Often one sees Bushmen mothers kissing their babies just as European mothers do, and when they become sick they are tenderly cared for. The fathers are stern and rough often, but they are never brutal to their children.

"They will respond to kind treatment as any other people will. They do not show their feelings readily, but that they feel grateful for kindness I have no doubt. They are light-spirited, full of merriment, especially the women, irresponsible, improvident and care-

less. They have much pleasure in their lives. On the other hand
they have equally great faults. They are wayward, obstinate, im-
patient of control, and when opposed or thwarted, savage, vindictive and cruel to a degree. Of their bravery there is no need to
speak at length. They will do anything for a person who has earned
their respect and confidence. If one is face to face with an angry
lion, the Bushman tracker will stand by one's side and never quail.
If the hunter goes down in the fight, so will the Bushman, and
cases are on record where a Bushman has killed a lion on the body
of his master. I heard of a Bushman who seized a lion by his
mane, when he had his master down and was mauling him, and
endeavoured to drag him off. Courage could not go much farther.
A knowledge of the habits and thoughts of the Bushmen enables
one to realise how very human they are after all. The Bushmen
were great gluttons when they had abundance of food. With them
life was either a feast or a famine, more often the latter."

Dr. Stow says of the Bushmen that "They never appear to have
had great wars against each other; sudden quarrels among rival
huntsmen, ending in lively skirmish, which, owing to their nimble-
ness and presence of mind caused little damage to life or limb, appear to have been the extent of their tribal differences. Even an
habitually quarrelsome man was not tolerated among them; he became an intolerable nuisance, and his own friends assisted in
putting the obnoxious individual on one side; while their very
enemies acknowledge them to have been, when left to themselves,
a merry cheerful race."

Unfortunately this remarkable people is almost extinct. Just a
few scattered groups still linger in the Kalahari Desert of South
Africa, and in a few years the world will know them no more.
Well may we join with Professor Sollas (*Ancient Hunters*) in
mourning the disappearance of this remarkable race, so valuable
to us in that they represent a stage of culture which reveals many
analogies to that of the Old Stone Age in Europe.

The Veddahs of Ceylon

The Veddahs and the Predravidian tribes of Southern India are
the remnants of the original population of their countries. The

Veddahs live in rock shelters in communities of relatives, and each community has its own hunting-grounds, over the boundaries of which members of other communities rarely, if ever, trespass. In behaviour they are quite peaceful. Professor and Mrs. Seligman describe them as "Extremely courteous and merry . . . in the main they have retained their old virtues of truthfulness, chastity and courtesy." Each Veddah "readily helps all other members of his own community, and shares any game he may kill or honey he may take" with the rest. The Veddahs are strictly monogamous, and exhibit great marital fidelity. These writers also say that "In every respect the women appear to be treated as the equals of the men; they eat the same food; indeed, when we gave presents of food the men seemed usually to give the women and children their share first. . . . Veddahs are affectionate and indulgent parents." Professor Seligman also states: "It may be noted that even at the present day the sexual morality of the Veddahs is extremely high; they are strictly monogamous, and both married and unmarried are habitually chaste."

Another writer says of the Veddahs: "In a general way these people may be described as gentle and affectionate one to another. They are strongly attached to both their children and their relatives. Widows are invariably supported by the local community, receiving their share of fruits and grain and the products of the chase. Altogether they appear to be a quiet and submissive race, obeying the slightest expression of a wish, and being very grateful for any assistance or attention. They consider themselves superior to their neighbours and are unwilling to change their wild forest life for any other."

A most illuminating account of the Veddahs is that of Mr. J. Bailey in the *Transactions of the Ethnological Society* for 1863. He spoke from an extensive personal knowledge of them. He describes them as "very harmless" and he says "they are as peaceful as it is possible to be. They are proverbially truthful and honest. They are fond of their children, who early become fond of them. . . . Their constancy to their wives is a very remarkable trait in a country where conjugal virtue is not classed as the highest of domestic virtues. Infidelity, however, in the husband or the wife, appears to be unknown, and I was very careful in my enquiries on the subject. Had it existed, the neighbouring Singhalese would have had no hesitation in accusing them of it, but I could not find a trace of it." Mr. Bailey goes on to say that the Kandyans divorce freely, that husbands and wives desert one another for the most trivial reasons, even a slight sickness affording sufficient excuse. "But the Veddahs have not yet arrived at such a pitch of civilisation. Divorce is unknown among them. They are kind: and constant to their wives, and few of their Kandyan neighbours could say as I have heard a Veddah say, "Death alone separates husband and wife." "The idea of such constancy was quite too much for one of the bystanders; an intelligent Kandyan chief, on one occasion when I was talking on these subjects to some Veddahs. 'Oh, Sir,' he exclaimed apologetically, 'they are just like Waneroos' (monkeys). He was perfectly scandalised at the utter barbarism of living with only one wife, and never parting till separated by death."

The Semang and the Sakai of the Malay Peninsula

The Malay Peninsula is the home of several food-gathering tribes, both of Australoid and Negrito stock. The Negritos are called the Semang. They are described by Messrs. Skeat and Blagden as living in a state of equality, with communal property, and are said by them to be happy-go-lucky, cheery little hunters. They are monogamous, and observe the marital tie with great fidelity. A recent account by Mr. Schebesta adds further corroboration. He says they live in small groups, with no tribal organisation and no chief class. There is no form of government, but the father of the family is respected. "Freedom, but not anarchy, is the characteristic of each Semang group and the characteristic of each individual." They do not build houses, but sometimes make wind-screens. But as a rule they have no fixed dwelling-places. They live chiefly on vegetable food, but occasionally some hunting is done for meat. They practise agriculture to a small extent. All members of the group eat in common, and share their food. If there is plenty it is said that some is given to other families of the same "clan," but not to members of other clans that happen to be with them. Marriage is a condition

of equality between husband and wife. Polygamy is allowed, but is rarely practised. Many of the Semang tribes observe pre-marital chastity, and regard adultery as a great crime, to be punished by death. Children are very highly prized. They are the link that binds the parents together. For, while newly married couples often dissolve partnership, those with children very rarely separate.

Mr. Schebesta states that murder, theft and drunkenness are unknown among them. "The better I knew the dusky dwarf, the less reason had I for thinking evil of him. He certainly was not evil, but *eitel, rechthaberisch und stolz.*"

The Sakai are Australoids. They are mainly hunters. They have neither warfare nor intertribal fighting. They are simple, kindhearted, upright, truthful and scrupulously just. They are generally monogamous, but some of them have adopted polygamy. Mr. Hale wrote (1886) of them in these terms:—"Where not demoralised by Malay intercourse, they are most kind and simple-hearted, always anxious to do their best to assist any white man that happens to be in want of any assistance, and I find that the opinion of other people out here who have had dealings with them coincides with mine in this respect." Curiously these people only hunt game when they are very hungry. "They love their women-folk and children."

Mr. F. W. Knocker remarks of a tribe of mixed Semang-Sakai blood living in the Ulu Plus district that they have no agriculture except a little cultivated tapioca, no chieftainship, and only one wife at a time, who comes from a neighbouring camp. Another group of peoples, called the Jakun, are largely hunters. They are quite inoffensive, good-natured, mild, excellent in temper, innocent, contented, liberal and generous. They never steal. They are fairly strict monogamists, and observe great post-matrimonial fidelity. Messrs. Skeat and Blagden say that they are far superior morally to the peoples who threaten to absorb them.

The Andamanese

The next peoples to be considered are those living in the Andaman Islands, in the Bay of Bengal, close to the track followed for many ages by migrants between Southern India and the Straits of Malacca. Although Food-Gatherers, their social organisation is more complicated than that, say, of the Semang or Sakai, who have just been considered. They live in definite settlements, each with its bachelors' sleeping-place, a feature of culture which they share with many peoples of the neighbouring region who are Food-Producers. The village is properly planned, and the different families have their huts, each family to a hut. These permanent camps serve as the headquarters of the local group. Formerly there used to be communal huts, but the practice is now being given up.

Professor Radcliffe Brown has given a detailed account of the social organisation of these people. Though hunting belongs to the group in common, each member having equal rights over the whole of it, there is a certain amount of personal property. A man may reserve a tree for himself. A pig belongs to the man whose arrow first struck it, even though it did not kill. A man's weapons are his personal property. In the same way anything that a woman makes belongs to her, and her husband may not dispose of it without her permission. Certain things, such as communal huts and canoes, are made and held in common, with certain reservations.

Andamanese communities have no organised government, but there is a great respect for seniority. "Beside the respect for seniority there is another important factor in the regulation of the social life, namely the respect for certain personal qualities. These qualities are skill in hunting and in warfare, generosity and kindness, and freedom from bad temper." There is, in each community, no real authority; influence is the force at work. Indeed, "women may occupy a position of influence similar to that of men."

Professor Radcliffe Brown's account of the general behaviour of the Andamanese is so illuminating and significant as to be worth quoting verbatim. "There does not seem to have been in the Andamans any such thing as the punishment of crime. We may distinguish the two kinds of anti-social action which are regarded by the natives as being wrong. The first kind are those actions which injure in some way a private individual. The second are those, which, while they do not injure any particular person, are yet regarded with disapproval by the society in general."

Amongst the anti-social actions of the first kind are murder or wounding, theft and adultery, and wilful damage of the property of another.

"No case of one Andamanese killing another has occurred in recent years. Quarrels sometimes occur between two men of the same camp. A good deal of hard swearing goes on, and sometimes one of the men will work himself up into a high pitch of anger, in which he may seize his bow and discharge an arrow near to the one who has offended him, or may vent his ill-temper by destroying any property he can lay his hands on, including not only that of his enemy but also that of other persons and even his own. At such a display of anger the women and children flee into the jungle in terror, and if the angry man be at all a formidable person the men occasionally do the same. It apparently requires more courage than the native usually possesses to endeavour to allay such a storm of anger. Yet I found that the slightest show of authority would immediately bring such a scene to an end. A man of influence in his village was probably equal to the task of keeping order and preventing any serious damage from taking place. It was probably rare for a man so far to give way to his anger as to kill his opponent."

Such murders did, however, occasionally take place. In view of an earlier statement in this quotation, this presumably refers to the past. "The murderer would, as a rule, leave the camp and hide himself in the jungle, where he might be joined by such of his friends as were ready to take his part. It was left to the relatives and friends of the dead man to exact vengeance if they wished and if they could. If the murderer was a man who was much feared it is probable that he would escape. In any case the anger of the Andamanese is short-lived, and if for a few months he could keep out of the way of those who might seek revenge, it is probable that at the end of that time he would find their anger cooled."

It is said that they do not practise marriage between relatives. They have premarital intercourse between the sexes, but "the girls are always modest and childlike in their behaviour, and when married they make good wives and become models of constancy." Sometimes after marriage they display great bashfulness. To this may be added Sir Richard Temple's remark that "divorce is rare and unknown after the birth of a child, and there is no polygamy or incest."

One of the most noteworthy authorities on the Andamanese was the late Mr. E. H. Man. His references to their original qualities are very emphatic. "It has been remarked with regret," he wrote (in the *Journal of the Anthropological Institute* in 1883) "by all interested in the race, that intercourse with the alien population has, generally speaking, prejudicially affected their morals, and that the candour, veracity, and self-reliance they manifest in their savage and untutored state are, when they become associated with foreigners, to a great extent lost, and habits of untruthfulness, dependence and sloth engendered." He then goes on to describe their domestic relationships. "Much mutual affection is displayed in their social relations, and, in their dealings with strangers, the same characteristic is observable when once a good understanding has been established." The life of the community is harmonious. "Every care and consideration are paid by all classes to the very young, the weak, the aged and the helpless, and these, being made special objects of interest and attention, invariably fare better in regard to the comforts and necessaries of daily life than any of the otherwise more fortunate members of the community."

The treatment of children is noteworthy. "Andamanese children are reproved for being impudent and forward, but discipline is not enforced by corporal punishment; they are early taught to be generous and self-denying, and the special object of the fasting-period . . . seems to be to test the fortitude and powers of endurance of the lads and lasses before entering upon the cares and responsibilities of married life. The duties of showing respect and hospitality to friends and visitors being impressed upon them from their early years, all guests are well treated; every attention is paid to their wants, the best food at their host's disposal is placed before them, and, ere they take their leave, some tokens of regard or goodwill are bestowed, or, to speak more correctly, interchanged. Strangers visiting an encampment for the first time are welcomed if introduced by some mutual friend.

"Selfishness is not among their characteristics, for they frequently make presents of the best that they possess, and do not reserve, much less make, weapons of superior workmanship for their own private use; at the same time it must be confessed that it is tacitly understood that an equivalent should be rendered for every gift."

With reference to their domestic relations Mr. Man writes: "It is generally admitted that one of the surest tests of a man's character may be found in the treatment women meet with at his hands: judged by this standard these savages are qualified to teach a valuable lesson to many of the fellow-countrymen of those who have hastily set them down as 'an anomalous race of the most degraded description.' The wife is not the slave of her husband. His authority is often more or less nominal, the wife often being the master. In short, the consideration and respect with which some women are treated might with advantage be emulated by certain classes in our own land."

As we have seen, their manifestation of anger is curious. When out of temper they do not defame relatives or use improper expressions. They say, for instance, 'you liar, you fool, you log-head, you longnose, you skin and bone.' In case of wrong-doing the aggrieved one sometimes flings a blazing faggot at the offender, or discharges an arrow at, "or more frequently near" him. All present flee until the quarrel is over. Friends often intervene, seize the quarrellers and take away their weapons "which are not restored so long as there appears any risk of their using them." If a man murders another, nothing necessarily is said or done to him, though the friends or relatives of the victim may take vengeance. "In most cases, however, the murderer succeeds in striking such terror in the minds of the community that no one ventures to assail him or even to express any disapprobation of his conduct while he is within hearing." Ill-temper is sometimes shown by the destruction of property. The women sometimes quarrel and fight and destroy property.

The Andamanese sometimes have feuds, which originate at tribal meetings. The reasons for such quarrels are a matter of fundamental importance for their bearing upon the problem of human nature. For, in spite of the statements that the anger of the people is generally short-lived, standing feuds between certain groups may survive for centuries.

As in the case of the Bushmen, it must be clearly understood that expressions of cruelty and violence are not foreign to the Andamanese. Mr. Portman, for instance, writing in the *Journal of the Anthropological Institute* in 1896, says of the Andamanese that "they are gentle and pleasant to each other, but have no legal or other restraint on their passions, are easily moved to anger, and shoot and kill."

The reason for the vicious tendencies in the particular group of Andamanese of whom Mr. Portman writes is not far to seek, for he tells us that "they have suffered much in the past from the depredations of Malay pirates, and consequently much of their behaviour is to be expected." In the *Journal of the Anthropological Institute* for 1885 Mr. Man also discussed the significance of the change in the behaviour of the natives. "So widespread is the evil influence that has been exercised, that on no point probably will future writers differ so strongly as on the social and moral virtues of the Andamanese. I wish, therefore, to make it clear to my readers that my remarks and observations on all, and especially on these points, are restricted to those communities who have been found living in their primitive state, and who may therefore be fairly considered as representatives of the race, being unaffected by the virtues or vices of so-called civilisation." Here again, when we find this flagrant contrast between the behaviour of one section of a people and the rest of the communities, it is not difficult to discover the cause of the demoralisation in some alien influence.

The Kubu of Sumatra

The Kubu of Sumatra, a people still in the food-gathering stage of culture, with no social classes, who wander about as bands of relatives, are quite peaceful by nature, being shy and timid. They are monogamous. The elders settle disputes and impose punishments for offences. Until a few years ago they wore no clothes. The late Dr. H. O. Forbes, from whose writings these statements are taken, states in another place (The *Journal of the Anthropological Institute* for 1885): "What struck me most in [the Kubus] was their extreme submissiveness, their want of independence and will; they seemed too meek ever to act on the offensive. One cannot help feeling that they are harmless overgrown children of the woods. Within the memory of the chief of the village in which I first met these Kubus, have they only come to possess a sense of shame; formerly they knew none, and were the derision of the villagers into whose neighbourhood they might come."

The Punan of Borneo

The Punan of Borneo are among the most primitive people, culturally speaking, in the world. For untold ages they have lived in the forests of Borneo, well out of the way of the great movements that have swept through the Archipelago, carrying culture from India to the East. There is no reason to believe that they had been influenced strongly by any food-producing people until the Kayan and kindred tribes came up into the central watershed on their way towards Sarawak. The central part of Borneo, so far as is known, is practically devoid of any archaeological remains. The only objects that have been discovered are some stone bulls of Hindu workmanship.

In the Punan we have a food-gathering people of good physique and bright intelligence who have remained comparatively undisturbed, and therefore present to us typical conditions among really primitive peoples in general. We owe to Dr. Hose and his collaborator, Professor McDougall, a most illuminating account (quoted in the next pages from *The Pagan Tribes of Borneo, 1912,* and *Natural Man, 1926*) of these people, which has been mainly responsible for raising for discussion during the last fifteen years this fundamental problem of human nature. It is one of the most charming pictures ever drawn of the uncivilised peoples of the world. What adds to the interest and instruction of the evidence relating to the Punan is the profound contrast they present to their neighbours, akin to them in race and living under similar geographical conditions.

It may seem strange that a people richly endowed by Nature physically and mentally should be content to live without houses or much in the way of clothes, and retain an engaging cheerfulness and goodwill towards their neighbours, in spite of the immense discomfort and anxiety of such a mode of existence. But such a phenomenon becomes infinitely more significant when it is realised that these people have for many centuries had the opportunity of acquiring from their neighbours many of the elements of what we call "culture." Yet they have ignored it. Moreover, neighbouring tribes that have adopted some of the customs and beliefs of civilisation present the sharpest possible contrast to the Punan in manners and morals. Some of the most notorious headhunters are their nearest neighbours.

It is instructive to quote the account of three of these peoples—the Sea-Dayaks or Ibans, the Kayans and the Kenyahs—to bring out the contrast with the really primitive Punans, concerning whom it is enough to quote the actual words of Drs. Hose and McDougall. Of the Sea-Dayaks they write: "They are a vain, dressy, boastful, excitable, not to say frivolous people—cheerful, talkative, sociable, fond of fun and jokes and lively stories; though given to exaggeration, their statements can generally be accepted as founded on fact; they are industrious and energetic, and are great wanderers; to the last peculiarity they owe the name of Iban.

"The good qualities enumerated above render the Iban an agreeable companion and a useful servant. But there is another side to the picture: they have little respect for their chiefs, a peculiarity which renders their social organisation very defective and chaotic; they are quarrelsome, treacherous and litigious, and the most inveterate head-hunters in the country; unlike most of the other peoples, they will take heads for the sake of the glory the act brings them and for the enjoyment of the killing; in the pursuit of human beings they become possessed by a furious excitement that drives them on to acts of the most heartless treachery and the most brutal ferocity."

Of the Kayans who are widely distributed throughout central Borneo, Drs. Hose and McDougall write: "They are to be found in large villages situated on the middle reaches of all the principal rivers with the exception of those that run to the North coast. They are a warlike people, but less truculent than the Sea-Dayaks, more staid and conservative and religious, and less sociable. They do not wantonly enter into quarrels; they respect and obey their chiefs."

The third people, the Kenyahs, they describe as "perhaps the most courageous and intelligent of the peoples; pugnacious but less quarrelsome than the Sea-Dayak; more energetic and excitable than the Kayan; hospitable and somewhat improvident, sociable and of pleasant manners; less reserved and of more buoyant temperament than the Kayan; very loyal and obedient to their chiefs; more truthful and more to be depended upon than any of the other peoples, except possibly the Kayans."

In sharp contrast to these three peoples the Punans are the only people who do not dwell in villages established on the banks of the rivers. They "cultivate no crops and have no domestic animals. They live entirely upon the wild produce of the jungle, vegetable and animal. . . . The Punan dwelling is merely a rude low shelter of palm leaves, supported on sticks to form a sloping roof which keeps off the rain but very imperfectly, and leaves the interior open on every side."

"A Punan community consists generally of some twenty or thirty adult men and women, and about the same number of children. One of the older men is recognised as the leader or chief. He has little formally defined authority, but rather the authority that is naturally accorded to age and experience and to the fuller knowledge of the tribal history and traditions that comes with age. His sway is a very mild one; he dispenses no substantial punishments; public opinion and tradition seem to be the sole and sufficient sanctions of conduct among these Arcadian bands of gentle wary wanderers. Decisions as to the movements of the band are arrived at by open discussion in which the leader will exercise an influence proportioned to his reputation for knowledge and judgment. From the point of view of physical development the Punans are among the finest of the peoples of Borneo.

"There are no distinctions of upper and lower social strata as among the other tribes, and thus the mixture of blood, which in the Kayan and Kenyah communities results from the adoption of war captives into the lower class, does not occur to them; and they present none of the wide diversities of type such as are common in the other tribes, especially between the upper and lower social classes. They correspond, in fact, to the relatively pure bred upper classes of the other tribes, and present the same high standard of physical development and vigour.

"When gathered in friendly talk with strangers, even those whom they have every reason to trust, they prefer to remain squatting on their heels, rather than to sit down on a mat; and the tension of their muscles, combined with the still alert watchfulness of their faces, conveys the impression that they are ready to leap up and flee away or to struggle for their lives at any moment. It is doubtless this alertness of facial expression and bodily attitude that gives the Punan something of the air of an untameable wild animal.

"In spite of his distrustful expression (which is merely the natural result of the fact that men living as they do must ever be alert to defend themselves against sudden danger) the Punan is a likeable person, rich in good qualities and innocent of vices. He never slays or attacks men of other tribes wantonly; he never seeks or takes a head, for his customs do not demand it; and he never goes upon the war-path, except when occasionally he joins a war-party of some other tribe in order to facilitate the avenging of blood. But he will defend himself and his family pluckily if he is attacked and has no choice of flight; and, if anyone has killed one of his relatives, he will seek an opportunity of planting a poisoned dart in his body. In a case of this kind all the Punans of a large area will aid one another in obtaining certain information as to the identity of the offender; and any one of them will avenge the injury to his people, if the opportunity presents itself. They do not avenge themselves indiscriminately on all or any member of the offender's village or family, but they will postpone their vengeance for years, if the actual offender cannot be reached more promptly.

"That the Punan will not allow the slaying of any one of their number to go unavenged on the person of the slayer is well known to all the people of the country, and this knowledge does much to give them immunity from attack.

"Their only handicrafts are the making of baskets, mats, blow-pipes, and the implements used for working the wild sago; but in these and the use of the blow-pipe they are very expert. All other manufactured articles not made by them—clothes, swords, spears —are obtained by barter from the other peoples. Unlike all the other peoples they have no form of sepulture, but simply leave the corpse of a comrade in the rude shelter in which he died. They sing and declaim melancholy songs or dirges with peculiar skill and striking effect.

"Each man has usually one wife. We know of no instances of polygamy amongst them; though we know of cases in which a Punan woman has become the second wife of a man of some other tribe. On the other hand, polyandry occurs, generally in cases in which a woman married to an elderly man has no children by him. They desire many children, and large families are the rule; a family with as many as eight or nine children is no rarity. Marriage is for life, though separation by the advice and direction of the chief, or by desertion of the man to another community, occurs."

Dr. Charles Hose gave the author his sanction for these extensive quotations from his writings to provide in the observer's own words the most impressive testimony as to the true character of Natural Man.

The Aru Islanders

On the Aru Islands, immediately west of New Guinea, dwells a tribe of Food-Gatherers, ignorant of metal-working, with no social classes, who are quite peaceful in their behaviour.

Certain Peoples of the Philippines

Negrito tribes still linger in the Philippines. Mr. Schaderberg says they are monogamous and keep strictly to the union. The old are respected, and when they get beyond looking after themselves they are fed by their children. Women are not considered by them as important as the men.

Mr. Morice Van Overbergh, a missionary in the Philippines, has given a detailed account of the Negritos of Northern Luzon. They have been considerably influenced by the neighbouring peoples, but they retain enough of their original nature to show their cultural similarity to the other Food-Gatherers. Usually they live in houses, not generally a trait of food-gathering culture, and one family to the house is the rule. One case is mentioned of a house occupied by four related families. The houses are scattered over a wide area, and never more than four of them are together.

"They never keep two wives at a time, although this practice is indulged in very often by Isneg and Kalinga alike; married people very rarely separate, although this is a very general custom among the other pagan tribes.

"Two vices generally recognised as being common to many uncivilised people are lying and stealing. It would seem almost against the nature of a Negrito to tell a lie, and one reason for this is perhaps his apparent inability to conceal his own thoughts. Whatever he knows he, like the "enfant terrible," makes public. Stealing, if it occurs at all, is very rare. The fact that we left our belongings for several days where every passing Negrito could have taken from them whatever he liked, is a sufficient proof of his honesty. Only once . . . have I heard the imputation of a Negrito having stolen something, and this was in the way of eatables, which might readily excuse hungry men, as everybody has a right to live; but . . . this was told me by a Kagayan, a member of a race that is far from respecting the Negritos. Anyway, stealing is certainly abhorred by them. . . ."

They are very peaceful. "Whatever may be the case with other Negritos, and whatever writers may have said about them, the Negritos I saw are of a very peaceful character. Only on one occasion did I hear of a Negrito having wounded one of his fellow Negritos: it was Allapa, who had to arrest the other fellow; as the latter was not willing to follow, Allapa became angry and wounded him; he then gave himself up to the authorities and was sentenced to prison for one year.

"There is no question of warfare between the different Negrito groups; they usually know one another; and, even when unknown, they are always very friendly; they seem to consider the whole Negrito Race as a big family, any representatives of it being welcome to their homes at all times. . . . When I asked Masigun if they would allow even Negritos from farther away to hunt in their forests, he candidly answered me in the affirmative and added: 'We cannot forbid them; if they like to come here and hunt on our forests, they are allowed to do so; why not?' When I asked him if his people would not object or shoot arrows at them, he simply laughed, seeming to find the idea a very funny one, and said, 'No, never.' . . . To conclude, we find the Negritos living in happy intercourse with everybody else, but entirely isolated and kept away, from Isneg and Christians alike, by a deep social gulf."

Mr. Van Overbergh's opinion of the Negrito may be summed up in his words:—"A Negrito is always happy, he laughs more than he weeps; he is devoted to his friends (and he has no enemies): and is always ready to succour them; he is very polite and he is hospitable to a remarkable degree. . . . To the Negrito life seems to be a very joyous affair, and he does not seem to have any preoccupation at all. To him each day has its cares, and, if he cannot find to-day what he is in need of, he expects to find it at some other time, not seeming to care a fig for disappointment of any kind."

Australians

The peoples of Australia, though still in the food-gathering stage of culture, have many elements of culture so complicated, and so similar to those of other islands in their neighbourhood, that it is impossible to look on them as primitive people in the sense in which we may regard the Punan of Borneo. In *The Children of the Sun* Dr. W. J. Perry has given in detail the reasons that compel us to adopt this view and its important bearing on the consideration of the problem of warfare. He has discussed the relationships between the Australian social organisation and that of the peoples of the neighbouring regions. Nevertheless, it is necessary to study the Australians along with the really primitive peoples and contrast their behaviour. The study of warfare and cruelty among certain of them serves to throw a flood of light on the questions of the influence of institutions on human behaviour.

The Australians are ignorant of pottery-making and of agriculture; they also have no domesticated animals that they use for food. Although they are organised under an elaborate social system of clans and territorial bodies, yet the family, as Professor Malinowski has pointed out, is the unit of society. As a rule the Australians have no ruling class, although in certain cases chieftainship is hereditary. Usually the authority in the tribe or other group rests, according to Dr. Howitt, in the council of initiated men. Their marriage rules, the outcome of an·alien form of social organisation, are responsible for the fact that the institution of monogamy is not so definite as among other Food-Gatherers. Nevertheless there is a distinct family life. The old men in Australian society, who are vested with much power, appropriate many of the women, so that the younger men have to wait a long time for a wife.

The domestic characteristics of the Australian are summed up by Dr. Howitt as follows: after showing that there is a sharing-out of food according to definite rules, he goes on to say: "The instances given in this chapter of the division of the food among the kindred and relations, and the special provision for the old people, give an entirely different idea of the aboriginal character to that which has been usually held. The latter is derived from what is seen of the Blacks under our civilisation. The oft-repeated description of the black fellow eating the white man's beef or mutton and throwing a bone to his wife who sits behind him, in fear of a blow from his club, is partly the new order of things resulting from our civilisation breaking down the old rules, but it is also in part the old rule itself. I have shown that in some cases the wife is fed by her own people, and the throwing of food to another person is not an act of discourtesy. Its reason is that there is a deep-seated objection to receive anything which can convey evil magic from the hand of another person, and in many instances that applies to the two sexes.

"Such contrasts between the old and the new conditions of things struck me very forcibly at the Kurnai *Jeraeil*. The people lived for a week in the manner of their old lives, certainly with the addition of the white man's beef and flour, but without his intoxicating drinks, which have been a fatal curse to the black race. That week was passed without a single quarrel or dispute."

In his latest work on *The Arunta* of Central Australia, Sir Baldwin Spencer makes a few comments that serve to supplement those of Dr. Howitt. "In their ordinary condition the natives are almost completely naked, which is all the more strange, as kangaroos and wallaby are by no means scarce, and one would think that their fur would be of no little use and comfort in the winter time, when under the perfectly clear sky, which often remains cloudless for weeks together, the radiation is so great that at night time the temperature falls several degrees below freezing point. The idea of making any kind of clothing does not appear to have entered the native mind." They "usually wander about in small parties consisting of one or two families, for example, two or more brothers with their wives and children." As regards their general behaviour he says, "As a rule the natives are kindly disposed to one another—that is, of course, within the limits of their own tribe— and, where two tribes come into contact with one another on the borderland of their respective territories, there the same amicable feelings are maintained between the members of the two. There is no such thing as one tribe being in a constant state of enmity with another so far as the central tribes are concerned. Now and again, of course, fights do occur between the members of different local groups, who may or may not belong to the same or to different tribes. . . . To the children they are, one may say, uniformly, with very rare exceptions, kind and considerate, carrying them when they get tired on the march, and always seeing that they get a good share of any food. . . ." Moreover, "there is no such thing as doing away with the aged or infirm people; on the contrary, such are treated with special kindness, receiving a share of the food which they are unable to procure for themselves."

An important feature of their behaviour which, however, is common to all primitive men, is the lack of care for the future. "He stores nothing, except for a few days in preparation for a ceremony, and has no idea of agriculture or domestication, partly perhaps because the animals around him are not adapted to act as beasts of burden or givers of milk, but still more because he believes that, by means of magic, which plays a large part in his life, he can increase their numbers when he wishes to do so. When food is abundant he eats to repletion; when it is scarce he tightens his waistbands and starves philosophically."

These accounts may be supplemented by what is said by one who lived in close touch with the natives during the early part of last century, and knew them well. He says much in their favour. "The natives are a mild and harmless race of savages; and where any mischief has been done by them, the cause has generally arisen, I believe, in bad treatment by their white neighbours. Short as my residence has been here, I have, perhaps, had more intercourse with these people, and more favourable opportunities of seeing what they really are, than any other person in the colony. . . . They have usually been treated, in distant parts of the colony, as if they had been dogs, and shot by convict-servants, at a distance from society, for the most trifling causes." This, of course, produced retaliations on the part of the natives, with the usual sickening story of revenge on both sides. But when left alone the picture is evidently that painted by Dr. Howitt. Mr. Dawson says that "they are savages in the common acceptance of the term, although they exhibit stronger traits of natural gentleness and good feeling towards their white brethren, and towards each other, than people under that denomination are generally found [it would be more accurate to say "supposed"] to do."

On the other hand a few pages later he gives an illustration of the influence of alien culture: "when a poor gin offends her sable lord, he taps her over the head with his club in no very gentle manner." Speaking of the women in general he says, "These poor creatures are made to do all the drudgery. . . . They carry the wood for fires, make the nets for fishing, and carry everything else that they move about with, except their instruments of war."

This is an important fact, namely, that once men begin regular fighting the work falls on the women. Mr. Dawson says, "They are remarkably fond of their children, and when the parents die, the children are adopted by the unmarried men and women, and taken the greatest care of. They are exceedingly kind and generous towards one another: if I give tobacco or anything else to any man, it is divided with the first he meets without being asked for." The Rev. John Mathew says of them in his work, *Eaglehawk and Crow:* "In the aboriginal character there are many admirable, meritorious elements, but there is a lack of strong, inherited, combining, marshalling will or self-determination, and, as a natural consequence, the moral qualities are prone to operate capriciously. The natives are not insensible to promptings of honourable feeling, but generally, unless when repressed or constrained by fear, they act from impulse rather than from principle, and their best inclinations are easily overpowered by pressure from within or without. You could rely upon a black fellow being faithful to a trust only on condition that he were exempt from strong temptation." He then goes on to quote condemnatory evidence against these people on the part of Mr. James Davies, who knew the natives well. He said, very forcibly, "Hundreds of them would take your life for a blanket or a hundredweight of flour. I wouldn't trust them as far as I could throw a bullock by the tail. . . . They are so greedy that nothing can come up to them. . . . They are the most deceitful people that I have ever come across. . . . The father will beat the son, and the son the father. The brother will lie in ambush to be avenged on the brother; if he cannot manage him in fight, he will lie in ambush with a spear or club."

Mr. Mathew dissents from this harsh judgment. "This, I am sure, was stating the case against the poor creatures too strongly. They are not wantonly untruthful; they are not deficient in courage; they are not excessively selfish; and they are by no means lacking in natural affection. But Mr. Davies corroborates what I have said of the presence of that defect of character that may be termed instability. It may be said that the whole fabric of their moral character is in a position of unstable equilibrium. The slightest strain will destroy the poise." He goes on to say that they have courage which enables them to perform marvellous feats. They may be very covetous, but they are very generous. "As a rule, the blacks are sympathetic and affectionate, especially the women. Sufficient evidence of this is the way in which white men have been treated who have been cast on their mercy. Relatives are usually fondly attached to each other. The attachment between parents and their offspring is very strong, and exhibits itself in kindness to the aged, who are tenderly cared for, and indulgence to little children." They are gay of heart and love jokes. Their laughter is unrestrained, but it easily turns to anger. "Settlement by the British has usually proceeded without much resistance. The blacks have kindly assisted in their own dispossession and extermination, guiding the aliens through their forests, giving them much of their own strength at a beggarly rate of compensation, submitting contentedly to indignity and oppression, and rewarding injuries and insults with gentleness and service. They have committed robbery, rape, murder, and perpetrated several massacres. True, but they have often been trained to such offences by the lawless, brutal, indecent, tyrannical behaviour of the white men with whom they have come into contact, for as a matter of fact the outskirts of civilisation have a strong admixture of barbarism."

Mr. R. Dawson also says, "I have never known a single instance of want of probity and honesty in the natives when confidence had once been placed in them; but if no trust was put in them they would sometimes pilfer."

A letter written by William Thomas to the Governor-General of Victoria, presumably about the year 1847, entirely supports these opinions. The writer says that the natives of Victoria were much given to wandering about, making temporary encampments for the night. He comments on their behaviour while so engaged. "The harmony that exists among them when none of another tribe is in the party is surprising. I have been out with them for months without a single altercation. . . . Theft is of rare occurrence, and is punished by blows on the head of the thief by the party wronged. I never knew but one case of this kind."

Mr. F. Bonney, writing in 1884, speaks in much the same terms about them. "Though ugly and unprepossessing in appearance they are most kind, gentle and of quite average intelligence and morality." Moreover, "both men and women are very fond of children, and the kindest attention is shown to them by young and old alike. They are not spoilt by this kind treatment all round; one word from the parent generally is sufficient to check a child when doing wrong, and the greatest respect is shown to parents by their children. Altogether the treatment of children by these people, after they are once taken up and nursed, is judicious and very creditable."

On the other hand, Mr. Jos. Bischofs, writing in 1908 of the Niol-Niol of Beagle Bay, Dampier Peninsula, says that mothers showed little affection to their children in the first months of life. But when the children are grown a little, the mothers take more notice of them.

The Australians are not as peaceful in their behaviour as such peoples as the Punan of Borneo, the Semang and Sakai of the Malay Peninsula and others. On the other hand they do not engage in regular wars between communities. There are a certain number of inter-tribal feuds, which, according to one author, have helped to keep down the population. Mr. Worsnop speaks of "their constant feuds . . . with contiguous tribes." Dr. Howitt gives an account of a big feud which involved several tribes in Victoria. Professor Radcliffe Brown mentions fights between communities in

Western Australia. This shows that the Australians were not so peaceful as other Food-Gatherers. They also had fights within the community. These often occurred in conjunction with breaches of their marriage rules, and were parts of an organised mode of behaviour, since the punishments inflicted on erring members were fixed by custom. The cruelty is not due simply to an individual's anger and loss of control but is the remedy prescribed by tradition in the community. In his writings Dr. Howitt has established the truth of this statement.

Mention must be made in this connection of another definite cause of fighting among the Australian tribes. At certain intervals certain tribes hold ceremonial gatherings, at which they initiate men into manhood. Among the tribe near Maryborough in Queensland this gathering was called the *Dora*. After the termination of the meeting there is a curious ceremonial practice connected with marriage. There is a dancing corroboree, and after it the people disperse. When this has happened, the young men of the community "capture" wives. The girls' friends protect them if they can, but often there is a severe fight. Sometimes a man marries a woman from a distant place. "Sometimes a ceremonial combat occurs between the tribe of the woman and that of her husband. In this case the husband fights on the side of the tribe of his wife. He may even fight against his own father." Dr. Howitt makes the significant remark that: "Fighting being a pastime with them, a few blows or a deep cut or two are considered as nothing, and the men being in first-rate condition, the wounds soon heal." In case of a hostile attack a woman belonged to her captor. "Nearly all their fights were the result of the capture of women, either after the ceremonial combats, or in raids for that special object."

More light is thrown on this subject by William Thomas, whose knowledge of the natives was intimate. After saying that the natives live very harmonious lives, except when different "tribes" are collected together, he goes on to say: "There is seldom a marriage without much fighting, as there is a great preponderance of males over females, and the old chiefs not being satisfied with less than two and sometimes four, the value of the women is increased. . . . The woman is handed over to her spouse who has scarce got her when some others—those who were desirous to obtain her——may be seen naked, discharging wonguims at the bridegroom. A general family fight takes place, and the bridegroom seldom gets off without a broken head. . . . Most tribes have intercourse or hold a kind of alliance with three or four neighbouring ones, with whom they barter for lubras (women). They generally once a year at least, unitedly assemble. There are many disputes, imaginary or real, to settle which cannot be done without some fighting. When all is settled, they will corroboree night after night till they separate. All the tribes beyond the district of their friends are termed wild black-fellows, and when found within the district are immediately killed." In spite of this fighting, "there is one particularly amiable trait in the aboriginal character, which is, that no animosity remains in their breasts nor does any shrink from punishment. At the close of a fight or punishment, those who have inflicted the wounds may be seen sucking them and doing any other kind office required."

Very often two groups meet to fight by previous arrangement. Mr. Dawson gives a lively account of one of these meetings, the cause of which was the spearing of a shepherd. The man to be punished for the crime was called Corbon Wickie. He had to stand and protect himself from spears thrown at him by the opposite side. Then a man named Wallis advanced towards him to fight with his waddy (club). "After some abuse and flourishing with their waddies, Wickie struck Wallis a tremendous blow on the crown of his head, which he purposely held forward, without any defence. In an instant he was seen dancing in the face of his opponent like a harlequin, brandishing his waddy, while the blood streamed down his cheeks and chest. Wickie now held forward *his* head to Wallis, who struck him a similar blow, when Wickie was seen dancing and bleeding in like manner. At this moment I dashed in between them, and insisted upon their desisting. They were all instantly silent, and but the slightest opposition was made; but Wallis, who had always great attachment towards me, entreated that I would allow him to give Corbon Wickie one blow more, which should hurt him, and then Wickie would give him another also. 'Only a little bit, massa,' he said, 'bael hurt it, den no more coulor (anger); black pellow always do so.'

"The sight was most sickening to me, and I would allow no more of it. I reasoned and argued with both of them, and told them to shake hands. They seemed to be quite astonished, that I should suppose that they were enemies. . . . Wallis said, 'I like Corbon Wickie always, dat good pellow.' 'Why, then,' I said, 'do you wish to hurt each other?' They both laughed outright at this question, which, as well as my reasoning, appeared quite incomprehensible to them."

Mr. Dawson also says that the spear attacks on these occasions are always conducted fairly, for no spears are thrown without warning. They are more of the nature of ordeals than anything else, and do not rank as fighting pure and simple. Seldom are any people killed in this way, for they are very skilled in avoiding the spears thrown at them.

Another form of cruelty is inflicted as part of the death ceremonies. The Australian natives have a widespread theory that death is caused by magic. It is usually thought that someone has abstracted and eaten the kidney fat supposed by them to be the seat of life. Nothing short of the kidney and fat of another will appease the dead. So when a man dies attempts are made to detect the wrongdoer responsible for his death. After due deliberation an avenging party is then sent out to kill the murderer. (Dr. Howitt; also Sir Baldwin Spencer and Mr. Gillen.)

The foregoing account shows plainly that violent behaviour exists among the Australian natives, especially in connection with breaches of marriage rules. Mention is also made of feuds between "tribes," and it would seem from the descriptions already given that these feuds are also associated with marriage. The theory of the causation of death also brings out vengeance in the shape of an avenging party, or of the ordeal of spear-throwing. The evidence therefore establishes beyond doubt that the cruelties practised by the Australian natives are due to certain organised customs and traditions of behaviour. In this they differ profoundly from truly primitive peoples like the Pygmies, Veddahs, Punan et cetera. Particular attention has been given to this matter because it serves (with many of the associated customs) to distinguish the Australian natives from the rest of the Food-Gatherers. In their marriage classes and in the strict rules for the regulation of marriage they are quite exceptional, and have long been studied in detail by anthropologists for that very reason.

But it is a profound mistake to regard the customs of the Australians as primitive. They derived their cruelty from the same source as their "culture." Perhaps it would be truer to express this by saying that the customs and beliefs adopted from alien peoples have imposed upon the Australians habits that involve forms of brutality which are not natural to mankind.

CHAPTER VI

PRIMITIVE MAN (II)

The Eskimo

THE Eskimo, whose domain extends right across the northern part of America and as far as Greenland, provides important evidence for the study of human behaviour, and in particular the circumstances that give rise to warfare and other forms of violence. In some regions they have come into contact with peoples of higher culture, and as the result their original form of social behaviour becomes profoundly modified, so as to provide a peculiarly instructive contrast to that of other Eskimo who have usually been exempt from such disturbing factors.

The following description holds fairly well for all the Eskimo. They live together in harmony. Warfare and fighting are practically unknown, except in the case of those living near Bering Strait where, for reasons to be explained in the following pages, the provocation of Europeans has made a formerly peaceful people quarrelsome and vicious. They have no word for "war." They neither scold nor swear. Children are kindly treated and are well-behaved and quiet. As a general rule the Eskimo are monogamous. The women are on an equality with the men: no contract is settled until ratified by them: and not even the shortest trip is taken without their advice. They have no ruling class. Social grades are unknown, and property is communal. The Eskimo deal with grievances in the following manner. The offended man composes a song, and invites everyone, including the offender, to listen to it. If the audience approves of the song, the complainant is considered to have justified himself: if not, his failure as a composer is regarded as an adequate punishment. If an Eskimo should lose or break some article that he had borrowed, the owner usually reassures him. If, however, he shows resentment, the culprit remains quite calm, for the Eskimo consider that only one person need be annoyed at a time. This general description might be corroborated by quotations from the writings of many travellers. For example, Dr. Frithiof Nansen describes his experiences in the following terms: "When I see all the wrangling and all the coarse abuse of opponents which form the staple of the different party newspapers at home, I now and then wonder what these worthy politicians would say if they knew anything of the Eskimo community, and whether they would not blush before the people whom that man of God, Hans Egede, characterises as 'These ignorant, cold-blooded creatures, living without order or discipline, with no knowledge of any sort of worship, in brutish stupidity. With what good right would these "savages" look down upon us if they knew that here even in the public press we apply to each other the lowest terms of contumely, as for example "liar," "traitor," "perjuror," "lout," "rowdy," etc., while they never utter a syllable of abuse, their very language being unprovided with words of this class, in which ours is so rich. . . . It is wonderful in what peace and unity they live with each other; for quarrelling and strife and covetousness are seldom heard of among them. . . . When they have seen our dissolute sailors quarrelling and fighting, they regard such behaviour as inhuman, and say: "They do not treat each other as human beings." In the same way, if one of the officers strikes a subordinate, they at once exclaim "He behaves to his fellow-men as if they were dogs." '

"The contrast typifies a radical difference of character. The Greenlander is of all God's creatures gifted with the best disposition. Good-humour, peacefulness and evenness of temper are the most prominent features in his character. He is eager to stand on as good a footing as possible with his fellow-men, and therefore refrains from offending them and much more from using coarse terms of abuse. He is very loth to contradict another even should he be saying what he knows to be false; if he does so, he takes care to ward his remonstrance in the mildest possible form, and it would be very hard indeed for him to say right out that the other was lying. He is chary of telling other people truths which he thinks will be unpleasant to them; in such cases he chooses the vaguest expressions, even with reference to such indifferent things, for example, as wind and weather. His peacefulness even goes so far that when anything is stolen from him, which seldom happens, he does not as a rule reclaim it even if he knows who has taken it. . . . The result is that there is seldom or never any quarrelling among them." Dr. Nansen makes this further comment: "Upon the whole the Eskimo is a happy being, his soul being light and cheerful as a child's. If sorrow overtakes him, he may perhaps suffer bitterly for the moment; but it is soon forgotten, and he is once more as radically contented with existence as he used to be. . . ."

"What chiefly cuts the Eskimo to the heart is to see their children starving; and therefore," says Dalager, "they give food to their children even if they themselves are ready to die of hunger; for they live every day in the hope of a happy change of fortune—a hope which really sustains life in many of them."

Professor Boas, in his study of "The Central Eskimo," (*Sixth Annual Report of the Bureau of American Ethnology,* 1884-5, published in 1888) has much to say about the characteristics of the Eskimo. "Real warfare or fights between settlements, I believe, have never happened, but contests have always been confined to single families. The last instance of a feud which has come to my knowledge occurred about seventy years ago. At that time a great number of Eskimo lived at Nuitang, in Kingnait Fjord, and many men of this settlement had been murdered by a Qungamio of Anarnitung. For this reason the men of Nuitang united in a sledge journey to Anarnitung, to revenge the death of their companions. They hid themselves behind the ground ice and killed the returning hunters with their arrows. All hostilities have probably been of a similar nature.

"One tradition only refers to a real fight between the tribes. On the steep island Sagdluagdjung, near Naujateling, ruins of huts are found on the level summit. They are said to have been built by Eskimo who lived by the seashore and were attacked by a hostile tribe of invaders. . . . The occurrence of huts upon the top of an island is very unusual, and this tradition is the only one referring to any kind of fights or wars. Even the tradition of the expulsion of the Torn itself, a fabulous tribe said to have lived with the Eskimo on those shores, does not refer to a combat." It is important to note that the provocation to disorderly conduct was the work of aliens.

The domestic relations of the Eskimo seem to be harmonious. "The parents are very fond of their children and treat them kindly. They are never beaten and rarely scolded and in turn they are very dutiful in obeying the wishes of their parents and taking care of them in their old age. The husband is not allowed to maltreat or punish his wife; if he does she may leave him at any time and the wife's mother can always command a divorce. . . . Children are treated very kindly and are not scolded, whipped, or subjected to any corporal punishment."

The community has no laws beyond a tradition of correct behaviour. "There is no way of enforcing these unwritten laws and no punishment except the blood vengeance. It is not a rare occurrence that a man who is offended by another man takes revenge by killing the offender. It is then the right and duty of the nearest relative of the victim to kill the murderer. In certain quarrels between the Netchillirmuit and the Qivillirmuit, in which the murderer himself could not be apprehended, the family of the murdered man has killed one of the murderer's relations in his stead. Such a feud sometimes lasts for a long time and is even handed down to a succeeding generation. It is sometimes settled by mutual agreement. As a sign of recognition both parties touch each other's breasts, saying Ilaga (my friend).

"Their method of carrying on such a feud is quite foreign to our feelings. Strange as it may seem, a murderer will come to visit the relatives of his victim (though he knows that they are allowed to kill him in revenge) and will settle with them. He is kindly welcomed and sometimes lives quietly for weeks and months. Then he is suddenly challenged to a wrestling match, and if defeated is killed, or if victorious he may kill one of the opposite party, or when hunting he is suddenly attacked by his companions and slain." A man who has committed murder or made himself obnoxious is simply killed as a matter of justice. "The man who intends to take revenge on him must ask his countrymen singly if each agrees in the opinion that the offender is a bad man deserving of death. If all answer in the affirmative he may kill the man thus condemned and no one is allowed to revenge the murder. In the report of the Hudson Bay Expedition of 1886, Lieut. A. Godron remarks that the same custom is reported from Port Burwell, near Cape Chidleigh, Labrador. He says: 'There lived between the Cape and Aulatsivik a good Eskimo hunter whose native name is not given, but who was christened by our station men Old Wicked. He was a passionate man and was continually threatening to do bodily harm to the other more peaceably inclined natives. . . . His arrogance and petty annoyance to the other natives became at length unbearable. It appears that these unfortunates held a meeting and decided that Old Wicked was a public nuisance which must be abated, and they therefore decided that he should be shot, and shot he accordingly was one afternoon when he was busily engaged in repairing the ravages which a storm had made in his "Iglu" or snow house. The executioner shot him in the back, killing him instantly. The murderer or executioner (one hardly knows to which title he is more justly entitled) then takes Old Wicked's wives and all his children and agrees to keep them . . . that they shall be no burden on the company.'

"The fact that the custom is found among tribes so widely separated will justify a description of those events which came under my own observation. There was a native of Padli by the name of Padlu. He had induced the wife of a Cumberland Sound native to desert her husband and follow him. The deserted husband, meditating revenge, cut off the upper part of the barrel of his gun so that he could conceal it under his jacket. He crossed the Sound and visited his friends at Padli, but before he could accomplish his intention of killing Padlu the latter shot him. When this news was reported to the 'eqerten,' the brother of the murdered man went to Padli to avenge the death of his brother, but he also was killed by Padlu. A third native of Cumberland Sound, who wished to avenge the death of his relatives, was also murdered by him. On account of all these outrages the natives wanted to get rid of Padlu, but yet they did not dare to attack him. When the pimian of Akudnirmiut in Niaqonaujang learned of these events he started southward and asked every man in Padli whether Padlu should be killed. All agreed: so he went with the latter deer hunting on the upper part of Pangnirtung, northwest of Padli, and near the head of the fjord he shot Padlu in the back."

Eskimo tribes have a definite method of dealing with strangers. "If a stranger unknown to the inhabitants of a settlement arrives on a visit he is welcomed by the celebration of a great feast. Among the southeastern tribes the natives arrange themselves in a row, one man standing in front of it. The stranger approaches slowly, his arms folded and his head inclined towards the left side. Then the native strikes with all his strength on the right cheek and in his turn inclines his head awaiting the stranger's blow. While this is going on the other men are playing at ball and singing. Thus they continue until one of the combatants is vanquished." The western tribes have similar greeting ceremonies, but in addition "boxing, wrestling, and knife-testing" are mentioned by travellers who have visited them. In Davis Strait and probably in all the other countries the game of "hook and crook" is always played on the arrival of a stranger. Two men sit down on a large skin, after having stripped the upper part of their bodies, and each tries to stretch out the bent arm of the other. These games are sometimes dangerous, as the victor has the right to kill his adversary; but generally the feud ends peaceably. The ceremonies of the western tribes in greeting a stranger are much feared by their eastern neighbours and therefore intercourse is somewhat restricted. The meaning of the duel, according to the natives themselves, is "that the two men in meeting wish to know which of them is the better man. The similarity of these ceremonies to those of Greenland, where the game of hook and crook and wrestling matches have been customary, is quite striking, as is that of the explanation of these ceremonies."

The following account by Mr. Hawkes of the Labrador Eskimo agrees with those of Dr. Nansen and Professor Boas. "We might define an Eskimo village as a sort of communistic settlement. Every one is free to do as he pleases, so long as he does not infringe on the general welfare of the people. When anyone oversteps traditional bounds or makes himself obnoxious to the people, he is admonished by some of the old men or women. 'Somebody speaks,' they say. This usually so humiliates the offender, that no further punishment is necessary. If he continues 'bad-hearted,' he is practically ostracised; he is not allowed to take part in village affairs; he is forbidden to enter the iglus; no one will speak to him or have anything to do with him. This social death is the worst thing that can happen to an Eskimo." If he commits a murder, the men of the village get together and await an opportunity to kill him. No concealment is made of the act, and it is not open to the usual blood-revenge, being considered desirable.

"In the case of ordinary murder, it is the duty of the next of kin to avenge it. Sometimes this act is delayed for many years, as in the case of a man leaving a small boy, who waits until he is old enough to avenge his parent. But the duty is never forgotten. In the meanwhile the murderer may be treated by the relatives of the deceased as if nothing had happened: a situation which is unthinkable to us, but which does not conflict at all with Eskimo ideas.

"In the meantime the murderer is constantly on the watch for the avenger. He never knows when a knife will be thrust into him or when he may be shot or speared from behind. His eyes acquire a shifty look, which the Eskimo says is the mark of a murderer. Sometimes the avengers may come to his own house, as in one case which came to my attention, and are treated as usual guests, until the day of reckoning comes.

"Generally speaking, murder is looked upon with horror by the Eskimo, and the spot where such a deed has been committed is shunned. But they do not scruple to take life, when they feel justified by hard conditions or customs. Aged people who have outlived their usefulness and whose life is a burden both to themselves and their relatives are put to death by stabbing or strangulation. This is customarily done at the request of the individual concerned, but not always so. Aged people who are a hindrance on the trail are abandoned. Deformed children who exhibit some monstrosity which arouses the supernatural fear of the Eskimo are strangled at birth.

"Under ordinary conditions the Eskimo live together in the greatest unity. In times of plenty they feast together, and in times of famine the lucky hunters share their game with the less fortunate. Murder is committed only when jealousy, caused by some love affair, awakens a man's passion, or brooding over a perhaps unintended slight produces a sort of melancholia. But after a man has once committed a murder, he becomes bloodthirsty, and is apt to look for another victim, unless he is put out of the way by the community. Most of these killings have a psychological background. During the dark days of midwinter when the polar winds are blowing, the Eskimo are unable to hunt. They sit inside and gorge themselves with meat, and take little exercise. The congested body reacts on the nervous system and the usually amiable good-natured native becomes sullen and moody. The gloomy surroundings add to his mental depression. He recalls old slights and grudges, and, in this abnormal condition, these often assume exaggerated proportions. It is under such conditions that most of the murders among them occur.

"The good nature and docility of the Eskimo have been emphasised, and rightly: but this does not preclude their committing as barbarous acts as any other savages, particularly when they are subjected to conditions which are favourable to the same. Many of their murders are extremely cold-blooded and unprovoked. The victim is never given a fair chance, but slain when off his guard." (Hawkes, 1916.)

The behaviour of the Eskimo of Alaska differs profoundly from that of their kinsmen further east. "Blood revenge is considered a sacred duty among them, and it is a common thing to find men who dare not visit certain villages because of a blood feud existing, owing to their having killed some one whose near relatives live in the place." . . . "Owing to this custom, a man who has killed another watches incessantly, and in the end acquires a peculiar restless expression which the Eskimo have learned to recognise at once. Several of them told me that they could always recognise a man who had killed another by the expression of his eyes, and from cases observed by myself I think that this is undoubtedly true. The desultory feud existing between the Kotzebue Sound Malemut and the Tinne of the interior partakes of the character of blood revenge, except that each side seeks to revenge the death of relatives or fellow tribesmen upon any of the opposing tribe."

According to Mr. Nelson "the neighbourhood of Bering Strait is particularly noteworthy on account of the warlike habits of the

Eskimo living there. Previous to the arrival of the Russians on the Alaskan shore of the Bering Sea the Eskimo waged an almost constant inter-tribal warfare. At the same time, along the line of contact with the Tinne tribes of the interior, a bitter feud was always in existence. The peoples of the coast from the Yukon mouth to Kotzebue Sound have many tales of villages destroyed by war parties of Tinne. Back from the head of Norton Bay and Kotzebue Sound, during the time of my residence in that region, several Tinne were killed by Malemut while hunting reindeer on the strip of uninhabited tundras lying between the districts occupied by the two peoples. During the summer of 1879 a party of three Malemut from the head of Kotzebue Sound ambushed and killed seven Tinne who were found hunting reindeer in the interior. Warfare was common in other parts of this region. The battles usually took place in the summer, the victors killing all that they could of the males of the other side, including infants, so that they should not grow up enemies. The women were taken as slaves. Young men fighting in their first battle were given some enemy's blood to drink and made to eat a small piece of the heart of an enemy. This was in order to make them brave.

"The Malemut at the head of Kotzebue Sound are another vigorous, overbearing tribe. As among the Eskimo of Bering Strait, they are quarrelsome and have frequent bloody affrays among themselves. The Unalit and Yukon people regard them with the greatest fear and hatred and say that they are like dogs—always showing their teeth and ready to fight. The Malemut are the only Eskimo who keep up the old feud against the Tinne, and are a brave, hardy set of men. They are extremely reckless of human life, and a shaman was killed by them during my residence at St. Michael, because, as they said, 'he told too many lies.' " They buy whisky and have drunken orgies during which men are hurt or killed. "They also had the reputation of being extremely treacherous among themselves, not hesitating to kill one another, even of their own tribe, when opportunity offered while hunting in the mountains—a gun or a few skins being sufficient incentive. As a consequence, hunters among this tribe would not go into the mountains with each other, unless they chanced to be relatives or had become companions by a sort of formal adoption."

The same author states that the Eskimo of Alaska consider that stealing from people of the same village or tribe is wrong, and the man is talked to while in the kashim. "The only feeling of conscience or moral duty that I noted among the Eskimo seemed to be an instinctive desire to do that which was most conducive to the general good of the community, as looked at from their point of view. Whatever experience had taught them to be best was done, guided by superstitious usages and customs." They are very honest, paying all debts contracted with traders. "A curious part of this custom was that very often the same Eskimo who would be perfectly honest and go to great trouble and exertion to settle a debt would not hesitate to steal from the same trader. Among themselves this feeling is not generally so strong, and if a man borrows from another and fails to return the article he is not held to account for it. This is done under the general feeling that if a person has enough property to enable him to lend some of it, he has more than he needs. The one who makes the loan under these circumstances does not even feel justified in asking a return of the article, and waits for it to be given back voluntarily.

"Hospitality is regarded as a duty among the Eskimo, so far as concerns their own friends in the surrounding villages, and to strangers in certain cases, as well as to all guests visiting the villages during festivals. By the exercise of hospitality to their friends and the people of neighbouring villages their good will is retained and they are saved from any evil influence to which they might otherwise be subjected. Strangers were usually regarded with more or less suspicion, and in ancient times were commonly put to death." Nelson usually found them hospitable. Sometimes they were sulky and disobliging. At some places their reception was bad. "On the contrary, at Askinuk and Kaialigamut, in the same district (mouth of the Kuskokwim River) the people ran out at our approach, unharnessed our dogs, put our sledges on the framework, and carried our bedding into the Kashim with the greatest goodwill."

The comments of other travellers are worth noting. Dr. Rink thinks there is no justification for the claim that the Eskimo of Greenland are liars and thieves. Dr. Nordenskiold found the Eskimo of Alaska "friendly and accommodating, honourable in their dealings, though given to begging and to much haggling in making a bargain." The women are regarded as the equals of the men, and the children are well brought up. They have not much personal property.

An American (R. D. Moore) who has recently visited the Eskimo of Bering Strait says that they move about in small groups of relatives, with little authority except what is vested in the old men. He remarks that this is a recent form of government. They have fierce fights over women, who are well treated. "The marriage tie is . . . fully as stable as among the whites and probably more so." Polygamy was formerly common, as among the Eskimo of Indian Point, Siberia. "The St. Lawrence Islander is very fond of his family. He spares the rod, but this does not seem to spoil the child. The older members of the family, especially fathers and older uncles, are treated with extreme reverence and respect, accorded them because of their age and the wisdom garnered from years of experience. To make a request of an old man is not common, to give him advice, the height of impertinence, and to command him, unthinkable.

"The children get on very well together, spending much time in one another's company, playing their simple little games or singing their songs. Only once during the writer's stay on the island was a children's quarrel seen, a record which he never expects to see equalled in a white community where a like number of children are as much thrown together." Mr. Moore finds the people truthful and fairly honest, and he sums up: "On the whole it might be said that these people are possessed of many very likeable qualities, and during his short stay on the island the writer became much attached to them. They have many virtues and their faults might better be called weaknesses which harm no one so much as themselves, while those factors which have made most for their moral and much for their physical degeneration have been introduced from without."

Dr. Rae saw the Eskimo in various places about the middle of the last century (1866). He says of them "They are sober, steady and faithful; generally speaking, honest, and never begging, as is the practice of the Red Indian; comparatively speaking, provident of their own property, and careful of that of others when under their charge. . . . Socially the Esquimaux are a lively, cheerful and chatty people, fond of associating with each other and with strangers, with whom they soon become on friendly terms, if kindly treated. . . . They are hospitable, for they always prepared food, if they had any, for their visitors. . . . In their domestic relations they are exemplary. The man is an obedient son, a good husband and a kind father, nor did I notice a single instance of harshness either to wife or child. The wife is treated as an equal, and indeed generally rules the establishment, which are said to be signs of civilisation. . . . The women show great affection for their babies—I particularly mention this, because a very common opinion prevails that they will give away their child in exchange for a knife, file or other trifle. This mistake has arisen from the mother having pointed to her child and then to the present given herself, meaning thereby, that you were to give something to the child. . . . The children when young are docile, old-fashioned little creatures. When grown up they are dutiful and kind to their parents; so much is this known to be the case, that a large family is considered a great boon, as the old people have then more certainty of being well cared for when they become unable to hunt for themselves." Rae states that the Eskimo are "as a rule truthful." "That they are a well disposed people may be inferred from the fact that for some weeks a number of families, with at least twelve grown men, had been encamped beside the three persons left in charge of our property at winter quarters, and although this property was placed on the rocks and protected by an oilcloth only, not an article was touched or stolen, nor the slightest annoyance given to my men, although sometimes only one of them could remain at home. When the snow thawed about our winter huts in spring, many articles that had been lost, mislaid, or thrown aside, came into view. When the natives found any of these, they were brought to us to find out if we required them."

Rae mentions an interesting contrast in behaviour between the Eskimo of the Coppermine River and those of the Mackenzie River. The first group are "gentle and courteous" and the others are "as turbulent and fierce as the latter are well disposed and peaceable." He goes on to say: "The only reason I can assign for these Eskimo being so different in temper and disposition from their countrymen to the east is, that they have always been at war with the Souchoux Indians, who hunt on the lands in proximity to the sea coast." He sums up his account by saying: "The more I saw of the Eskimo the higher was the opinion I formed of them."

Finally the opinion of Mr. Walter Wood may be quoted. He comments on the behaviour of a community which he observed throughout an Arctic winter. "Throughout the long Arctic winter these 38 men, women and children lived in one room, eating, drinking and sleeping, and mourning and merry-making; yet there was nothing in the nature of a breach of the peace. This amiability and toleration is one of the most notable characteristics of the Eskimo people; indeed they have no word to express scolding, nor have they the equivalent of 'war.'" He speaks of their family relationships: and says that "despite the casual nature of their marriage bond relationship is highly valued, and there is a strongly-developed wish to continue the species, with a particular desire for male descendants: consequently there exists a real regard for children and the little mortals are treated with a care and kindness that could scarcely be expected from parents reared in such a depressing environment. From the cradle to the grave the Eskimo has to fight for his existence, yet everything it is possible to do is done for the children. The youngsters are docile and contented, and rarely know the meaning of harshness or unkindness. Orphans are readily adopted, even when the parents have a number of children to provide for; and it seldom happens that these newcomers are not treated with just the same kindness and consideration that are shown to the parents' own offspring."

Similar testimony is borne by the late Sir Clements R. Markham. "The visitor who first sees a party of Arctic Highlanders will be at once struck by their merry good-natured countenances, their noisy fun, and boisterous laughter." He quotes Dr. Kane as saying that "when troubles came upon him or his people, never have friends been more true than these Arctic Highlanders."

The Dene Indians

South of the Eskimo live the Athabascan Dene, who, with the exception of some branches who have come into contact with the coastal peoples, wander about in bands with no chiefs. They have, it is said, no religion in the ordinary sense of the term, yet they rank high (according to Mr. Hill Tout) in all moral qualities except courage. They never resort to arms, but, in the case of a conflict, opponents lay aside their knives and wrestle with each other, grasping each other's hair. Their folk-tales show that "their lives were moral and well-regulated: that deep shame and disgrace followed a lapse from virtue in the married and unmarried of both sexes. The praise and enjoyment of virtue, self-discipline, and abstinence in young men is no less clearly brought out; whilst the respect and consideration paid by the young everywhere to their elders affords an example that more advanced races might with profit copy."

The Salish

South and west of the Dene people of North America live the Salish. Those on the coast have social classes and at times are warlike, but the inland branches live in small communities of hunters. They were formerly "well-regulated, peace-loving, and virtuous people, whose existence was far from being squalid or miserable." Father de Smet says that "the beau-ideal of the Indian character, uncontaminated by contact with the whites, is found among them. What is most pleasing to the stranger is to see their simplicity, united with sweetness and innocence, keep step with the most perfect dignity and modesty of deportment. The gross vices which dishonour the red man on the frontiers are utterly unknown among them. They are honest to simplicity. The Hudson Bay Company during the forty years that it has been trading in furs has never been able to perceive that the smallest object has been stolen from them. The agent takes his furs down to Colville every spring, and does not return before autumn. During his absence the store is confided to the care of an Indian, who trades in the name of the company, and on the return of the agent renders him a most exact account of the trust. The store often remains without anyone to watch it, the door unlocked and unbolted, and the goods are never stolen. The Indians go in and out, help themselves to what they want, and always leave in place of whatever article they take, its exact value."

The Algonquian

The Eastern Algonquin peoples of Canada, north of the St. Lawrence, were formerly, as a rule, peaceful. The Ojibway, for example, were divided into two branches. Whilst the Southern division, who were partly agricultural, were very warlike, the Northern Ojibway, called Chipewas, were generally mild and harmless, little disposed to make war upon other tribes.

The Beothuk

The Beothuk, the former inhabitants of Newfoundland, were harmless and tractable, mild and gentle in disposition, with strong family affection, and great love for children.

The Paiute

In pre-Columbian times the territory we now call the United States was occupied for the greater part by peoples who had a warlike organisation, and sometimes hereditary chiefs. They made pottery, worked metals and grew maize. But certain peoples were peaceful. Some of these still survive. Prominent among them are the Paiute of Nevada, Utah and Arizona, who generally wander about in small bands. They are relatively uncultured, neither making pottery nor practising agriculture. "As a rule they are peaceful, moral and industrious, and are highly commended for their good qualities by those who have had the best opportunity for judging. While apparently not so bright in intellect as the prairie tribes, they appear to possess more solidity of character, and have steadily resisted the vices of civilisation." (Handbook of American Indians, Vol. II, p. 187, 1912.)

Californian Indians

Professor Kroeber of the University of California says that "from the time of the first settlement of California, its Indians have been described as both more primitive and more peaceful than the majority of the natives of North America."

Speaking of the Cahuilla Indians, Mr. Hooper says, "Unselfishness and respect for the old people is their ideal of right living.

Children are taught from infancy to be generous and kind to the old. . . . Liberality and generosity were considered the most important virtues. The man who was the best hunter was held in very high esteem. The woman who could do the most work in the shortest time was the ideal woman. Nowadays these things do not seem to matter so much.

"There was always real affection between the members of an Indian family but very little outward demonstration of it." He goes on to say that "the Cahuilla, like most of the Californian Indians, have been a very peaceful people. Their main troubles were between villages, and were caused by boundary disputes."

Among the Hupe, according to Dr. Goddard, "children are seldom punished or handled roughly when small. They are thought to be above the natural and likely to disappear, going to the world of immortals if they are ill-used." Also "disagreements were common among (them). They arose more frequently over personal injury or insult than over matters relating to property. . . . Personal insult or injury is followed by absolute non-intercourse."

Among the Californian Indians we find a characteristic that is reminiscent of the peoples of Australia. "Warfare in California," according to Professor Kroeber, "was carried on only for revenge, never for plunder or from a desire for distinction. The Mohave and Ymua must indeed be excepted from this statement, but their attitude is entirely unique. Probably the cause that most commonly originated feuds was the belief that a death had been caused by witchcraft. No doubt theft and disputes of various sorts contributed. Once ill feeling was established, it was likely to continue for long periods."

The Tierra Del Fuegians

The peoples of Tierra del Fuego are said to be affectionate, but very undemonstrative. Parental and filial affection exist, as is shown by the care taken of children and the deference paid to parents. Although quite nude these people are modest. They are generous and share with each other. Lying is allowed, but murder is banned. The different groups are hostile, and occasional rows occur in which one or more men may be killed. But in the same group friends interpose to pacify the disputants.

Siberians

Some of the peoples of Siberia are so lacking in culture as to be classed with the Food-Gatherers. They keep reindeer, but do not cultivate the soil, which, indeed, is impossible in the greater part of their lands. Professor Ratzel states that "by far the greater number of testimonies to the character of the Hyperboreans are favourable. Honourable, good-tempered, inoffensive is the praise given by the Russians to nearly all the peoples of Northern Asia. It is doubly strong, if we consider the mass of wickedness with which for some decades the deportation of criminals from Russia has been leavening the whole mass. Russian hunters say that only in cases of extreme necessity will an Orochone touch the store of provisions that a hunter has left for his own use. Middendorf asks with surprise, 'Whence comes such exemplary honesty among these poor starving wretches?' And one may well say that the history of Arctic travel would have a far larger list of disasters to show but for the effective help and open-handed assistance of the Hyperborean races. Their way of life is an admirable teacher of the social virtues. The Samoyedes are good-tempered and peaceful: the Chuckchis live in a state of the greatest unanimity: the Ostiak of the Ob have retained a great part of their childlike good-temper, their contentedness and honesty. But all are united by a certain cheery composure, far removed from the melancholy imagined in them by those who meditated on their life under the inspiration of civilised nerves." The Lapps are said to be "of a cheerful temperament, fond of gossip, very hospitable, and much given to merry meetings and family gatherings, at which the feelings whether of joy or sorrow find ready vein in copious weeping" (Keane). They are fond of drink. In other respects they are described as "extremely peaceful, possessing no effective weapons, carrying on no inter-tribal feuds, kind, good natives, and, except in Russia, strictly honest and trustworthy." In another place they are described as "these kindly and inoffensive nomads." Another writer describes them thus, "All have to struggle equally hard for existence. They are, however, cheery and contented. They endure with indifference and even manage to enjoy hard conditions of life under which more civilised peoples could not possibly exist."

The Samoyedes, as Ratzel says, are given a good character by all who have known them. "No one could be more sociable than the Samoyede. He is extremely hospitable to his tribesmen and to strangers; he delights in gossip; his smile is almost continuous, and his harsh laugh loud and frequent. Visiting each other seems the favourite social occupation—a Samoyede will go a long way out of his road in order to put in an appearance at a choom which he knows to be in the neighbourhood; and during the whole time I was in the country I never saw a blow struck, or even witnessed a serious squabble. It will be interesting to some of my readers, perhaps, to hear that the women are also on the best of terms with each other, and, as far as I could learn of course, there was no wrangling and little backbiting" (Jackson). Both father and mother are kind to their children, who, on their side, show no fear of their parents. (Rae, *Land of the North Wind*). Benard states that *"les moeurs sont familiales et paisibles."* Another traveller who knows them says the same. They are "affectionate, even-tempered, honest, and possess a certain pride of independence, which it would not be difficult to convert into a sense of self-respect. They work hard, and to beg they are ashamed; hospitable to a degree they are preeminently a sociable people." They are "honest, cheery, capable *'compagnons de voyage.'"* (Montefiore.) They are said by another writer to be a "kindly and cheerful people, very hospitable and generous in sharing the things that come into their possession."

The Character of Natural Man

This extensive series of quotations, which might easily have been multiplied a hundred fold, represents an impartial and unbiassed picture of the real character of mankind when free from the complications and embarrassments of civilisation. The Food-Gatherers include members of races as different as the Australian, Negro and Mongol and live under conditions as varied as it is possible to be—ranging in climate from the tropics to the Arctic, and in environment from the tropical heart of the continent of Africa, and the small islands like the Andamans, to the icy regions of Greenland, Alaska and Northern Siberia.

As there is no reason for supposing that all these varied peoples have lost a culture they once enjoyed, it seems justifiable to assume that they represent the survival of the state that was common to all mankind before civilisation was created about sixty centuries ago. In those times men were without houses and clothes, without social or political organisation, without property or any restraints upon their freedom other than such as common decency and consideration for other human beings imposed. Free from the common causes of exasperation, envy and malice, the innate goodness and kindliness of Man found unhampered opportunities for expression. Men were happy and peaceful, kind and considerate. In spite of the discomforts and anxieties of daily life men cheerfully enjoyed a state of Arcadian simplicity. It was indeed the Golden Age of which poets have been writing for thirty centuries. The contemptuous denials of cynics and philosophers that mankind was ever peaceful and contented are rendered nugatory by the unimpeachable testimonies quoted in the foregoing pages. It still remains for us to consider the circumstances that were responsible for the introduction of the serpent of discord into this Garden of Eden.

Behaviour in Family Groups

Let us now consider the significance of the evidence that has been submitted. Writers with a personal knowledge of various peoples have been made to record their observations of the societies with which they came into contact. Thus the evidence we are discussing is objective: the total effect of the quotation of a large number of independent witnesses describing what they actually saw is to eliminate any suspicion of bias in estimating the real character of primitive Man.

The peoples who have come under observation—Negritos from Africa, the Andamans, Malay and the Philippines; Australoids from Ceylon, Malay, and Australia; Mongoloids from Borneo, America and Asia—are a miscellaneous assortment that includes members of three of the great racial divisions of mankind, the Alpine, Mediterranean and Nordic being excluded.

These people live in every possible variety of climatic environment. The Negritos live, as a rule, in the tropical forest, whether in Africa or in Southeastern Asia. The Eskimo, Samoyedes and Ostiak live in the Arctic regions. Between these extremes of climate and environment are the tribes of the woodlands of Canada; the natives of Utah, Nevada, and other states of the western plains in the United States; and the Californian Indians, situated in one of the most comfortable climates in the world. The Australian natives enjoy a variety of climatic conditions, for they live, or in the past have lived, in all parts of the continent, from the dry plains and barren deserts of the centre to the hilly and rainy districts of and delightful East coast.

The descriptions do not warrant us in assuming that this racial and climatic diversity has had any profound influence upon the character of the primitive people we have been considering. Obviously the Eskimo must deal with the peculiar conditions of the frozen North as must the Australian with the more genial hills and plains. The one eats walrus, and the other kangaroo. Local materials must of necessity influence crafts. But it does not seem possible to discover particular types of behaviour distinctive of the various peoples. On the contrary, their geniality and morality are surprisingly uniform in spite of the variety of discomforts and exasperations to which they are subjected. The failure of racial or climatic conditions to influence social behaviour in the case of this widespread series of peoples is obviously a fact of fundamental importance in estimating the true character of primitive Man— and a striking commentary on the efforts of those historians who from the time of Bodin in 1566 onwards have claimed a decisive influence for climate in determining human character and achievement.

No evidence has appeared throughout the whole range of Food-Gatherers of any division into social classes. Differentiation of rank has not yet begun. Equality is the rule.

The fundamental social element of this primitive society is the group of relatives, the Family, in the wider sense of the term. The people go about in small bands, consisting either of a single family, sometimes of three generations, or of two or more brothers and their families. Village life, in the sense of the more or less permanent grouping of families not related to one another, is only mentioned in the Andamans; and there is no doubt that, in these islanders, external influence is responsible for this definitely alien practice. For the Andamanese village reveals features resembling, and clearly borrowed from, those of agricultural peoples in the neighbouring lands. A conspicuous example is the "bachelor's house." But there are other reasons for concluding that Andamanese culture is strongly tainted with external influence.

Each of the family groups among all truly primitive peoples ranges over a limited area, which other groups respect as their domain. They rarely make any permanent settlement. As a rule they do not have any intercourse with the other family groups of the same tribe. Even in those cases where village life of a sort has begun, the family is still the fundamental unit of society, for each family lives apart from the others. The family is therefore the constant and essential unit of primitive society.

The family is the grouping invariably formed in the absence of an alien influence not only in human communities but also in the Man-like Apes. It is thus the social unit that gives expression to Man's innate tendencies. Important corroboration of the essential importance of the family as a genuinely primitive feature of human society is revealed by the similarity of the habits and the social arrangements of the anthropoid apes to those of primitive Man. These significant comparisons are brought out with conspicuous lucidity in Dr. S. Zuckerman's memoir on *The Social Life of the Primates* published in *The Realist* (July, 1929). If, therefore, any other organisation is found superimposed upon the family groups, such, for example, as the village, there must be some specific reason for it.

Village life, in the sense of an association of independent families, cannot be ascribed to the working of any innate tendency common to the whole of mankind. It was entirely absent until a very special set of circumstances compelled men to resort to such a close association as life in villages involves. Anyone who has lived in a village will realise how unnatural such a mode of life is and how perilous it is to the chance of survival of those primitive qualities of geniality and forbearance displayed by the nomads living in family groups. The artificial aims created by civilisation provoke in a village all kinds of rivalry and jealousy, which in most part of the world lead to physical violence, but in Western Europe (and the countries that draw their cultural capital from it) usually to nothing more than violent or abusive language or malicious scandal-mongering.

These considerations have a bearing on the theory of the so-called "Herd Instinct." They go to show that, whatever meaning may be assigned to this speculative term, the evidence we have been collecting reveals no hint of the assembling of any "herd" other than the family group, either for self-defence or any other purpose. Parents, children and their grandparents remain in association to form the family: but it is not a herd in the sense of the speculative psychologists and sociologists.

The "primal horde" of Mr. J. J. Atkinson (*Primal Law* 1903) and many recent writers, including Professor Freud (*Totem and Taboo,* 1919), is fiction pure and simple and the ethnological theories based upon it are illusory. The "Herd Instinct" belongs to the same category of misleading speculation. Reference is made to these popular fads here only to impress upon the reader that they are not forgotten but definitely discarded.

With certain exceptions, which will have to be considered later, there does not appear to be any tribal organisation among peoples ignorant of agriculture or stock-rearing. Although there are tribes in the sense of groups speaking a common language, and occupying a more or less continuous tract of land (and sometimes, as in Malaya, distinguished from other tribes by certain physical characteristics), yet there is no tribal cohesion. The tribe has no corporate existence. It is misleading to speak of tribal rites. When we refer to, say, the Semang, what we mean is not a complex coordinated form of society differing from the family, but a series of independent family groups, similar in physical type, language and habitat. There is no observable tendency among these lowly folk to weld together these scattered, autonomous groups into such an entity as many popular writers understand by the word tribe.

Much social theory rests upon the supposition that the social organism, the tribe, the state, has some organic structure which must be preserved. Age-grades analogous to the "classes" in an American College are often called "tribal" in East Africa and have been claimed to be necessary to the preservation of the life of the association of family groups. In his work on *The Andaman Islanders,* Professor Radcliffe Brown has recently attempted to analyse the customs of these people on such a basis. Their marriage practices and their mourning customs are claimed to have as their purpose the maintenance of the corporate life. Yet the evidence already set forth in the preceding pages indicates that there is nothing to warrant the belief in anything other than the family as the natural or inevitable mode of social grouping, based on biological foundations, as the analogy with the anthropoid apes proves. There is no valid reason for the belief in any innate or inevitable tendency to develop larger and more complicated modes of grouping. Such groupings have come into being, as everyone knows, but their mode of origin calls for explanation. Only when their raison d'être has been satisfactorily explained will it be possible to build up a theory as to their rôle in society.

It is often said that social classes began with the domination of the strongest man of the tribe. But if there is no such thing as the tribe this theory falls to the ground. The domination of the strong man in a form of society consisting mainly of family groups is a contradiction in terms. The only instance of the sort is mentioned in the case of the Bushmen, but even there the domination does not last, and it certainly is not perpetuated from generation to generation, as it is when many families have agreed to live together in a community with a definite social organisation. The persons who effected such an organisation became a ruling class and created the hereditary principle.

The family group is the fundamental social unit among three at least of the six races of mankind. We may assume, as a working hypothesis, that originally it was also the unit of the three remaining races.

Much has been written concerning the original matrimonial arrangements, whether monogamy or polygamy was the natural state of Man. The dominant school of sociologists in England, led by Professors Westermarck, Hobhouse and Malinowski, adopts the view that originally monogamy was the usual custom among mankind, but in certain cases polygamy developed later. The evidence quoted in the foregoing pages provides definite support for this contention. The Food-Gatherers as a whole are credited with being mainly, and sometimes wholly, monogamous. Time after time special comment is made by observers upon this feature of primitive society. The strict monogamy of these lowly folk is contrasted with the looseness of the surrounding peoples. In Man's ancestors, as Dr. Zuckerman has pointed out, polygamy seems to have been the natural mode of behaviour. But it is probable that new circumstances arose when the earliest human beings became nomadic hunters and these imposed upon Man the monogamous custom. How frail is the monogamous impulse, however, is shown by the readiness with which polygamy is adopted when the primitive mode of life gives place to civilisation. Then Man tends to revert to the methods of the gorilla and displays his power by the acquisition of women and the creation of harems.

The evidence of Mr. Schebesta concerning the Semang of Malaya is of interest, for it suggests that the union of the sexes is not the only factor that conduces to monogamous union. He says, it will be remembered, that young married couples who have no children will often dissolve partnership; but once children are born, the union becomes stable. Marriage among Food-Gatherers is usually stable. This is expressly stated to be the case among the Congo Negritos, the Veddahs, the Semang, the Sakai, the Punan and others. Adultery is said to be very rare, in contrast to the conduct of the surrounding agriculturalists and stock-rearers.

The family group, whether monogamous or polygamous, is invariably said to be harmonious. The children are well treated, and are rarely scolded or punished. Contrary to expectation, they behave themselves, and do not quarrel among themselves. The Semang children, for instance, are said to be a model for civilised children in this respect. As would be expected, the children, being well treated by their parents, in their turn look after them when they grow old. The common rule is for these family groups to be described as cheerful, happy and in every way harmonious.

The harmony within the group of relatives extends to all forms of behaviour. There is almost complete absence of strife. Food is shared in common, and there is no evidence of the tendency of the individual to keep what he has found or hunted. He sinks his personality in the interests of his relatives. No mention is made of any tendency to share with groups who are not related.

Each individual, man or woman, has his or her weapons or other paraphernalia which are necessary for personal use. Beyond that there is no trace of any accumulating of property beyond what is necessary for immediate needs. Theft is practically unknown to these people when free from alien interference. Moreover, they are invariably honest, until they become contaminated by peoples of higher culture.

These lowly peoples are hospitable to strangers who are usually received in a friendly manner, and without violence. In certain peoples, for example the Bushmen and Veddahs, each group has its own hunting grounds, and violently resists any intrusion on its preserves. But other peoples, such as the Negritos of Luzon, do not seem to resent such intrusion. This conflict of evidence makes it doubtful whether the violent resistance is original, or whether it is not due to the past experience of these peoples. The Bushmen, it is well known, have suffered for centuries from aggression on the part of the neighbouring Bantu and Europeans, and this can well have engendered a violent resistance towards intruders. Similarly in the case of the Congo Pygmies and the Veddahs. The general rule among Food-Gatherers appears to be one of mutual toleration, each group respecting the territory of the others.

Within the group of relatives there is a strong feeling of respect for the elders. This is mentioned by more than one writer. This respect does not seem to be based on fear, for, as has been seen, the practice of violent punishment is negligible. The elders control the small community, so far as any control is needed, and constitute the sole source of authority. There is little or no government among such peoples, and little or no organisation for maintaining peace. It is hardly necessary among people who do not lie or thieve or break the marriage tie to any formidable extent. A harmonious group will carry on its life practically without the need of any organised authority. The natural respect accorded to elders serves to conduct such common affairs as are necessary, and to take the proper decisions for the best ordering of the life of the community.

The elders carry on a certain amount of education. The children are taught to behave themselves, to be hospitable, and generally to conduct themselves as decent members of society. Judging from the results, it is the most efficient form of education in the world, since it produces a more complete balance within society than any other.

Since primitive men are cheerful, happy folk, fond of their families, and living in groups of relatives, it is not surprising that violent behaviour in the group is rare. Murders do sometimes occur, but only very rarely. Nothing, however, is known about the actual causes of its occurrence in these rare instances, so we do not know whether it is due when it occurs to an unstable mind, and therefore is to be discounted altogether. But some of the Food-Gatherers, certain of the Eskimo, for instance, are said to commit murders, and to make them an excuse for fighting. Murder also occurs among the Australian natives, but usually in certain definite circumstances. For the present it can be said that among undisturbed primitive peoples any sort of violence is surprisingly rare.

Warfare, in the sense of organised conflicts between groups, is virtually non-existent among truly primitive peoples. Certain groups, notably the Eskimo, the Andamanese and the Australians have definite warfare, in the sense that different groups come into more or less regular conflict. But the others do not manifest any tendency to fight, and certainly lack any military organisation or training. Before complete confidence can be placed in this generalisation, the exceptions will have to be discussed.

Primitive people are innocent of the more horrible practices that are found among mankind. They are not addicted to head-hunting, nor do they practice human sacrifice. They are never cannibals. They do not torture other human beings. They are not wantonly cruel.

The fact that primitive people do not, in their original condition, display any well-marked tendency towards violence, either within the community or between communities, does not mean that they are incapable of it. They often display great bravery, such, for example, as the instances already mentioned in the accounts of the Congo Pygmies and the Bushmen. They can and do fight when necessary in defence of their lives or their means of subsistence. When provoked they can be very cruel, as in the case of the fights between Europeans and Bushmen, or Europeans and Tasmanians. There is not the slightest doubt, however, that this cruel behaviour is a reaction to aggression, and, it must be confessed, an imitation of behaviour exhibited by those of more advanced culture. The majority of the Food-Gatherers do not, when undisturbed, display cruelty or violent behaviour. Their behaviour is stable and peaceful.

The manifestation of anger is of interest in connection with the exhibition of violent behaviour. Professor Radcliffe Brown states that Andamanese, when angry, will not attempt as a rule to harm the person with whom they are angry, but will shoot an arrow near him, or will destroy property, often their own. Such incidents suggest that aggression on the person of the offender is not the necessary result of an insult.

The quick reaction to aggression manifested by otherwise amiable primitive people has been regarded by some writers as a sign of instability of character. The natives of Australia have been described by the Rev. John Mathew and others as unstable in their behaviour. It is easy to turn the cheerful, well-disposed Bushman into a remorseless enemy, capable of malicious cruelty, not ready to forget cruelties or injuries practised upon him. His equilibrium is soon disturbed, for it is supposed not to rest upon a stable foundation. The readiness with which an otherwise gentle and considerate man can suddenly become vindictive and spiteful cannot be regarded, however, as a token of unstable character. It is rather a manifestation of the reality of his inborn goodness. For the man who knows no other code of morals than honesty and kindness will naturally react much more violently against the novel discovery of human beings so devoid of real humanity as to be dishonest and cruel. Even a civilised man who tries to be considerate and generous is apt to react much more violently to chicanery in others than would a hardened villain. Thus it is not surprising to find the most violent and wholesale display of savagery amongst "the gentle and noble savages" after the shock of their contact with a civilisation which first reveals to them the, to them, unnatural vices of envy, malice and all uncharitableness. When we recall the sort of practises which most primitive men have learned from their first impact with alien culture—head-hunting, other forms of human sacrifice and a variety of other forms of violence—it is not surprising that unsophisticated people, who do not fully understand the meaning of these things (beyond realising the gross injustice and inhumanity of the new experience), should resort to the only kind of reaction they understand and try to meet cruelty with more cunning forms of cruelty, and treachery with even more vindictive and malicious reprisals. For once the innocence of the Golden Age is demoralised it requires all the wisdom and magnanimity of the highest form of culture to recover the primitive virtues of tolerance and generosity.

So far nothing has been said of the more definitely intellectual aspects of the lives of the Food-Gatherers. Attention has been concentrated on the moral aspects of their social behaviour. The Food-Gatherers have survived since the birth of mankind without learning much, certainly not originating much. But there is one feature of their lives which impresses everyone who has lived with them. They know all that there is to be known about the behaviour of the animals and the obvious properties of the plants they use for food. They are always expert hunters and trackers: they know all about the products of the jungle, or whatever region they live in. Their attention is fixed on their food-supply, and they readily accumulate knowledge on this subject, and pass it on to their children. But in spite of this constant preoccupation with their food they do not seem to have acquired any degree of foresight. They are universally improvident. When there is plenty of food they eat to repletion without attempting to store it up for the future. They share it with their relatives and do not seek to keep any for themselves. When it is lacking they starve. No doubt they realise the fact that most foods tend to putrefy. They may appreciate the difficulty of hoarding food, without knowing how to cope with the problems involved in such attempts. Even cereals and edible seeds are apt to germinate when no proper receptacles or dry places for storing them have yet been invented. But such difficulties are merely illustrations of the factors that discourage the attempts to look ahead and be provident on the part of a people who have not yet learned to appreciate even the possibility of storing up food. They have lived through countless ages, and have not found it possible to invent any of the arts and crafts that seem to us to be so obvious and so imperative for existence to be tolerable. The people who first got the idea of the possibility of storing up food were thereby definitely committed to the task of creating civilisation.

This review makes it clear that human societies can exist with hardly any more trace of culture than a chimpanzee displays. Take from the Negrito his bow and arrow, which he presumably borrowed from another people, and nothing is left but a society that only differs from that of the apes in enjoying a greater skill in capturing game, in being able to communicate information to one another, and in utilising that information. Of constructive efforts of originality there is little or no trace. Apart from implements of stone, bone and wood they invented nothing. These people evidently had not begun to make houses, to clothe themselves, to practise any of the various arts and crafts except making implements, to develop tribal organisation, to create ruling classes, or to form such a society as exists among many other peoples. The cultural level of the Food-Gatherers, in fact, may be defined as a lack of everything we call culture. It is, we may say, as innocent of institutions, of forms of behaviour common to groups of men, as can well be imagined.

The family as the only form of social grouping is so common to all Food-Gatherers that it must be classed as the innate biological association, and not as having been deliberately planned or produced by social influences. It is, in fact, the form of society that is found among the apes.

The family group is a complicated affair. It consists of a man and a woman, in the first instance, and the children produced by their union. Whatever may be the innate tendency of the man as an individual, or the woman as an individual, they tend when associated together to live harmoniously under primitive conditions. The union is stable. This may be due to the equality of the sexes, to the desire of the woman for one mate, and the power to restrain the supposed polygamous tendencies of the man. Whatever the reasons, the result is the monogamous union. Economic causes may well play a part. It may not be possible for a man to keep more than one wife. Or it may be that the monogamous habits are the reflection of the democratic nature of the society, no man being in a position, or desiring as a rule, to outdo his fellows, if it be that he considered the possession of more than one wife a superiority. Dr. Zuckerman has suggested that the contrast between the sexual behaviour of Man and the apes may be due to the fact that the human male, having to spend most of his time hunting for animal food, could not guard a harem as the ape does. The real meaning of the pronounced monogamy of the Food-Gatherers, however, still awaits a satisfactory explanation. One further fact must be borne in mind. The family includes children in addition to parents, and these may play a decisive part in stabilising the union. For the Semang marriages are not stable until children are born. Children are universally loved and petted by these people, so that they may play a fundamental part in rendering matrimonial union durable. Children are the cement of society.

The discovery that the group of relatives, the family in the larger sense of the term, is the fundamental group of society, makes it possible to go one step further, and to establish the standard of behaviour to which all others can ultimately be referred. Harmony, cheerfulness, affection, mutual help, are the common characteristics in such groups. That is to say, when human beings are subjected to no other influences than those of the family, they will be cheerful, happy and peaceful. Any deviation from this normal type is, therefore, to be ascribed to the influence of some institution or other, when it is not due to pathological causes in the individual.

When it is found that the Food-Gatherers of to-day are so harmonious in their lives, it is inevitable to institute some comparison between these communities, and those, say, of Western Europe of to-day, whose life certainly is not so harmonious. Many observers of primitive peoples make such comparisons, and speak in enthusiastic terms of the "moral" behaviour of the primitives. But it must be realised that in making this comparison such observers are forgetting that the experience of primitive communities has been vastly different from ours. Now the Food-Gatherers represent the type of community that has persisted for untold ages with practically no advance whatever in culture. For ages their parents and forbears have lived quite untroubled simple lives, and have elaborated, or have inherited from their simian ancestry, the harmonious type of behaviour so characteristic of their type of social grouping. Such behaviourism confers an obvious biological advantage. Family groups which hold together so harmoniously would be greatly favoured in the struggle for existence, their chance of survival obviously surpassing those who indulged in violence towards each other. The consideration shown by primitive people for their children's welfare and happiness is essential for preserving the babies throughout their long childhood. For these and for other reasons harmonious family behaviour would be the most profitable for early men. But these communities differ greatly from our own in their circumstances. For various reasons we have acquired habits of violence, and have adopted vicious habits that were unknown to our food-gathering forbears. The life of an ordinary civilised man or woman thus consists often in a struggle with desires that must be repressed. It does not follow that these desires are so active among peoples of low culture. It is this element of struggle, of choice between good and evil, that enters into ethical questions; and to import such considerations into the discussion of the behaviour of the Food-Gatherers is to prejudge the whole question. It is evident, of course, that the facts cited in the preceding pages cannot be ignored by those who are discussing ethical questions. That, however, is not a matter for this book, the aim of which is to describe and explain various types of behaviour so far as that is possible, but not to evaluate them.

The study of the Food-Gatherers will serve in the end to help in the elucidation of the problem of instinct in Man. For their form of society manifests human behaviour at its simplest. They have so far escaped many of the complexities of civilisation, and can thus provide a basis of discussion.

A typical primitive people manifests the working of two great groups of innate tendencies. First there is the preservation of life, getting food and avoiding danger. This form of activity is common to all living creatures. Without it the organism would perish. The other great group of innate tendencies comprises those centring round the function of procreation, which is necessary for the survival of the species. But the innate tendencies concerned with reproduction are involved in the complicated grouping of sentiments that centre round the family, and include the relationship of man and wife, as well as those of parents and children, with all their interactions.

There is a tendency in every human being to exhibit himself in the best possible light, to show his superiority over all others. This is revealed, for example, in situations in which degrees of skill or courage can exhibit themselves. The Bushmen honoured the best hunter. This makes men strive to hunt better than their fellows. The biological significance of this tendency is obvious enough. It is clearly an essential element in the individual's struggle for existence. It is an innate mode of behaviour.

Primitive Man has been credited with an acquisitive instinct. Using the term to mean the accumulation of objects beyond personal needs, there does not seem to be any reason for supposing that Food-Gatherers display such a tendency. On the contrary, they do not thieve, and they share what they possess among their relatives. These facts suggest in the first place a lack of any tendency to get objects for the sake of acquiring them, it suggests that there is no tendency to hold objects once they are obtained. It may be, of course, that the influence of the social group prevents the manifestation of this selfish characteristic, that it represses it. In this case an individual who became released from these repressing agencies might display acquisitiveness.

A similar argument may be brought forward with regard to violence. While it seems certain that the family group is predominantly peaceful in its behaviour, it may be that what really is happening is a repression of the pugnacious and violent tendencies of the individual. If the children were not taught by precept and example to behave themselves, they would be quarrelsome and violent. What seems to happen in this case is that the interaction of sentiment in the family group produces a form of behaviour that is mainly peaceful. This peacefulness even extends itself towards strangers.

The cheerful, happy frame of mind is really the normal condition in human beings. Manifestations of violence and anger are neither normal nor healthy. They produce bad physiological effects in the individual. The over-secretion of adrenalin which happens under the influence of such emotions as anxiety and anger, and is inevitable during fighting, is not good for the organism as a whole. While our bodies are so fashioned as to enable us to fight in self-defence and to display anger and violence, such reactions are intended only for use in exceptional circumstances. A contented mind is "the divine gift." The society in which all is peace is the healthy society.

The conclusion suggested by the facts is that the type of behaviour in family groups is stable, happy, cheerful, and lacking in violence. This may therefore be regarded as the standard of behaviour for human society.

CHAPTER VII

THE BEGINNING OF CIVILISATION

THE creation of civilisation was the most tremendous revolution in the whole course of Human History. Within a few centuries so profound a change was effected in the mode of life, the aims and occupations, and in the size of the population and in the areas affected by these changes, as to open a new chapter of Man's career with new standards of values and new social conditions and aspirations.

Civilisation is not simply a jumble of new arts and crafts. It is an amazingly complex organisation which gave Man an entirely new outlook on the world and his activities in it. It involved a great deal more than the mere invention of even so impressive a list of new occupations as irrigation and agriculture, cattle-breeding and pottery-making, weaving and house-building, working gold and copper, carpentry and stonemasonry, architecture and boat-building, the making of clothing and the brewing of beer, the use of arithmetic and the devising of calendars. It was responsible for the origin of the kingship and for conferring upon the king the reputation of being not merely the distributor of the waters of irrigation, but also the actual Giver of Life to the land and to the seed which the inundation made fertile; of being not merely the measurer of the year and the predictor of the time of inundation, but also the actual cause of the inundation and the Creator of the dry land that emerged when the waters subsided. The king was the Giver of Life and the Creator. He was regarded as the source of the life of the whole population and the creator of the State. In a much more absolute sense than was involved in the famous boast of the King of France, the earliest king in the history of the world was regarded as "The State."

When it was discovered, by observation of the heliacal rising of the star Sirius, that the Sun was a more accurate measurer of the year than the moon and, as the early Egyptians thought, also the cause of the inundation, they identified it with the king, who had already been credited with the same functions. The dead king was then believed to pass to the sky and become one with the Sun. This idea of the Sun-God involved the creation of a sky world as the home of dead kings, who attained immortality by becoming identified with the great Giver of Life in the celestial regions.

The conception of a State System in which the king was the sole source of life and prosperity and the arbiter of every happening in the whole universe completely transformed the conditions of existence for his subjects. They became puppets who had to dance to the tune he called. As the influence of this artificial conception was diffused throughout the world the acceptance of civilisation involved the imposition of the shackles of this amazing tradition. Civilised societies suffered this tyranny for thirty centuries before an Ionian trader, enjoying the newly found freedom which the invention of a metallic currency had given private individuals, defied the dominant system and restored to human reason the right of Man to think for himself, no longer hampered by theocratic shackles.

We must now in turn examine the circumstances under which these two miracles were wrought—the Creation of Civilisation and the Emancipation of Reason from the tyranny of the early theory of the State.

In the preceding chapters evidence has been cited to demonstrate that for hundreds of thousands of years before the inauguration of the social system of city life we call civilisation, men of different races had been wandering throughout the whole extent of the continental areas of the world. Apart from the making of such simple implements of flint, bone and wood as were necessary for the capture of animals for food or for protecting themselves from wild beasts, these primitive men were devoid of any arts and crafts. They were simply nomads wholly occupied in the pursuit of food and in an unceasing vigil to safeguard their existence. In these pursuits their distinctively human qualities of vision and understanding enabled them to acquire amazing skill and cunning, so that they survived in competition with the greater strength and speed, and the power to inflict damage, possessed by many animals. They led a life of happy innocence. The world was theirs. They had neither houses nor farms to tie them to one place. They had neither clothes nor property to carry about with them. They had no leaders to command their actions or hampering social or political regulations to restrict their freedom.

What then were the circumstances that brought to an end this era of Arcadian simplicity with its "liberty, equality and fraternity," to use the phraseology which the French Humanists of the eighteenth century devised from their study of Natural Man?

Before embarking on this enquiry it is important to get some idea, however rough and lacking in precision it must necessarily be, of the fewness of early nomads. It is estimated that the present population of the world is roughly 1700 millions of human beings. "The descendants of a single pair of human beings increasing at the rate of 1 per cent per annum (the present rate of increase of the world as a whole) would amount in little more than 200 years to this figure" (A. M. Carr-Saunders, *Population*, Oxford 1925). The Australian statistician, the late Sir George Knibbs (*The Shadow of the World's Future*, 1928), estimated that, at the present rate of increase, within two centuries the numbers will have exceeded what the earth can feed! In view of these considerations, especially when we remember how tremendous a part the practice of Food-Production has played in making possible a rapid increase in numbers, it is probable that in the times before the invention of agriculture the population of the world must have been singularly small and sparsely scattered.

This fact incidentally enables us to understand something of the factors involved in the differentiation of races and of the possibility that racial traits may have been acquired in a relatively short period of time. For if a very small community were completely isolated from all communication with other human beings the individual peculiarities of this restricted group of interbreeding people would rapidly accumulate and be intensified to produce a distinctive racial character. However, this problem does not concern us at the moment. At the close of the Glacial Epoch the removal of the great barriers that until then had kept these small racial communities apart made the nomads free to roam further afield and to mingle with members of other races. But what is of chief interest to us in this chapter is that, soon after the melting of the Glacial Ice, perhaps sixty centuries ago, the races with whom we are now concerned occupied the territories (Figure 29) which we associate with them as their areas of characterisation.

Archaeological investigations during the last quarter of a century have thrown enough light upon the conditions that obtained in the world at the beginning of the third millennium B.C. to justify the inference that, excepting in Egypt, Mesopotamia, Western Asia and Crete, the whole world was still in the food-gathering phase. In attempting to arrive at a solution of the much disputed problem as to which of the closely associated peoples, all members of the Mediterranean Race, was the pioneer in creating civilisation, we can eliminate Crete, not only because its dependence on Egypt and Western Asia for its cultural capital is generally recognised, but also because it is obvious that until sea-going ships had been invented—and their invention was the work of a people already committed to the regimen of civilisation—neither population nor culture could have reached this island in the Mediterranean. With reference to Syria and Western Asia no traces of early culture are known which cannot be referred to the inspiration of Egypt or Mesopotamia. At the moment, therefore, the issue is reduced to the question whether Egypt or Sumer (with Elam) was the pioneer. The essential similarity of the two earliest manifestations of culture-development in these two localities and the identity of their peculiarly distinctive repertory of strange practices allows no room for doubt that, whichever was the pioneer, the other place drew its inspiration from the more precocious inventor.

In 1926 Professor James H. Breasted, having then recently returned from a critical study on the spot of the new archaeological discoveries in Egypt, Syria and Mesopotamia, expressed his opinion in no uncertain voice. In *The Conquest of Civilisation* he announced that "it is now a finally established fact that civilisation first arose in Egypt." The constant repetition since then by other scholars, of the statement that Sumerian (and Elamite) civilisation antedates Egyptian, makes it necessary to emphasise the fact that all the discoveries which have been made in Sumer since 1926 add further corroboration to the accuracy of Professor Breasted's judgment. Taking the dates, which every archaeologist accepts, it is a simple problem in arithmetic to reach the conclusion that civilisation was growing and flourishing in Predynastic Egypt at least five centuries before the earliest evidence revealed in Sumer. Moreover, in addition to the unassailable testimony of chronology, it can be demonstrated, as the following pages will show, that the peculiar form early civilisation assumed, not only in Egypt but in every part of the world, was determined in large measure by the practice of mummification on the banks of the Nile in the middle of the fourth millennium B. C.

The ancient tradition of Osiris recorded by Plutarch probably represents an essentially accurate report of what actually happened nearly forty centuries before the Greek essayist wrote. "When Osiris came to his kingdom" he is said by Plutarch to have found "the Egyptians living a life such as animals lead. He taught them the art of agriculture, gave them laws and instructed them in the worship of the gods. Then he traversed the whole world on a mission of civilisation." Archaeological research has revealed the fact that Egyptian civilisation is vastly older than that of any other part of the world, and the form this earliest civilisation assumed affords a complete demonstration of the fact that it was actually created on the banks of the Nile. In the following pages the evidence in substantiation of this claim will be set forth. Hence Plutarch is probably right in claiming that Egypt's first king found his subjects "living a life such as animals live." For if the Egyptians created civilisation they must have been living the life of Natural Man before they began their pioneer work. Osiris also devised the art of agriculture, created the State System, and was the first god of whom antiquity has preserved any record. Though it is unlikely that Osiris himself travelled abroad there is no doubt that his works "traversed the whole world on a mission of civilisation." Plutarch had clearly rescued an ancient tradition in which was crystallised the true story of the origin of civilisation.

When for the first time in the history of the world the group of people who happened to be living in Egypt abandoned the nomadic life and began to till the soil, they were accomplishing a vastly greater revolution in the affairs of mankind than the mere invention of the crafts of the farmer and the irrigation engineer. They were committing themselves to the much more formidable task of erecting the complicated edifice of civilisation and formulating the fantastic doctrine of the State System which has dominated the world ever since. The creation of the State involved not only the invention of a multitude of arts and crafts, but also a complicated social and political organization under the rulership of a king endowed with peculiar powers and an authority over the lives of his subjects and the control of his kingdom, which was believed to be, in the fullest sense of the word, absolute. The identification of the State with the life of one man, making the welfare of the whole community and every individual citizen utterly dependent upon his ability to perform certain ritual acts, is the amazing phenomenon we have to study and, if possible, explain.

The natural crop of barley, which was growing wild on the banks of the Nile, seems to have provided the lure to attract the earliest settlers in Egypt. As the population increased and a more abundant supply of grain was needed, some man of exceptional insight imitated the natural processes, which people had probably been witnessing for untold generations. He dug channels to allow the innundation to extend more widely. Hence arose the system of basin irrigation and with it the beginning of agriculture. Baskets and pottery were devised to hold the seed, and granaries were invented to store it—which may have suggested to men the possibility of erecting houses to protect themselves also, one of those apparently obvious things Natural Man had neglected to do. Incidentally the makers of baskets and matting discovered that they could make a much finer "matting" from the flax growing in their fields. Thus they invented the spinning and weaving of linen.

The vital importance of irrigation compelled the Egyptians to study the habits of the river, to measure its rise and fall, to count the days that intervened between the inundations—in other words to invent arithmetic and devise a calendar. The yearly measurement of time, which originally was made by observations of the river, involved complicated calculations. But time was also being measured by the more easily calculated periods, the months which the phases of the moon determined. The similarity of these cyclical changes with the physiological periodicity of women suggested the belief that there was a causal relationship—that the moon was controlling the lives of individuals upon the earth, and in particular

the life-producing functions of womankind. This conception of a
celestial influence over mundane affairs was strengthened when it
was realised that Sirius, one of the seven stars in the constellation
known to modern astronomers as Canis Major, after being invisible
from the beginning of June, reappeared in the east a few minutes
before sunrise in July, exactly at the time when the Nile flood began
in Middle Egypt. This coincidence of course applies only to one
particular circumstance and one particular place. Hence it affords
decisive evidence upon the question of the place of origin. The
inundation of the Nile was the most vital and impressive natural
phenomenon in Egypt. It provided an assurance of food and
prosperity for the whole community and every individual. The
coincidence of the rising of Sirius with the inundation was believed
by the Egyptians to have the relation of cause and effect. Hence it
played an essential part, not merely in corroborating the hypothesis
of celestial control of human affairs, which the moon's cycles had
previously suggested, but also in helping to build up a comprehen-
sive theory of the regulation by the sky of all really vital affairs of
the earth. This archaic form of astrology was destined to exert a
far-reaching influence upon thought and speculation for the next
sixty centuries. It played a tremendous part in provoking the enquiries out of which eventually emerged our conception of the
universe.

Several centuries after the first measurement of the year in Egypt
the growth of astronomical knowledge led some man of conspicuous ability to suggest the replacement of the old calendar, based
upon observations of the river, by a new calendar determined by
observations on the sun and Sirius. In the world of belief this application of astronomical knowledge was responsible for transfer-
ring the home of the dead from the earth to the sky, and for
emphasising the solar attributes of the king-god. Hence the Sun-
God Re seemed to usurp the place of the River-God Osiris. It is
probable however that, contrary to the views now current, the
Egyptians had only one god, whose river-controlling powers were
at first most obstrusive (namely Osiris the Giver of Life and Measurer of the Year by the river), and later, when the solar attributes
were emphasised, the same god was called Re (who in the form of
the sun measured the year).

The tremendous influence of the belief in a Sun-God on the development of human thought and belief, as well as of social practices, is one of the cardinal facts in the history of the world. In the light of the considerations set forth in the preceding pages it is certain that the invention of the Solar Calendar and the creation of the Sun-God occurred at Heliopolis.

Thus the simple fact that in Egypt men began to practise irrigation and agriculture led them also to make pottery, granaries, houses and linen, to invent arithmetic and the calendar, to create the kingship, to develop ideas of celestial control of human destiny and of such mundane affairs as affect Man's welfare, and to create a Sun-God. But a host of other significant results followed in the train of these momentous events.

A settled mode of life in the fertile valley of the Nile and the impressive discovery that cereal food supplies could be increased almost without limit by artificial cultivation may have suggested the idea of also increasing their supplies of animal food by breeding cattle. They had already domesticated the dog (Chapter 3): hence the feasibility of doing the same for the ox, goat and sheep was not altogether a novel procedure.

Figure 33—The Divine Cow as the Sky.

The domestication of the cow had far more momentous results than the mere supply of meat for food. The discovery that human children could be fed on cow's milk came to these simple-minded people as a most miraculous revelation of Man's relationship to the universe. For if the cow was able to provide milk for man-

Figure 34—The Divine Cow giving the king divine life in the form of milk. Note the moon between her horns.

kind she must be their foster-mother or even their actual parent. She came to be admitted to the family circle of mankind as a blood relation. Hence the cow was apotheosised as the Mother of Mankind and her attributes merged with those magical amulets, at once cowrie and woman (Figure 3), which were also regarded as the Givers of Life. But the Great Mother had already been identified with the moon as the controller of the life-giving functions of women. Hence the Divine Cow, as the Mother Goddess Hathor was called in Egypt, was also identified with the moon in the sky. Throughout the whole of Egyptian history, as well as that of Sumer and Babylon, and even until the present day in India, these ideas of the Mother of Mankind and of veneration for the cow have exerted a far-reaching influence.

A pre-Islamic poet, writing more than thirteen centuries ago, has given expression to the ancient ideas:

> "She, the white cow, shone there through
> the dark night, luminous like a pearl of
> deep-seas, freed from the string of it."
> (From the Mu'allaqa of Labid in
> Wilfred S. Blunt's *Seven Golden Odes*).

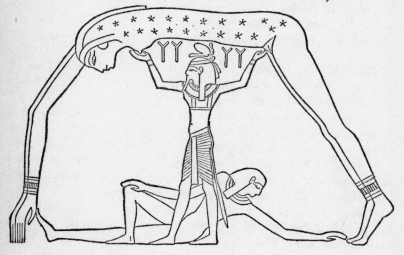

Figure 35—The Mother Goddess being raised up to become the Sky.

This identification of a cow with the moon and a pearl is true to the ancient symbolism of these three Givers of Life. The Divine Cow was not only the Moon Goddess but the sky itself and the vehicle whereby the dead were raised to the celestial abode.

Thus the craving of the early pioneers to safeguard their lives led them into far-reaching speculations. They were formulating hypotheses about the nature of life and the means of protecting it: but in the absence of knowledge they lacked the means to control their roving fancies. They wove a fantastic theory to embrace earth and sky and all the forces of Nature and when they became entangled in this web of their own making they entrusted their destiny to the man of outstanding genius, who had spun the first threads. Like all human communities throughout the ages they listened to the voice of authority. The man who had made himself the artificer of the new order also made himself king. When he foretold the future behaviour of the river and measured the year his subjects believed that he was something more than a prophet: he was the cause of the changes he had accurately predicted. People believed that the king controlled the forces of Nature. He not only caused the river to rise and then made the dry land, but by doing this, so they imagined, he created the earth and conferred upon the waters their life-giving powers.

The Story of the Flood, diffused throughout the world in an infinite variety of forms, preserves the tradition of the creation of civilisation and of the kingship.

We have to study not merely the discovery of agriculture (to which another section will be devoted) but the miracle of civilisation—the means whereby mankind, in the face of its first great adventure in constructive thought, got caught up on the wings of extravagant fantasies, which dominated his unrestrained imagination for more than thirty centuries. During these centuries the magical properties attributed to gold, for reasons which will be discussed in Chapter IX, had conferred upon the metal a standard of value which made it the appropriate material for a currency. The invention of coinage not only provided commerce and industry with its most potent instrument but incidentally it also made the individual citizen engaged in international maritime trafficking independent of the State System. Nearly six centuries before the Christian era Thales of Miletus seized the opportunity this freedom conferred and, in the intervals of his commercial pursuits, freed the human mind from the incubus of authority and conferred upon it a reliance upon its own resources and an emancipation from the cruder forms of superstition.

In many other ways the adoption of agriculture transformed the conditions of life. The rapid accumulation of population in a narrow valley that was flooded every year necessarily involved the concentration of the dwelling houses on those isolated elevations that rose above the level of the inundation. Hence communities became herded together in villages and people were forced into more intimate association than they had experienced during their career as nomads.

The creation of the village was a momentous event in Human History. Not only did it determine the conditions that are implicit in the literal meaning of the word civilisation and compel Man for the first time to devise a social organisation, but in addition the circumstances under which it developed promoted certain incidental results of far-reaching influence upon the subsequent history of mankind.

Perhaps the more intimate contact of human beings herded in villages may have played some part in preparing the way for the development of the habit of wearing clothes. To the scattered nomads nakedness was a natural state. When special circumstances led men and women to cover their bodies, wholly or in part, the conditions of village life would promote the rapid development of the new fashion.

The cultivation of the soil and the congregation of people in villages were responsible for profound changes in the treatment of the dead.

Primitive Man had been in the habit of leaving his dead wherever they happened to die. The new circumstances that developed among the Food-Producers made it incumbent on him to bury his dead and to make cemeteries beyond the limit of the cultivated area in the sand of the desert. This practice led to surprising results which were in large measure responsible for shaping the subsequent history of civilisation.

The burial of the dead in the hot dry sand was often followed by the desiccation of the body, which became exempt from the forces of corruption. This natural preservation of the body was made known to the living by the depredations of jackals. The early Egyptians were thus led to associate this phenomenon with these carnivores and also to devote much more attention to the corpses of the dead than they had formerly received. If we may judge from the writings of Egyptians several centuries later, or, what is more important, their immediate reaction to the wonder of desiccation, we can be confident that they regarded the preservation of the body as an obvious token of the prolongation of the deceased's existence. As the body was not destroyed neither was the deceased man's (or woman's) existence at an end.

Whether this is the true interpretation or not, the graves themselves provide definite evidence that increasing attention was devoted to the care of the corpse during the Predynastic period. It was wrapped in linen, and around the swathed body the skin of an ox or goat was wrapped to protect it from contact with the soil. Implements, ornaments, and other precious objects, as well as food, were put in the grave.

As this provision for the deceased's comfort and welfare became more lavish the size of the grave increased to accomodate the growing needs, and produced a series of experiments in grave construction, which produced very important results—the invention of brick-making, carpentry, stone-working, and mummification, the evolution of architecture, and the vast revolution in thought and speculation that emerged from the belief that the mummies were not merely spared the fate of corruption but could be reanimated to continue living. This subject is so important that a special section will be devoted to it.

The Life Quest and the Creation of Civilisation

The importance of the Life Quest, which was emphasised in the Introduction, in its relation to the most momentous event in the career of mankind—the creation of civilisation—suggests the desirability, even at the risk of repetition, of summarising the argument for the connection between the general impulse involved in that vital factor and the peculiar incidents involved in the making of civilisation.

True civilisation began when Man adopted a settled mode of life based upon the practice of agriculture. The realisation of the possibility of obtaining a secure means of sustenance without giving up his whole time to the daily search for food induced Man to settle in a definite place, which he made his home. It also provided him with the leisure and the inducement to devise arts and crafts and a social organisation the lack of which was not felt by simple nomads.

If the assurance of a generous supply of life-sustaining cereals was the determining factor in creating the conditions which made the development of civilisation possible, the other aspects of the Life Quest were not neglected when Man first became a farmer. On the contrary this initial success and the increased opportunities it gave him for reflection and experiment seem to have given added zest to the search for objects and devices to satisfy his dominating motive. For long ages he had been using such Givers of Life as blood and blood-red objects, shells, teeth of animals and models representing the forms of generously maternal women. These things were not abandoned when Man began to cultivate barley. He used some of his leisure to grind red carnelian to make beads. At puberty his sons made a blood offering from their life-giving member by means of a primitive operation known as "incision," which was soon superseded by true circumcision.

New expressions of the search for Givers of Life were devised. The river was the source of the barley's fertility. In it the early Egyptians saw the source of all life and they associated with it all the blessings that came to them. Even its greenness at the beginning of the inundation and the green colour of the crops whose growth it promoted were credited with the magic of life-giving. Hence in self-protection the early Egyptians and Sumerians used malachite as a green cosmetic; and out of this practice probably came the chance discovery of how to extract copper from the ore. Thus the search for Givers of Life and the magic of greenness were responsible for the inauguration of the Age of Metals, and the profound transformation of the arts and crafts of civilisation, which the use of metal tools effected.

In the belief that by protecting the corpse a man's existence would be prolonged, the first practical use made of copper was in the making of chisels to shape wood and stone for the purpose of protecting the bodies of the dead. The craft of the carpenter seems to have been devised first for the making of coffins, as the stonemason's was for the shaping of sarcophagi.

The early Egyptians seem to have detected in the shape of the barley grain a resemblance to the cowrie. Hence they conferred upon it all the mystic symbolism of the shell. The reputation of the barley was thus enhanced to so great a degree that it became "divine," in the sense that the power was attributed to it of conferring life and a continuation of life. Hence we find an Egyptian king, while claiming in his coffin text his identification with Osiris, adding the comment: "I am barley."

When the natural history of the life-giving river was intensively studied, its rise and fall measured, and the intervals between its annual inundations estimated, these enquiries not only created arithmetic and the calendar, but they impressed upon the observers the relationship of the sun and certain stars to the regimen of the river. The moon had, probably long before then, been associated not only with the measurement of time but also with the control of human destiny, and in particular of the life-giving functions of women. But the coincidence between the heliacal rising of the star Sirius and the beginning of the inundation seemed to prove that the sky, and in particular the sun, controlled the measurement of the year, as it obviously did of the day, and therefore was causally related to the river and its inundations and especially to its life-giving powers. Hence the sun stole the magic of the river and acquired the reputation of being the chief Giver of Life. But as the king had, for reasons to be discussed in the following pages, already acquired the same reputation he—or more properly the dead king—was identified with the sun. For this purpose he had to be transferred to the sky to become the Sun-God, the Giver of Life and Light to the universe. Hence light, the sun's light, became a symbol of life-giving. The sun was also fire: hence fire was identified with life, and such expressions as the living flame acquired the symbolic meaning that survives to this day.

If civilisation, by relieving Man of the increasing quest for food and the necessity for the intensive concentration of the tracker on one exclusive aim, provided him with the opportunity to devote his skill and understanding to other purposes, it also brought him into closer association with fellow men not of his own family. It also created an increasing number of new aspirations and new opportunities for rivalry. These new pursuits provided material for jealousy and called for a severer hold on the natural impulse not to be outdone. In other words, civilisation provided ampler opportunities and more stirring reasons for quarrelling. By a curious irony Man's creation of the artificial value of gold brought to an end the Golden Age. As Shelley expressed it:

"The harmony and happiness of man
Yield to the wealth of nations."

In the early phase of civilisation, however, this new risk of violent behaviour was in large measure kept in check by the autocratic power of a beneficent ruler who exercised extraordinary control over his subjects because they regarded him as the source not merely of their sustenance and their prosperity but of their very lives. The king was the Divine Creator, the Giver of Life, the Controller of the Flood and the Bestower of Harvests. He was the State and he was also the Cosmos. Hence his power over his subjects was infinitely more absolute than that of any more recent sovereign. He could exact proper behaviour from all his subjects, who were his devoted followers bound to his service by a mystical devotion to the very source of their lives.

When a second kingdom developed on the banks of the Nile—another State firmly knit together by the same spirit of loyal solidarity, but depending upon the same river for its life and prosperity—the stage was set for the first serious conflict in the history of the world. What the cause of the dispute was we do not know. The traditions of the sacred passion of Osiris have been told innumerable times through thousands of years. They are the source of most of the world's folklore. They have come down to us in such a bewildering variety of versions, and have been embellished with so rich a decoration of varied symbolism and moral principles, that we are unable to pierce the obscurity and discover exactly how Osiris met his death. Did his brother kill him because his powers were failing? Was he slain on the field of battle in warfare against Set? Was he drowned in the river? Did Set simply slay or mutilate him so that he might seize the throne? All that we know for certain is that he was slain by Set and his body mutilated; that there was fighting between their respective followers; and that Horus, the son of Osiris, was impelled to seek revenge for his father's death.

In addition the duty was imposed upon Horus of putting together the fragments of the body of Osiris, making a mummy of his remains, and performing the necessary ceremonies to reanimate his mummy and secure the continuation of his existence.

The Invention of Agriculture

The origin of agriculture is a problem of such fundamental significance in the argument of this book that the issues at stake must be set forth fully. Obviously the discovery of the meaning of cultivating grain was the essential factor in bringing to an end the career of food-gathering.

The remains of Early Predynastic Egyptians, which the writer studied, were unearthed in 1901 and the following years by the Hearst Expedition of the University of California under the direction of Professor George A. Reisner, now of Harvard University. Examining the cemetery excavated by Mr. Albert M. Lythgoe, now of the Metropolitan Museum in New York, it was discovered that the hot, dry sand in which the bodies had been buried nearly sixty centuries ago had in many cases desiccated them and naturally preserved them in so wonderful a manner that every tissue in the body, whether brain or muscle, skin or heart, and in fact any organ or structure, could be studied. In addition, the contents of the alimentary tract were available for examination. Many examples of this material were submitted for examination to Professor Netolitzky, the leading European authority on ancient food stuffs. In the writer's little book, *The Ancient Egyptians,* the nature of the last meal eaten before death by these Egyptians of the fourth millennium was described in these words: "Almost every sample contained husks of barley, and in about 10 per cent, husks of millet could be identified with certainty. . . . Root tubers of *Cyperus esculentus* [the nut rush] were found both in the intestinal contents and in pots placed in the graves alongside the bodies. These tubers were of very small size, which Dr. Netolitzky regards as evidence of either the utilisation of the wild plant or the beginning of its cultivation."

Thus there is the suggestion that many centuries before agriculture is known to have been practised in Mesopotamia or India, and perhaps two thousand years before China began to make use of cultivated cereals, the Egyptians were either cultivating barley or eating the barley growing naturally on the banks of the Nile. The presence of the barley in the stomachs of these very early Egyptians obviously affords proof that the grain was growing in Egypt. Only two alternative explanations of this fact are possible. Either barley was growing wild in the Nile Valley when the Egyptians settled there; or they imported the grain and cultivated it. There is no evidence to show that agriculture had been invented at this early period and nothing to suggest the likelihood of the importation of the seed. Thus it is in the highest degree probable that barley was indigenous in Egypt. In the following pages other reasons in substantiation of this will be given.

The vast significance of this fact and its bearing on the history of civilisation were first pointed out by Professor Thomas Cherry of the University of Melbourne, whom the Great War took for five years from the School of Agriculture at Melbourne to serve in Egypt and Palestine with the Australian Medical Corps. The results of his study on the spot of the problems of early agriculture were published in the Report of the Australian Association for the Advancement of Science in 1921. As this most important memoir is not easily accessible to most readers the actual words in which Professor Cherry expressed his observations and his interpretation of their meaning will be freely quoted.

Barley was found in a series of Predynastic Egyptian burials ranging from, say, 4000 B.C. to 3400 B.C. The next indication of the use of cereals in Egypt is provided by a series of early burials of ambiguous type and unknown date, which have been distinguished as Badarian. A charred fragment of ivory found in a grave of the First Dynasty (3400 B.C.), i.e. about six hundred years later than the first known use of barley as food, is also an interesting representation of a cereal. On the ivory was carved in relief a grain of conventional design. The long beards on the ear in this drawing raise a doubt as to whether the grain was intended to represent barley or bearded wheat, but it is commonly assumed to represent wheat, which recent excavations have shown to have been in use in Egypt at this time and, shortly afterwards, also in Sumer. At about 2900 B.C. one of the earliest scraps of literature that have survived from antiquity relates how four goddesses came to Heliopolis to superintend the birth of the triplet sons of the lady Rud-dedit, the first of the children of the Sun-God. After consultation with her husband, the high priest, she gave the nurses a bushel of barley as a thank-offering. A few weeks later the happy mother wished to brew beer to make a feast, and it was found that this bushel was all the grain there was in the temple. In contrast with this dearth we find "heaps of wheat" as a common royal gift to the temples some seven hundred years later. By that time barley seems to have become less significant than wheat. In the tale (about 2000 B.C.) of the *Sekhti and Hemti* the husbandman is said to have had wheat and barley growing on his farm in the Fayum; and both cereals are mentioned by Senuhi amongst the products of the South of Palestine. The Biblical references to the corn of Abraham and Isaac at Beersheba are centuries later.

When we pass to Asia, flint sickles (i.e. wooden sickles studded with flint "teeth") have been found in the lowest stratum at Susa, Elam and other early sites, including Anau to the east of the Caspian. The sickles are of the same peculiarly distinctive shape and mode of construction as those found in Egypt, and the design must unquestionably have been derived from the *earlier* Egyptian models. It is not probable that any of this Asiatic material can be assigned to a date as early as 3400 B.C., at which time the use of cereals as food was a long-established practice in Egypt. All the evidence at our disposal affords good grounds for believing that agriculture was the special gift of the Nile, and that it was introduced into Asia from Egypt.

Coming down to much more recent times, there was a widespread belief amongst all European peoples that the cereals came from the East. The word for barley is similar in many Indo-European languages, while wheat has different and unrelated names. Hence it is probable that these people knew barley before wheat. But it is doubtful if any of the evidence found with the Neolithic implements in European lake dwellings, kitchen middens and tumuli, is of very great antiquity. These European remains belong to a period at least twenty centuries later than the invention of agriculture in Egypt. In the case of the Swiss lake dwellings, wheat, barley, millet, flax, copper and perforated stone axes are all found together. The presence of millet goes far towards solving the mystery of these settlements. Millet was not indigenous nor is it now grown in Switzerland, although it still survives on the plains of Italy. But the latter approximate to sea-level, while the Swiss lakes are 1,500 feet higher. The experience of failure in an average year in the mountain valleys has made the Swiss abandon millet and pin their faith to the cereals. Probably a generation or two would be sufficient to teach the pioneers that the risk of frost was too great to allow of millet becoming a staple crop. As millet, therefore, was clearly not an indigenous product of the country, it must have been brought from abroad. Professor Breasted traces copper blades from Egypt, through the Mediterranean area, to Denmark. The Swiss baked clay spinning whorls, with flax attached, also recall Egypt. The probable date of the European lake dwellings and megalithic monuments is not earlier than 2000 B. C., and most of them may be nearly a thousand years later.

At first sight it might seem highly improbable that Man began agriculture as an irrigator. Nevertheless it is true that the first traces of civilisation are found in two practically rainless regions, Egypt and Sumer. With the recent laying bare of the foundations of history as distinguished from tradition, it seems certain that the Egyptian civilisation was evolved in the valley of the Nile, and equally certain that the germs of Sumerian and Babylonian civilisation were imported. In the Nile Valley every phase may be followed, from simple nomadism to the highest culture, and this without a break. It is idle, therefore, to turn to some hypothetical land, as so many writers are doing to-day, and assume that the Egyptians acquired their cereals and their knowledge of agriculture from elsewhere, and adapted this knowledge to irrigation in order to meet the new and quite unique conditions of the Nile. Nor is it likely that Man cultivated the vine and olive first, and subsequently applied this hypothetical experience of agriculture to the cereals. As a matter of fact, the two oldest civilisations, Egypt and Elam-Sumer, depended entirely on irrigation, while the second group, which clustered round these—Assyria, Persia, Phoenicia and Syria—were all noted for their skill in irrigation. The earliest known people of Indo-European speech—the Kassites and Mitanni —appear to have had no culture before they came into contact with the civilisation of the Ancient East. It may also be something more than a coincidence that the Hittites arose on the edge of the salt treeless tract in Central Asia Minor. In this district irrigation for summer crops is now practised. The Hittites may also have been acquainted with the art.

In the history of mankind there is a mystery that is insoluble unless we assume that the Egyptians were in reality the first of mankind to cultivate cereals.

The population of the world was probably quite insignificant and perhaps almost stationary in numbers throughout the many thousand years of the Old Stone Ages. But the Egyptians at the epoch 4000 B. C. put an end to this stagnation, and mankind has been steadily increasing in numbers ever since. The Chinese, for instance, are said to have doubled their numbers during the historic period at least once in each 250 years. Reversing the process, the conclusion is forced upon us that before men discovered how to increase their food supplies by agriculture and cattle breeding the number of human beings must have been very small. The scantiness of human remains is a sure indication that the population of the world was insignificant until progress began on the banks of the Nile. There was a complete transformation of the conditions of life at the dawn of civilisation in Egypt.

In the early stages of his career Man probably lived for the most part on food of animal origin, the wild fruits and roots contributing only a small percentage of the total supply. Comparative anatomy and physiology suggest that Man was not evolved as a vegetable feeder, for the structure of his alimentary canal and its length in proportion to that of the body is much nearer to the ratio found in some of the Carnivora than to that of the Herbivora. Primitive Man probably lived for the most part near the seashore, and on the banks of the great rivers, where he could get shell fish as well as the vertebrates for food. But the extent to which berries, acorns and nuts were used was probably never very great. If one is reminded of the coconut and banana, it must be remembered that civilisation did not begin in places where these grew wild. Hence the reliance on cereals was a new factor in

Human History, the far-reaching significance of which it would be difficult to exaggerate. Natural Man, as we have seen in Chapter VI, did not preserve the surplus food from times of plenty to meet the deficiency in times of scarcity. Primitive Man was always near the edge of want, because the family was dependent from day to day on the results of the day's collecting. The coming and going of bird, fish and beast cannot be controlled by Man, but it was possible for him to domesticate fowls and cattle.

It is doubtful whether Man domesticated any animal except the dog until he had become an irrigator on the banks of the Nile. The small groups of hunters living far back in the grass lands may never have learnt the special value of milk as food for human beings, nor have had the idea of trying to improve their food supply by taming cattle. Such areas have always been subject to low rainfall and years of drought. Otherwise they would have been covered with forests. The population was kept small by the exigencies of the rainfall alone. At all events we are able to say for certain that there was no overflow of population from the grass lands until more than a thousand years after the increase had become marked in Egypt, when the practice of agriculture induced a rapid growth of population.

If we assume for the moment that barley and millet were found growing wild, the art of cultivation may have been learnt in Egypt from the simple experiment of imitating on one part of the flood plain what was done naturally by the river. The people saw that wherever the waters of the inundation spread the soil became fertile. Irrigation began by imitating the natural process: scooping out channels to extend the area flooded. Throughout all the area of the valley under flood there were in Egypt unique features *such as are not found elsewhere in the world*. The most important of these was the seasonal incidence of the floods. The plain was soaked at the very end of the hot season, so that the land remained moist for several months. During the cool season evaporation was small compared with what it would have been if the flood had come at the beginning of the summer. The slope of the plain was such that very large areas were soon clear of the water. Stagnant swamps were not a great feature of the valley. At the same time the temperature in the cool season was high enough to keep millet, barley, and flax steadily growing until the opening of the following summer.

The Nile is unique, not only in flowing from the tropics to a much cooler zone, but in having a double source of water supply. The equatorial source, gathering in the Great Lakes and the other branches of the White Nile, keeps up a regular daily flow of 50,-000,000 cubic yards at Khartoum. The same quantity issues from Lake Victoria. The great tributaries are just sufficient to make good the loss by evaporation during the first 1,200 miles of the river's course. It is joined in the Sudan by the Blue Nile and Atbara from Abyssinia, which carry little water during most of the year, but are subject to immense floods in August and September. The volume of water may reach 1,000,000,000 cubic yards a day. The natural flood is, therefore, an inundation lasting only a few weeks. The cool part of the year is from October to March. Professor Cherry has emphasised the fact that *this natural cycle of flood and cool weather exactly suits the seasonal growth of millet and barley. Hence in all probability it was here that the cultivated varieties of these plants completed the last stages of their natural evolution long before Man came into the valley.*

The plants appear above the ground a few days after the water drains off, and ripen at the beginning of the hot season, before the soil is parched by the oncoming summer. The seeds lie on the surface of the land without injury until next flood season, when it is again soaked and the cycle begins anew. These unique circumstances, combined with the knowledge that barley was the staple food of the earliest Egyptians, force us to conclude that the Egyptians must have been the inventors of the art of agriculture.

If we suppose that the Egyptians gathered the wild seeds and discovered that they could be preserved from year to year simply by keeping them dry, we have discovered a reason to account for the increase in population. The fact that Egypt is a rainless land makes it possible for the seed to lie on the surface of the ground, or buried a few inches, without losing its power of germination. The same dry atmosphere makes it easy to store the grain without its being injured by mildew or weevils, the two pests which make it very difficult to carry on from one harvest to the next in all the moist regions of the tropics. Such continuous losses from these and other causes are experienced by even the most skillful European farmers, so that, were it not for very cheap labour, no tropical colony could be made an economic success. In the face of these difficulties it is very unlikely that primitive Man ever discovered in the tropics the secrets of agriculture without outside assistance. In learning how to store grain the exemption from such risks in the milder climate of Egypt was a most important consideration. In any other place mildew and insect pests might have discouraged the early farmers from persisting in such attempts.

With the wild plants, the soil, the time of the floods and rainless climate all favourable, the Egyptians had an annual demonstration of the facts relating to the natural history of barley and the conditions necessary for its cultivation. Hence we may draw the only possible inference and assume the invention of agriculture in Egypt, where Nature was annually pointing the way so clearly.

Thus, to repeat and reëmphasise the fact, the most momentous event in human history occurred when some Man first scooped shallow channels to extend the area of inundation. Experience would soon lead to the closing or deepening of these first channels at given periods, and so the first steps towards "basin irrigation" would be made. In basin irrigation the flood water is led in this way from the first to a number of other level areas in succession, the necessary works in the shape of channels and banks being small affairs. The surface of the flood plain needed no levelling or adjustment to prepare the way for effective irrigation. The tops of the banks have become the pathways from village to village.

Working the land by means of a stick or hoe may have resulted from the observation that where the mud was well marked by the footprints of wild animals, the crop in the following year was more luxuriant than elsewhere. The tomb pictures at Sakkara show pigs and sheep treading in the seed. The following hint from Herodotus may suggest that cultivation began from imitation: "When the river has come of its own accord and irrigated their fields, and having irrigated them has subsided, then each man sows his own land and turns swine into it, and when the seed has been trodden in by the swine he waits for the harvest."

The earliest device in agriculture was clearly an imitation of the hoofprints by means of a stick.

The first steps towards agriculture were thus very simple in some parts, at least, of the Nile Valley. Subsequently larger banks would be made and channels dug to control the water, and by the primitive *shadouf* the water could be lifted from the river or channel in order to help the crops in parts which appeared to be too dry.

Irrigation was thus made perennial by a simple and natural course of development. That this was the real order of events is confirmed by the earliest beliefs of the Egyptian people—the ideas which became the foundation of their religion. An obvious scientific explanation is forthcoming if we assume that the order of events was: first, the use of wild millet and barley and the gathering and storing of the seeds: second, the use of sticks to till the land, combined with simple improvements in the method of regulating the flooding and drainage of the land, in other words, imitating the natural basin irrigation: third, transforming backwaters and lagoons into canals from which the water was lifted into small channels by the *shadouf*.

The conditions that have always existed in Egypt are paralleled by those of no other river in the world. The other rivers on the banks of which high civilisations have arisen are the Euphrates and Tigris, the Indus and Ganges, and the great rivers of China. In all these cases irrigation is practised, but not in the way that is normal in Egypt.

In Mesopotamia, the flood reaches its maximum at the end of May, and the rivers are again within their banks in June. But this is full summer, and plants that appear after the flood has left the plain have no chance of reaching maturity. The soil dries so rapidly that the mud is replaced by dust in the course of a few days. The flood is caused chiefly by the melting of the snow on the mountains of Armenia, which, of course, begins with the return of late spring. The plain of Mesopotamia is rainless in summer, so that the dry mud remains a barren waste. The few showers that mark each year occur in midwinter. These floods, therefore, require regulating before the water can be used for profitable irrigation, for the single application of water, which comes naturally each year, is not capable of bringing any crop to maturity. As Sir Hanbury Brown has pointed out: "under the extreme conditions of heat and dryness, which prevail in summer, it would be lost labour to sow seed, which, though it might germinate, would wither away before coming to maturity."

These circumstances in Mesopotamia must be borne in mind, because they are all-important in their bearing on the question of the priority of Egyptian or Sumerian civilisation, as well as on the still more fundamental question of the most probable localities for the evolution of barley and wheat before Man interfered with the process. From these considerations it is clear that the Sumerians must have learned from the Egyptians how to use the river water for irrigation.

In India, the two great rivers are fed from the snows of the northern mountains, and the floods come early in summer, so that conditions there are similar to those of Mesopotamia. In China, the floods are caused chiefly by the heavy local rains, which occur during the summer months. Thus the incidence of the flood season is all in favour of Egypt as the place where the art of irrigation originated. It is the only land where the annual flood produces crops without any assistance. On the Euphrates, the preliminary requisites are an embankment to keep off the flood and a canal to bring the water from the river at the proper time of year. It is unlikely that such technical knowledge was acquired without the help of the natural object-lesson which the Nile alone provided.

The common assumption that cultivation began by making use of the rainfall instead of by irrigation presents difficulties which on examination appear to be insuperable. The aboriginal Australian has been gathering and crushing seeds for untold ages, even robbing the ants of their store of such seeds. Yet it never occurred to the Black Man to devise the art of cultivation, nor have we any justification for assuming that primitive Man had a knowledge of plant-breeding and the prophetic vision to cultivate natural grasses until he bred plants like barley and wheat, which would be useful for food. It is surely an anachronism to credit primitive Man with a knowledge of genetics! The less cultured of savage people have little foresight or perseverance. It was easier to follow the river beyond the limits of the drought rather than stay behind and see how the new-fangled experiments of barley cultivation were likely to succeed. Charles Darwin quotes evidence as to the wretched food used by savages, and tells of the Australian blacks cooking many kinds of vegetables in the hope of rendering them innocuous or more nutritious. After mentioning the Africans gathering grass for food, he continues: "The savage inhabitants of each land, having found out by many and hard trials what plants were useful would, after a time, take the first steps in cultivation by planting them near their usual abodes." He states that Australia, New Zealand, Cape Colony, and North and South America beyond Mexico and the Plata respectively, have yielded no plant useful as food for Man. He then suggests that as Australia produces 107 species that might be useful to savage man, it may be only a question of cultivating them for thousands of years to enable them to compete with those already in use in the civilised world.

But if the Australians, who know what hunger means as well as most savages, have no idea of the meaning of cultivation, how should savage man in any part of the earth have got the idea of improving the food value of the grain? If it required many centuries for the dwellers in the Valley of the Nile to appreciate the plain object-lesson in agriculture being given by nature year after year, it is idle to pretend that thousands of years earlier some man began breeding plants without such guidance. But we have to go much farther than this. Not only did one man begin the new task, but he was able, by his example, to stimulate the first of a long succession of enthusiasts to imitate him, to hand on the secret, to preserve the best of the seed through times of famine, and thus to accomplish what no one else before that time had been able to do—make a permanent increase in the size of the grain of wheat and barley. If the cereals began as small seeds, what conviction of ultimate success, or what instinct led some primitive Man to begin the task? Presumably, if there is any truth in the supposition, hundreds of grasses were experimented with, but only two—wheat and barley—turned out a success. The conception of starting to improve a seed is very different from cooking roots to make them eatable. Dr. Aaronsohn, who found wild wheat with large seeds growing in Palestine, argues that primitive Man would not select a useless and inconspicuous grass for cultivation. "It would have

taken a wonderful power of divination on the part of our prehistoric ancestors to pick out one grass and to find that this grass
had such possibilities. We have done no such thing with the thousands of other species of grasses."

The adoption of clothing would appear to be a much simpler
step for a savage to take than the discovery of agriculture. Speaking of the habits of the naked Australian, Sir Baldwin Spencer and
Mr. Gillen tell us: "The idea of making any kind of clothing as
a protection against cold does not appear to have entered the native
mind, although he is keen enough upon securing the Government
blanket when he can get one." Yet these people are continually
hunting fur-bearing animals for food, and at night in winter the
temperature often falls several degrees below freezing point for
weeks together.

Agriculture is like the use of fire—the invention was a sudden
inspiration and not the result of a gradual change. There is no half-
way house. A people either tills the soil or it does not, and if it cultivated anything in the Ancient East we may be sure that it knew
something of wheat or barley. The limited amount of time that is
available for the spread of this knowledge all round the world is
forgotten, and was not known to earlier writers on the subject.
Because Man of the Old Stone Age lived apparently as a non-
progressive being, perhaps for hundreds of thousands of years, it
was assumed that civilisation took a correspondingly long period
to evolve. But, by accepting the modern dates for the beginning of
progress in Egypt, and by recognising the evidence of the spread
of culture, we are able to see the history of mankind as a consistent
whole. Thousands of years may no longer be evoked to suit the
theory of the historian, for the evolution of civilisation in Egypt
covered less than the single millennium which fell between 4000
and 3000 B.C.

If this is the true account of the history of barley, the origin of
civilisation was due to the accidental discovery of valuable food
plants growing in the Nile Valley. Man did not deliberately set to
work to solve the problem of becoming a tiller of the soil, but discovered the possibility of cultivation accidentally and without effort.
He helped the river to do the business just a little better than it had
been doing it before his advent. Of his early plants, wild millet is

easily able to hold its own in the valley, but barley had not a very great margin for safety. Wheat can be best accounted for by its evolution on a small island in the Aegean Archipelago. Here it was found by men who had already learned from their experience in Egypt how to cultivate millet and barley.

Perhaps the most remarkable fact of all this story is that Man should have discovered so many plants, animals and metals of special importance at the dawn of civilisation in Egypt. Many of these are still the most important factors in the economic and industrial life of modern men, and they have not been superseded by newer products from other parts of the world. In the course of the next thousand years after agriculture was invented, when Syria, Asia Minor and Mesopotamia had been added to the domain of the civilised world, and silver, iron, fruit trees, cotton, the camel and the horse added to Man's equipment, it may be said that the list of essential raw products was almost complete. Before the epoch 4000 B.C. Man had hardly begun to appreciate the world's resources; soon after the year 2000 he had gained most of what the earth affords.

The breeding experiments of such investigators as Professor Sir Rowland Biffen of Cambridge and the late Mr. Aaronsohn dispose once' for all of the popular view that Primitive Man more than sixty centuries ago produced the barley and wheat which have been the staple foods of a large section of mankind since then by an elaborate and long-continued process of experimental breeding. Having disposed of this anachronism, one is in a better position to appreciate the cogency and conclusiveness of Professor Cherry's claim in the foregoing paragraphs that the Nile Valley was the place where barley was found growing in a natural state, and the agriculture associated with basin irrigation was invented simply by imitating the natural conditions, which the proto-Egyptians had constantly before their eyes. In Egypt alone the climatic conditions and the seasons of the inundation are favourable for the natural growth of barley: and we know that it was the staple diet of the earliest Egyptians. The climatic conditions in Mesopotamia, Syria and Asia Minor are such that the cultivation of barley became possible there only when men applied the lessons of artificial irrigation which they had learned in Egypt. Dr. Cherry believes that wheat must have grown naturally on some of the smaller Aegean Islands

—he suggested Melos or Naxos—and was first cultivated centuries after barley, and by men who had learned the art of agriculture directly or indirectly from Egypt. But before the close of the fourth millennium the Egyptian technique of agriculture and irrigation had been adopted in Sumer and probably also in Crete, Syria and Asia Minor. Soon afterwards it was to spread north from Sumer and Elam to Turkestan and east to Baluchistan and the Valley of the Indus. But it probably took another millennium before it spread in Europe as one of the distinctive features of the Neolithic culture there.

CHAPTER VIII

THE KINGSHIP

FROM the circumstances of his origin the king is the impersonation of the health and prosperity of the whole community, of which he was believed to be the Creator and the Life-Giver. Hence it was a matter of the most vital personal interest to every individual in the community to safeguard his health. Any sign of the failing of the king's health and strength, and in particular, of his virility, the most obvious witness of his power of life-giving, endangered the welfare of the State. The killing of the king to make room for a more youthful and vigorous head of the State was regarded as the logical course for a prudent people to adopt. But the dead ruler when mummified was believed not merely to recover his lost virtues but also to acquire power greater than that of a mere king. He became a god.

Amongst really primitive peoples in which there is no social organisation except the family groups there is no hereditary leader. In fact the circumstances of life are so simple and uncomplicated that there is little scope for leadership. When decisions have to be made one of the old men takes the lead or several of them form a council of elders. As the social system develops there are councils of elders for the village, and a combination of such for the clan, and representatives of the clans form a tribal council which governs the whole community. This system of government is wholly independent of the kingship, which was devised for a special purpose to safeguard the community's welfare and to confer prosperity on it. The king was the controller of irrigation, the rainmaker, the man who regulated his people's destiny by astronomical observation and prediction of seasons and auspicious times for doing things.

But his functions as the titular ruler had to be brought into correlation with those of the Council of Government. In Egypt it seems that this was in part effected by making the king's son his vizier or prime minister, whose duty it was to preside over the council of ten charged with the administration of Upper Egypt.

The irrigation-engineer who devised the system of agriculture and so regulated the distribution of water that every community throughout Egypt should get its proper share, necessarily became the organiser and controller of the whole community. He was the first king, the first human being to direct the work and dominate the lives of any large group of people. He was able to do so in virtue not only of the fact that he gave his people the assurance of an adequate supply of food, but also because he had the knowledge which enabled him to predict when the flood would come. Such esoteric knowledge of the river's behaviour and of celestial events had never previously been displayed by any human being. It was miraculous and incomprehensible. Hence there grew up the belief that the king actually controlled the river and was identified with it. He caused it to inundate the fields: after the appointed time of flooding he withdrew the water and so created the dry land. He came to acquire the reputation of creating not only the world but all that was in it, including his own subjects. The king was in fact the universe. He was the microcosm that was identified with and controlled the macrocosm. If his health failed and he became senile the fact that he was unable to perform the ritual ceremonies of creation was regarded as a danger to the State. Hence it was considered desirable to kill him and replace him by a more virile and younger man.

The original lack of any form of social organisation other than that of such family grouping as Man inherited from his simian ancestors could not survive under the conditions that developed in Egypt. On the numerous hillocks in the Nile Valley that were converted into islands during the inundation many family groups had to be accommodated as the population increased. These became herded together in towns, and some sort of administration had to be devised by the irrigation-engineer who had become their ruler. The conditions were profoundly different from those that prevailed when the people were simple nomads free to maintain their independence of other families and to respect their unwritten territorial rights. Whether they wanted to do so or not, the families living side by side in the same village had to cooperate in their economic and social life. Moreover the conditions that arose from the practice of agriculture with its dependence on one river made all the people in a village subjects of one ruler. As the population increased and the just distribution of water became a condition of survival, it became necessary to link together all the villages into one composite state with a single controller. Just as the compelling motive for this was the common need of the benefits the river bestowed, so the river itself formed the link to bind the State together. Boats were essential to permit people dwelling on one bank to get into touch with those of the other: and the river also became the highway for trafficking throughout the land of Egypt. Just as the king was identified with the State, so he was the river and the personification of its life-giving and prosperity-bestowing powers.

In our own times we have repeated demonstrations of the common love of the sense of power. It is often a matter of surprise how staid and serious men can be elated by the exercise of even trivial powers of patronage or of the control of the actions of their fellows. History is mainly concerned with the actions of kings and statesmen who are using for good or ill their power over nations. For it is an undeniable fact that history is not shaped by communities or nations but by individuals who by some means or other have acquired the power to dictate the actions of their fellows. It is difficult for us to realise what must have been the prestige of the first man in the history of the world to attain such preeminence and to acquire the reputation for controlling the powers of Nature in ways beyond the comprehension of his subjects. It must have seemed marvellous that a man in other respects like themselves could confer the boons of life and prosperity upon them. Is it surprising that they attributed supernatural attributes to him or that he became so inflated with his own importance and sense of power as to regard himself as differing from those other men who had become his subjects?

In Egypt the control of irrigation necessarily involved centralised power. It has always been the case that the controllers of irrigation in Egypt have dominated the country. More than thirty years ago the distinguished scholar, Professor Alfred Wiedemann of Bonn, emphasised this consideration in his *Religion of the Ancient*

Egyptians (1897, p. 7): "The control of the canals was necessarily far more centralised than that of the rest of the country, for the regular irrigation of Egypt can only be secured when directed by a single authority which opposes in the common interest any attempt to cut off and divert the water for the gratification of private ends."

The apotheosis of these powers of controlling the river is revealed in the words put into the mouth of the dead king by a scribe of the twentieth dynasty:

"I have made the heaven and the earth, I have ordered the mountains and formed all that is thereon. I am he who made the water, creating the inundation. . . . The water of the Nile riseth at my command; the gods know not my name. I make the hours and create the days; I send the festival of the New Year and form the river."

The invention of the means for extending the range of the inundation of the Nile necessitated not only the devising of the tools for digging channels and for raising and distributing the water, but also the study of the problems of simple hydrodynamics, the planning of the irrigation basins, the measurement of the height of the river and the invention of the Nilometer, and a host of other considerations. It involved also the counting of the time from one inundation to another so as to organise the arrangements for the distribution of the water. The measurement of the year so given by the river had to be brought into relationship with the natural monthly periods determined by the phases of the moon. Thus the early Egyptians were compelled, once they began to till the soil, to study the natural behaviour of the river and celestial events and devise simple mathematical rules for such measurements and calculations.

There is an innate tendency in all human beings to interpret the results of experience for their own satisfaction and guidance. It is not what we see or hear that matters so much as our interpretation of such sensory experience. This impulse to rationalise and to embark on speculation is irresistible: for every man must in self-defence attempt to understand such facts of experience as are forced upon his attention. In proportion as the methods of enquiry lack the strict discipline which only the accumulations of knowledge and centuries of critical experiment can give, such speculations must of necessity be little more than rationalisations—finding plausible explanations for experiences that are still beyond the scope of real understanding. Hence the attempt to correlate the measurement of the year provided by the annual inundation of the Nile with the movements of the moon (and later of the sun and stars), inevitably provoked the idea that there must be a causal connection between these terrestrial and celestial events. The early theorists rightly assumed that the luminous objects they observed moving in the sky were regulating mundane affairs. Moreover when they had already accepted the belief that the moon was regulating the life-producing functions in women, the early astrologers came to regard the celestial influence as one personally affecting the welfare of human beings and in particular their powers of life-giving. The sky controlled not only the river that brought abundant harvests of food, but also the very birth and life of human children. It measured not only the length of the day, the month and the year, but also the span of human life. The celestial world provided a horoscope for every human being.

This seems to have been the train of speculation that developed when men first began to cultivate the soil. The settled life of the farmer, rooted in one definite place, prepared the way, as we saw in the last chapter, for the domestication of cattle, which so long as men were nomadic does not seem to have been attempted. With the domestication of the cow, the discovery of the fact that cow's milk could be used as food for human beings impressed the earliest people who used milk as a most startling mystery, the strangeness of which long familiarity has deprived us of the ability fully to appreciate and assess. For at this time the strange creature that acted as a wet-nurse for children came to be regarded as a real foster-mother. The amulets these people and their predecessors had been making in representation of maternal women or as symbols of birth and life-giving were now identified with the milk-providing cow. The Mother of Mankind was now called the Divine Cow and often represented as a life-giving and death-averting symbol simply as a cow or as a goddess (afterwards known as Hathor) equipped with a cow's horns and ears.

But this process of syncretism went much further. For if the

Divine Cow controlled the life-giving powers of women, so also did the sky and the moon that dwelt there. Hence the moon was identified with the Great Mother and the cow with the sky. To the cow's horns on Hathor's escutcheon was now added the moon's disc. (Figure 34.)

Before discussing further the evidence relating to the rapid development of these astrological speculations, which provoked men to study celestial phenomena with particular intensity, we must first consider other effects of the practice of agriculture.

The cultivation of the soil would not have been possible unless men had realised the necessity of saving seed for planting, and devised means for doing so. The storing of grain was probably responsible for a host of new discoveries. Whether or not the invention of baskets and pots can be attributed to this cause, lack of evidence makes it impossible to decide. But obviously when it became the practice to save seed for planting, the step to the building of granaries for the storing of grain for food was perhaps inevitable. But it must not be forgotten that Natural Man had no thought for the morrow. It never seems to have occurred to him in times of plenty to save food for the leaner times in the future. But once necessity compelled the farmer to save grain for planting he would be forced to contemplate the possibility and to appreciate the desirability of hoarding food for human consumption.

With his newly acquired knowledge of the length of the year, and of such arithmetic as would enable him to foretell when there would be another harvest, the Egyptian farmer had all the data to enable him to estimate how much barley he should store up to provide the year's food. But when he had made a storehouse for his food this object lesson would compel him to ask himself the further question—if he had not already done so without such prompting—why not make a house to protect himself and his family also?

The Egyptians seem to have been the first to build real houses— of wattle and daub—and they did so about the time when circumstances compelled them to devise granaries. But the storing of barley, before a primitive people had fully realised the importance of dryness, must often have provided the circumstances that promoted germination and fermentation. It is not surprising, there-fore, that these first cultivators of barley should have discovered how to make beer. Nor need we wonder that a people who had already come to attach to their staple diet, not only a special life-sustaining importance, but also a peculiar magical value as a Giver of Life (in virtue of the cowrie-like form of the grains of barley) should have regarded the fermented drink made from it as the divine (i. e. life-giving) essence of the sacred grain. Did not the exhilarating effects of drinking this beer afford corroboration of the reality of its divine power? It created a new personality. It was indeed a maker of gods.

The experience derived from the storing of grain impressed upon the early Egyptians the importance of dryness in preserving food from decomposition. This may possibly have played some part in teaching them how to preserve animal food, such as fish, by drying and salting, and in acquiring the knowledge which a few centuries later enabled them to embalm human bodies, and so to inaugurate a practice which had the most profound and widely extended in-fluence upon the arts and beliefs of every civilised people during the last fifty centuries.

Indeed, before we fully appreciate the attributes of the god and the nature of his powers and reputation, it is necessary to examine the circumstances under which the practice of mummification arose and how the material arts and crafts, and the spiritual beliefs and aspirations, became crystallised around this strange practice. The embalmer's art became the nucleus of civilisation and of its ritual.

The accumulation of increasing numbers of people in the small villages which every year became islands isolated in the vast stretch of water made it altogether impracticable for the earliest Egyptians to continue the practice observed by many groups of Natural Man of leaving the bodies of their dead wherever these happened to die. As we have already seen, they took the dead just beyond the limits of the irrigated land and put them into shallow holes scraped in the sand. They wrapped them in hides (and the linen they made from the flax growing in the fields of barley) to pro-tect them from contact with the soil. The depredations of jackals soon made the people aware of the surprising fact that in many cases the corpse did not suffer corruption but was preserved in an incorruptible form by natural desiccation. What was the meaning of this mystery? If the dead survived in this way did it mean that their existence was being prolonged? Were they simply sleeping in their eternal subterranean world? Whether the Predynastic Egyptian really thought such thoughts as these we have no written evidence to tell. But we do know that they began to lavish on the bodies of their dead and the graves containing them increasing attention and material equipment. The bodies were more carefully wrapped and elaborate pains were taken to save them from contact with the soil—perhaps the Predynastic Egyptians even invented the crafts of the carpenter and the brickmaker for this special purpose—and increasing supplies of food and equipment in the shape of weapons, articles of toilet, and jewellery were provided. So vast was the provision made for this purpose that by the time of the First Dynasty (circa 3400 B.C.) large subterranean chambers (needing a stairway to afford access) were made to house the equipment (Figure 53).

The successful attainment of this phase had most paradoxical results—for in making this lavish provision for the material wants of the dead by building large rooms the corpse itself no longer survived in the incorruptible form it often assumed in earlier times, when contact with the hot dry sand desiccated it. By the time this ironical fact was discovered tradition had already established the necessity for all the elaborate tomb-equipment. Hence there was no question of returning to the old type of simple grave. Instead of this the people set to work to devise some artificial means of preserving the corpse. The importance of desiccation had been deeply impressed upon them for many years. Perhaps they had also acquired experience of preserving fish by drying and salting. They were also familiar with the properties of resin, which they had been using (for centuries before the time of the First Dynasty) as an adhesive for their cosmetics. Whatever the explanation may be we know as a fact of observation that already in the Second Dynasty—and probably in the First also—attempts were being made to preserve bodies by drying and salting and to apply to these earliest mummies a paste made of resin and soda.

The Apotheosis of the King

Thus more than the great reputation he had acquired was needed to complete the king's apotheosis. The full appreciation of what his powers meant for his people was only reached when he died: his deification was completed when by mummification his body was saved from destruction and he was believed to be resuscitated in an imperishable form. The prosperity of the whole State thus became centred in the king's mummy, which, though immured in a subterranean vault, was regarded as the incorruptible body of the living god, who was known as Osiris.

The apotheosis of the king's attributes to transform him into a divine being who controlled the powers of life-giving and was himself a candidate for immortality increased the gap that separated him from his subjects. They were mere mortals. He was a divine being. As a result it was not considered proper that he should be free to choose his consort from them. There was no one except his own sister of celestial rank fit to be the mother of a king. Moreover, in virtue of the principle of matrilineal descent his own son could acquire royal rank and the right of succession only through his mother. Hence the apotheosis of the king had as one of its many strange results the inauguration of the practice of incest as the approved marriage of a ruler. As sister-marriage was regarded as the king's divine right, a practice devised to meet his special circumstances as a divine being, it was made the most heinous of all offences on the part of the common people to imitate his actions in this respect. Hence in all the earliest forms of civilised society the severest penalties were imposed upon those who had sexual relations within the forbidden limits of relationship prescribed by law or custom. Yet these same peoples prescribed the marriage of brother and sister as the proper procedure in the case of their rulers. (See Perry's *Children of the Sun,* p. 445.)

Such ideas were not restricted to ancient Egypt but were common to all early civilisations, both in the Old World and the New, as the written histories and surviving traditions of India, Japan, Peru and many other peoples reveal.

With the multiplication of kingdoms and the increasing influence of the people, which made the feeling of repugnance against incest stronger, kings began to seek for consorts in the divine families of other rulers. In some countries the lack of consorts of equal rank also played a part. Hence the incestuous practices gradually became modified until in most countries they were completely abandoned; and the king in this respect became subject to the same sort of code as his subjects.

But the mutual influence of the marriages of the Children of the Sun and of commoners was much more profound. It would be misleading to suppose that the change in practice was an assimilation of the customs observed in the royal family to those of their subjects. It would, in fact, be nearer the truth to say that, except in the matter of incest, the development of the marriage ceremony was due mainly to the imitation by the commoners of the customs that were originally wholly royal. The bridegroom and the bride, even of the lowliest members of the community, pretended for the ceremony to be the king and queen. They were crowned as they still are in Eastern Europe, Russia, Burma and elsewhere, and treated as sovereigns. Moreover, when kings began to seek for their consorts outside the limits of their own realms, their subjects also adopted exogamous practices, until it became a rigid discipline, disregard for which was considered a sin as heinous as incest. (Hocart's *Kingship*.)

These ideas do not represent the whole explanation of the practice of exogamy: but they probably explain one of the factors that played a part in the creation of this puzzling social institution.

The original institution of the royal type of marriage was intimately wrapped up with the ceremony of consecration of the king, whereby he acquired the power to confer life and prosperity upon his people. The ceremony of coronation was not complete or efficient unless the king was associated with a consort of solar rank equal to his own. Without such a wife divine rank could not be conferred upon him: he was unable to attain the immortality whereby he acquired the powers of giving life to others.

These ideas, so enigmatic to our reason, developed in times when inheritance was matrilineal. The queen, rather than the king, conferred royal rank upon her progeny. The rights of succession were determined by the mother. Hence to secure the succession for his son—or perhaps it would be more in accordance with the available evidence to say the birth of a son upon whose ritual performances the king's prospect of immortality wholly depended —the king could not attain divine rank unless his coronation was also his marriage. It was the firm belief that the queen's son, as the next king or Horus, was alone competent to perform the cere- monies necessary to convert the reigning Horus at death into the living god Osiris (or Re). Hence the ritual of deification was assimilated with that of coronation, and the marriage ceremony in the case of commoners was an imitation of a king's coronation, which was also his marriage. By the ceremony of union with his queen he acquired his regal powers, which, like the physiological consummation of the marriage itself, were essentially in the nature of life-giving.

The whole thought of early civilisation was dominated by the idea, which has already been repeatedly mentioned with tedious but unavoidable insistence, of the possibility of obtaining security —both of life and prosperity—by resurrecting the dead god, who alone was believed to be able to bestow such boons. We can perhaps get a truer perception of the real attitude of mind of the people who first formulated the possibility of such life-insurance by regarding their beliefs, not simply as articles of faith or religion, but rather as the all-inclusive scientific theory of the time, a doctrine that was supposed to be founded upon observation of the facts of nature and an essentially rational attempt to interpret them.

We know how profoundly every aspect of physical nature was transformed when Copernicus, Galileo and Newton devised a new interpretation of the facts and enunciated a theory that dominated all our conceptions of the universe and the nature of the forces at work in it. Charles Darwin's work compelled all seri- ous men to recognise the reality of biological evolution and to make it the foundation of the interpretation of vital phenomena, which utterly revolutionised our conception of Man's Place in Nature. In much the same spirit more than fifty centuries earlier some un- known genius in Egypt formulated an interpretation of the world and a view of life, and the factors which produce and control it, which dominated speculation to such an extent as to compel all theories of the universe and the living things in it to be brought into conformity with the general theory of creation and life-giving.

The practical application of this archaic theory of the universe was based upon the view that the death and resurrection of Osiris was essential for the maintenance of life. Hence it was considered necessary repeatedly to give a dramatic representation of the passion of Osiris, in other words, of the creation. By imitating as realistically as possible the incidents by which life was conferred on Man by the dead king it was believed that the existence of human beings, and in fact of the whole world, could alone be assured. We may smile at the idea that any people could seriously adopt such a childish belief. But throughout the history of the world, not excluding the present time, men have been enslaved by theories of knowledge. The vast majority of people accept such ideas blindly, without any real understanding, simply because other people believe in them, or they are persuaded that a theory is valid.

For the very existence of the archaic community it was considered essential periodically to give a realistic dramatic representation of the death, mummification and reanimation of Osiris. In this performance the conflict of the followers of Osiris with those of his enemy Set was enacted, often with ribald jesting. The actual mummy of the king, some relic or a bundle to represent it, was the essential ritual object in this Mystery Play, because the actual presence of the dead king was necessary so that he might be reanimated and (having been given a new name and new powers) perform the ceremony of creation. In its original form the act of creation was represented by the king, who appeared in the rôle of the god, actually engaging in the consummation of his marriage with the queen. The ceremony of creation was both the coronation of the king and his marriage, the creation of life.

Drama and dancing, music and comedy all had their origin in this ritual ceremony for maintaining the life of the community. Perhaps the most brilliant achievement in ethnological research within the present generation is Dr. W. J. Perry's demonstration of the deep motive underlying all primitive ritual and mythology. Merely by quoting the translation of the ancient Indian ritual from the Sathapatha-Brahmana, the folk-lore of the Pawnee Indians of North America as recorded by the Bureau of Ethnology of the

United States, and the beliefs of the aboriginal Australians studied by Dr. A. P. Elkin, he has demonstrated that the primitive rituals of these and other peoples involve the idea of mummifying a dead ruler, of dramatic representations of the conflict which brought about his death, of reanimating him, and of the creation of life. Though Dr. Perry's *Gods and Men* is a small book, judged by size, it expounds this vast and fundamental theme with such convincing lucidity as to deserve the reputation for greatness. He shows conclusively that Creation Stories are a vital part of the primitive ritual, seriously believed to be effective in maintaining the life of the community. A mummy, or a "medicine bundle" to represent it, is an essential part of the ritual performance. The myth is the official interpretation of the ritual, and the correct recitation of the verbal formulae is essential if the dramatic performance of the ritual is to be effective.

The vast literature of mythology and of the early history of the drama, dancing and music, only becomes really intelligible if these facts are given their due significance. In such books as Mr. Ivor Brown's *First Player* and Miss Evelyn Sharp's *Here We Go Round,* illuminating sketches are given of parts of this fascinating theme. But such great treatises as Sir William Ridgeway's *Dramas and Dramatic Dances* and Mr. F. M. Cornford's *The Origin of Attic Comedy* provide a fuller statement of the evidence without actually giving the interpretation of it.

In these ritual performances also were devised the germs of most of the games and athletic contests that, often in much modified forms, absorb so large a part of people's time and interest to-day. Not only the bull-fighting of Spain and the cock-fighting of Asia are relics of such ritual combats, but also the tug-of-war, football, hockey, tennis, cricket, polo, and in fact all ball games are the modified survivals of the Osirian competitions in which representatives of the rival parties struggled for the mummy of the king-god or his head, the ball.

In a Theban tomb men representing Upper and Lower Egypt are shown in a bas-relief engaged in a tug-of-war to obtain possession of the mummy, just as at the present time in Burma, according to Sir Richard Temple, there is a tug-of-war at a monk's funeral to decide who will take the body to the pyre. In ancient times in India a tug-of-war between the good (corresponding to the followers of Horus) and the evil beings (the followers of Set) effected the churning of the amrita, or elixir of life, which provided the gods with the divine food and drink to make them immortal.

The intimate association of ball games with churches and religious festivals persisted until modern times in Europe, just as cock-fighting still takes place in Hindu temples in Bali, for example, and bull-fighting at the funerals of rulers in Madagascar.

If we trace back the history of these singular proceedings we shall find records of ritual contests between royal combatants (for example, at polo in ancient Persia), in which kingdoms were at stake, or earlier still the attainment of immortality was the prize, for the kingly victor, like Osiris, attained the elixir of life, which conferred the rank of a god upon him.

Throughout the world these ritual ball-games and contests, like the dances and dramatic performances, add their corroboration to the fact that, as Plutarch of old expressed it, "Osiris wandered throughout the world on a mission of civilisation."

For a wonderful storehouse of information concerning the questions discussed in this chapter the reader is referred to Mr. A. M. Hocart's book *Kingship* (Oxford University Press, 1927) and H. J. Massingham's *The Heritage of Man* (London, 1929).

CHAPTER IX

THE GLAMOUR OF GOLD AND THE SANCTITY
OF THE FLAG

LONG before the development of an organised society on the
the banks of the Nile, men had been accustomed to the use
of amulets, supposed to be life-giving or death-averting. With
the adoption of a settled mode of life belief in such talismans
was not abandoned: on the contrary, under the influence of the new
stimulus, the number and variety of the objects credited with life-
giving rapidly increased. Among these was gold.

It is a very remarkable fact that a soft metal of relatively slight
intrinsic value should have exerted an influence so profound and
far-reaching, both for good and ill, throughout the whole history
of civilisation. The significance of gold does not depend wholly
upon the fact that it has become the material of currency, the
substance by which standards of monetary value and exchange are
estimated. It played a great part in Human History for thirty
centuries before a metallic currency came into common use. The
metal represents something more than mere riches; its influence
pervades our common speech, in which it has become the usual
token of excellence and uprightness, and in religious literature a
symbol of immortality and untarnishable incorruptibility. No
other substance—not even the pearl—has acquired such a
glamour. No other material consideration can compare with gold
in the vastness of its influence in Human History.

In attempting to obtain some insight into the nature of the
factors responsible for so curious a phenomenon, which has been
made to seem obvious and inevitable by more than fifty centuries
of tradition, it is essential not to forget that Man has no instinctive
craving for gold. Even at the present day uncultured peoples in
Australia, New Guinea, Africa and elsewhere do not attach any
value to the metal, which they do not bother to pick up when they

find it lying about in their natural domains. Thus the value of gold is arbitrary and has been created by civilised men as the outcome of a series of historical events, the evidence of which can be discovered and interpreted.

In the ancient literature of every people whose writings are known, there is ample evidence of peculiar magical properties attributed to gold. Thus, for example, in the ancient Indian Satapatha-Brahmana, gold is said to be immortal, born of fire, the rejuvenator of mankind, conferring long life and many offspring upon its possessors. It is said to be the seed of the god Agni, even a form of the gods themselves. It is not only regarded as immortal and imperishable, but also identified with fire, light, and immortality. Gold was endowed by the sun with its beautiful colour and lustre, and shone with the brilliancy of the Sun-God. Hence it was regarded as a source of life, as well as of light and fire. Thus we have clear evidence of the divine nature of gold among the Indians. It was the Sun-God, it was his seed, it was the source of life and fertility.

But there are indications of other kinds to reveal that the search for gold played a dominant part in influencing men's behaviour in India many centuries before the Satapatha-Brahmana was written. If the wanderings of the earliest Aryan-speaking invaders of India are plotted out on a map, as Dr. W. J. Perry has done, it will be found that every place mentioned in the Rig-Veda which Sanscrit scholars have been able to identify happens to be a site where gold occurs. The coincidence is much too exact to be merely accidental. It affords a precise demonstration of the fact that the earliest speakers of the Indo-European language to make their way into the Punjab were searching for "the divine substance," and settled at first only in those places where they found it.

The same story can be read in the early wanderings of the Persians from the references in their earliest writings, the Avesta.

But in Southern India also, archaeological evidence gives an even more emphatic proof of the fact that the earliest civilisation was introduced into the Deccan by the gold-miners. The most ancient stone structures (dolmens and stone circles) are found in vast numbers in certain regions of the States of Hyderabad, Mysore, and elsewhere, but always in close association with extensive and

long-forgotten gold mines, the very existence of which was quite
unsuspected and forgotten even in folklore until archaeological
exploration revealed them in recent years.

As to the uses of the gold thus laboriously obtained, the Vedas
inform us that the Aryan-speaking immigrants attributed magical

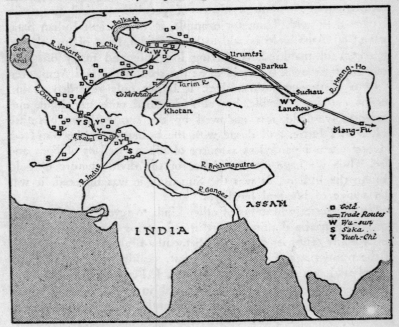

Figure 36—Map to illustrate old migration routes in the heart of Asia and their
close correlation with the distribution of gold deposits. (W. J. Perry, *The Growth of
Civilization,* Methuen.)

powers to the aboriginal people (Asuras). They could bring the
dead to life. They had vast stores of gold, jewels, and pearls, all
of them life-giving.

However, it was not only in India and Persia that men were
searching in ancient times for the golden elixir of life. Many
centuries earlier still, in Mesopotamia, the chief deities of the
Sumerians were called Lords of Gold.

Going still farther west, and to an even more remote epoch in
time, the Egyptian sun-god Re, in the Pyramid Age, was believed

to be the procreator of kings. He gave them life, strength, and endurance, so that in their veins coursed "the liquid of Re, the gold of the gods and goddesses, the luminous fluid of the sun, source of all life, strength and persistence."

Thus we find in Egypt, more than two millennia earlier, the same strange beliefs of the Indian Satapatha-Brahmana, expressed in almost the same peculiar phraseology.

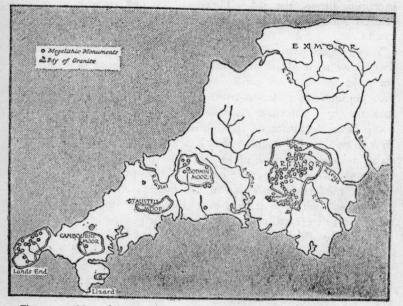

Figure 37—Map of Devonshire and Cornwall to show the coincidence of the distributions of megalithic monuments and gold-bearing granite. (W. J. Perry, *The Growth of Civilization*, Methuen.)

One could quote from the literature of Greece and China and the folk-lore and mythology of every part of the world where men sought for the yellow metal in ancient times, to emphasise the reality and wide geographical diffusion of these strange beliefs regarding the divine nature of gold and the potency of its magical virtues. But enough has been said to call attention to the reality of these ideas in antiquity.

In almost every part of the world where gold is found there is evidence, either in the form of ancient monuments or the survival of distinctive customs and beliefs, to reveal the former search for the metal on the part of people, who directly or indirectly, had acquired some part of the heritage of civilisation. Witness, for example, the remarkable coincidence (Figure 37) in the geographical distribution in Devonshire and Cornwall of the rude stone monuments we know as dolmens and the gold-bearing granite. Even the exception proves the rule! There are no old monuments in St. Austell Moor because the granite was covered in thirty feet of kaolin.

What we are particularly concerned to do here is to get some clues as to how such ideas came into being. The history of the search for gold in our own times is familiar enough. It has attracted vast populations, collected from all parts of the world to definite localities in California, Australia, South Africa and Alaska. In some cases, for instance in California and Australia, the people thus drawn to the neighbourhood of a goldfield have settled down to an agricultural mode of life after the harvest of precious metal began to dwindle. These are matters of common knowledge which provide modern illustrations of the process of cultural diffusion, which has been in operation ever since, more than fifty centuries ago, men first created an artificial value for gold, and then searched the whole world for it.

We know how obtrusive a part the pursuit of gold played in prompting the great maritime adventures in the sixteenth and seventeenth centuries. While the alchemists were busy in their laboratories, striving to convert base metals into gold, more enterprising men were roaming the world to discover natural deposits of the metal. The great voyages were essentially treasure hunts, the search for Eldorados and Isles of the Blest, where golden elixirs of life were to be had for the taking. Our maps of the world are studded with such names as the "Gold Coast," "Costa Rica," and the "Solomon Islands," which preserve the records of the chief motives for mediaeval enthusiasm in geographical exploration. Such phrases as "The River of Golden Sand," "The Mountain of Gold" (Altai), reveal even more ancient searching. But in still more remote periods the myths of the Golden Fleece, the stories of Golden Apples, and even the Golden Bough, represent a combina-

tion of traditions of the search for the metal and its magical attributes. The latter perhaps find more definite recognition in the
life-giving reputation expressed in the phrase: "Danae pregnant
with immortal gold." This gives expression to the very ancient
belief preserved, as has been already noted, in the literature of
China, India and Egypt, and more vaguely elsewhere, that gold
was the seed of the gods, the givers of life upon earth. Going
back still earlier in the history of ideas, when the source of all life
was attributed to the Great Mother, the Divine Cow Hathor, gold
was identified with her. The ancient Egyptian word for gold,
Nub, which was particularly associated with her and the deter-
minative (a necklace of gold pendants, probably models of cowrie
shells) of her divinity, gave its name (Nubia) to the place where
the metal was obtained, which also was regarded as Hathor's own
province. The Golden Hathor of Egypt was undoubtedly the prototype of the Golden Aphrodite of the Greeks. This does not mean,
as some modern interpreters of Homer pretend, that the Cypriote
goddess was a blonde of Nordic race, but it certainly does imply
that she was the daughter of the Egyptian Mother of Gold.

Thus there can be no doubt that when it first came into use,
gold had the reputation of being a divine substance. It was identified
with the gods and goddesses who controlled the giving of life. But
the bare statement of this fact affords no adequate idea of the
vast significance such a belief implied. At the time when civilisation came into being and the idea of a masculine deity was formulated the god (Osiris) was simply the dead king, whose existence
was supposed to have been prolonged by means of mummification and certain animating ceremonies. The essential difference
between the gods and men was that the former had acquired, if
not immortality, a prolongation of existence. So a distinction was
created which survives in our common speech in the use of the
term "mortals" for mankind. Substances credited with the power
of prolonging existence were therefore called "divine," in the sense
that they were the instruments whereby the distinctive attribute
of divinity, that is, a prolongation of existence, could be conferred
upon a dead king to transform him into a god.

During the past fifty centuries the Kingdom of Heaven has
become so democratised that it is now open to all mankind; but

originally the divine right of attaining immortality was the king's exclusive privilege. Hence the attribution of these vast potentialities to gold, its identification with the life-giving powers of the Great Mother herself, gave the metal a tremendous respectability and reputation for magical power. Not only did it prompt early rulers to send out expeditions to obtain the means of attaining immortality, but it also laid the foundations of the glamour that has crystallised around gold in later ages.

The earliest evidence of the use of gold has been provided by the examination of the Predynastic cemeteries in Egypt, which proves that the metal had already come into use (as a material for covering beads of clay or soft stone) before 3500 B.C. But the most instructive examples of early gold work are the objects found by Professor George A. Reisner at Naga-ed-Der in Upper Egypt, and Mr. J. E. Quibell at Hierankopolis, which belong to the time of the first Egyptian Dynasty (circa 3300 B.C.).

In a grave referred to the middle of the First Dynasty (possibly synchronous with King Zer) Dr. Reisner found ten beads (each made of an egg-shaped case of beaten gold filled with a light cement), twenty-four models of shells (snail-shells) made of heavy beaten gold, and a model of a male gazelle in beaten gold, with the representation of a band around its neck bearing the design of the goddess Hathor's head.

Thus the earliest examples of gold-work represent shells and other objects definitely associated with the goddess Hathor. As we have seen already, the goddess was herself identified with gold, and her hieroglyphic symbol was a necklace with pendants that probably represent cowrie shells. Similarly in the early Sumerian graves Mr. Woolley has found large numbers of golden objects, in particular models of shells made of gold.

In the *Evolution of the Dragon* the writer has put forward a tentative suggestion for linking all these positive facts into a coherent explanation of how the metal acquired the reputation for life-giving and became identified with the Great Mother herself. The study of early Egyptian writings makes it clear that many of Hathor's attributes were afterwards conferred upon Osiris and especially—still later—upon the Sun-God Re, with whom and with whose life-giving seed gold was identified and rationalised as the colour, light and brightness of the sun. Hence the fundamental problem is to discover how Hathor, the Mother of Mankind, came to be associated with gold.

Long before the earliest use of gold, shells, as was explained in the introductory chapter, seem to have acquired a definite magical significance. Thus in Southern Europe, bodies buried during the so-called Upper Palaeolithic period had a variety of sea-shells placed upon them. At Laugerie-Basse, in the Dordogne, Mediterranean cowries were used for this purpose; whereas at Mentone fragments of the shell *Cassis rufa* were found in the same stratum as the skeletons of Palaeolithic men. As this shell is not known to occur in the Mediterranean, the possibility is suggested that it was brought all the way from the Red Sea. This symbolism of shells is as old as *Homo sapiens* himself.

There can be little doubt that the magical significance attached to shells originally referred to the cowrie, probably upon the shores of the Red Sea. In his book, *Shells as Evidence of the Migrations of Culture,* Mr. Wilfrid Jackson has explained how the cowrie came to be regarded as a symbol of the life-giving powers, and so developed into an amulet potent to protect the living from the risks of death and to confer upon the dead a prolongation of existence. Hence in course of time a shell endowed with such maternal powers became apotheosised as the Great Mother and identified with Hathor (see Figure 3).

Before this happened the virtues originally associated merely with the cowrie itself (because of its shape) came to be attributed to it as a shell, and were then transferred to many other kinds of shells, even to many devoid of the form that gave the cowrie its magic. This is seen in the use of a variety of shells in the Upper Palaeolithic period, in the snail shells chosen for representation in gold as the Protodynastic Egyptian models found by Dr. Reisner, and the golden models of the shells found by Mr. Woolley in Sumer.

Putting together all these facts, and not forgetting that Hathor's hieroglyphic symbol, the Nub-sign, meaning gold, represents a necklace with pendants which are probably models of cowries, a tentative explanation can be suggested to link up all the established evidence in a rational way.

The wearing of cowrie shells still survives upon the upper reaches of the Nile and is widespread through East Africa, as well as in widely scattered places throughout the world, at the present day. When this custom began, the use of shells that were supposed to be potent to confer such considerable boons as the protection of life and the prolongation of existence created a widespread demand for them, which it soon became difficult to supply. The people of Egypt began to make models of these and other magical shells in clay, stone and any other material that came to hand. These were believed to have the magic of the real shells as life-giving amulets. In the course of these experiments people travelling between the Nile and the Red Sea, whence the cowries came, discovered that they could make more durable and attractive models by using the soft plastic metal which was lying about unused and unappreciated in the Nubian desert (Hathor's special province). The lightness and beauty of the untarnishable yellow metal made an instant appeal. The gold models soon became more popular than the original shells, and the reputation for life-giving was then in large measure transferred from the mere form of the amulet to the metal itself. Thus in all probability gold acquired the arbitrary reputation as an elixir of life by transference of the magic from the cowrie shell. Its sanctity was still farther enhanced by the fact that the shell had already been identified with the great Giver of Life herself, the goddess Hathor, who thus became known as "the Golden," and was identified with gold (Nub) and the gold country (Nubia) as far as the Red Sea, where the symbolism of the cowrie shell probably originated.

This hypothesis offers an explanation of all the known facts concerning the acquisition by gold of the divine reputation as a Giver of Life. This suggestion explains not only why it became an amulet, but also why it was identified with the Great Mother, and associated particularly with her reproductive functions and those of her successor, the Sun-God Re, whose powers of procreation were identified with gold. Dr. Perry suggests that the discovery of copper may have been made first and that gold may have been regarded as a sort of copper. But we still lack the evidence to decide this issue.

When the kings of Egypt accepted the belief that the prolongation of their existence after death (and the consequent attainment of the immortality to make gods of them) depended upon making adequate material preparations for effecting their purpose, expeditions were sent to collect gold. It was used with the almost incredible lavishness made known to us in the case of Tutankhamen's tomb, to make certain the dead king's attainment of divinity. The pictures in the tomb of Tutankhamen's vizier Huy had already made us aware that vast quantities of gold were being obtained from the Sudan in the fourteenth century B. C. Dr. Reisner's investigations in the Sudan itself have completed the story of the exploitation of the south by the Egyptians for gold.

When it became a matter of national policy thus to obtain gold, the mere demand for the metal further enhanced the value that its use for making amulets had created. Hence even in very early times the search for gold extended beyond the frontiers of Egypt. In Mesopotamia, even as early as 3000 B. C., gold is said to have been imported from Anatolia. Mr. Leonard Woolley has demonstrated that the Sumerians had access to a very fertile source of supply. The arbitrary value which the search and the magical reputation had given it is said to have found expression even then (in Sumer) by making a gold currency—small stamped pieces of the metal which became a standard of values for buying and selling. It took another twenty-five centuries, however, before people adopted this system of coinage in their ordinary commercial transactions; but there can be no doubt that long before a gold currency was commonly adopted as an instrument of commerce, gold rings and bars were in common use in the Ancient East for purposes of tribute between nations. Hence the metal acquired a recognised position as a medium of exchange long before it became used, at any rate widely, as ordinary currency.

One factor that played a very significant rôle in establishing the estimation of gold and maintaining its value throughout the ages has been its use for making jewellery. It is clear that the earliest jewellery was worn primarily as amulets. Gold was the favourite material by reason of its magical significance as a giver of life, which incidentally was supposed to bring the protection of the guardian deities with whom, from the beginning of its use, the metal was identified. But the aesthetic factor in the golden amulets, their beauty and lightness, as well as their durability and freedom from corrosion, must in time have developed an affection for such objects that was not wholly religious or magical. The love of beautiful adornments simply because they were beautiful and becoming to their wearer led to the survival of golden amulets as jewellery long after their original magical significance was forgotten.

The Dark Ages, when men were still searching for the elixir of life and the philosopher's stone to transmute base substances into divine gold, represent the stepping-stone from ancient times, when the semi-religious and magical reputation of gold was still obtrusive, to the frankly commercial and aesthetic value of gold, respectively as currency and jewellery, in modern times.

If it be true that the arbitrary value of gold was acquired as the outcome of the peculiar set of circumstances suggested here, it is utterly unlikely that such a remarkable concatenation of events should have occurred more than once. Hence the mere fact that men have embarked upon the most hazardous adventures, involving untold dangers by sea and land, to obtain a metal of little intrinsic value, is in itself the most emphatic demonstration of the reality of cultural diffusion in ancient times. Not only does it prove the diffusion of culture, but it also represents the chief lure which impelled men in antiquity to engage in maritime adventure and long expeditions by land. It also determined the localities where these wanderers settled, and incidentally planted in foreign lands the germs of the civilisation of their own country. Such events have been the chief factor in the spread of civilisation in the world for fifty centuries.

It is also important not to forget that the story of gold and the circumstances that were responsible for conferring a value on the metal are Egyptian and not Sumerian.

If the search for gold was responsible in greater measure than any other factor in disseminating throughout the world the germs of our common civilisation, it must not be forgotten that its influence was not wholly beneficent. The growth of the appreciation of gold made it not merely the basis of currency, but also the instrument of greed and an incentive to strife. Gold has, perhaps, played a more important part in exciting discord and provoking warfare than almost any other material factor; and there can be no doubt that the era of peace and happiness among men, which Hesiod with unconscious irony has called the Golden Age, was, in fact, brought to an end mainly by the quarrelling excited by the greed for gold.

Copper and the Age of Metals

Among the magical influences that acquired a particularly potent force for life-giving was the colour green—the colour of the new life that manifested itself when the fertilising waters of inundation awakened the apparently dead grains of barley to reveal their new life. The copper ore malachite, apparently by reason of its green colour, as Mr. Donald A. Mackenzie first pointed out, shared in this reputation as an elixir of life and it became a common practice, in

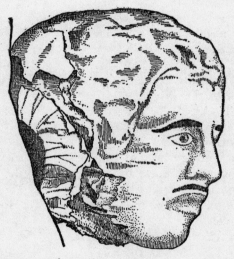

Figure 38—The mummy of Ranefer, a noble of the Pyramid Age (about 2600 B.C.). The pupils, eyelids and eyebrows are represented in green paint.

Egypt to apply to the face a paste of powdered malachite made adhesive by admixture with resin (see Figure 38). So important a part did this remarkable custom play in early times in Egypt (as also in Sumer) that slate palettes for grinding up this life-giving cosmetic are amongst the commonest objects found in Predynastic graves, and the kings had ceremonial palettes made and engraved with elaborate designs (see figures 39 and 40). The malachite seems to have been obtained from the Eastern deserts, especially of Nubia,

as is revealed by the exceptional abundance of the ore in the Predynastic graves south of Assouan.

After this green cosmetic had been in daily use for several centuries it was discovered, no doubt as the result of oft-repeated
accidental happenings, that in a charcoal fire malachite could produce a metal like gold. Some man of insight applied this empirical
knowledge and invented the practice of smelting. The copper which
was thus obtained was in fact used as a substitute for gold for many
years before some genius discovered that even a metal like copper
could be usefully employed for making chisels and other tools such
as axes. From this discovery, which occurred shortly before the time
of the First Dynasty, the Age of Metals developed. For implements
made of copper, especially when mixed with impurities such as
oxides of the metal, can be given a steel-like edge when hammered.
It is true the edge only lasts for a few strokes, but it is enough to
have enabled men to inaugurate the working of stone even as hard
as granite. The crafts of the stone mason and the carpenter were
made possible by this invention and out of their practice the art of
architecture developed. As was pointed out in the previous section,
Dr. Perry thinks copper may have been extracted from malachite
before any attention was paid to gold.

But if the discovery how to cast metal implements made such
crafts possible, other circumstances suggested to the Egyptians the
ideas of stonemasonry, carpentry and architecture. For all three
were first practised for the purpose of protecting the bodies of the
dead more effectively. Moreover the slag produced in smelting
copper ore revealed how to make glazes, and out of this practice,
which was widely adopted, there emerged some centuries later the
invention of glass.

Thus metallurgy and the Age of Metals, the glazing of pottery
and the making of glass add further examples of industrial progress which was the result of the Life Quest. Copper was added
to gold as another substance for which men ransacked the world.

The Sanctity of the Flag

We have now examined some of the manifold ways in which the
insistent search for the means of safeguarding life shaped men's
behaviour. The whole range of Man's thoughts and aspirations was

so dominated by this natural impulse that when the invention of civilisation, which was due to this very desire, enormously extended the range of ideas and actions, Man's craving for safety found expression in a bewildering variety of new devices of what we would now call magical practices.

Abstract thought is the rarest manifestation of the human mind even in modern times. Every schoolboy and student can make a pretence of abstract thinking by reproducing scraps of wisdom (and folly) acquired from the writings of scholars or the everyday currency of polite conversation. But when it comes to original observation and real thinking, the influence of the traditions and fashions of the time tends to inhibit abstract thought and keeps most men's attention fixed on stereotyped ideas and concrete demonstrations.

Primitive Man, who lacked the accumulated knowledge and traditions of our age, had nothing else save a few concrete ideas. At first he had not even acquired the knowledge that death was the inevitable fate of all living creatures. He knew that the existence of other men and animals could be brought to an end by injuries and loss of blood, but it seems not to have occurred to him that his own existence would inevitably be similarly terminated. Such a concrete fact obviously could not come within the range of his own experience. He had not at first framed the general conception that the usual fate of living creatures must include his own fate also. But when eventually the inevitability of death was forced upon his realisation, he devoted all his thoughts to the problem of understanding the nature of life and of devising means to avert its extinction. The concrete facts that came within the range of his experience were the loss of blood or the damage inflicted by the teeth and claws of animals as the causes of death, and the phenomena of birth as the means of acquiring life. Hence blood and blood-substitutes, the teeth and claws of animals, and maternal figurines and cowries become elixirs of life—objects which by a process of reasoning that was not wholly illogical, even if the premisses were false—led primitive Man to believe these things to be life-giving or death-averting.

When, in later ages, it was realised that these devices were devoid of adequate justification they were called magical. But it is important to recognise the fact that the ideas which we brand as magic and superstition were originally based on rational attempts to interpret natural phenomena. Magic is really nothing more than the scientific theories of the past, which have been shown to be unsound, but survive as popular superstitions. Yet in popular language the practice still survives of calling anything we cannot understand, or any conspicuous achievement, magical. Unless this principle (that magic is the survival of discarded science) is understood, the fashionable statement of modern scholars that medicine was founded on magic is meaningless jargon. In face of the mystery of disease, which primitive Man was less able to interpret than we are to-day, he applied his theories of knowledge much as we do. Disease was regarded as something that imperilled life. Hence the practitioner—it matters little whether we call him magician, physician or priest, for there was originally no distinction—put into practice his rational ideas of the only means known to him for prolonging life and averting extinction. If this is magic much of the medical procedure of the present time will half a century hence fall into the same category.

The process involved in the growth of magic can be witnessed in operation at the present time. Even in this century serious investigators, by pushing just a little farther than the evidence warrants the application of a bright idea, can make it nonsensical. There is an age-long tendency in all human thinking to adopt speculations such as we call magic and superstition. It is important to keep in mind this human frailty when we try to put ourselves in the position of those pioneers who more than fifty centuries ago, without the guidance of the accumulated knowledge to which we have access, or the control of the modern apparatus of critical discrimination, did seriously try to interpret the universe and put it at the service of Man.

Nearly sixty years ago Sir Edward Tylor discovered so many examples of a peculiar phenomenon discussed in the latter part of this chapter—the attribution of life and mind to inanimate objects —that he put forward a theory of universal animism, which distorted the vision of ethnologists for more than half a century.

The new ideas that emerged from the discovery of agriculture and the creation of the kingship involved, as we have seen, the belief that the world was actually created by the king and that he not only controlled the phenomena of Nature, such as the annual changes in the river, but actually conferred upon water its property of life-giving and upon human beings their very life. This was not a theological dogma, but a perfectly rational attempt to frame a scientific theory to interpret the things that seem to affect human welfare.

How seriously this theory of the kingship was adopted and applied in practice, not only in Egypt, but also throughout the civilised world, is revealed in Mr. A. M. Hocart's illuminating book, *Kingship* (Oxford 1927), which has not received the acknowledgment its profound significance merits. Dr. W. J. Perry's brilliant book, *Gods and Men* (London 1927) expounds the wider application of the theory.

In the intensive study of this theory of knowledge the principle involved was applied in a bewildering variety of ways. One of these led to the practice of mummification and the development of architecture. Another was destined, as we have seen in the preceding pages, to confer upon gold its glamour and power as an economic instrument of tremendous importance, and to inaugurate the Age of Metals. Yet another found expression in a peculiar social system, commonly known as "totemism," which exerted a profound influence in Human History, and survives in the civilisation of modern times as beliefs regarding blood relationship, the sanctity of the flag and the symbolism of national and family crests.

The belief that the king was, in the strictly literal meaning of the words, the life of the community, made it a matter of the deepest personal interest to every individual in the State to safeguard his life. The pious expression of the wish "God Save the King" was not simply a token of loyalty: it was rather a personal appeal for life and protection. Translated into its real meaning the prayer was "God Save *my* life and bring *me* prosperity." The devices invented for safeguarding the king's life were manifold and varied. One of the most curious results of such attempts emerged in the social system of totemism, with which is intimately associated the theory of the soul and the use of flags—a strange association of apparently irrelevant social practices and spiritual beliefs.

The study of the physiology of birth is as old as Man himself. The reason is to be sought not merely in idle curiosity concerning a strange human phenomenon, so much as in the hope that the discovery of how life was acquired at birth might suggest means for safeguarding life. The palaeolithic symbolism of shells and blood reveal the remote antiquity of such speculations. Under conditions of civilisation they assumed a more elaborate and sophisticated form, which the abundant evidence provided by Predynastic Egypt and later survivals throughout the world enable us to recover and interpret.

For many centuries it was—and in fact still is among many peoples—the belief that a child was formed in its mother's womb from the blood that was not shed during gestation. At the time of birth what was regarded as the accumulated blood not used in forming the body of the child was delivered with the child as the "afterbirth" or "placenta." It was united to the child's body by the umbilical cord. The placenta thus came to be regarded as a reserve of vital material, which from the circumstances of its origin was intimately related to the child's life and welfare. It acquired the reputation of being the child's "secret helper" throughout life, and even during his existence after death. It was his twin-brother, his protecting genius. When in the evolution of the tombs in Egypt the mummy, for the sake of safety, was buried in a deep shaft and a statue was made to preserve the deceased's likeness above ground (Figure 54, p. 334) his "twin" was believed to use the statue as its body. The statue was a material fact that compelled men to consider the possibility of a man's personality surviving apart from his body. The statue could be animated by the personality of the deceased which was dissociated from his body. Conversely, as the dead block of stone could be animated, so a living being could be petrified.

It has been claimed by Professors Seligman and Margaret Murray that the curious object carried on a standard before the king in Egyptian ritual processions was intended to represent the placenta, the king's "secret helper." For some reason that is not altogether clear the place of the placenta might be taken by a jackal (as well as by other animals or objects) and the umbilical cord by streamers of red, white, and sometimes also blue, hanging down from the standard. Figures 39 and 40 represent the two sides of a ceremonial slate palette found thirty years ago at Hierankopolis by Mr. J. E. Quibell. The chief scene in Figure 39 represents King Narmer,

Figure 39—The Slate Palette of King Narmer of the First Dynasty.

Figure 40—The other side of Narmer's Palette.

wearing the white crown of Upper Egypt, and demonstrating his power and his ability to subdue his enemies. The king is also represented symbolically on the right as a falcon with a human hand, holding captive on a rope a human head, behind which are six papyrus stalks, and below it a single barbed harpoon and a rectangle to signify a lake.

Professor Breasted interprets this picture as a record of the Falcon king's exploit in taking captive from Lower Egypt the people of the Harpoon Lake.

This is the earliest attempt (circa 3400 B. C.) in the history of the world at writing, which is not simply pictorial; and it is instructive to note that its purpose was to bolster up the king's reputation for power. When such omnipotent functions were attributed to the ruler as to put him on a plane vastly superior to that of his subjects, it must have been difficult for the king "to live up to," as we say in colloquial phrase, the glory that had been assigned him. The invention of writing seems to have been made primarily as a device to maintain the king's prestige by means of preposterous boasting of his omnipotence.

On both sides of the ceremonial palette the king is under the protection of Hathor, who is represented by a pair of heraldically grouped human heads equipped with cow's horns and ears.

Thus on one side of the palette (Figure 39) the king is represented as a human-armed falcon and his mother Hathor as a cow with a human face. On the front of the king's kilt four pendants hang down from his belt, upon each of which is the representation of the head of Hathor (Figure 41). This prototype of the Scottish sporran is peculiarly interesting because the cow's heads, representing the Mother Goddess, take the place of the cowries (also symbols of motherhood) upon the belts of primitive peoples still living in Africa and Oceania, and upon those displayed in the ancient monuments of India and Central America. On the other side of the palette (Figure 40) the king is represented wearing the red crown of Lower Egypt in a ceremonial procession. To the right are the decapitated bodies of his enemies, and in front of the king four attendants carry standards, which are shown on an enlarged scale in Figure 42.

The standard nearest the king has been interpreted as the placenta

with the umbilical cord hanging down. The second standard bears
a jackal, and the other two birds representing Upper and Lower
Egypt. It is important to note that upon the third and fourth stand-

Figure 41—King Narmer's Sporran (see Fig. 39).

ards the place occupied by the umbilical cord in the first standard
is taken by the streamers alongside the pole of the standard. Examination of the large series of Egyptian standards—the use of which
survived for more than thirty, or even forty, centuries—suggests
that this similarity of position was not due to mere chance: but

Figure 42—King Narmer in ritual procession.

was an intentional demonstration of the symbolic identity of the umbilical cord and the streamers of red, white and blue. In early times in Egypt such standards seem to have been regarded as ani-

Figure 43—A Protodynastic warrior carrying a falcon standard.

mate representatives of the king as the bestower of life and protector of his subjects.

A soldier in battle would carry the standard (Figure 43), not at first as a national or regimental emblem, but as a life-saving, i. e., victory-bringing, device. Even to this day the king in person presents the flag to his regiments with elaborate ceremonial: but it is not recognised that he actually presents to his soldiers a symbol of his own life-protecting powers. For the flag is the lineal descendant of the coloured streamers of the earliest standard (Figure 42), which in turn was supposed to represent the king's umbilical cord. As the representative of the king the animated standard could also seize the king's enemies (Figure 44). Originally all the symbols on the standard represented the king, but as two of them expressed his dual nature, as king of Upper Egypt and king of

Figure 44—Animated standard seizing the king's enemy.

Lower Egypt, the standards acquired a secondary significance as territorial badges, not merely of kingdoms but also of districts or nomes.

Thus by the time of the Pyramid Age each nome had its own distinctive standard. King Mycerinus was represented in a wonderful series of slate triads found by Professor George A. Reisner at the Giza Pyramids. In these sculptures the king is shown with the Goddess Hathor on his right side (not shown in Figure 45) and a woman (or sometimes a man) representing a particular nome bearing the appropriate standard above her head. The standard was animated in the form of a woman. In the symbol of the jackal nome reproduced in Figure 45 it will be noticed that a feather is stuck in the jackal's back.

From the Pyramid Age onward it was the custom to represent

Figure 45—Two figures from a slate triad of Mycerinus (George A. Reisner).

such a conventional feather on the standards. For example, two crocodiles from standards of the Eighteenth Dynasty (Figure 46) have such feathers respectively on the back and head. Their precise significance is not known: but the feather may be a symbol of identification with the sky. The idea involved in the symbolism of the placenta was that the *ka* was a something in the home of the

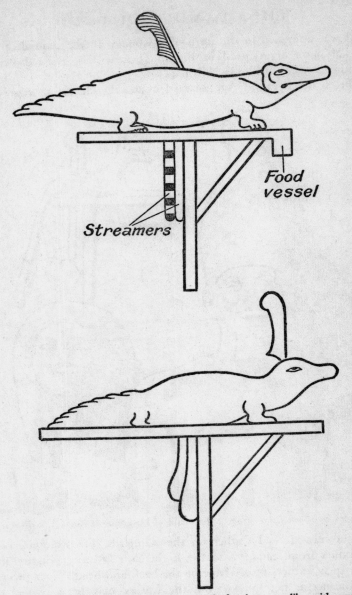

Figure 46—Two Egyptian standards (1500 B.C.) showing crocodiles with symbolic feathers.

'dead in the sky, which protected the deceased and prolonged his existence.

Discussing the Naga standards from Alor and Pantar (small islands in the Malay Archipelago) in the Rijks Ethnographisch Museum at Leyden some years ago (*The Year Book of Oriental Art and Culture 1924–1925*, London, 1925, p. 70) the writer called attention to the surprisingly complete and exact way in which these modern objects from the Netherlands East Indies reproduce the

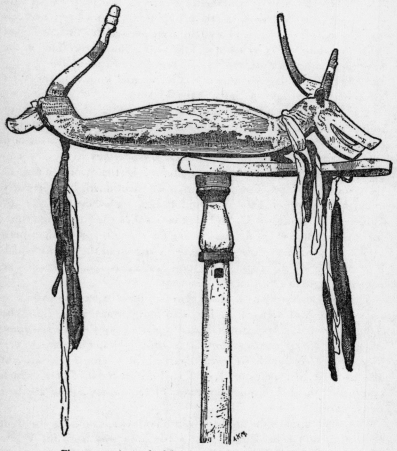

Figure 47—A standard bearing the Ular Naga from Alor.

peculiar features of the ancient Egyptian standards, the history of which can be traced back to the time of the First Dynasty fifty-four centuries ago. The form of the perch, the presence of a food vessel at one end, the coloured streamers, the conventional feather stuck in the tail of the Naga (in the Pantor standard the feather is on the head), and the curious headdress suggestive of the crowns of Upper and Lower Egypt are each and all peculiar and arbitrary features, which in combination can be reasonably explained only in one way. The standards that are still being made in the East Indies and elsewhere, and in particular those of Alor (Figure 47), are certainly survivals of the symbols that were in use in Ancient Egypt for more than thirty centuries. The Cobra and Crocodile of the Egyptian prototypes are replaced in the Indonesian models by the Sacred Serpent (Naga) or the fish-tailed animal known in the West as the Capricorn and in India as the Makara.

The substitution of an animal or some other object, plant or mineral, for the placenta is a curious phenomenon. Since the publication of the writer's memoir on this subject (in 1925) much new information has come to light which corroborates in a very emphatic manner the hypothesis adumbrated in that work. Three of these sources of new illumination may be mentioned. In a privately printed "Report on Totemism and Religion of the Dinka of the White Nile" Professor C. G. Seligman makes the important statement that "Most of the Dinkas derive their origin from a man born as one of twins, his fellow twin being an animal of the species which is the totem of his clan." The twin-brother is the placenta. The totem is the man's brother, his placenta.

That this conception of the totem is not restricted to Africa is revealed in Mr. Richard E. Latcham's important work on "The Totemism of the Ancient Andean Peoples," published in the *Journal of the Royal Anthropological Institute* (Vol. 57, 1927, p. 55). These people of South America regarded the totem as "the ancient ally of their first ancestor, bound to him by a blood-pact, which constituted them as mutual protectors of each other and of all their descendants."

The ally bound to the ancestor by a blood-pact is nothing else than the placenta. If it be objected that it is a long way from the White Nile to the Andes, the reader's attention may be called to the statements made by the writer ten years ago (*The Evolution of the Dragon*) concerning the widespread distribution of such ideas concerning the placenta in Egypt, Mesopotamia, Persia, India, China, Indo-China and Indonesia, representing so many stages in the diffusion of the idea from Africa to America by way of Oceania.

In the course of his important memoir on "Dualism in Western Bantu Religion and Social Organisation" (*Journal of the Royal Anthropological Institute,* Vol. 58, 1928, p. 225) Dr. E. Torday refers to "the leopard, *Ngo,* the only totem known to the Kongo nation," and makes this very explicit and decisive statement:— "Every person claims descent from Kongo, and whenever a woman bears a child she is delivered at the same time of a leopard, for that is the name '*ngo*' by which the afterbirth, 'the brother born at the same time,' goes" (p. 237).

This quotation affords quite conclusive corroboration for the hypothesis that the totem originally was "the twin" or placenta.

The reasons for regarding the standard bearing the placenta or the totem animal as the representative of the king and for conferring upon it a territorial significance have already been mentioned. What remains to be explained is the identification of the placenta with a totem-animal. The goddess Hathor, whose symbols are so obtrusive on Narmer's palette (Figures 39 and 40), was regarded as the mother of the king Horus. She was the Divine Cow who provided him with the elixir of life in the form of milk (see Figure 34). Once this blood-relationship with an animal was admitted it was not a difficult process to bring other animals into the cycle. Other factors may have helped in this assimilation. As the creature who preyed on the dead, the jackal seems to have acquired a reputation for protecting the dead. There is no doubt that Anubis, the jackal, was identified with the dead king Osiris—and perhaps the identity was based upon the concrete fact that the corpse had been devoured. It was the chief function of Anubis to take care of the dead and he became the director of mummification. In an ancient text (Middle Kingdom) Anubis is said to have come down from the sky to embalm Osiris. In his work, according to the Pyramid Texts, he was assisted by the sister goddesses Isis and Nephthys, whose symbols, the het-bird and the falcon, appear on the third and fourth standards (Figure 42).

In addition to being identified with the Divine Cow Hathor was also the Moon, who was believed to control the menstrual cycle and to be the celestial repository of life.

The underlying principle of totemism is found among many peoples who are not usually regarded as totemic. We do not apply the name totem to the "Ka" of the Egyptians, the Babylonian "god who walks by my side," the Persian "fravashi," the Roman "genius," the "kelah" of the Karens, the "ngarong" of Borneo, the "churinga" of the aboriginal Australians, but essentially the same idea underlies all these beliefs. Nor does it matter that some of them are given a material form as a standard or an object of wood or stone (like the churinga), whereas others are merely names defining an immaterial essence, like the Persian "fravashi" or our "soul." The details of the expression of this amazing, and even fantastic, conception of human affinities are so peculiar and arbitrary as to afford a definite proof of the ancient diffusion of this primitive theory of genetics throughout the world.

The attempt to interpret totemism by the intensive study of any one people in isolation is doomed to failure. Only by studying the history of the factors involved and the circumstances of the diffusion of a primitive theory of biology can we get any real illumination for the solution of this difficult problem. Without the use of the historical method it would be as impossible to interpret totemism in Australia as it would be to explain the presence of Mohammedan mosques in Java, or Hindu temples in Bali.

Flags and banners of all kinds derive their origin from the Egyptian standards we have been considering. Mesopotamian standards were constructed on much the same lines. The oldest Roman standard is said to have been a bundle of hay tied to a pole linking up, according to Mr. G. C. Rothery (*The A. B. C. of Heraldry*), with the Scythian horse-tail standards, still retained by the Turkish Pashas. "The more formal Roman standards were also of the Egyptian type, long poles, with short cross-bar, supporting a series of discs and rings, with figures of animals, almost invariably the open right hand (the sword hand held up in sign of command), and later portraits." In Rome the most ancient form of Egyptian standard (Figure 43) survived as the eagle. Constantine placed the monogram of Christ at the top of his Imperial standard pole, and thus gave rise to a long list of cross and crucifix standards.

The sanctity of the flag, then, is due to the fact that originally it was supposed to be functionally active as the life-giving power of the king and the celestial source of all life represented by the king's placenta. The king was identified with his people by a blood-bond. He was regarded as their creator and, as his own mother was the Divine Cow, his people were all knit together by a common origin. The form assumed by this blood-kinship was very peculiar.

The Divine Cow was the parent of the king and the king's placenta. The people were all created by the king, which established their kinship, and his placenta was their totem. The fact that this fantastic idea of blood relationship still survives in Africa, Australia and America, and in earlier times probably among all civilised peoples, is the most striking testimony of the diffusion of culture from Egypt, where alone the history of this system can be found.

Animal Symbolism

The development of the belief in the king's omnipotence set men speculating on ways of interpreting his attributes and powers, which so transcended those of all other men as to put him into a distinct category of beings. He was an immortal, while they were mere mortals. He was of the sky and the Giver of Life: they were of the earth and receivers of life from him. But how were these early people with limited knowledge and more limited vocabularies to express the superhuman powers of the king? They were familiar with animals which were bigger and stronger than any man, more fleet of foot or with subtler powers of death, or with abilities, such as flight, denied to men. Hence in striving to express the idea that the king was a superman, they were tempted to resort to the symbolism of animals. The Great Mother had already been identified with a cow, and subsequently with death-dealing cobras and lionesses to express her homicidal actions in sanctioning human sacrifices to obtain life-giving blood. The king was identified with a falcon as a symbol of his power of flying up to his divine Father, the Sun, to confer with him. The jackal's partiality for dead bodies led to the identification of Horus with him as the caretaker of the dead or the director of mummification.

In the famous story of the Destruction of Mankind the slaughter was done by the goddess Hathor, but not in her cow form. She assumed the likeness of a lioness and did the destructive work which earned her the name Sekhmet. To this day in Egypt it is firmly believed that certain persons are able to assume the form of a cat and go abroad doing "catty" acts of malice.

This strange belief has in past ages been so widely diffused throughout the world that the barest record of the doings of were-beasts would fill many volumes. Even in Europe alone the legends of were-wolves would fill a shelf in any representative library. In Further India and Indo-China the stories assume a more gruesome form as the common were-animal is a tiger. But hardly any country is free from the results of the evil reputation Hathor acquired when she destroyed mankind.

Another rich stream of folk-lore arose from the same exploit when her homicidal zeal led to her being compared to a cobra. Worn upon the king's forehead, however, the cobra acquired merit and a good reputation by spitting poison on the king's enemies. In fact the king was even identified with the sacred *uraeus* or cobra. Under the influence of such beliefs when Egyptian civilisation began to shape the nascent culture of Southern India, the Dravidian kings were called Cobras or *Nagas*.

Winged Disc

At an early phase in the development of the Egyptian architecture the custom developed of embellishing the lintels of temple-doors with the symbol of the winged disc in token of the fact that in passing through the door the worshipper was entering the sky world— the domain of the Sun-God.

The design is a curious association of the sun's disc, representing the god Re, embellished with the wings of Horus's falcon, and the cobras of the two goddesses. It represented a concatenation of all the most potent forces of life-giving to prepare the worshippers for admission to the celestial world of the temple. This symbolism was adopted far and wide in Palestine, Syria, Anatolia, Mesopotamia, and in modified forms in India, Indo-China, Indonesia and China, Oceania and America. The very eccentricity of the association of the sun, a falcon's wings and a pair of cobras, confers upon this symbol a unique distinction that makes it easy to recognise any-where. The evidence of the spread of this fantastic and incongruous assemblage of motifs thus affords peculiarly exact and significant corroboration of the spread of an element of Egyptian culture, via Western Asia, India, Indonesia and Oceania to America.

In the course of its wanderings it underwent strange vicissitudes. The place of the Sun-God's disc is often taken by other deities. The cobras' heads may become so conventionalised as to be unrecognised, leaving the bodies and tails of the serpents free to be variously in-terpreted by the puzzled sculptors. Or again, a sculptor recognising wings may think it necessary to provide an eagle's head in place of the sun's disc, but leaving tell-tale appendages to indicate that the heads and tails of the cobras were once parts of the design. One of the most interesting variants is the terrifying goggle-eyed head of the kalimakara, which embellishes so many temple-lintels in India, and especially in Java (Figure 49). As a rule its wings become trans-formed into complicated decorative designs, from which there some-times emerges the snake-like body of an elephant-headed makara.

The Winged Disc flew across the Pacific Ocean to embellish the lintels of some of the Maya temples in Central America. Although it has the typical wings and definite traces of much-altered cobras, the design is reversed so that the wings are upside down, making it necessary for the sculptor to deal with the now meaningless cobras' tails. In the best preserved of these lintels (Figure 48 lowest design) the characteristically goggle-eyed head of the Javanese kali-makara is in the Sun-God's place.

Before this distinctive emblem began its wanderings from the Ancient East it had already been brought into association (Figure 50) with a floral scroll, the Greek honeysuckle, the diffusion of which can be traced from Alexandria and Greece, to India, to Indo-China, to China (where it is one of the distinctive features in the art of the Tang Period), and to Java. But it also accompanied the Winged Disc in its flight to America, as Mr. Maudslay has shown in his beautiful atlas of Maya art. Here then is one more instance of an artistic motif created in Hellenic Egypt spreading to the ends of the earth. It would, indeed, have been almost inexplicable, when we recall the frequency and the prominence of this floral motif in the temples of Java, and in fact the whole of Eastern Asia from the

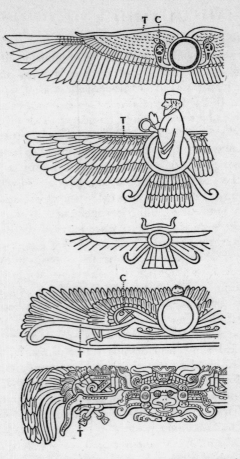

Figure 48—Five examples of Winged Discs. At the top the typical Egyptian symbol from the lintel of a Theban temple in the fifteenth century B.C.

A Persian variant.

An even more conventionalised Babylonian form.

Below two Central American (Maya) lintels. In the upper one (from Ocosingo) the reversal of the wings necessitates a re-interpretation of the conventionalised head (C) and tail (T) of the Cobra in the original Egyptian design. The lower symbol is Dr. Maudslay's representation of what he calls the serpent-bird from the wooden lintel of a temple at Tikal. From comparative studies of Maya art Dr. Maudslay arrived at the conclusion that the geometrical design above (and including) the tail (T) represents a serpent's head upside down, without a jaw. The writer by comparison with Indonesian motives arrived at the same conclusion. The loss of the jaw by the conventionalised serpent occurred in India and was emphasised in Java and then adopted in Maya America.

eighth century A.D. onwards, if this design had not been taken to
Central America along with all the other cultural influences during
these centuries.

Figure 49—A gateway in the Sivaite temple of Prambanan in Java (ninth century
A. D.) to show the kalimakara lintel with the wings conventionalised into geometrical patterns in the centre of which the serpent (with an atrophied lower jaw) is
shown performing the somersault the effects of which are seen in the American design from Tikal. Note also the kalimakara head (without a lower jaw) which gives
the Maya design ("serpent bird") its distinctive character.

Mythical Monsters

So far we have been considering the symbolic use of animals to
express the magic of the king's superhuman powers. But the most
significant aspect of this strange practice is the combination of the

Figure 50—Three examples of the wavy floral design, respectively from a Phoenician temple at Byblos (in association with a conventionalised Winged Disc) from
a Sivaite temple at Aihole in India, probably seventh or eighth century A. D. (Report
of Arch. Survey of India, 1907–8), and from the Great Ball Court at Chichen Itza
in Yucatan (after Maudslay).

parts of several animals to express the variety, and, so to speak, the
cumulative force of the king's powers.

From the very beginning of civilisation it has been the practice
to create wonder-beasts by adding to human beings certain parts
of other animals such as horns, ears, wings, fish scales and an endless variety of other derivatives, or alternately to make composite
animals by adding the head of an eagle to the body of a lion, or
the head of a goat or ram to the body of a fish; or again by using
natural animals by attributing to them powers and behaviour that
are wholly mythical. It would be difficult to estimate the wide influence of such symbolism in the history of civilisation. We see its
effects to-day in the use of coats of arms for our cities and countries,
in the crests of the nobility, the national standards and flags and in
many other symbols of kings and states. The English lion, the
Welsh dragon, the American eagle, the dragon of China, the
double-headed eagle of several European states are instances of the
present-day use of such symbols. If we look at mediaeval and
modern buildings we see gargoyles and a variety of embellishments
that are conventionalised animals. Animal symbolism is widespread in ancient architecture in Egypt, Babylon, Greece, Rome,

India, China and America. Mythical monsters thus play an obtrusive part in the development of architectural ornament. If we
turn to religious literature, the Bible is packed with references
to the mythical monsters borrowed from the epic stories of Babylon
and Egypt. Egyptian literature is largely concerned with the conflict of Horus and Set who are often given animal forms or appear
as composite creatures, which are really the parents of most mythical
monsters. In Babylon the great story of creation and the flood is
intimately entwined with the story of Marduk's conflict with the
dragon Tiamat. In Indian literature we find the same thing. From
the time of the Vedas onward the greatest episode in all the stories
is the conflict between Indra and Vritra. Ancient Persian literature
tells the same story. In China the exploits of the dragon are the
endless theme of much of the literature: it is no exaggeration to
say that such beliefs influence almost every incident of the daily
life of the people. In Greek and Roman times the stories of Zeus,
Oedipus, Perseus et cetera are largely concerned with the pursuit
of mythical monsters; and if we turn to the sagas of Europe the
exploits of Thor and the stories of Beowulf and Spenser's *Faerie
Queene* again tell the same story, with endless variations.

Throughout the whole history of civilisation people have been
intensely preoccupied with the problem of creation, not simply
from idle curiosity as to their origin, but from the belief that their
own safety and their welfare are wholly dependent upon repeating as a ritual performance the process of creation by which life
might be conferred upon them. In these narratives a series of
mythical creatures played a part.

Long after men refused to accept the stories at their face value
the themes persisted as the plots of innumerable romances and
folk tales, with which children are regaled in their early years even
to the present day. Apart from this wide religious and literary
interest in mythical monsters, such beliefs have had a fundamental
influence upon the development of social organisation. In most
cases the attributes of the animal with which a totemic clan was
believed to be related by blood-kinship were wholly mythical and
closely akin to the behaviour of composite monsters. There is a
close kinship between wonder-beasts, which are made by blending
series of parts of different animals to make a composite monster,

typifying the various attributes of a single deity, and the natural animal which is endowed with a series of supernatural attributes and identified with a particular group of the community. In studying mythical monsters it is essential that we should at the same time not forget the totemic animals and their mythical kinship with different human groups.

In one particular department of modern life the survival of mythical monsters plays a conspicuous part. The system of heraldry, blazoning the arms of different rulers and families, symbolises their totemic relations.

Even in Predynastic times in Egypt combinations of human with animal attributes were made. The goddess Hathor was represented with cow's horns and ears. In the First Dynasty King Narmer is shown on his palette as a falcon with a human arm. In the Fourth Dynasty the Pharaoh Kephren was modelled as a gigantic lion with the king's head to form the famous Sphinx of Giza. When the Egyptian gods were transferred to Babylonia composite animals were created: animals such as goats and rams were given the bodies and tails of fish to symbolise the fact that they had emerged from the waters of the Persian Gulf. When the Mesopotamian Capricorn was carried to India it acquired further attributes. In addition to the head of sheep, ox, goat or lion, it also assumed that of the elephant. The crocodile-like composite animal known in India as the makara became confused (especially in the Indian colonies of Indonesia) with the actual crocodile. But even this transformation has not been able to delete the unmistakable tokens of the original Egyptian ancestry of this mythical monster, who wears the crowns of Upper and Lower Egypt and the tell-tale feather in its tail (Figure 47).

The Dragon

The Naga and the Makara are merely two types, and not the most important, of the mythical beasts. The most interesting and peculiar symbol of the king's omnipotence is the dragon, for in this wonder-beast survive many of the attributes of the earliest king in the history of the world. Like Osiris, it is the special function of the dragon to control the waters of irrigation and to superintend the processes of life-giving and life-destroying. But although the dragon draws his original inspiration from the Egyptian Flood, Mesopotamia is the great breeding-place of mythical monsters.

In Babylonia too the superhuman powers of kings and gods expressed in the symbolism of animal forms were enhanced by combining the varied attributes of different creatures so as to make composite monsters. Hence a single wonder-beast may be built up with the forepart of a lion, the legs and wings of a falcon or eagle, and the scales of a fish. Once this process was started, as it was in quite early times in Elam and Sumer, and in the more restricted fashion already mentioned in Egypt, no limit was placed upon the fantastic combinations which heralds, both in ancient and mediaeval times, created. This strange fashion spread from the home of its original invention to India and Greece, to China and Europe, and it was swept across the Pacific in the fantastic forms it had assumed in Indo-China and the Malay Archipelago. Hence the weird combinations of monstrous snakes and elephants, crocodiles and eagles, intertwined with the peculiarly distinctive floral and symbolic designs, which flourished so luxuriously in Java and Cambodia between the eighth and thirteenth centuries A. D., suddenly made their appearance in Central America and Peru during the same centuries.

The dragon and its strange progeny of wonder-beasts are all forms of the king and Osiris. They are crude attempts to give concrete expressions to the marvel of his supernatural powers, his control of the waters of life, rejuvenation and protection from danger.

Throughout the whole history of civilisation the mystic symbolism of animals has exercised a profound influence on artistic designs and on literature. Mythology and folk-lore, poetry and religious writings have been concerned in large measure with the exploits of these mythical wonder-beasts. But it is not so much the use of these motifs as themes for epic literature that concerns us at present, as the evidence they afford of the reality of that diffusion of culture which this book has sought to elucidate.

CHAPTER X

MUMMIES AND ARCHITECTURE

REFERENCE has already been made to the fact that in Early Predynastic times in Egypt the bodies of the dead, lying flexed upon the left side, were often desiccated by the hot dry sand and so preserved indefinitely (Figure 51).

The body was not always preserved in this way, but more often suffered the usual fate of a buried corpse of becoming reduced to a mere skeleton (Figure 52). Even from the earliest times, centuries before any attempt was made to embalm bodies artificially, the Egyptians were familiar with the materials which their successors were to use for making mummies. Thus in the Predynastic grave shown in Figure 52 a large cake of resin was found upon the knee of the upper body. This material was treasured because it was used as the adhesive vehicle for a cosmetic including malachite, which, as was mentioned in the last Chapter, had the reputation of an elixir of life by virtue of its green colour.

At first the grave was nothing more than a shallow hole scraped in the sand. The hide of an ox or a goat was employed to keep the linen-enshrouded body (supported on a floor of matting) from contact with the sand. Then the Egyptians invented a variety of devices in their experiments to protect the corpse. Instead of the skin of an animal to prevent contact with the soil a wall of some sort was made to line the grave, and the use of the skin was discarded. The wall was sometimes made of sticks of wood pushed vertically in the ground to form a palisade, or rough slabs of stone were set upright, or more often mud-bricks were built up to form a retaining wall. Witnessing year by year the mud deposited by the inundation break up into lumps as the sun dried it, the Predynastic people got the idea of imitating these natural bricks by shaping mud into more regular forms of uniform size. The use of bricks determined the rectangular form of the grave.

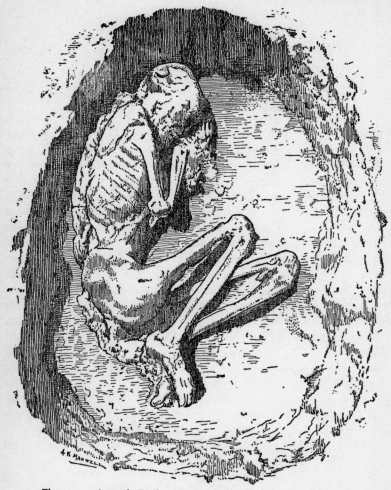

Figure 51—An early Predynastic Egyptian body, naturally desiccated

After using the palisade of sticks for many years as a means of holding back the sand, the Egyptians discovered that it was possible to use copper for making chisels, and the first use they made of their metal chisels seems to have been the shaping of slabs of wood to put into the grave instead of the palisade of

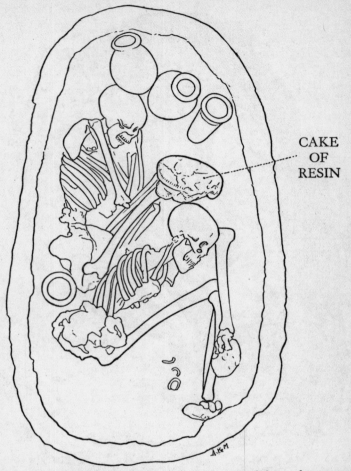

CAKE
OF
RESIN

Figure 52—A Predynastic Nubian grave containing two skeletons, four pots, and, near the feet, a little ivory cosmetic-holder. Note especially the large cake of resin on the knees of the upper skeleton.

sticks. Then it occurred to some man of inventive mind that instead of putting four vertical boards into the grave to wall in the corpse, which was lying on a sheet of matting, it would be more effective to make a box into which the corpse might be put. The invention of the coffin reveals the earliest instance of carpentry in the history of the world. The circumstances in the Egyptian necropolis created the need, and the discovery of copper provided the tools for the carpenter's craft.

As the provision of food and equipment for the dead increased, probably as the result of the growing appreciation of the significance these early people attached to the preservation of the corpse, the grave became larger and deeper, until eventually it became necessary to cut steps to provide access to the grave (Figure 53)

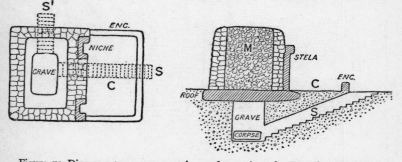

Figure 53–Diagrams to represent a plan and a section of a Protodynastic Egyptian grave. S the Stair leading to the burial chamber, the roof of logs of wood, upon which is a mound of rubble (M), kept in position by a retaining wall of mud-brick. On the face of the superstructure looking towards the Nile there were niches for false doors and sometimes stelae, and there was an area (C) enclosed by a low wall (ENC). (Figures 53, 54, 55 and 56 are copies of illustrations from the author's contribution to *Essays and Studies presented to William Ridgeway* (Cambridge University Press, 1913) which the late Sir William Ridgeway gave him permission to borrow.)

as a sacred place where the relatives of the dead placed the offerings of food. The stairway (S) usually opened on the side that looked toward the river, but sometimes, apparently to avoid the sacred enclosure, it was on the north side (S¹)

During the first two Dynasties the grave and superstructure underwent a process of gradual elaboration. In addition to the wooden coffins, made in imitation of houses, large pottery coffins were also made, and sarcophagi formed of stone slabs or by hollowing solid blocks of stone. As the burial chamber increased in depth the stairway necessarily became more and more oblique, until eventually it became quite vertical, and its upper part now opened through the tomb superstructure (Figure 54).

As the burial shaft was dug deeper, the more effectually to pro-

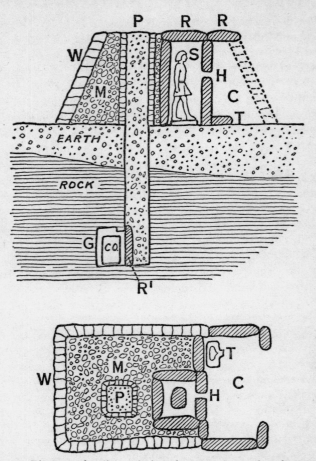

Figure 54—Diagrams of section and plan of an Egyptian tomb and superstructure (mastaba) of the Pyramid Age.

P—burial shaft filled with rubble.

G—burial chamber containing the coffin (CO) and closed by a stone slab 'R.'

M—rubble mound of the mastaba enclosed by a stone retaining wall W.

C—the court of offerings surrounded and roofed by slabs of stone 'R.'

S—a chamber (serdab) made of large slabs of stone and containing a statue of the deceased. The large slab H is perforated to permit communication to be made between the statue and the court of offerings.

T—table of offerings.

tect the body from desecration by men or jackals, the rock was reached and cut into. This happened at Sakkara at the end of the Second Dynasty (circa 3000 B. C.). For the first time in the history of the world Man cut into the rock and did serious stonemasonry. For many thousands of years previously men had been shaping flint implements. For several centuries they had been using stone slabs to build rough coffins or to pave the tombs. But it was not until the end of the Second Dynasty that the real work of the stonemason began. At the same time shaped blocks of stone were used to make the retaining walls of the superstructure of the tomb (W), which archaeologists now call by the Arabic word *mastaba*.

As the belief in the reality of prolongation of existence developed, and ampler supplies of food and equipment were made, the tomb had to be made larger, until eventually it became a suite of large rooms, in one of which the corpse was lodged in a coffin of wood, stone or pottery. But it soon came to be realised that these ampler provisions for the welfare of the dead defeated the very object that had prompted them. For in the large tombs the body was no longer preserved as it often was when placed in contact with the hot dry sand in the simple grave. But the importance of such preservation had become so deeply impressed upon the minds of the people as the essential condition for prolonging existence that (somewhere about the time of the First Dynasty, 3400 B.C.) attempts were made artificially to preserve the body, using common salt, perhaps also crude natron, and various resins for the purpose.

The realisation of the possibility that barley might be stored up to feed the community during the lean periods of the year naturally suggested the problem whether other food-substances might not also be collected in times of plenty for use in the leaner periods of the year. The attempt to store fish and meat in their natural state would of course lead to the inevitable result. The picture of fish hence became a symbol of the corruptibility of a dead body. But in the dry climate of Egypt no doubt it was soon discovered that an eviscerated fish exposed to the heat of the sun might become desiccated and incorruptible. It was also discovered at an early period that the use of salt made such preservation of the flesh much more sure and efficient. One of the things that impressed Herodotus during his tour of Egypt was the preservation of fish by drying and salting. We know from the pictures in Egyptian tombs that this practice was many centuries older than the Father of History, and in all probability existed over 3000 years earlier. For the Egyptians could hardly have devised the difficult and exacting technique of embalming the human body unless they had some knowledge of the feasibility and experience of the practice of salting fish. If this suggestion is accepted it is easier to understand how such technical devices as evisceration, salting and drying were invented and successfully practised.

This causal connection of the measures of the production and storing up of food with one of the strangest and most significant inventions of a nascent civilisation affords yet another illustration of its organic unity. The intimate correlation of the ingredients that went to the making of human culture, all inspired by essentially the same motive of safeguarding life and human existence, is a convincing demonstration of the fact that civilisation was not built up piecemeal but as an organic and closely knit whole.

The custom of burying valuables with the dead led indirectly to the acquisition of the knowledge of the effects of desiccation which suggested the idea and demonstrated the possibility of the artificial preservation which we call mummification. The earliest Egyptians at present known to us had already commenced those nefarious practices of grave-plundering which have been continued by their successors ever since then. When powerful Pharaohs like Rameses the Great, whose acts were accomplished in the glare of the publicity that illumines a throne, dared to mutilate his own father's monuments, merely to attain a greater fame or notoriety, and others, like Akhenaton, who desecrated even his royal father's tomb out of spite against his religious professions, or, rather, the better to emphasise his devotion to a new religion, is it to be wondered at that the common people should have satisfied their more insistent desires and obtained useful and valuable objects from the graves of their contemporaries, when they could do so in secrecy and without running any of the risks that attended the royal vandalism?

However strong a restraining influence their religious beliefs may have exercised against the committal of such acts of desecration, we have the most positive and conclusive evidence that the temptation of the immediate gains that might accrue from grave-plundering often proved too strong for these people: and at every period of their history from the most remote times until the present day, the inhabitants of Egypt and Nubia freely indulged in such easy methods of enriching themselves in defiance of their belief in the sanctity of the remains of their dead.

Thus it happens that a considerable proportion of graves, even of the earliest known Predynastic period, are found to have been desecrated and their contents damaged to a greater or less extent; and in many of these there is unmistakable evidence to show that the robberies were committed by contemporaries of the deceased— that is, by people who knew whether the graves contained the bodies of rich or poor, men or women.

This practice of rifling graves had very important consequences, for at every stage in the history of Egypt people were getting repeated demonstrations of the succcess or failure of their efforts to care for the dead. Mummification was invented to make more certain the prolongation of the king's existence. He had been raised to such a pinnacle of fame and credited with such vast powers of life-giving as to make it inconceivable that he himself should die and the country and people who drew their vitality from him should perish. Hence it became a matter of the utmost importance to the State to save the king and afterwards perform a complex ritual to animate his mummy and confer upon the deified king the ability to continue his life-giving functions.

Before discussing the vast significance of these historical events we must consider the curious incidental phase that led to the making of portrait statues.

The aim of the embalmer was to preserve not merely the corpse but also the life-like appearance of the dead whereby he might be recognised. When it was realised that the preserved body lost its resemblance to the man when alive, the attempt was made to convert the wrapped mummy into a portrait statue, by modelling and painting. When this was found to be impracticable a statue was made of stone, wood or plaster (apart from the body) and painted to reproduce the life-like appearance of the deceased.

The ideas that inspired this new art are revealed by the words used by the Egyptians themselves to define their achievement. The sculptor was called the "vivifier," and the word for "to carve" was "to give birth," "to create," "to give life." The artist was, in fact, believed to have made "a living image," a reproduction of the deceased that was so life-like as to ensure the continuation of his existence. It gave him a fresh lease of life, a new birth: it was, in very truth, a recreation of his existence, the creation of the conditions necessary for reanimating him as a living being. This was the origin of the widespread beliefs concerning the possibility of bringing the dead to life.

During the time when architecture was being created in Egypt foreign intercourse was being extended by the needs of the embalmer and the builder. Trafficking with Palestine and Syria, with Crete and the Aegean, and also with the South, became more and more fully cultivated as expeditions went out to obtain timber and resins, gold and copper, and the various other materials for which the new developments in Egypt had created a demand.

When an important Egyptian colonist died abroad his associates attempted to give him the rites of burial he would have had if he had died at home. Though the service of skilled craftsmen, the masons and the sculptors of statues, were in most cases lacking, the colonists tried as best they could, using native labourers, to observe their own customs. In the attempt to make the mastaba type of tomb it might be beyond the ability of their workmen to cut a shaft in the solid rock or to make a statue of stone. Hence their attempt would take the form roughly shown in (Figure 55).

Naturally the most essential part of the tomb, that upon which its function as the eternal home of the dead depends, would become the salient feature to be emphasised in a crude copy. The serdab, as the residence of the dead man or his statue, thus emerges as a holed dolmen (S) with or without a mound and retaining wall. The dolmen represents the serdab of a mastaba. Though the scheme suggested in Figure 55 is hypothetical—an attempt to represent the inevitable results of degradation, when unskilled workmen attempted a task beyond their ability—actual remains exist to reveal the truth of the principle enunciated. In Sardinia there are funerary monuments commonly known as the "Giants' Graves" (Figure 56) in which all the essential features of this hypothetical degraded mastaba are shown.

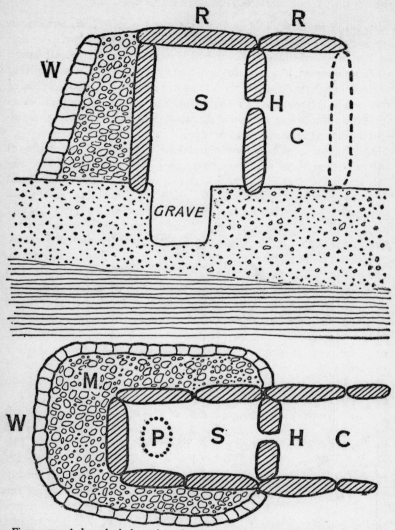

Figure 55—A hypothetical tomb such as might be made for an Egyptian in a foreign land without craftsmen sufficiently skilled to make a proper mastaba tomb such as is shown in Figure 54.

Scattered more widely, in Palestine, the Caucasus, France, India (Figure 57), and elsewhere, holed dolmens are found which undoubtedly represent crude copies of the serdab of the Egyptian mastaba without the tumulus. Far more widely diffused in other far distant parts of the world, ranging from Ireland, Britain, Scandinavia, Holland, France, Spain, Portugal, Northern Africa, Palestine, the Black Sea littoral, India, Further India, Indonesia, Corea, Japan, Oceania and America, dolmens without the holed stone blaze the track of the diffusion of a very distinctive type of archaic culture, which was the earliest to encircle the world. But the

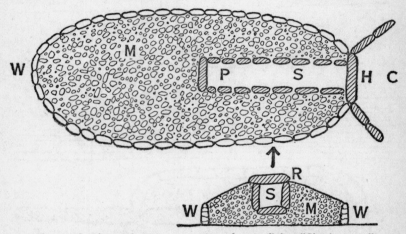

Figure 56—Plan and transverse section of a Sardinian "Giant's grave."

spread of the practice of building megalithic monuments is not so simple a matter as the foregoing statement may suggest. The types of dolmens we have been considering make their first appearance in Western Europe in association with what is known as the passage dolmen, which, as Professors Montelius, Sophus Müller, Déchelette and others have clearly demonstrated during the last thirty years, is an imitation of the rock-cut tomb. In his chapter on "The First Civilisation of England" in Marvin's *England and the World* (1925) Dr. W. J. Perry gave reasons in corroboration of this view, as well as the further suggestion that the type of Eastern Mediterranean rock-cut tombs imitated was invented in

Egypt not earlier than 2000 B.C. and afterwards adopted in Crete. The date of diffusion to the west was the time when the new alloy, bronze, was coming into use in Crete and Egypt. The people of the Eastern Mediterranean were searching for supplies of tin, which could not be obtained in their own country. Hence the paradoxical conclusion is forced upon us that the beginning of the Bronze Age in the Levant provoked the development of the Neolithic Age in the West. The civilised people of the Ancient East (perhaps for not more than a couple of centuries or so)

Figure 57—A holed dolmen from India—built by ancient prospectors for gold in Hyderabad.

exploited Britain and Western Europe for tin and other metals, which were shipped East. This surprising inference is corroborated by the peculiar geographical distribution of megalithic monuments in such places as Cornwall and Devon (Figure 37) and in Galicia and Northern Spain. These sites coincide with the distribution of tin and gold, as well in some cases as copper and lead.

The reader will find a clear exposition of this important interpretation in Mr. H. J. Massingham's *Downland Man,* Chapter III.

Presumably the people of the Eastern Mediterranean who introduced the ancient type of (serdab) dolmen, which was an ancient survival in the Levant, also introduced simultaneously the idea of copying, above ground, the plan of the rock-cut tomb which was not invented in Egypt until eight centuries later than the former. It is important to recognise that stone architecture

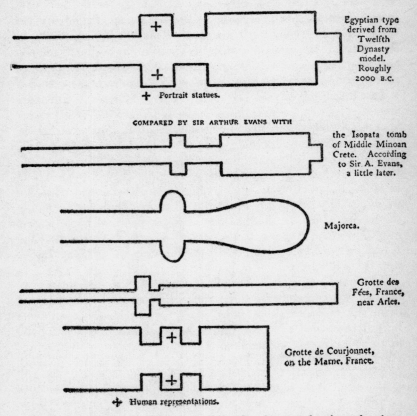

Egyptian type derived from Twelfth Dynasty model. Roughly 2000 B.C.

✚ Portrait statues.

COMPARED BY SIR ARTHUR EVANS WITH

the Isopata tomb of Middle Minoan Crete. According to Sir A. Evans, a little later.

Majorca.

Grotte des Fées, France, near Arles.

Grotte de Courjonnet, on the Marne, France.

✚ Human representations.

Figure 58—Diagrams to illustrate the comparison between the plans of rock-cut tombs of the Eastern Mediterranean and the passage dolmens of Western Europe. (H. J. Massingham, *Downland Man*, Cape.)

developed from the idea of making the essential parts of the mastaba as durable as possible. The forecourt of the tomb super-structure (Figure 54 C) eventually developed into a temple of offerings, the original purpose of which was for the performance of the ritual offices, opening the mouth, incense burning and libation-offering, for reanimating the dead and presenting food and drink for his sustenance.

Dwelling houses were for many centuries much humbler buildings made of less durable materials.

When we attempt to reconstruct the history of architecture and realise that the whole art was evolved from the stone temple, it is important to remember that the Cretans did not build temples and the Sumerians did not use stone. Architecture was created in Egypt and assumed its distinctive qualities from the fact that it was in essence a part of funerary ritual. When the Egyptians were devising a colossal stone tomb for the king to symbolise both his identity with the Sun-God and his everlasting existence, the Cretans were building a palace in which the living king could administer a beneficent rule over his people. The Sumerians and Babylonians were at the same time erecting stepped pyramids of mud brick, which were neither eternal homes for the dead nor dwellings for the living king, but lofty buildings to symbolise the sky, to which the king gained access by means of steps (Figure 59). There he performed the ritual ceremony (such as King Narmer is represented as doing in Figure 42), whereby he assumed the divine rank of a god.

When mummification was first practised, the embalmer's attention was concentrated for a time on attempts to preserve the living likeness of the mummy. After a variety of experiments he was compelled to recognise that he was unable to make of the mummy or of the material and paint applied to its wrappings even a passable likeness. Hence he invented the substitute head, modelled in plaster, stone or wood, which was made apart altogether from the actual head of the mummy. The next step was to make a life-size model of the whole body and put it above ground in a special chamber (serdab), instead of in the burial chamber, as was done when the substitute head was made. About 2600 B.C. the practice was introduced of inscribing upon the walls of the burial chamber hieroglyphic inscriptions to assist the deceased to attain the source of eternal life in the sky world. In the Middle Kingdom (2000 B.C.) the literary texts were inscribed upon the coffin containing the mummy. In the tomb around the coffin were placed many objects, such as boats and models of "food-producing," as Dr. Perry would express it, to assist the dead man on his celestial journey and provide him with subsistence.

By the time of the New Empire (1500 B.C.) the process of concentration of life-giving devices on the mummy itself was carried another stage. The coffin-texts were now inscribed on papyrus ("Book of the Dead") and put with the mummy inside the wrappings. The funerary equipment around the coffin was also enormously increased both in number and variety of the objects provided for the dead man. In the Twenty-First Dynasty

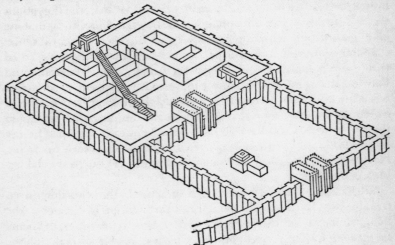

Figure 59—An early Babylonian Ziggurat. (After Hilprecht and Fisher.)
This type of building was destined in later centuries to become the prototype of numerous stepped pyramids made both of brick and stone, in India and Ceylon, in Cambodia and Java, in Polynesia and eventually in Mexico, Central America and South America.

(900 B.C.) the mummy itself was converted into the portrait statue, so that instead of the dead man's personality being housed in a statue and the mummy, it acquired, so to speak, a permanent habitation in his own body, upon which all the life-saving equipment was being concentrated. During the next five centuries this process continued until eventually even the furniture, such as the funerary couches which were to waft the deceased to heaven, were depicted on the mummy. The mummy then became, so to speak, self-contained and fully equipped to become one with Osiris.

The persistence with which, for nearly forty centuries, the Egyptians maintained this practice and developed it with such a constant and steady aim affords the most convincing testimony of the tremendous significance they conferred upon the mummy and how all their efforts were concentrated on it. At the same time there developed, as we have already seen, the custom of making life-sized portrait statues. When such statues were made to represent a king, who on his death was deified and identified with the god Osiris, the statue became the body of the god which, so they believed, could be animated by appropriate ceremonies. The custom of making idols and worshipping such images of wood and stone grew out of this Egyptian practice.

Even when Christianity was introduced into Egypt, and the early bishops of the Church forbade the practice of mummifying the dead, people refused to abandon a practice to which their ancestors had been habituated for more than thirty centuries. But if the exhortations of such devout bishops as St. Anthony failed to put a stop to embalming, the more vigorous methods of the followers of Islam did succeed, after the Arab conquest of Egypt, in destroying the most distinctive invention of Egyptian civilisation.

Though the practice of mummification was thus brought to an end in Egypt, it has survived elsewhere. In early times it was adopted in Palestine and Syria, and at least as early as the sixth century B.C. along the whole North coast of Africa. But it also was adopted in Nubia and the Sudan, in Uganda and the basins of the Niger and the Congo, as well as in the Canary Islands. Later on it spread farther afield in Africa, for example to the Zimbabwe region of Rhodesia and also in Madagascar.

But with the wider diffusion of culture in later centuries it spread to Europe and India. From the latter and Ceylon it appeared in Burma, the Malay Archipelago and Indo-China, was adopted in New Guinea, Australia and Melanesia, and then in the early centuries of the Christian era, reached the islands of Polynesia, Peru and Central America. At the same time it was being diffused around the eastern littoral of Asia, along the Aleutian Islands to the Northwest coast of America.

Thus the practice of embalming affords one of the most unmistakable tokens of the influence of Egypt in devising elements of civilisation which in time were diffused throughout the world. Its influence was much more profound and widespread than the distribution of the actual making of mummies suggests. In Egypt, the art was intimately associated with the development of the idea of immortality, when "this corruptible shall put on incorruption and this mortal immortality." This belief and the correlated idea that objects credited with the power of life-giving, such as cowries, pearls, gold, jade, et cetera, were also efficacious in preventing the decomposition of the corpse has survived in many places where the practice of mummification itself is not known or at any rate is only rarely practised. In the folklore and the religious literature of China this idea finds frequent expression, and in the mythology of many North American tribes who do not mummify their dead references to such ideas are not infrequent.

The art of mummification, in fact, is the nucleus around which the fabric of civilisation, its architecture, its stoneworking, carpentry and portrait statuary was crystallised. It represents the essential inspiration of the assurance of resurrection and immortality.

In most places the art of mummification rapidly deteriorated and eventually was abandoned. But the influence of the ideas associated with the practice have persisted in the rituals of initiation, coronation, marriage and the creation of witch doctors, in the use of magic bundles (so-called "medicine bags" or "medicine bundles"), in the veneration of relics and the attribution of magic powers to the mortal remains of kings and saints, and in a thousand and one customs and phrases in daily use at the present time amongst every people.

The practice of embalming is the nucleus around which civilisation was crystallised in Egypt somewhere about 3500 B.C.; and the persistence of vestiges of the ideas associated with mummification in the intimate texture of civilisation throughout the whole world affords the most emphatic corroboration of the influence of Egypt as the pioneer in the creation of civilisation. But apart from this fundamental significance of Egyptian embalming as the inspiration of the crafts and the innermost beliefs of civilised peoples, a sufficient number of undoubted instances of the actual survival of characteristically Egyptian methods of mummification at the present day afford the most concrete evidence of the reality of the early diffusion of culture and of its Egyptian origin. Moreover the fact that the most widely diffused method is the highly complex and very distinctive procedure devised (after twenty centuries' experience of other devices) to meet a very peculiar set of circumstances in Egypt during the Twenty-First Dynasty (900 B.C.) adds the strongest possible corroboration of the reality of the derivation from Egypt and of the fact that the major activities in cultural diffusion, beyond the Ancient East, were later than 1000 B.C.

The evidence that is now available in substantiation of these statements is enough to fill many volumes. Fifteen years ago the writer called attention (*The Migrations of Early Culture*) to the facts that establish the identity of the methods used during the present century for embalming bodies in the islands of the Torres Strait, between New Guinea and Australia. Since then Mr. Warren R. Dawson has added further corroborative detail with reference to mummies from the Canary Islands, Australia and America, and has recently summarised the conclusions in his book *Magician and Leech,* which provides also the bibliographical references.

In China the practice of embalming is not wholly extinct: but the custom of using materials like jade, gold, pearls, cowries et cetera and pretending that they preserve the corpse from putrefaction suggests the influence of mummification. The essential beliefs concerning the dead in China are based upon the supposition that the body is fully preserved and would be devoid of intelligible meaning unless in former times it had been the practice to mummify the dead. Nor is there any doubt as to the particular phase of Egyptian history that provided the incentive. When we recall the fact that during the Twenty-First Dynasty in Egypt it was the custom to put animal-headed figurines with the important viscera—in the Nineteenth Dynasty the practice arose of providing with representations of the heads of animals the lids of the so-called canopic jars in which the liver, lungs, stomach and intestines were placed—special significance can be assigned to the statement of the late Professor de Groot that it is "strange to see the Chinese fancy depict the souls of the viscera as distinct individuals with animal forms."

In Egypt the embalmers' early failure to preserve the lifelike appearance of the mummy was responsible, as we have seen already, for the creation of portrait-statues to take the place of the mummy. The widespread extension of this practice in Sumer and Babylonia, in Greece and Europe, in Africa and India, in Eastern Asia, Oceania and America and the practices known to us comprehensively as idolatry are so well known as to make it unnecessary to attempt to cite the voluminous details here.

But as we have been considering the evidence for the influence of mummification in Chinese customs it is important to note that the Chinese make funerary tablets and have a ritual for animating them that is essentially identical with the Egyptian procedure.

In consideration of the obtrusive part played by Elamite and Sumerian civilisation in providing China (during the third millennium B.C.) with her original cultural outfit, it is important to remember that Babylonia had these practices. In the journal of the Royal Asiatic Society for 1925 Mr. Sidney Smith, of the British Museum, has translated an important tablet of the sixth century B.C. describing "the Babylonian Ritual for the Consecration and Induction of a Divine Statue," which may be compared to the account given a century ago by the missionary Ellis of the similar ceremonies in Tahiti in distant Polynesia. The statues made in Egypt, Babylonia, Eastern Asia and Polynesia did not represent the deceased until ceremonies for animating them had been performed. Then the actual individual was believed to take possession of his statue, or as it was expressed by the late Sir Gaston Maspero, to "inhabit his image." So at the present day the Dravidian peoples of Southern India make images of their village deities, which are not regarded as the actual deities, but as the bodies into which these deities can enter to perform their divine acts. These beliefs were originally implicit in the widespread traditions of bringing the dead to life, powers which the earliest Aryan-speaking invaders attributed to the aboriginal peoples of India, who had learned from the West to make not only idols but also dolmens to house them.

But far more widespread than even the actual practices of mummification and "idolatry" are the ceremonies of initiation, which Dr. W. J. Perry has shown to be based on ideas derived from the ritual associations of Egyptian embalming.

When the king died and his body was converted into a mummy, incense and libations were offered to it and the ceremony of opening the mouth was performed—all for the purpose of restoring life. The dead king thus reanimated as a god was believed to have attained enormously enhanced powers and an immunity from death. To emphasise the acquisition of this divine personality the dead king was no longer called Horus but was given the title Osiris.

Hence the typical procedure in ceremonies of initiation is first that the initiate should die, then be embalmed and reanimated and given a new name to designate his new rank.

In the case of a coronation the prince is anointed with the embalming oils and swathed in special robes representing the mummy-wrappings. Then the ceremonies of reanimation are performed and the prince receives a new name as a king. From the earliest times in Egypt (and Sumer) the tradition of the reanimated Osiris's intercourse with Isis for the procreation of Horus determined one episode of the coronation ritual. The king entered a special booth and consummated his marriage. The coronation was both an initiation into the kingship and a wedding. In Sumer the booth (called *gigunu*) was said to be "like heaven": it was erected on the top of the Ziggurrat, the pyramid-like structure in the temple enclosure. Mr. Sidney Smith quotes a Hymn to Ishtar which says:—"They (Ishtar and Anu) abode together in the chapel, in the *gigunu* that is the seat of joy": and calls attention to the statement of Herodotus that the top part of the great tower of Babylon had a shrine containing a bed and a golden table, but no statue. A woman slept there and was visited by the god. There was a certain appropriateness in the action of the god when assuming his function as a Giver of Life providing a practical demonstration of his life-giving powers. The intense phallicism of certain religions, especially in India, is not primarily the result of a perverted sexuality but rather an exaggeration of this ancient conception of the god's life-giving functions.

What is significant for us at the moment is to discover why the form of coronation, based as it is primarily on the ritual of mummification, should have determined the ceremony of marriage.

Other Elements of Culture

As we look into the constituent elements of civilisation, one after another, we eventually arrive with almost wearisome monotony at the same conclusion which emerges from the study of the system of civilisation as a whole. The search almost invariably leads us back to Egypt as the place of origin and to the Life Quest as the motive that inspired the particular custom or belief we are investigating.

If for example we study the history of clothing, a topic of never-ending interest to every civilised man and woman, we can establish the fact that our clothes evolved from a girdle of life-giving cowrie-shells. A treatise might be written on the evidence afforded by clothes in demonstration of the diffusion of culture. Egypt was the home of the kilt, the full-length dress and the shirt. Sandals and hats were probably invented there also, at first as sacred symbols (see Figure 39, especially the sandal-bearer) of the kingship. The feathered head-dress of the Egyptian queens of the New Empire (fifteenth century B.C.) were widely copied by both sexes in the early diffusion of culture, attaining wide popularity in Indonesia and Oceania, and particularly in America, where it became the symbol of the American Indians and as such the favourite toy of modern European children. Thus at the present day the head-dress such as Queen Aahmes wore in Egypt thirty-four centuries ago can be seen on an Indian brave in Arizona and an English boy in London. The helmet worn by Roman soldiers at the beginning of the Christian era was still being roughly imitated by islanders in the Pacific within the present generation. Pectoral ornaments such as were worn by Pharaohs of the Pyramid Age have survived in India, at any rate from the times of Asoka onwards, and cruder copies of the same device are worn by potentates in Further India, Indo-China, Indonesia and Oceania, as they were by the Maya and Inca people of the New World.

The study of dress tells the story of the world-wide diffusion of culture. It also sheds a clear illumination on the psychology of human motives and human behaviour. It also provides a simple test of the distinction between a Food-Gatherer, who is naked and unashamed, and a Food-Producer, who is clothed and shame-faced.

The Flowing Bowl

Who can assess the part the use of alcoholic drinks, beer, wine, mead, soma, kava, and all the varieties of ritual beverages, has played in the history of civilisation—not merely in provoking jollity or degradation, in promoting friendship and geniality, or in exciting discord and criminal irresponsibility, but also in the ritual of almost every religion? As we have already seen, the dis-covery of alcoholic beverages began with the storing of the life-giving barley and its reputation was enhanced by the practical demonstration it provided of its ability to confer a new personality on the imbiber.

The study of the part played by drink in the religious rituals of Egypt and Greece, India and Europe, Oceania and America affords yet another inexhaustible commentary on the reality of diffusion and the varying reactions of different communities to a practice rich in its social possibilities and the temptations it provides for the defiance of traditional ways of behaviour.

Such a vast quantity of beer was provided for the celebration of New Year's Day that not only did the Mother Goddess Hathor and all her priestesses become intoxicated, but the volume of red fluid was supposed to symbolise and to play a magical part in producing the inundation upon which the prosperity of the whole nation was dependent. Moreover the Nile flood was the begin-ning of the year and the control of the inundation was believed not merely to provide sustenance and measure time, but also to control human destiny in the widest sense.

But the association of beer with these divine attributes was deeply rooted in religious belief for other reasons. Beer was made from barley which was not only the staple food of the earliest civilised community, but the particular crop that revealed the beneficence of the god Osiris and so to speak the foundation of his divine reputation. But over and above its material importance as the chief sustenance of the people barley had magical virtues attributed to it. We have already referred to the fact that the grain of barley was identified with the mother-goddess (who was regarded as the corn mother) as a giver of life, and afterwards with Osiris also. Thus in the Egyptian Coffin Texts of about 2000 B. C. the dead king is reported as saying: "I am Osiris. I live as the gods: I live as grain: I grow as grain. I am barley." (Breasted's translation.) It was a common practice to represent Osiris's body sprouting as barley or to make models of Osiris's mummy in barley and allow it to sprout to symbolise the resurrection of the god. Perhaps the references in the old texts, which are usually regarded as traces of cannibalism, have no meaning other than the symbolic reference to barley as the god's body. "Thou art the father and mother of men, they live on thy breath, they eat of the flesh of thy body." This idea survived in early Christian folk-lore. Sir Wallis Budge translates some Christian (Chaldean) texts of the fourth century in which wheat is described as having been formed by plucking pieces of flesh from the dead body of Adam (or Christ). There is no doubt that such staple articles of diet as barley, wheat, rice et cetera were regarded in primitive times by different peoples not only as material sustenance but as the life-giving substance of the gods themselves.

When the practice of storing barley developed it was discovered that fermentation of the grain produced beer which provided new evidence of the vital properties of barley. So potent was its influence in altering personality that the newly discovered drink was regarded as in truth the divine essence of the life-giving barley which was potent to make new men or women of those who partook of it.

But non-alcoholic drinks have also played a very significant part in Human History. It is unnecessary to say more about water or do more than mention the ritual use of milk as an elixir of life. Throughout the world, even in places where milk itself is not used as human food, the influence of its reputation as a sacred elixir has spread, so that many milk-like substances, such as the juices of plants, fig trees, nuts and in particular the Mexican maguey, share the sanctity of Hathor's Cow.

In his *Myths of PreColumbian America* Mr. Donald A. Mackenzie has written a brilliant essay on the ritual significance of milk and the symbolism of the milk-pot. The persistence of the worship of the Divine Cow in India naturally stimulated the greatest development of the ritual use of milk and ghee. Hence in Ancient America, which drew its original cultural capital mainly from Indian sources, we find the paradoxical fact that the milk-symbolism was actively cultivated there, as Mr. Mackenzie has shown, without the cow or any actual milk. No more emphatic testimony of the reality of diffusion to the New World could be imagined.

In return America gave cocoa and chocolate to the Old World in the sixteenth century, with the surprising result that the people of Europe became educated in the use of warm drinks of that type. Hence a century later coffee and tea were enthusiastically adopted. Who can assess the far-reaching social influence of the coffee house (the first was opened in London in 1652) and the salon? It was at the salon of the Marquise de la Sablière that the practice of putting milk in tea was started in 1680. These customs profoundly affected the politics and manners of Europe in the seventeenth and eighteenth centuries. In addition they also influenced the advancement of learning. For the famous learned societies and literary academies were created in the days when tea-drinking and coffee houses were first adopted and there was an intimate relationship between these social institutions and the cultivation of scientific discussions and the work of the scientific societies.

CHAPTER XI

ELAM AND SUMER

AFTER many years of fluctuating diversities of opinion it is now widely admitted that there is a very close genetic relationship between the earliest civilisations of Egypt and Western Asia. The identity of their burial customs, their methods of agriculture and irrigation, the use of bricks, cylinder-seals and mace-heads, the use of gold, copper and painted pottery, the weaving of linen and the choice and methods of preparing cosmetics, and above all their beliefs and religious practices—these and scores of other customs reveal the fact that the cultures of the earliest peoples of Egypt, Sumer, Elam, Northern India, and of a wide area contiguous to those countries, were derived from a common source.

If Egypt was the real home of the invention of agriculture and irrigation, of the working of gold and copper, of the weaving of linen and the making of bricks, of the building of sea-going ships and the use of incense, the probability is suggested that Sumer and Elam acquired these practices from Egypt, especially as the spread of culture took place mainly by sea-routes. The Babylonians themselves tell us that their culture was brought to them by a man who emerged from the waters of the Persian Gulf. Hence they equipped the animal representatives of their gods with the bodies and tails of fish. As neither the Sumerians nor the Elamites are known to have built sea-going ships, nor to have had any motives for doing so, one naturally assumes that the Egyptians (as the builders of the earliest known sea-going ships) took the initiative in opening up Sumer. The discoveries made by Mr. Woolley at Ur have provided material for a surer estimate of Sumerian chronology, whereby the First Dynasty of Ur is now put at between 3100–2900 B.C., instead of a millennium or more earlier. These spectacular discoveries, however, have distorted the judgment of certain authorities, who claim to see in them a civilisation superior to that of Egypt at the end of the Predynastic Period. Even if this were admitted, which is not the case, for the superiority of Egypt over Sumer at the time of the First Dynasty of Ur is unquestionable, this would not give Sumer the priority in invention.

This subject is at present in a state of confusion. Hence a useful service will be achieved by the effort to disentangle it, even if the attempt does nothing more than to make clear what the problem really is. It is claimed by writers such as Dr. H. R. Hall (see for example *Antiquity,* March, 1928) and Mr. Woolley that Sumerian civilisation preceded that of Egypt, whereas the civilisation of Egypt had existed for centuries before any trace of cultural achievement in Asia or any possible Sumerian influence in Egypt.

Excavations carried on in Western Asia since the war have made the situation much clearer, though they have done no more than verify the general conclusions set forth in the writer's article on Anthropology in the twelfth edition of the *Encyclopaedia Britannica* (Supplementary Volume, 1922). The trend of opinion is to reduce the dating in Sumer to a reasonable figure, so that where a few years ago the First Dynasty of Ur, the earliest historical Dynasty of Sumer, was assigned to 4200 B.C. the date is now estimated at between 3100 and 2900 B.C. Explorations during recent years have revealed the existence of a civilisation extending from Eastern Europe to the furthest confines of China, and from the basin of the Danube and Dneiper to northern India. This, the earliest known civilisation in this great area, is easily identified by the characteristic painted pottery. There is a striking similarity between the designs of pottery found in China by the Swedish scholar, Professor Andersson, and those found in Elam by the late Professor J. de Morgan. They are undoubtedly the product of one and the same civilisation. The sites in which painted pottery and other remains have been discovered are now numerous. They include Susa, the ancient capital of Elam, and the surrounding area:—Persia; Baluchistan; the Punjab and Sind in India; Egypt; Asia Minor; Armenia; the Caucasus; Turkestan, both Western and Eastern; China; and the Danube valley. It is highly probable that other sites will be discovered in the intervening areas; but it seems unlikely that beyond the limits of the continuous area, ranging from Eastern

Europe to China, in Western Europe for instance, such painted pottery will be found. The recent discoveries of Professor Andersson in Western China have revealed the importance of this early civilisation in Eastern Asia.

The significance of the painted pottery in the study of Human History lies in the fact that it is quite distinctive of early civilisation representing at least two phases. The earliest known occurrence of this fabric in Western Asia is at Susa in Elam, where it was found in the lowest level of the mound excavated by de Morgan. This pottery was followed in the same site by ware of a similar make, but less well made, of inferior paste, and of less artistic merit. This sequence has led to important conclusions concerning the early history of Sumer and Western Asia in general.

It will be necessary to refer briefly to certain centres of this early civilisation, so as to define its relationship to the civilisation of Egypt. Susa was excavated by a group of French archaeologists, under the leadership of the aforementioned de Morgan. The results of their investigations were published in a series of sumptuous volumes just before the Great War. The significance of their discoveries in relation to the problem of the origin of civilisation was discussed by the writer in the article "Anthropology" in the edition of the *Encyclopaedia Britannica* issued in 1922, and all the information that has since come to light corroborates and strengthens the argument then set forth.

The mound of Susa represents the débris of an occupation ranging from the earliest settlement to the time of its abandonment by the Arabs in the fifteenth century of our era. The lowest layer revealed the existence of a people who practised agriculture. They made flint sickles exactly like those made by the Predynastic Egyptians; rectangular houses of sun-dried bricks; polished stone axes, chipped flint implements of various types, and arrow heads with the pressure-flaking technique which is also characteristic of Predynastic Egypt; copper implements, particularly chisels; pear-shaped maces; spouted jugs; paste beads, vases of various hard stones, some of them in the form of animals and birds; slate palettes; linen, the presence of which shows that this people either already knew how to spin and weave or had access to some country where linen was made; necklaces of turquoise and lapis lazuli beads; figurines, both of

women and animals; metal mirrors and face veils. The greatest
claim to fame of the early people of Susa is their pottery, which is
remarkable for its beauty and for the skill displayed in its manufacture. The specimens found in the lowest layer of the mound
are the best: those found in the layer above are inferior in every
way. Thus it affords very definite evidence of the reality of
degradation. There is not only no trace of a progressive improvement, but very definitely a loss of the skill the makers once displayed. The painted pottery of the earliest settlement of Susa stands
practically alone in Western Asia. That derived from the other
centres is akin to the second style of Susa, the degraded pottery.
It is clear, and the fact is generally recognised, that the first population of Susa came there from elsewhere and brought their high
culture with them, but there is at present no general agreement
as to their provenance. Nevertheless for the present Susa may be
taken as the starting-point in Western Asia of the painted pottery. Thence the manufacture of the ware spread into other areas,
including Sumer, where its manufacture was part of the culture

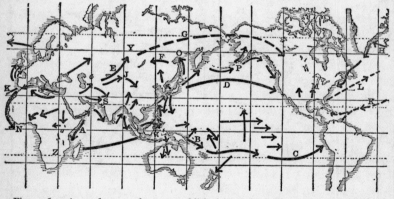

Figure 60—A rough copy of a map published in 1917 to illustrate the diffusion of
early culture.
S—the two lines of diffusion to India.
J—the route of diffusion to China.
E—the diffusion to Siberia (Y).
G—the route taken by the earliest *immigrants* into America.
P, D, B and C—the lines of diffusion of *culture,* across the Pacific into America
many centuries later.
H, L, and K—possible lines of diffusion across the Atlantic, which have not been
definitely established.

of the prehistoric civilisation of that region. For instance the excavations of Dr. Hall and Mr. Woolley at Al Ubaid have revealed a settlement of people making painted pottery, who preceded the First Dynasty of Ur. The same type of civilisation has been discovered at Abu Shahrain in the neighbourhood of the ancient Eridu.

Discussing the spread of proto-Elamite culture to the East, twelve years ago the writer published a map graphically expressing Dr. W. J. Perry's tentative suggestion that the pursuit of gold and copper probably led early Elamite and Sumerian prospectors into India both in the Punjab and into the lower valley of the Indus just east of the little village of Nal in Baluchistan. Part of a world wide map (of which figure 60 is a very rough copy) drawn in

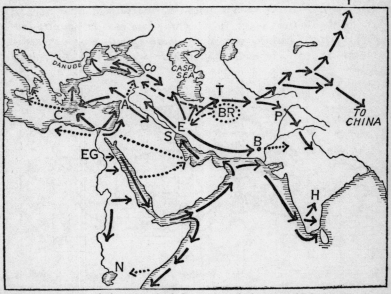

Figure 61—Part of the original of figure 60, which was published in 1923, to show the diffusion of culture earlier than 1500 B. C.

B and P—the lines of diffusion to India from Elam (E). BR—the probable home of bronze.

S—Sumer.

T—Anau in Turkestan.

H—the Megalithic Area in Southern India.

CO—Colchis—the Megalithic area in the Caucasus.

1916 and published in the Proceedings of the Manchester Geographical Society in 1917 was reproduced in the form shown in Figure 61 in the writers' *The Ancient Egyptians* (p. 191) in 1923. In the *Encyclopaedia Britannica* (Supplementary Volumes, 1922, Art. Anthropology, p. 150) a fuller explanation was given of the reasons for making these suggestions and for tentatively assigning the date 3000 B.C. to such a diffusion of culture. After this fore-

Figure 62—Map to show where the archaic sites were actually discovered in 1924, at Harappa in the Punjab and at Mohenjo-Daro in Sind.

The writer's argument in 1922 was that the archaeological remains found at Nal were certainly inspired by Elam contemporaneously with the manufacture of Susian Pottery, circa 3000 B.C., and further that it was inconceivable a diffusion from the West as far as Nal could have failed to reach the Indus. Moreover it was also argued (see Figure 36) that the intensive search for gold could not have failed (at the same time) to have brought culture-bearers to the Punjab.

cast was made Sir John Marshall, the Director-General of Archaeology in India, announced (in September, 1924) the discovery of Indo-Sumerian—or perhaps it would be more accurate to call them Indo-Elamite—remains, the age of which he estimated at 3000 B.C., in the two places to which by a happy guess the two arrows in the writer's old map (Figure 61, P and B) point, to Harappa in the Punjab and to Mohenjo-Daro just beyond Nal (see Figure 62). This corroboration of the prediction is specially emphasised here because in archaeological enquiries the experimental methods of investigation by which hypotheses are tested in physical and biological science are inapplicable: suggestions in explanation of the facts can only be tested by the confirmation of predictions. In 1916 the evidence seemed to point to the diffusion of culture from Elam into the valley of the Indus about 3000 B.C., but archaeologists ignored (or at any rate were sceptical of the cogency of) the argument. The confirmation of the prediction is a new argument in support of the general theory of diffusion, of which the prediction was merely one specific application.

The investigations of Mr. Hargreaves have helped to establish the reality of the connection between the early civilisation revealed at Nal in Baluchistan and that of Mohenjo-Daro in Sind. Sir John Marshall was impressed by the excellence of the roomy and well-built houses and in particular the wonderful drainage systems of the people in the Indus valley who were responsible for this early Indian culture.

With reference to the amazing skill of their craftsmen Sir John Marshall's eloquent appreciation may be quoted in his own words: "Among the smaller antiquities found by Mr. Dikshit, the most interesting perhaps are the engraved seals with pictographic legends, of which he has obtained a remarkably fine series, numbering 146 in all. The most beautiful of them is one bearing the effigy of a Brahmini bull, which in the stylish treatment of the dewlap, the modelling of the muscles, the slenderness of the hoofs, recalls the best glyptic efforts of Mycenean Greece. Another interesting specimen depicts a *pipal* tree (Ficus religiosa), the Indian "tree of life," with twin heads of some horned animal, real or fabulous, springing from its stem; others represent elephants, tigers or rhinoceroses, with a trough, as a rule, placed beneath their heads;

others, again, are engraved with pictographic legends only. Buried beneath the floors of the houses Mr. Dikshit found a number of copper vessels and utensils, including a curved saw; and in one of the larger vessels he recovered a valuable collection of jewellery. They comprise gold and silver bangles, ear-ornaments, gold netting-needles, charms and two particularly handsome necklaces or girdles (kanchi) made of tubular beads of carnelian, with terminals and smaller beads of copper gilt. The gold ornaments are so well finished and so highly polished that they might have come out of a Bond Street jeweller's of to-day rather than from a prehistoric house of 5000 years ago.

"Of the character of the other objects of bone, ivory, shell, terra-cotta and the like which Mr. Dikshit found in the houses, what is particularly striking and not a little anomalous is the great disparity in the quality of their technique. Rough flakes of chert, for example, which served as knives and scrapers, have been found in hundreds all over the site, and these utensils are as crude as such objects could well-nigh be. But mingled with them, and contrasting strangely with their primitive appearance, are finely made objects of gold and blue faience and exquisitely engraved seals, such as could only have been turned out by a people possessed of marked artistic ability as well as great technical skill; while the construction of the buildings themselves is far superior to anything of the kind in later India. Iron, of course, was unknown in this early age, but gold, silver, copper and lead were all being worked, and the discovery of some specimens of cinnabar suggests that the Indo-Sumerians knew how to extract mercury from this mineral."

Excavations carried out by the Archaeological Survey of India, under the general direction of Sir John Marshall, have since revealed more of this ancient civilisation. (See the *Annual Report of the Archaeological Survey of India,* 1923–4; 1924–5; *Illustrated London News* 1924, Sept. 20, 27, Oct. 4; 1926, Feb. 27, March 6; 1928, Jan. 7 and 14). The sites at present in course of excavation are those of Mohenjo-Daro in Sind and Harappa in the Montgomery district of the Punjab. Harappa has long been known to archaeologists as the source of seals engraved with effigies of bulls and with an unknown script. (*Ann. Rep. Arch. Surv. India,* 1923–4, p.

47.) Little else was known until 1920–21, when Sir John Marshall caused excavations to be begun on the site. Work was begun at Mohenjo-Daro during the following season. These excavations soon revealed a civilisation similar to those of Elam and Sumer. The following abstract of Sir John Marshall's account in the Reports for 1925–26 will make this clear.

The preliminary work carried on at Harappa, along the banks of the Ravi, on which Harappa stands, and in Baluchistan, shows that the two sites were part of an extensive civilisation. This civilisation probably will be found in the end to cover a large area, linking up ultimately with Elam and Sumer, as well as with other areas. The excavations at Mohenjo-Daro have revealed the existence of an early city, beneath which are the remains of successive settlements, built on top of one another, as is the rule in Elam, Sumer and elsewhere. The buildings on the uppermost stratum are of two classes; temples and private houses, both of brick, sun-dried, and kiln-burnt. Some of the walls have the bricks laid "header and stretcher" fashion. The smallness of the chambers and the thickness of the walls suggest that the temples were several stories in height. In them have been found some remarkable rings, requiring four or five men to lift them, made of stone, faience or other substances. The dwelling-houses are excellently constructed, and possess bath-rooms, fire-places, brick flooring and elaborate drainage, all pointing to a high degree of civilisation. In their every-day life the people used stone scrapers and knives; they worked copper, gold, silver, lead and probably mercury, as well as ivory. They made jewellery and other articles of gold, fine paste, and glazed blue and white faience. Among the gold objects were circular flower-shaped ear-ornaments; pointed cylindrical pendants; gold hair-ornaments with hair-clasps at the back; barrel-shaped beads and little hooks with eye-holes. "A noteworthy find made beneath the floor of one of the houses was a group of copper vessels and implements, and in one of the larger vessels a collection of jewellery of polished gold, silver, carnelian and other stones, including a particularly handsome necklace or girdle of carnelian and copper gilt, talismanic stones in polished gold settings, 'netting' needles of the same metal and bangles of silver were found."

Seals were engraved with great skill. The animals on the seals were provided with a food-bowl, as were the animals on the Egyptian standards (Figure 46) from late Predynastic times onwards, and on a Proto-Elamite bone cylinder. Terracotta figurines of human beings and animals were found. Most of the human representations were of women. Among the animals were lions, rhinoceroses, stags, boars, cattle, buffalo, sheep, goats, dogs and monkeys. The representations of birds are of particular interest as they include the earliest known evidence of the domestic fowl. Traces of malachite have been found on some of the ducks and geese. Terracotta was much used: balls and rattles were made for children; beads and pipes for ornament; circular ring-stands, triangular tablets and spindle-whorls. Gaming pieces were made of terracotta, ivory, shell and stone. They made many beads of various shapes and of different kinds of stone, including, it would appear, agate, carnelian, crystal and chalcedony. The people were stone-carvers. Two statues of bearded men have been excavated at Mohenjo-Daro, one of alabaster and the other of limestone with a veneer of fine white paste. They represent men, bearded, with low forehead, prominent nose, fleshy lips and narrow oblique eyes. "The culture of these people was also similar to that of Elam and Sumer: they both made painted pottery. The colours used were red ochre, yellow ochre, kaolin white and lamp black, some of which were found in shells, for inlay and for ornament, the commonest shell used being the Indian conch. Examples of exact imitations of shells in terracotta probably indicate a ceremonial significance to the form of the shell." In the latest city of Mohenjo-Daro the dead were cremated. But "At Mohenjo-Daro it is true some complete skeletons in excellent preservation are now being unearthed, but these appear to have been interred at a much later age, probably about the beginning of the Christian era. At Nal, however, in the Jhalawan country of Baluchistan Mr. Hargreaves has discovered a burial ground of the same period, where the dead were buried either in graves of sun-dried brick or directly in the ground. In the former case, the skeleton was complete; in the latter only a few bones and the skull of each body were found, instead of the whole skeleton, and they were accompanied by numerous earthenware vases, copper implements, beads, grind-stones and other small objects. All these objects are analogous to those found at Mohenjo-

Daro and Harappa; but the painted potteries from this burial ground constitute an exceptionally fine series, most of them being superior in fabric and design to those from the city sites." In other words there is evidence of a loss of skill in the easterly diffusion.

The date of the later sites at Mohenjo-Daro and Harappa may perhaps be indicated by the similarity, pointed out by Dr. E. Mackay, formerly Director of the Oxford American Expedition to Kish, between a seal found in the débris under a temple of Hammurabi's time, and those of the Indian cities. The report further states that Mohenjo-Daro must have been abandoned about 2000 B.C., after an occupation of many centuries (Rep. 1924–5).

The finds at Harappa are of like importance. They include earthen jugs with carved handles representing heads of crocodiles. The painted pottery resembles that found at Kish in Sumer. Terracotta cones were offered in the temples. The dead were cremated as at Mohenjo-Daro. The body was burned on a pyre: then what remained of the bones was placed in an earthen vessel or in a brick structure resembling a modern samadhi. Sometimes the ashes were placed in a large pot, set mouth downwards in the ground. Some stone pestles and mortars were found with the dead in one case, a practice recalling that of Mesopotamian sites.

Turkestan

Another settlement of painted-pottery-makers has been excavated at Anau in Turkestan near Askabad on the railway to Merv (see Figure 61, T). The lowest level revealed the existence of a people growing wheat and barley, probably by irrigation, who made rectangular houses of sun-dried bricks, and flint implements of pressure-flaking, but not, so far as is known, polished stone implements. Stone mace-heads; spindle whorls, witnessing to spinning and weaving; copper and lead; mealing stones and turquoise beads were all found at this site. Slightly higher up in the same mound the people were using lapis lazuli for their beads, and were making small pottery figurines of women and cows. Copper was used for chisels and knives among other things.

The culture of the people of Susa, Sumer, Mohenjo-Daro and Harappa, Anau and China in the days when painted pottery was made is so similar as to leave no reasonable room for doubt that it all belongs to the same civilisation. There is an unmistakable difference between this and, say, the civilisation of the builders of megalithic monuments in Western Europe at a somewhat later time. In the one case we have the use of brick and painted pottery; in the other we have monuments of large stones and no painted pottery. Lapis lazuli was used by the one and not by the other. There are similarities; arrowheads made by means of pressure-flaking; polished stone implements; spindle-whorls and other things, which suggest that there is some underlying unity connecting the two civilisations. But the contrast is marked enough to enable them to be distinguished with ease. It is, indeed, almost possible to write down what is likely to be found in the future in any settlement in which the archaic painted pottery occurs. We should expect to find the people practising pressure-flaking; making polished stone implements; using sun-dried bricks and copper chisels; and wearing beads of turquoise, carnelian, and lapis-lazuli. Some of these may be absent, but enough will be found to reveal the fundamental similarity with typical stations.

This civilisation suddenly appears as a whole in each place, obviously having come from somewhere else. No traces have as yet been found of its origin in Asia. Most writers are emphatic in their refusal to admit that the origin of this civilisation should be sought in Egypt. It is at this point that the element of confusion creeps into the argument. In regard to the Asiatic discoveries the agreement is fairly general: but when comparison is made with Egypt objections are immediately raised. No doubt is expressed by some authorities as to the similarity between the cultures of Predynastic Egypt and early Susa and Sumer. For instance M. Edmond Pottier, the distinguished authority on ceramics at the Louvre in Paris, writing in the year 1912, said: "Examining Egyptian monuments of prehistoric times and those of the earlier dynasties everyone will be impressed by their numerous points of resemblance to the objects found in the earlier Elamite deposits. In Egypt the forms, subjects and the details in technique remind one of the antiquities of Susa." De Morgan himself was so impressed with the similarities between the civilisations of early Susa and Predynastic Egypt, that he wrote a long article in *l'Anthropologie,* claiming an Asiatic origin for Egyptian civilisation. He goes through the catalogue of similarities; arrow-heads; polished stone implements; pressure-flaking; mace-heads; writing; pottery, painted and incised; stone vases, animal vases and figures; feminine figurines; art motifs; inlay; metal mirrors, spinning and weaving; vase supports; cylinder seals; architecture and copper chisels, to emphasise the essential similarities between the cultures of early Elam and Predynastic Egypt. That the early civilisation of Elam should agree practically point by point with the Predynastic culture of Egypt is strong evidence for some connection between the two. This connection was emphasised by the writer in 1922, and in 1923 Dr. Perry added further cor-roboration in his *Growth of Civilisation* (Chapter 3).

De Morgan has shown that the pottery is funerary in both cases, just as Professor Andersson demonstrated its association with burials in China. It is, therefore, the product of very exceptional circumstances, which are so complex and distinctive that they can hardly be imagined to have been repeated independently. Moreover, both De Morgan and M. Pottier have emphasised the similarities in the designs on the two series of potteries, as is evident from the following quotations. Speaking of the painted pottery De Morgan says: "This pottery in Egypt is probably contemporaneous with that found by us in the lowermost Susian deposits and presents such analogies with the latter as naturally to suggest a comparison between the two arts. Taking into account the differences that exist between Egypt and Susiana, we see in the two countries the wheel used with the same perfection: the technique is identical. . . . It is in the ornamentation that the most curious analogies are revealed, for in Egypt we find reproduced a large number of the ornamental motives which are painted on fragments of Susian vases." He refers especially to the representations of birds on the two series of pots. "Such analogies cannot be due to chance, but I shall not report here the reasons that support the view for a Mesopotamian origin of the earliest civilisations in the Nile valley."

His colleague, M. Edmond Pottier, goes into even more minute detail to emphasise the amazing likeness of the pottery and its painted ornamentation in Egypt and Elam. He goes on to say that, without attempting to minimise the importance of the resemblances, there are profound differences in technique. The commonest form of the Egyptian goblet differs notably from the Susian.

The Egyptian does not approach the fineness of the Elamite pottery. The method of painting is quite different; white on red or reddish on a clear ground. The Egyptian never knew the solid lustrous black, comparable to that of the Greeks, which is one of the beautiful discoveries of the ceramic ware of Elam.

In his recent book (*The Most Ancient East,* 1928), Professor Gordon Childe has agreed that there is a connection between Early Susa and Predynastic Egypt. He says "An approximate synchronism between the Second Predynastic culture and the First Prediluvian (i. e. the earliest settlement of Susa) is indeed quite likely. And some relation between the two is quite beyond dispute; common to both are the pear-shaped mace, spouted jugs, needles, flat celts of copper, dark-on-light ceramic decoration, as well as the use of obsidian and lapis. But one of these elements, for instance the spouted jugs and of course the obsidian and lapis, look like foreign intruders in Egypt, whereas they are at home in the domain of the Asiatic Prediluvian culture whose frontiers had extended at least into Syria. Accordingly a better case could make out for treating Susa as the parent of the Egyptian Second Culture than for the contrary relationship postulated by Perry; the only objects at Susa for which an Egyptian inspiration might possibly be claimed are the paste beads, and they differ materially from any Predynastic Egyptian specimens known to me. In other respects Susa seems to be ahead of Egypt."

To argue that the paste is different, that the pigments are different, and that other technical procedures differ in the two cases is beside the point: such differences are inevitable when an art or craft is transferred to another home. But this form of argument cannot be given the weight claimed for it. The painted pottery of Susa, it must be remembered, is an integral part of a civilisation which shows so many points of similarity to certain phases of the Predynastic period of Egypt that no reasonable doubt can be entertained of their relationship. It is not justifiable to isolate the painted pottery from both cultures, and to argue from it alone. The whole culture of one place must be compared with that of the other. The central fact is that both peoples had painted pottery for funerary purposes, and incised ware for everyday use.

The Predynastic period of Egypt was divided into three distinct periods, Early, Middle and Late. To these have recently been added the so-called Badarian civilisation, which has been claimed to precede the Early Predynastic Period. But whether this new period be accepted or not does not affect the matter. As Professor Childe admits, the comparison is between Susa and the Middle Predynastic Period of Egypt. They have in common painted pottery; incised pottery; lapis lazuli beads; copper chisels; polished stone implements; stone vases; vases of animal and bird forms; slate palettes; flexed burials.

This culture came ready-made to Susa from somewhere else. It must have been evolved somewhere. Although it is true that advances take place rapidly, yet there must be some sort of development. In Egypt the Middle Predynastic culture was not due to an alien influence. Professor George A. Reisner has shown conclusively that it was in unbroken continuity with the Early Predynastic culture and was developed from the latter in Egypt without foreign interference of any sort. In the earlier period copper was used, but the broad chisel had not yet been invented. Copper was first used in Egypt exclusively for ornaments, beads, foil and needles. Only at the end of the Early Period were thin graving chisels made; while it was not until the beginning of the Middle Predynastic Period that broad chisels were made. In the Early Period vases were made of aragonite and calcite, and in the Middle Predynastic Period a start was made with the use of harder rocks such as basalt, syenite, diorite and granite. These vases had tubular handles, and from them were developed animal-shaped vases of hard stone, which are also distinctive of this phase. The people of the Early period were already using lapis lazuli. They were making slate palettes in various animal shapes. That is to say, certain elements of the culture which has been claimed as Susian already existed in the Early Predynastic Period in Egypt, before the Egyptians had arrived at the general stage of development of culture such as was found in the earliest level at Susa. Thus Predynastic Egypt displays the process of evolution of some of the cultural elements which make their appearance in Susa suddenly and ready made. For instance, the use of copper is found in Egypt in a stage of development definitely earlier than that found in Susa or anywhere else in Asia.

The Middle Predynastic Period differs from the Early period in the addition of certain elements such as painted pottery. But it retains several elements of the Early period, and thus cannot be ascribed to a new beginning. The most that can be claimed by those who refuse to give the Egyptians sole credit for the new development is that a new influence came in from elsewhere, and added its contribution to the culture the Egyptians were already enjoying. But whence came this influence? The only place, so far as we know at present, with a culture as old as the Egyptian Middle Predynastic, is Susa. Suppose, merely for the sake of argument, we were to admit that Susa conferred upon the Middle Predynastic culture in Egypt its characteristic features, we should then have to discover how the people of Susa got their culture. It is to be noted that the latter presents certain features characteristic of the Early Predynastic Period of Egypt, for example, the use of lapis lazuli, calcite, slate palettes, incised ware. Where did it acquire these things? It certainly did not give them to Egypt, for they were present in Egypt already. The culture of Susa begins with the arts and crafts in a stage at which they had not arrived in Egypt until the end of the Early Predynastic Period. Therefore it is certain that the early Elamites got their original cultural capital from a source exactly similar to that of Egypt in the Middle Predynastic Period. They had acquired a culture which included elements that were characteristic of a summing up of the development in Egypt up to that time.

Theories must be founded on facts, not on possibilities. Here we have a civilisation—Susa—suddenly appearing, and similar to that of another place—Egypt, which has a long history of development leading up to that phase. The civilisation which suddenly appears in Elam is composed of two sets of elements: those characteristic of a still earlier stage of development in Egypt, and those that appear later in Egypt. If it be held that Susa influenced Egypt, then the question is, how did it manage to acquire certain elements that were already in Egypt, if the two countries had previously been without contact? Those who admit the similarity as evidence of genetic relationship are therefore caught in the toils of their own logic. They cannot adopt the favourite ruse of twenty years ago and dodge the difficulty by pretending that the culture of Susa might perhaps have been elaborated in Central Asia or some other remote spot, for they have emphasised the connection with Egypt. We have too much exact information to entertain such fantasies any longer. But if we were to agree to discuss such unlikely possibilities we should have to admit that the hypothetical civilisation influenced Egypt also. Thus we should be in a worse position than before, lost in a maze of useless speculation. The evidence, however, cannot be brushed aside merely to permit such day-dreams as we have been discussing. Elam acquired the use of steatite, calcite, stragonite, copper and other things, from a place with culture similar to that of Early Predynastic Egypt, and that place cannot be found anywhere but in Egypt. To postulate some unknown centre, say in Southern Arabia, is beside the point. What we have to do is to explain the known facts as best we may. The explanation that is staring us in the face, if only we keep our eyes open to see it, is that the earliest civilisation of Egypt is the most primitive so far discovered. In the course of time it developed into that of the Middle Predynastic Period. This culture suddenly appeared in Elam at Susa, where it took root and developed in a way distinctive of its new home. From there its influence spread over a wide area, and finally reached such distant regions as China (see Figure 61).

This question has been discussed at length to expose the hollowness of the pretensions of those who persist in denying the pioneer efforts of the Egyptians. But, as we have seen in previous chapters, the real reasons for recognising this fact are: first, the known culture of Egypt is of greater antiquity; secondly, the circumstances under which agriculture was invented are peculiar to Egypt; thirdly, it is utterly inconceivable that irrigation could have been devised originally under the conditions that are natural in Elam and Sumer; fourthly, whereas the Egyptians are known to have had the means of getting to Sumer by sea and land neither the Elamites nor the Sumerians had such means.

The prehistoric civilisation of Sumer was characterised by the use of painted pottery, resembling the later styles of Susa. This civilisation was followed by the historic Early Sumerian civilisation, which appeared in such centres as Eridu, Kish, Ur and elsewhere.

The excavations made at Ur on behalf of the British Museum and the University of Pennsylvania, and at Kish by the Field Museum of Chicago and Oxford University, have revealed much of this early civilisation, and many unexpected treasures. It is widely asserted that these discoveries establish the priority of Sumerian civilisation over that of Egypt. It is said that Sumerian civilisation was flourishing at the time of the First Dynasty in Egypt, and that Egypt owed its Dynastic civilisation to influences coming from Sumer. Thus, in a recent number of *Antiquity* (March 1928) Dr. H. R. Hall, of the British Museum, claims that "Ur, with its superior ceramic and metallurgical technique, seems to show us a culture more highly developed than that of the first Egyptian dynasty, though closely analogous to it. . . . If this impression is justified by the facts, its development must go back further than that of the contemporary Egyptian culture, and it must be the older of the two. . . . So far as the facts go . . . we seem to be confronted by the new Babylonian discoveries with the conclusion that of the two the Sumerian was slightly the older culture, and that Egypt borrowed from it not only the element which we have just noted, but, after the time of the First Dynasty, the knowledge of the potter's wheel and the socketing of weapons, which she adopted for the spear but not for the axe." But it is not enough to claim that Sumer "must go back further," when we have the most positive evidence that it did not do so.

It is asserted with confidence that Sumer was superior in culture to Egypt at that time. The chief reason given for this assertion is the claim for artistic superiority and the presence, in Sumer, of the socketed axe, a type of implement that was unknown to the Egyptians of the period. But if a people by special attention to one or two elements of a borrowed culture carry them to a higher pitch of efficiency, that does not disprove the fact that the art was borrowed. At the moment this sentence is being written the news comes of the exploit of an aeroplane far surpassing anything previously achieved. Neither the makers of this machine nor the pilot belong to the nation which invented the aeroplane. Yet this fact does not affect the fact that the art was borrowed. Moreover Egyptian civiliation involved something more than painted pottery and a particular type of axe! The statements of Mr. Woolley and Dr. Hall convey the impression that there was nothing in Egypt until the hypothetical coming of the Sumerian influence. The Predynastic civilisation is ignored. But it cannot be ignored. In his volume on the cemetery of Naga ed Der, Professor George A. Reisner in 1908 demonstrated quite conclusively that there was an unbroken continuity from the Earliest Predynastic to the Dynastic civilisation in Egypt. Many distinctive elements of the Dynastic culture were invented in the Predynastic Period. Moreover, the most that the Sumerians can be credited with are the cylinder seal, pear-shaped mace-heads, recessed brick walls, perhaps wheeled vehicles, and one or two other things, a frail foundation on which to build so far-reaching a theory!

It has already been made clear that the issue of priority lies between Susa and Predynastic Egypt. Egypt has the definite claim to priority, in the possession of its unique Early Predynastic culture. The early civilisation of Elam at Susa, is admitted on all sides to precede that of Sumer, which makes it unnecessary to enter upon this discussion once more. But it can be shown that much of the culture of Sumer was enjoyed by the Early Predynastic Egyptians, and by the Middle Predynastic Egyptians, and that the only possible place of origin of the culture of the early Sumerians was Egypt. The evidence recently brought to light by Mr. Woolley enables us to establish the relative chronology of Sumer and Egypt more precisely.

It is commonly asserted that the historic civilisation of Sumer influenced that of Egypt at the beginning of the Dynastic period. But considerations of chronology show that this is impossible. An examination of the burial practices revealed in the early cemetery of Ur has thrown a clear light upon this issue. The earliest burials found by Woolley reveal a variety of practices. The inhumed body may be wrapped in a mat; placed in an oval clay coffin; or in a rectangular wooden coffin. The most elaborate graves have corbelled and arched roofs of stone. These burial practices make their appearance suddenly in Sumer. Neither in Elam nor in Sumer is there any trace of the development of this complicated series of burial practices. The fact that so many forms of disposal of the dead were practiced suggests a fairly complicated history behind the culture of the early people of Ur. If, therefore, the development of this series can be demonstrated in any other country, it should have a good claim to be the pioneer of the culture revealed at Ur. In a recent article in *Man* (1929) Dr. W. J. Perry has shown that the complete history of these series of burial practices is revealed in Egypt, and that they were all in use towards the end of the Second Egyptian Dynasty, during the reigns of Perabsen and Khasekhemui. We have already seen that the Predynastic Egyptians wrapped their dead in skins or mats to protect them from the soil, and that this practice led ultimately to the making of coffins of various kinds. The poorer people continued to wrap their dead in mats during the time of the Old Kingdom, until long after the time of the Second Dynasty. The graves were often lined with wood in the later phases of the Predynastic period. After some time a portable wooden box was made—the first coffin. This was certainly made in the beginning for the rich. The poor people imitated the wooden coffins in clay or pottery. They made these clay or pottery coffins rectangular at first, and only at the end of the Second Dynasty, or the beginning of the Third, did they make them elliptical. This is a much more easily made shape for a pottery vessel. It is important to note that the clay coffins in the cemetery at Ur were, to the surprise of Mr. Woolley, those of poor people, while the wooden coffins, as in Egypt, were those of the rich. The wooden coffins of both places likewise resembled each other in having recessed panels. Thus by the beginning of the First Dynasty the burial practices had developed to a stage similar to those of Ur. The stone construction and vaulting, however, had not yet made their appearance. This was not invented until later. During the First Egyptian Dynasty a beginning was made of the use of stone for the construction of tombs. A notable instance is the granite floor of one of the chambers of the tomb of king Den. But the first large stone construction in Egypt was in the tomb of Khasekhemui of the Second Dynasty, who had a chamber made of worked limestone. During the latter part of this dynasty corbelled vaults are made in the tombs of nobles. Professor Reisner states that the first corbelled vault made in Egypt was in the tomb of either Perabsen or Khasekhemui of the Second Dynasty. Therefore the grouping found at Ur in the earliest cemetery was achieved in Egypt by the summation made during the period ranging from the late Predynastic to the end of the Second Dynasty.

Hence we can confidently claim that the early civilisation of Sumer was approximately of the same age as the later part of the Second Dynasty in Egypt 3000 B. C.

Civilisation was an Egyptian invention; Elam and Sumer were the sites where Egyptian colonists introduced the leaven of culture, as I have endeavoured to show. Only a part of the Egyptian culture really took root and many of the most distinctive elements were conspicuously absent.

CHAPTER XII

THE EARLY CIVILISATION OF CRETE

IN 1883 Dr. Milchhofer published a very suggestive essay on some strange objects picked up by Cretan shepherds, and he called attention to the possibilities of Crete as a promising field for archaeological research. In 1886 Dr. Halbherr, in cooperation with Dr. Hazzidakis, began the work of excavation and was rewarded by the discovery of double-axes, figurines and other interesting objects. Yet, even with these encouraging results, we had to wait for another eight years until Sir Arthur Evans began to reveal the richness of the harvest of important historical evidence that was awaiting a systematic exploration.

Some years before the awakening of interest in Crete Dr. Schliemann (in 1876 and 1877) had made the revolutionary discovery of a series of remains on the site of Troy and at Mycenae, Tiryns, and elsewhere on the Greek mainland, representing a phase of culture several centuries older than the classical civilisation of Greece. The wealth displayed in these discoveries lent peculiar appropriateness to Homer's reference to "Mycenae, rich in gold." Hence this pre-Homeric phase was distinguished as Mycenean civilisation. But the new discoveries in Crete nearly twenty years later revealed the still earlier Minoan civilisation as the chief source of the Mycenean inspiration.

In considering the origin of the Minoan civilisation it is a matter of fundamental importance not to forget that Crete is an island, which can be reached only after a considerable journey by sea. Hence neither people nor culture could reach this sea-girt island until the invention of some sort of sea-going ship and the cultivation of sufficient confidence in some ancient mariners' seamanship to induce the immigrants to undertake the hazardous adventure. The absence of any palaeolithic remains in Crete confirms the view that men did not reach the island until the beginning of maritime adventuring. The only people who are known to have been shipbuilders and seamen early enough to have colonised Crete and to have given it its cultural capital were the Ancient Egyptians, probably no earlier than about 3500 B.C.

These facts must be kept in mind during the subsequent discussion.

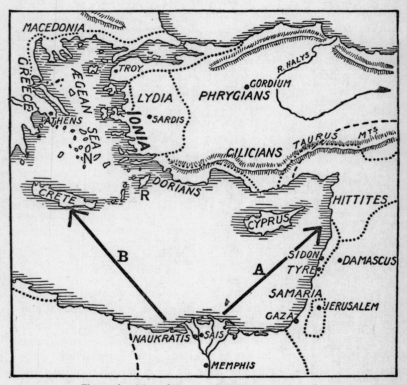

Figure 63—Map of Eastern Mediterranean.
A and B—Sea routes from Egypt to Syria and Crete.
R—Rhodes.
N—Naxos.

The persistent Greek tradition that assigned to Crete a preeminent place in the early history of the Mediterranean received startling corroboration in the years from 1894 onwards when Sir Arthur Evans and his fellow archaeologists laid bare the evidence of the brilliant civilisation that flourished in the island during the third and second millennia B.C. The legends of the sea-power of Minos were thus shown to have a definite historical foundation. Hence Sir Arthur Evans used the term Minoan to define the wonderful phase of culture revealed by his excavations.

The Minoan culture reached its zenith some fifteen centuries before our era, and was independent only in the sense that it early developed an individuality of its own which sharply distinguished it from other ancient civilisations. It was not independent, however, in the sense that it grew from nothing, untouched by influence from without. It is indeed certain that all the elements of civilisation were introduced into Crete from elsewhere, more particularly from Egypt. There were also influences from Asia Minor and Mesopotamia which must be taken into account. Not a single invention of any importance can be certainly attributed to the Cretans; but they nevertheless excelled the Egyptians and Babylonians in certain of their achievements in art, in domestic architecture, and in sanitation.

Sir Arthur Evans has divided the whole era of Minoan civilisation (roughly 2000 years) into three periods—Early, Middle and Late. There is no trace of any Palaeolithic phase of culture in the island. The first inhabitants were the men who introduced agriculture, and of course came in sea-going ships to colonise Crete. They brought with them a culture that was already well developed. They were members of the Mediterranean race.

The primitive houses built by the first colonists were made of mud and wattle, or unbaked bricks, and lasted but a short time. When they fell down the ruins were built on again; the rubbish was never cleared from the paths between the huts. Hence quite a considerable mound would rise on the site of a village in a comparatively short time giving archaeologists the idea of long periods of time, for which there is no justification. On the other hand, civilised people, such as the Minoans, building more substantial houses, often paving their floors, roads and courts, and probably keeping them clear whether paved or not, might live on a spot for centuries without adding much to the level of the ground.

The actual remains of Pre-Minoan culture give little clue as to their origin. They bear a general resemblance to the earliest cultures elsewhere, with pottery, stone maces, and rude female figurines. We cannot say whether it was derived directly from Egypt—the ultimate source of all food-producing cultures—or not. The pottery certainly is not like that of Predynastic Upper Egypt: we know little about the pottery of Lower Egypt in early times. Possibly early colonists came both from Asia Minor via Rhodes (the shortest sea-passage to Crete) and from Egypt or the coast of Libya.

Little progress can be detected in Crete in Pre-Minoan times. Towards the end of the period the influence of the Predynastic culture of Egypt becomes evident in the types of pots and stone vessels. A single copper axe was found at Cnossus well down in the earliest stratum: it was probably introduced from Egypt. With the introduction of copper into common use the early Minoan period began, and rapid progress in civilisation took place. Though it is clear from the ceramic evidence and from the types of houses that the transition from the Pre-Minoan to the Minoan culture was gradual, and that the new culture was developed in large measure from the old, and not suddenly substituted for it, it is highly probable that there was at this time a fresh immigration from the Egyptian Delta and that the intercourse was continuous.

There is a great mass of evidence, of which only the barest summary can be given here, indicating the derivation of much of Minoan civilisation from Egypt. Some of this evidence indicates influences from Dynastic Egypt; some indicates Predynastic Egypt; and some the particular Predynastic culture of the Delta. The people of the Delta appear to have been the founders of Minoan civilisation. They were conquered and subjugated by the founders of the First Dynasty. The remains left by the Earliest Minoan period are comparatively scanty; later periods, which have left more plentiful records of the appearance, clothes and religion of the Minoans, have added to the evidence for this colonisation of Crete by the Libyans of the Delta.

The copper weapons of Early Minoan times were similar to those of Egypt. Egyptian stone vases were imported into Crete and were there copied. It is unlikely that the Cretans could learn how to cut and polish vases of hard stone from examining imported Egyptian specimens; they must have learnt the technique from Egyptian craftsmen. The vases imported and copied were of both Predynastic and early Dynastic types. In the plain of Mesarà, in Southern Crete, have been found bee-hive tombs (Tholoi) similar to those made by Libyans. These were derived ultimately from the Egyptian mastaba tombs of the early dynasties; if they were built, as is probable, by immigrants from Libya, they must represent a diffusion of culture later than the First Dynasty. In these tombs were found figurines closely similar to Predynastic specimens from Hierankopolis and Nagada in Upper Egypt; and rectangular stone palettes exactly like those used in late Predynastic times in Egypt, for grinding malachite and antimony for cosmetics. Numbers of vases consisting of rectangular blocks of stone with cups hollowed out in them, and diagonal perforations on the upper edge, as if for suspension, or the attachment of a lid, were clearly derived from less decorated specimens found at Hierankopolis, and belonging to Predynastic times. A figurine similar to those mentioned has also been found at Cnossus.

The clothes of the Minoans, as we know them in later times, present striking similarities to those of the Predynastic Egyptians. The peculiar Minoan loin-cloth with cod-piece is similar to the Egyptian loin-cloth and phallic sheath. The later Minoan kilt suggests the kilts of the Dynastic Egyptians; the fact that girls taking part in the sports of the bull-ring at Cnossus wore the male loin-cloth has been compared by Sir Arthur Evans with the Libyan custom of women of high rank wearing male clothing. The cloaks of Minoan women seem to be derived from the Predynastic cloak, as see on ivories from Hierankopolis. The arrangement of the Minoan man's hair (which persisted into Late Minoan times), with long locks falling below the shoulders both behind and at the side in front of the arms, is similar to that represented in Nubia from Predynastic times onwards.

The double-axe, one of the most common religious emblems in Minoan Crete, was used as an amulet in Predynastic Egypt and drawn on Predynastic and First Dynastic vases; and there was an official called the "Khet-priest of the Double-axes" under the Fifth Dynasty. The double-axe was a common emblem in the cults of Anatolia, and it is generally supposed that it reached Crete from that side; but its use in Egypt is probably older than its use elsewhere, and it may have reached Anatolia from Crete. The sanctity of the bull, and of the bucranium, or bull's skull, was common to Crete and Egypt. Neïth, Goddess of Saïs in the Delta, and national goddess of the Libyans, has many features in common with the Minoan huntress-goddess. Her symbols were bows, arrows, and a shield of peculiar shape with incurving sides. These were the special weapons of the Libyans, and correspond with weapons used by the Minoans. The similarity of the bow, which was of simple shape, is unimportant, but it is worthy of note that two Middle Minoan seals show arrows with a chisel head instead of a point. Neïth's arrows were always of this type, as were the arrows used by the Libyans. The shield of Neïth seems to be related to the typical Minoan 8-shaped shield, which also had sacred associations. In other respects also Minoan religious ideas were affected by Egyptian influence.

The evidence is cumulative. It shows beyond doubt that Egypt was the source of Early Minoan civilisation. People from Egypt actually settled in Crete. Hence, when the Egyptians painted Cretans (Men of Keftiu) on the walls of XVIIIth Dynasty tombs, though they carefully showed, even caricatured, the peculiar facial features of Negroes, Syrians and Hittites, they portrayed the Keftians, apart from clothes and hair, almost exactly like Egyptians, though of a slightly lighter colour.

The First Early Minoan period shows not only Predynastic influence, but the importation of vases made under the first three or four Dynasties. The Predynastic types found in this period, Early Minoan times, and later, must be due to their survival in Crete or in the Delta, after the opening of the Dynastic period. There is therefore no reason to put the beginning of the Minoan civilisation any further back than the VIIth Dynasty of Egypt, probably not earlier than 3300 B.C. The second phase of the Early Minoan period may be called roughly contemporary with Dynasties IV to VI (circa 2800–2400 B.C.). Stone bowls and vases of new types were introduced from Egypt, and imitated in both stone and pottery, but Predynastic types were still made. Under Egyptian influence the Cretans reached the height of their stone vase technique. Their pottery became highly artistic; they learnt the art of making and moulding faience from Egypt, and also of cutting seals. The plans of their houses become much more complicated. The tomb superstructures, commonly known in the pedantic jargon of the archaeologist as Tholoi of the Mesarà, which we have seen were probably of Egyptian origin, and to a greater extent the tombs on the little island of Moehlos, with their wealth of gold ornaments, suggest a time of prosperity and progress. In this period too a system of hieroglyphs came into use which were engraved on seals. The Minoan signary was quite distinct from that of Egypt, but the Cretans probably owed the development of a hieroglyphic system to the Egyptian example. Some half-dozen of the signs seem to be derived from Egypt. The men of this age, if inferior in culture to the Egyptians or Sumerians, were yet immensely in advance of the peoples of Europe.

In the next period (contemporary with Dynasties VI to XI, circa 2400–2100 B.C.) the central government in Egypt failed, and Libyans once more invaded the Delta. The troubled times in Egypt were reflected in Crete. The importation of true Egyptian objects ceased; what influence there was from that side was from the half-barbaric Libyans in the Delta or elsewhere. The Minoans were much less prosperous, and progress slowed down, though the development in art continued. It was perhaps symptomatic of the decline of Minoan civilisation that a strong cultural influence from the comparatively barbaric Cyclades appeared at this time, bringing with it the spiral system of decoration.

The Cycladic Archipelago, the group of small islands in the south of the Aegean, were never inhabited before copper-using times. They were first settled in Early Minoan times, and their culture appears to have been an off-shoot of Cretan, though more subject to Anatolian influence. But the islands must have been visited in earlier times; for from Melos was obtained obsidian for high-grade knives, and from Naxos emery for polishing stone vases. Both substances were used in Predynastic Egypt and in Crete; while obsidian was obtained in Pre-Minoan Crete. Both Cretans and Egyptians must have obtained these materials from abroad, and it is probable that Naxos and Melos were their principal sources. At Cnossus a large number of cores, as well as flakes, of obsidian were found, showing that the Pre-Minoan people imported it in the rough state and worked it at home. This is exactly what we should expect if

Melos was as yet uninhabited. It was doubtless the people who visited the islands for these valuable substances who eventually settled there.

In the island of Siphnos were found pots with representations of ships upon them. The characteristic of these ships is a high prow surmounted by a fish emblem or ensign on a pole. Below the fish there hang from the pole some streamers. Exactly the same arrangement is found in a Predynastic representation of a ship from Nagada in Upper Egypt. This proves either that Egyptians visited the Cyclades (which is *a priori* extremely probable) or that the Cycladic people received this emblem from the Minoans, who in turn had received it from Egypt. We have no evidence of its existence in Crete, but as we have little information until much later times as to the form of Minoan ships, the lack of evidence is not significant. However the fish-standard got to Siphnos, it is clear that it, and the art of sea-faring, came to the Aegean from Egypt.

The slight retrogression in some respects which is noticeable in Minoan culture in this period seems to be connected with the more serious breakdown in Egypt. This points to the great importance to Crete of trade and intercourse with Egypt, of which we have had so much other evidence. By the island of Pharos at Alexandria, where in later days stood the famous light-house, there has been found a large harbour with great breakwaters of massive stonework, now sunk beneath the sea. Its date is uncertain, but it is older than Greek times, and was unknown, or unused, in the days of Naucratis and Alexandria. It is hard to resist the conclusion that it was used for trade with the Aegean or the West.

In Crete itself Sir Arthur Evans discovered a paved road, which led from Cnossus on the North coast to some port or ports near Komò on the South coast. Along it must have passed the traffic to and from Egypt. It is a curious fact, which is more intelligible in relation to this road, that almost all the actual Egyptain objects (not local copies) found in Crete have come from Cnossus. From Early Minoan times onwards Cnossus was evidently the political and commercial capital of the island, and was in closer connection with Egypt than the other towns.

The Minoans probably exported olive oil in Egypt: the rows of huge earthenware jars, some of them 5 feet high which stood in the store-rooms at Cnossus, and are known to have contained oil, suggest that the olive was the main source of their wealth.

As the anarchy in Egypt which divided the Old from the Middle Kingdom was reflected in Crete, so was the unification and prosperity of the country under the XIth and XIIth Dynasties. The first Middle Minoan period, contemporary with the latter part of the XIth and the early part of the XIIth dynasties (about 2100 to shortly before 1900 B.C.), was one of rapid progress and increasing wealth. Relations with Egypt were renewed on a greater scale; the road across the island was paved, probably for the first time; Egyptian objects, and Egyptian influence appear at Cnossus; and at the beginning of the XIIth Dynasty the influence of Minoan art appears in Egypt. Palaces on the grand scale arose at Cnossus, Phaistus and Mallia. The Cretan palaces, even of this early period, though they did not equal in grandeur the pyramids and temples of other nations, yet with their hundreds of rooms, their many staircases, and their elaborate drainage system, and scientifically designed earthenware drain-pipes, exceeded any other examples of domestic architecture which the ancient world could show. The Romans alone rivalled them, until they were surpassed in the Nineteenth century. The great palace of Cnossus was partially destroyed, altered and restored several times. Its destruction in one case certainly, and probably in other cases, was due to earthquakes—to which Candia is to-day still subject; but in various form it lasted as seat of the rulers of Crete until about 1400 B.C., when it was for the last time overthrown, probably by foreign arms.

Eastern influence at the same time became important—Babylonian cylinder-seals (of date about 2000 B.C.) have been found at Platanos and near Candia in Middle Minoan sites; the Minoans began to write a linearised version of their hieroglyphs on clay-tablets—an idea derived ultimately from Sumer; an axe found in the palace at Mallia, with its butt carved to represent the fore part of a leopard, suggests oriental work; and the Minoans began to make bull-shaped rhytons (sacred vessels used in rites for pouring libations), which were derived from early Sumerian types made some thousand years before. The latter phenomenon suggests an indirect connection with Sumer through some place (probably Anatolia) where early Sumerian types and customs might have survived.

Polychrome pottery came into fashion, and in the next period (lasting from the latter part of the twentieth to the latter part of the eighteenth centuries B. C.) reached its finest development. The magnificent, and often delicate and tasteful decoration of polychrome ware has rarely been surpassed by the potters of any nation. In the Middle Minoan also began the naturalistic style, in which the Minoans were later to excel.

In this second phase of the Middle Minoan period (contemporaneous with the Egyptian XIIth Dynasty and early XIIIth) the interaction of influences between Crete and Egypt increased. Among other things, the Minoans copied in pottery Egyptian flasks made of ostrich's eggs; Minoan pottery was imported into Egypt; and Cretan workmen even settled in Egypt. Senusert II (circa 1903–1885 B.C.) built himself a pyramid in the Fayum, and in neighbouring settlements made in connection with the work, at Lahun and Harāgeh, Cretan workmen lived, and left Minoan ware and imitations of it in the coarse local Egyptian clay. The town at Lahum lasted for some time after the pyramid was finished, but that at Harāgeh which was "of a somewhat more well-to-do character" seems to have existed only in the reign of Senusert. It is clear that Minoan workmen were engaged to work on the construction of the pyramid, and that some of them made Lahun their permanent home.

It is not easy to guess why Senusert should get workmen from Crete. He could hardly have thought that they were more skilled than the Egyptians, for that, in spite of the palaces, was by no means true. There may have been a shortage of labour in Egypt, and the Minoan labourers may have been attracted by high wages, or sent by the Cretan King as a sign of friendship for, or in return for favours from, the Pharaoh.

To the latter part of this period belongs a small Egyptian statuette (XIIth or XIIIth Dynasty) found at Cnossus. It is the figure of a man called User of the Wazet-nome (which is in Upper Egypt near Abydos); as it is of no commercial or artistic value we can only suppose that User himself visited Cnossus, perhaps as an ambassador to the Court of Pharaoh, or on commercial business, and left the statuette as a memento of himself.

At the end of the second phase of the Middle Minoan period, the palace at Cnossus was destroyed, whether by an earthquake, or by human agency we cannot tell; and a short interruption in the prosperity of Crete followed, coinciding with the collapse of the Middle Kingdom of Egypt before the Hyksos. But a rapid recovery soon led to the most brilliant period of Minoan civilisation, in the XVIth and XVth centuries B.C. In the third phase of the Middle Minoan official intercourse with a reunited Egypt was restored, as is proved by the discovery of the cartouche of Khyan on the lid of an Egyptian alabastron at Cnossus. Khyan was probably the first Hyksos to unite Egypt, and to be generally recognised. His date is about 1650 B.C. or shortly afterwards.

Towards the end of the Middle Minoan period (in the first half of the sixteenth century B.C.) the palace of Cnossus was again destroyed by an earthquake. The effect on Minoan civilisation seems to have been stimulating rather than otherwise. The palace was restored in magnificent style, and decorated with numerous and highly artistic frescoes. The great opportunity which the restoration gave to the painters and decorators of this period seems to have led to rapid changes in artistic style which brought in the Late Minoan epoch (circa 1550 B.C.). It is this restored palace which has been most clearly shown to us by Sir Arthur Evans' excavations.

The Minoan civilisation now surpassed that of Egypt in many ways. Though the Cretan artists never attained the skill and precision of the Egyptians, they had a keener aesthetic sense, and allowed themselves much greater freedom. In consequence, though Egyptian works of art are generally more perfect, the Minoan are often more vital and attractive to the modern eye. Yet in a hundred and one details the influence of Egyptian art is still known in Crete, and to a lesser extent the influence of Crete in Egypt, so that it is possible to speak of an Egypto-Minoan style of decoration.

During the XVIIIth Dynasty the Cretans, known to the Egyptians as the "Men of Keftiu," were in the habit of sending embassies with gifts to Egypt; and we see them painted on the walls of the tombs of the viziers who received them in the regency of Hatshepsut and the reign of Thothmes III. About 1400 B.C. the palace of Cnossus was, as mentioned above, destroyed, and with it, apparently, the power of the Kings of Crete. Akhenaton's short-lived "City of the Sun's Disk" at El Amarna shows sherds of pottery from the Mainland of Greece, but none from Crete; and from this date onwards the Men of Keftiu are rarely mentioned. But before this disaster overtook the Minoans, their civilisation had been firmly planted on the Mainland of Greece.

An early culture, somewhat different from that of Pre-Minoan Crete, had existed in early days in Greece, and persisted there long after the beginning of the Minoan Age. Probably about 2800 B.C. Southern Greece was conquered by the people of the Cyclades, who, as we saw above, were but recent arrivals in the islands. The "Helladic" culture thus established in Greece was at first but an extension of the Cycladic. Foreign influence soon appeared. About 2500 B.C. the so-called "Dimini" ware appears in Thessaly and sporadically in Southern Greece, assumed by some writers to be due to an invasion from the North; and it has been suggested that the people who introduced it were the Indo-European-speakers who first brought the Greek language into the Peninsula. Another invasion of later date is represented by what is called (by an unfortunate misnomer for which Schliemann was responsible) Minyan ware. It seems to be of Northwest Anatolian (Trojan) origin, and appears suddenly in various parts of Greece, and in the Cyclades, at the end of Early Helladic and Early Cycladic times. Thus the civilisation of the Mainland was of composite origin; and, though the Minyan ware represents a higher culture than that which it invaded, it was far behind the contemporary civilisation of Crete.

About the time of the earthquake in the Sixteenth century B.C. the full Minoan civilisation suddenly appears in the Peloponnese and in Boeotia. Colonists of high rank from Crete evidently settled and ruled at Mycenae, Tiryns, Argos, Thebes, Orchomenos and elsewhere, taking with them Minoan works of art and Minoan craftsmen. Professor Nilsson has suggested that this sudden establishment of Minoan culture in Greece may have been due to the conquest of Cnossus by the mainland kings; but there is no evidence of any foreign disturbance at Cnossus at this time—for the palace was destroyed by an earthquake, as Sir Arthur Evans has proved—and the completeness of the transplantation of culture precludes any explanation but that of colonisation from Crete. Conquerors from Greece would not have adopted Minoan fashions and religion in so wholesale a manner.

The Mycenaean civilisation, as this new Mainland culture is

called, from its chief site, was at first, with only a few modifications a mere copy of Minoan civilisation. As a whole it was slightly inferior, but Minoan, and probably Cnossian, works of art and craftsmen were imported, and some of the finest purely Minoan works of the great period, such as the Vaphis cups, have been found on the Mainland. The old Helladic culture was completely overlaid, though it survived in part and affected the later Mycenaean culture to a certain extent. For some time the sites on the Mainland accurately reflected the various phases of Minoan art, but finally developed a style of their own. On the final destruction of the Palace and the power of Cnossus about 1400 B.C. Mycenae became the political centre of the Aegean world. It is possible that the colonists revolted against the supremacy of the Kings of Crete, and themselves sacked the Palace. The typical Late Mycenaean culture, distinguished now from the contemporary Late Minoan in Crete, spread far and wide, and established a comparatively uniform culture all over the Aegean world, except in Crete. It spread to the Aegean coast of Asia Minor, to Cyprus and to Cicilia. In a debased form it was eventually carried to Palestine by the Philistines, who probably came from the southwest corner of Asia Minor; they were certainly not, as was once supposed, true Minoans from Crete.

The story of the various influences which went to the making of Minoan civilisation was by no means simple; but the main outlines are fairly clear. First there was the arrival of the early Food-Gatherers, who brought the Pre-Minoan culture. In the latter part of the Pre-Minoan period they were in contact with, and influenced by, the Predynastic Egyptians. During the first two Early Minoan periods, contemporary with the Old Kingdom in Egypt, two strands of influence from Egypt can be traced. One is marked by the importation from Egypt of objects made during the first six Dynasties, and of contemporary Egyptian arts and styles. The other is marked by the appearance in Crete of objects and styles connected by the archaeologists with Predynastic Egypt, and in particular with the early Libyan or Egypto-Libyan population of the Delta, but also with Upper Egypt of Predynastic times.

No very satisfactory solution has yet been given to the problem which arises from the apparent contemporaneity of the Dynastic and Predynastic influences. The settlement of Predynastic people in

Crete at the time of the unification of Egypt, and the survival among them of elements of culture which vanished in Egypt will partly explain it. But the tholoi of the Mesarà, and their associations with objects of Predynastic type, suggest a later invasion of Libyans. For the tholoi are modified mastaba tombs, and cannot therefore have been introduced into Crete at the beginning of the First Dynasty, when mastaba tombs had not yet been invented. But they bear a close resemblance to the particular modifications of the mastaba which were made by the Libyans. We may tentatively assume therefore that the second stand of Egyptian influence was due to the Libyans, among whom Predynastic styles had survived. After Early Minoan times Egyptian influence in Crete was almost continuous, and was the main cause of the great developments of Minoan culture: but other influences from the East and North complicate the issue. All were assimilated and combined into the specifically Cretan civilisation.

CHAPTER XIII

THE REBIRTH OF CIVILISATION

NO one can deny, even if some may fear, the magnitude of the gifts conferred by Greece on the world. As the late Professor John Burnet expressed it: "Rational science is the creation of the Greeks, and we know when it began" (*Greek Philosophy,* 1914). The Dean of St. Paul's tells us that "without what we call our debt to Greece we should have neither our religion nor our philosophy nor our science nor our literature nor our education nor our politics." (W. R. Inge in Livingstone's *The Legacy of Greece,* 1921).

The heritage of Greece has been so often and so eloquently acknowledged that no useful purpose would be served by repeating in halting phrases what has been so adequately expressed in noble prose. Yet there is an urgent need for a new assessment of the heritage of the Greeks. Most classical writers have underestimated both the extent of the Greeks' indebtedness to those who preceded them and the range and profundity of the influence the Greeks themselves have exerted on the world at large, and in particular on India, China, Indonesia, Oceania and America.

In this and the following chapters the attempt will be made to estimate the full significance of the Rebirth of Civilisation, which was effected in Ionia by Thales (585 B.C.) and his contemporaries, when they restored confidence in human reason and freed mankind from the shackles of hieratic tyranny and the domination of the State System.

Nothing but confusion can result from attempts unduly to minimise the achievements of the earliest civilisations of Egypt, Crete and Mesopotamia. Not only did they create and develop during several millennia the arts of agriculture, architecture, metallurgy, ship-building, writing, sculpture, music, dancing and the drama, and bring the material side of civilisation to a pitch of excellence

389

which, as new archaeological discoveries are made year by year, is a constant source of amazement; they also devised a system of government and a social and political organisation, and made laws and a political system. If their intellectual achievements are denied recognition as real science and philosophy, no one can refuse to admit that they collected the empirical observations which the Ionians used as the basis for their speculations. Nay, more than that, they devised many of the tentative explanations of natural phenomena, which are often cited as among the supreme achievements of Ionian rational thought. For example, Aristotle regarded as "the principle tenet of Thales" that "everything is made out of water," that "water is the material cause of all things." Professor Burnet expresses the opinion that the greatness of Thales "would live in his having asked the question" (of the cause of things) "rather than in the particular answer he gave it." But surely he is forgetting that for thirty centuries before the time of Thales both the question and the answer had been the bedrock of Osirian religion in Egypt! The same comment applies to Anaximander's teaching that all life, all living beings, came from the sea.

However the knowledge of the Egyptians may be disparaged, they must be given credit for inventing an empirical arithmetic and geometry, and for devising a cosmogony without which the Ionians would have had no bricks wherewith to erect their great edifice of rational knowledge.

The more fully we pay tribute to the knowledge and experience of those who preceded them the greater should be our admiration for the achievement of the Greeks in breaking down the highly organised and strongly defended citadel of stereotyped tradition. Let us try to understand what the Ionians achieved and why it represents a rebirth of civilisation.

When for the first time in Human History the Egyptians abandoned the nomadic mode of life and embarked on the adventure of civilisation they devised a theory of knowledge to direct their efforts and interpret the miracle their culture-hero Osiris had wrought. In accordance with this theory of the State System there was no distinction between natural and supernatural, between philosophy and religion, between medicine and magic. Every kind of activity was a function of the State and the king exercised an absolute autocracy over every individual. It was part of the theory of knowledge that he conferred life upon each of his subjects and controlled all their actions. They had no need to think for themselves, as all their doings were prescribed by rigid convention.

Perhaps a concrete illustration will make this matter more intelligible. In Turkey until ten years ago the Sultan was not only the absolute ruler, but also the Caliph, the head of the Mohammedan religion. He was, at any rate in name, the autocrat who controlled the religious, civil and moral organisation of the State, of which he was the legislator and whose armed forces were controlled by him. In building up the Turkish State in Asia Minor by non-Mohammedan invaders from Central Asia, who adopted the religion of Islam from their conquered subjects, the Sultan made his autocratic position the instrument of military glory, and gave sanction and support to religious, civil and imperial aspirations of the State, which presented, so to speak, a united front to all its enemies. The Great War completed the destruction of the ancient State System in Turkey, and the law of March 3, 1924, gave legislative recognition to this accomplished fact. The Caliphat was abolished: education was taken out of the exclusive control of the religious teachers and secularised: legislation was emancipated from religious control: polygamy was abandoned: the Gregorian calendar and the Latin alphabet were adopted: the Swiss civil code and the Italian penal code were substituted for the former Moslem juridical systems. Witnessing the breaking-up of a State System of archaic type helps us the better to understand something of what was involved in the Original State in which the king was the repository of all knowledge: the regimen of the river and the cosmic forces that controlled the flood and the life-giving forces, the mathematical knowledge for measuring the year, foretelling the inundation and predicting the seasons were his: he was the autocratic disposer of the lives of his people, to whom he was the legislator, the judge and the actual god.

The understanding of the genesis of such a system is essential for the interpretation of the history of civilisation. The real nature of modern civilisation's legacy from Greece cannot be appreciated unless we realise the nature of the tyranny of the State System which was first really overthrown in Ionia during the sixth century

B. C. Nor can we properly understand the present condition of the world or estimate the prospects for amelioration of society in the future unless we learn the meaning of the elements of the old system that still survive to-day.

In Egypt the sole conception of natural phenomena had become more and more centred on the idea that the dead king, having been mummified, became a national god, who controlled the affairs of the universe. No emancipation of reason could be effected until the incubus of this superstition was removed. The act of embalming the king's body and making it imperishable was the essential factor, according to the ideas of the ancients, in determining the prolongation which made it possible for him to become a god. His mummy was a national possession of supreme importance and the welfare of the community was dependent upon the preservation of that mummy and the periodical dramatic representation of the historical incidents of the king's death and resurrection. His body was supposed to represent the State and the four divisions of the State, north, south, east and west. Such ideas represent in a crude form the sterilising conception of the cosmos and microcosmos, the king in his own body being identified with the universe and the four parts into which it was traditional to divide the universe, the four parts which were under the protection of the divinities known as sons of Horus, each of which was given a topographical representation in the king's body.

Discussing the "Dramatic Element in Ritual" (*Folklore,* 1928) Dr. W. J. Perry clearly defined the point of view the Ionians were destined to destroy. He cited evidence from the American Indians, from the ancient civilisation of Mexico and Peru, from the Chinese Book of Rites of the Chau Dynasty, from India, Java, Burma and the more ancient civilisations of North and East Africa and Western Asia, to prove that the essential purpose of all ritual was the imitation of the ceremony of creation, as it was handed down from remotest antiquity—the creation of the world and the four quarters of it, East and West, North and South, with the king at the centre as the State itself. The peoples of antiquity regarded the identity of the king and the State as complete and absolute. Prosperity was wholly dependent upon his actions; he was the river, the inundation of which brought life and prosperity to the whole community. He was identified with the barley which provided them with sustenance. His life was the animating force which enabled the waters of inundation to fertilise the fields. *The aim of the ritual ceremony was to re-enact the original creation ceremony for the purpose of conferring upon the king a prolongation of existence,* not immortality in the sense in which we understand it, but the prolongation of his vital activities so long as his people performed the necessary ceremonies. These ceremonies were not at first regarded as acts of worship, but rather as the necessary physical processes whereby the dead king's life might be prolonged. Thus alone could he confer upon the community such boons and such prosperity as he was able to effect during his actual life on earth. The people at first did not pray to him for life, they performed certain ceremonies, certain ritual acts, for the sole purpose of conferring life upon the king himself, in the sure and certain hope that his own prosperity involved the prosperity of the world at large and of every one of his subjects. It is important not to forget that such ritual became a tradition which was handed down from one generation to another as the true history of the way in which the earliest people obtained from their king the celestial control of their prosperity. Such people did not pretend to understand or interpret the means, or their efficacy for obtaining such results. They accepted them as an act of faith; the myth had been transmitted to them in a particular form which it became an obligation to them to preserve inviolable. Seeing that they were not interested in explaining how the ritual can produce such effects, in other words how life can be obtained by certain dramatic imitations of the original way in which according to tradition it was obtained, they depended upon faith without reason. It is important not to forget that in the early days of civilisation no distinction was made between knowledge and religion, politics and society. The king was the State; he was the repository of all knowledge, and the measures that he adopted to control his subjects were individual acts which were not questioned by them. The great revolution in human affairs which was effected by the Ionians in the sixth century before Christ was due to the fact that they began to criticise the validity of ritual as a means of effecting such tremendous powers. The effect of such a critical attitude of mind was to break the hieratic tradition and separate science from theology. The belief that the State, society, knowledge and administration were all centred in the king, was abandoned and for the first time a rational system of enquiry was introduced.

This peculiar conception of the king's omnipotence enables us to understand why the introduction of a metal currency among a group of enterprising pirate-merchants of Ionia, by conferring upon them personal power, was able to destroy the fiction of the king's power and authority. With the fall of the king the State System with which he was identified disappeared also. In the next chapter it will be explained how for long ages before the Ionians definitely emancipated reason the way was being prepared for it by the growth of rationalism and a weakening of the hieratic restraints. When Egyptian civilisation was diffused to Crete and Mesopotamia it underwent many changes, which, particularly in the case of the former, gave greater freedom from the tyranny of convention and tradition. But as the range and intimacy of maritime enterprise developed there was a constant intermingling of peoples of varying traditions, which compelled them to think of their differences and encouraged them to eliminate inconsistencies by reason. There were special reasons why the Ionians should have been affected by such circumstances more than other peoples. They were brought into more intimate relations with a great variety of people of different traditions. They were engaged in wide-ranging traffic, which brought them into touch with Egypt at a critical moment in her history, when she was ready to suggest the lead to an enterprising and open-minded people. But above all, this series of propitious circumstances happened just at the moment when the Ionians acquired a metallic currency, the most potent instrument of commerce, especially for a people addicted to maritime trafficking. It is probably not an exaggeration to say that the invention of coinage purchased freedom of thought and action. It gave to the merchant an independence of the State and a personal power which encouraged him to think and act for himself, and no longer to behave as a mere cog in the national machinery. But as we have already seen, this was an instrument of revolution in that it involved the destruction of the kingship and the State System.

In his illuminating treatise on *The Origin of Tyranny* (1922)

Mr. P. N. Ure has given a brilliant sketch of the influence of "perhaps the most epoch-making revolution in the whole history of commerce" brought about "by the invention of a metal coinage like those that are still in circulation throughout the civilised world.

"It was no accident that the invention was made precisely at this time. Industry and commerce were simultaneously making enormous strides. About the beginning of the seventh century the new Lydian dynasty of the Mermnadae made Sardis one of the most important trading centres that have arisen in the world's history. The Lydian merchants became middlemen between Greece and the Far East. Egypt recovered its prosperity and began rapidly to develop commercial and other relations with its neighbours, including the Greeks. Greek traders were pushing their goods by sea in all directions from Spain to the Crimea. Concrete evidence of this activity is still to be seen in the Corinthian and Milesian pottery of the period that has been so abundantly unearthed as far afield as Northern Italy and Southern Russia. It was a time of extraordinary intellectual alertness. Thales and the numerous other philosophers of the Ionian school were in close touch with the merchants and manufacturers of their age. They were in fact men of science rather than philosophers in the narrow modern sense of the latter word, and most of them were ready to apply their science to practical and commercial ends, as for example Thales, who is said to have made a fortune by buying up all the oil presses in advance when his agricultural observations led him to expect a particularly plentiful harvest. A corner in oil sounds very modern, and in fact the whole of the evidence shows that in many ways this ancient epoch curiously anticipated the present age.

"The great developments of trade and industry that just preceded the age of tyranny in Greece had their parallel if not their origin in Egypt. At the height of this development in Egypt a new and powerful dynasty arises which bases its power on commerce and on the commercial and industrial classes. Already towards the end of the eighth century we find King Bocchoris (somewhat after the manner of the Argive Pheidon) devoting special attention to commercial legislation. His successor Sethon is said by Herodotus to have based his power on 'hucksters and artisans and tradespeople.' During these reigns the country was always being occupied or threatened by foreign invaders from Ethiopia or Assyria. The first Egyptian king of this period to rule all Egypt in normal conditions of peace and quietness was Psammetichus I, who rose to power about the same time as Cypselus in Corinth and Orthagoras in Sicyon. Psammetichus according to Diodorus converted his position from that of a petty Delta chieftain (one of twelve who shared the rule of the part of the country not in foreign occupation) into that of supreme ruler of the whole country as a result of the wealth and influence that he won by trading with Phoenicians and Greeks.

"It was probably in the Greek world of the seventh and sixth centuries B.C. that *all the main streams of modern thought and energy first took place*. It is among the Greeks of the seventh and sixth centuries B.C. that we first find men who intellectually and politically share our outlook in a way that is becoming more and more striking the more the world emancipates itself from the mediaevalism that it is in the process of casting off.

"The civilization that developed so remarkably in the age that we are about to consider does not appear to have been the result of a long period of evolution. It was a rapid and almost sudden renaissance."

The Diffusion of Minoan and Mycenaean Influence

Before we study the momentous events in Ionia it is important that the earlier exploits of the people of Crete and the Mainland of Greece, which prepared the way for the Ionian revolution, should be recalled to our memory. Reference has already been made to the fact that the influence of Egyptian civilisation, in particular the phase known as the Middle Kingdom (2000 B.C.), was active in promoting the development of civilisation in Western Europe. The effects of this westerly diffusion of culture are witnessed successively in the Neolithic and Bronze Ages. In the maritime adventures that led to this spread of Egyptian civilisation Cretan seamen played so prominent a part that in such distant lands as Spain, Ireland and the Orkneys it is difficult to dissociate the contributions of Egypt and Minoan Crete.

During the time when copper first came into use in the Aegean area this phase of culture was introduced into Central and Eastern

Europe. Peaceful farming peoples settled on rich fertile lands. A brilliant culture suddenly developed on the Western coast of the Black Sea, in Roumania and elsewhere in Eastern Europe. Its most notable site, Erosd in Transylvania, shows copper from the earliest times. This civilisation finally disappeared as suddenly as it came, leaving no trace.

A less brilliant culture was found among peaceful farmers on the banks of the Danube, but it does not seem to have included the use of copper. Its Mediterranean affinities are made more obtrusive by the use of bracelets of shells (*Spondylus gaederopi*), which must have been imported from the Middle Sea. The scanty anthropological evidence also suggests that the Danubians were of Mediterranean race.

This culture spread up the Danube, and into the Rhine and Elbe valleys, and was the first food-producing culture of most of Central Europe. From the Danubians the Swiss lake-dwelling culture acquired the character commonly described as Neolithic.

In Spain a flourishing civilisation was founded by immigrants who were searching for gold, tin and copper and built megalithic monuments of different kinds. The spread of this culture over Europe is proved to the satisfaction of even the most inveterate opponents of the diffusion theory by two groups of phenomena, proving *two* waves of diffusion due to *colonisation* and the *exploitation* of other countries; while a multitude of other evidence proves the influence of Spain in the rest of Western Europe.

The distribution of megalithic monuments in France, Britain, Holland, Scandinavia, and North Germany demonstrate the settlements of one people proceeding North from Spain, who seem to have been of Mediterranean race.

The distribution of a distinctive style of pottery, of which a handleless swelling mouthed "beaker" is typical, affords further evidence of diffusion. This so-called "bell-beaker" pottery is also clearly distinguished by a peculiar style of incised decoration. It also originated in Spain, and is found throughout Western Europe, particularly in Germany, as well as in Northern Italy. It is sometimes found in conjunction with megalithic monuments, but very often separate. It is associated in Spain and elsewhere with a broadheaded (Alpine) element in the population.

In the course of their search for precious metals, these two peoples, the Mediterranean Megalith Builders, and Alpine "Prospectors," carried culture from Spain. The latter first brought copper into common use in Central Europe.

The culture of South Russia was evidently introduced from the Black Sea into the Kuban in the Caucasus. The Kuban people may possibly be the Egypto-Colehians of Herodotus (Figure 61 CO), also in touch with Mesopotamia. The evidence of the diffusion of their culture is the battle-axes and megalithic single-burial graves. It spread through Central Europe to Denmark, where the single-grave megalith people, with their battle-axes, are clearly distinguished from the Iberian-megalith people who buried many bodies in a single grave. This culture early became associated with the Nordic Race (probably speaking the Indo-European language) and may have been associated with the spread of the latter. In the Caucasus it had copper: but the knowledge of it was lost as the culture was transmitted westwards. Thus the Neolithic stone battle-axes of Germany are copied from copper axes from the Kuban river.

Except possibly in Spain, it is not certain whether the Aegean peoples exerted a direct influence in the creation of European civilisation. But the subsequent progress of Europe may have been largely due to contact with Crete and Mycenae.

The extent of the influence of the Aegean in Europe can be judged from the following statement made by Professor Gordon Childe in his *Dawn of European Civilisation:* "The baetylic pillar, the holy tree and the double axe-objects, . . . had a sacral significance not only to the east, but throughout the Western Mediterranean, and in France and Britain. Doves and snakes in association with the divine cult again find echoes in Sardinia and Britanny. . . . We meet with similar objects (to the "Horns of Consecration" or double-mountain symbol) with the painted pottery of Eastern Galicia, sculptured on the pillars of Sardinian tombs, and surmounting Spanish altars. . . . Tauromorphic vases have a wide easterly range, but in Europe they recur in Bulgaria, Bukowina, and Spain." Tauromorphic vases (or rather "rhytons") were introduced into Crete in Middle Minoan times, having been derived from Early Sumerian types of a thousand years earlier.

The various peoples of the Aegean, all of whom came in contact with the first seafarers, contributed equally in the diffusion. Even before the close of the third millennium Minoan influence extended as far as the Western Mediterranean and Southern Russia. In the Middle Minoan period Crete began to come to the fore, although the others were still active. Later still, from the thirteenth century B.C., the Mycenaean culture of the mainland of Greece became the most important, though the influence of the Late Minoan period in Crete was not then wholly extinguished.

With the details of the diffusion of Aegean civilisation into Italy and the West, and by way of the Black Sea into the basin of the Danube and Central Europe, and also into Southern Russia, there is no room to deal here. In Professor Gordon Childe's recent books, to which reference has already been made, a precise survey of the whole evidence is available.

Enough has been said to make it clear that, long before the intensive intermingling of peoples in Ionia, with which the next chapter is concerned, the Aegean peoples had been actively participating for more than fifteen centuries in the widespread diffusion of culture.

CHAPTER XIV

THE GLORY THAT WAS GREECE

THE brilliant civilisation that flourished in the Aegean in the middle of the second millennium rapidly declined after the thirteenth century B. C. There followed a period of confusion. The palaces were sacked and burnt; many of the chief sites of the old culture were abandoned; art became degenerate, and stone-building seems to have ceased almost entirely; iron came into common use, replacing bronze in the manufacture of weapons; and great movements of population took place. From this "Dark Age" there eventually emerged the civilisation of Classical Greece, very different from the old Aegean civilisation, and rapidly surpassing the achievements of the men of Cnossus and Mycenae in every direction. We may assign the beginning of the renaissance to, say, roughly 800 B. C. It attained its culmination in the fifth century B. C. at Athens, but at first the leading part was taken by the Greek cities of Ionia in Asia Minor; in particular by Miletus. "The first prose historian mentioned by tradition is 'Cadmus of Miletus'; the first who has real substance and influence is Hecataeus of Miletus. The first Greek philosopher is Thales of Miletus, the second and third are Anaximander and Anaximenes of Miletus." (The Legacy of Greece.)

It is hardly exaggerating to say that the outstanding distinction of Greek civilisation was the creation of the Ionians. Even the early culture of Sparta, which excavations have shown to have been surprisingly well developed, was largely dependent on Ionia. We cannot of course deny that any contribution to the common culture was made by the rest of Greece; but Ionia was, in the eighth, seventh and sixth centuries, far ahead of the cities of the mainland.

It would be ridiculous to assume, as was once fashionable practice, that the mental superiority supposed to be inherent in the Greeks, and the clarity of the Aegean atmosphere, afforded an adequate explanation of their wonderful civilisation. It would be a blind defiance of the established facts of history and archaeology to pretend that the Greeks accomplished this alone and uninfluenced by the ancient civilisations of their neighbours. The cause of the sudden burst of progress between 800 and 400 B.C. is to be found in the peculiarly favourable social and economic conditions in Greece, and the stimulus of cultural influences from outside. It is the purpose of this chapter, as far as is possible in a short space, to examine those conditions, and to trace those influences. The question is the more complicated because Greece, lying close to the original centres of civilisation, had long been civilised itself and continually subjected to the cultural influences diffused over the waters that bathed its shores.

The first important fact to notice is that the old Minoan-Mycenaean civilisation was not completely extinguished during the Dark Ages between the thirteenth and the eighth centuries B.C. Surviving in part at least, particularly in Ionia, it formed the foundation on which the new civilisation was built. The period of transition between the "Aegean" and "Hellenic" ages is known to archaeologists, from the typical decoration on the pottery of the time, as "Geometric." For the most part the patterns are composed of straight lines, zig-zags and so forth, though conventionalised figures of animals and men are also common. There was no break in the development of style, however, between the Mycenaean and Geometric. In the later stages of Mycenaean ware, before its final decline, the designs were becoming more and more geometrical in character; and in the full geometric age the use of Mycenaean ornament can still be clearly traced. The gradual and continuous transition is shown in some early Iron Age tombs in Crete, and in many sites which were continuously occupied. The Geometric pottery of Athens, known as "Dipylon Ware," continues to show considerable technical and artistic ability; and it is perhaps worth noticing in this connection, that, according to Greek tradition, the Ionians set out from Attica to colonise the coast of Asia. The Geometric ware, in its turn, developed gradually and continuously into the pottery of Classical Greece. It should not be supposed that the deterioration in artistic talent shown during the Geometric period necessarily implies an equal degradation in all other departments of culture. Indeed, during the late Mycenaean period, when the decoration of pottery was becoming poorer, the quality of the material of the pots improved. This phenomenon is not unique: a new form of artistic expression often attracts the best craftsmen and impoverishes other forms of art. Moreover, art often declines, while technique improves. The Dark Ages of Greece coincided with the great revolution in metallurgy which transformed the Bronze into the Iron Age.

Although, as we have seen, there was no sudden change, influences from Northern Greece, and perhaps from Central and Eastern Europe, can be traced both in the Geometric decoration of pottery, and in the other articles made at this period. There may have been a continual movement of peoples from the North into Southern Greece, from the time when Mycenaean civilisation was at its height, until the full Iron Age. But the only immigration from the North of which we have any certain proof—the so-called "Dorian migration," which is established by traditional, philological and archaeological evidence—took place when the Geometric style was already in use. This Northern influence is the second element which entered into the composition of Greek civilisation.

Of the period of transition, or the Dark Ages, we know something also from the poems of Homer, the *Iliad* and the *Odyssey*. The age of which they tell is usually called the "Heroic Age," a name which implies that it is seen, as it were, through the highly tinted spectacles of the writers of "Heroic" verse. We see Greece ruled by a number of warrior-princes, most of whom, with their subjects, bear the name of "Achaeans." The greatest of the princes live in the chief seats of Mycenaean civilisation—Mycenae, Tiryns, Thebes among others; and that civilisation, though perhaps degenerate, has by no means completely disappeared. The wealthier princes live in luxury, in large richly decorated palaces, and possess many works of art in bronze, silver and gold. It has been found difficult to equate this "Heroic Age" with any known archaeological period, perhaps because the poet has mixed together the changing fashions of a century or more. But it is generally agreed that the poems represent mainly the conditions of a generation or generations falling somewhere at the end of the Mycenaean, or beginning of the Geometric Age, of the archaeologists. The important point for our purpose is that this "Heroic Age" is manifestly dependent culturally on the great age of Mycenae, and is equally clearly the beginning of Greek civilisation. The Epic itself is proof that the cultural tradition between the Heroic Age and Classical Greece was unbroken.

We need not here go into the questions of the origins of the Achaeans, and the introduction of the Greek language into the Aegean. The most diverse opinions have been expressed by scholars on the subject. It has been held that the Achaeans were Celts from Central Europe, who only learnt Greek from the inhabitants of the Aegean; that they were the invaders from the North who first introduced the Greek language; or that they were indigenous in Greece, or on the coast of Asia. Egyptian and Hittite inscriptions suggest the possibility that both the Greek language and the Achaean name existed in the Aegean in the twelfth, even the fourteenth century B. C., that is, in the Mycenaean Age, before the time with which we are concerned here. The disappearance of the name from the greater part of Greece suggests that it belonged properly only to a ruling group.

The poems of Homer show us a state of society in which local, tribal and racial ties seem to have been completely broken down. Even family ties seem loosened; and Homer mentions the tale of Orestes without any indication of the horror which it rouses in the mind or Aeschylus. The only important social bond was allegiance to a prince, who was often of different tribe and race from his subjects. Little consciousness of racial differences is shown; and combined with this internationalism, is extreme individualism. The Achaeans have been aptly compared to the Goths of the fifth and sixth centuries A. D., and to the Vikings and Normans of a later date. They seem also to have been peculiarly free from the domination of a priesthood: they had few hampering superstitions, and no mysticism in their religion. Though custom is held in great honour, it is a simple custom; there are no complicated taboos, no elaborate social organisation, no overwhelming immemorial tradition dominating every department of their lives, such as are found in ancient Egypt and in many savage tribes. Homeric religion, in strong contrast to much of Greek religion as we know it at a later date, is highly rationalised and purged of many savage characteristics, of which we find traces later. The general moral tone of the poems is high;

savage rites and superstitions, and barbarous acts, of which the legends as we know from later sources are full, are for the most part omitted in Homer, or else strongly condemned. This has been clearly demonstrated by Professor Gilbert Murray. The gods indeed were so rationalised and humanised that it is impossible to believe that they inspired any very deep religious feeling; they are often frankly burlesqued by Homer himself. How far all this corresponds to historic fact, and how far it is the invention of Homer, is a disputed point, but not one of great importance. Fact or fiction, its influence survived in Ionia, intensified by the troubles of the migrations and the abolition of Kingship, and was carried all over the Greek world. The Homeric poems themselves, for generations the best known literature in Greece, were used as the chief part in the curriculum of schools, and had an immense influence on the national character of the Greeks. The "Homeric" spirit was the main ingredient of Hellenism.

It was this freedom and secularisation of life in Ionia which made possible the great renaissance, and enabled the Ionians to profit by cultural influences from outside. In this connection we must mention another historical accident which was of great importance in the development of Greek civilisation—the rise of the City-State. That this form of social organisation, combining independence with opportunities of social intercourse and usually associated with extensive trade and considerable wealth, is particularly favourable to rapid progress in the arts and sciences, is shown by the history of all periods in which free cities have flourished. It used to be the fashion in text-books of history to describe the Greek City-State as the product of the geographical features of Greece—a land cut up by the sea and mountains into little compartments which would inevitably be independent. While there is no need to deny altogether the influence of these physical features, it is absurd to consider them of paramount importance. Physical features will not adequately explain why the City-State flourished in Greece for a few centuries only; nor why it has existed in other countries, such as Ancient Sumer and Mediaeval Germany and Italy. In reality two factors are involved; the independence of small territories, which means the absence of any strong unifying power; and the existence of towns, as distinct from village and scattered farms, to serve as centres of political life. These factors could only be explained by an exhaustive enquiry into the political and economic history of the period. We may regard it as a fortunate accident that both circumstances appeared in the Greek world in the first millennium B.C., and produced the City-State.

To return from this digression to the Homeric poems, the Creation of the Epic is the first gift of Ancient Greece to the world. The *Iliad* and the *Odyssey* are the first epic poems of which we have any knowledge, and were very probably the first ever composed. All later true epics, as opposed to mere collections of ballads, owe their inspiration directly or indirectly to Homer. This is universally admitted of the European epics.

The problem of the origin of the Homeric poems has been hotly disputed for more than a century. We are probably safe in saying that the poems were written between 1050 B.C. and 800 B.C. The Epic is primarily the creation of the "Heroic" state of society described above. The Achaean princes, we know from Homer himself, were entertained at their feasts by singers who sang of the exploits of their ancestors and contemporaries, like the skalds and bards of the Heroic Age of Northern Europe. Their songs, or at least the tales they told, were handed on to other generations of poets, who sang or recited in the homes of nobles, or in the market-place to the people. Finally some man of genius conceived the idea of composing, from the traditional tales and ballads, a long continuous poem; and produced, on a dramatic episode during the siege of Troy, and of the adventures of one of the heroes returning thence, the *Iliad* and the *Odyssey,* which are not only the earliest, but are considered by many to be the finest, epic poems ever written.

The above view of the origin of the epic is accepted by an increasing number of modern scholars. But Professor Gilbert Murray, in the *Rise of the Greek Epic,* follows the many scholars, who, since Wolf, have refused to believe that either the *Iliad* or *Odyssey* is the work of a single poet. He regards the poems as *"traditional books"* which grew slowly for many centuries in the hands of poets, rhapsodists and editors.

The Achaeans, whom we have been considering, ruled most of Greece, many of the islands, including Crete, and seem, even before the Trojan War, to have had a footing in Asia. They were a race of sea-farers, though pirates and raiders of coast towns rather than legitimate merchants. "Sackers of cities" was considered a proud title. They raided even the Nile Delta, as we know from Egyptian records and Homer; and it was probably they who spread the latest Mycenaean culture to Cyprus (where Teucer, son of Telamon was said to have settled after the fall of Troy) and to the coast of Cicilia. Shortly after the Trojan War, according to the traditions, they began to settle in Aeolis, the coast of Asia Minor north of Ionia. This tract of country had been thrown open to them by the destruction of Troy. Later, but probably some years before 1000 B.C., occurred what is known, rather incorrectly, as the "Dorian Migration." A number of Greek tribes from the Northwest corner of Greece, speaking closely allied dialects of which Dorian proper is only one, pushed into Greece and conquered the greater part of the mainland, the most southerly of the islands, and the Southwest corner of Asia Minor. The conquerors, Dorians, Thessalians, Boeotians and others, were less civilised than the Achaeans, destroyed most of the Mycenaean culture on the mainland, and intensified the Northern cultural influence which we noticed appearing in the Aegean with Geometric pottery. They were also in all probability responsible for the introduction of the use of iron in greater quantities, though that metal was not unknown before. Many of the former inhabitants of Greece fled overseas, and colonised Ionia, where they preserved the Mycenaean civilisation to a greater extent than elsewhere.

The central portion of the coast of Asia Minor, afterwards called Ionia, was already, before the coming of the Ionians, the seat of a civilised people. In the district of Smyrna and Magnesia are to be seen the most considerable prehistoric monuments which have yet been found near the coast south of Troy. Here on Mt. Sipylus are Hittite rock sculptures, and sanctuaries, and certain tombs distinguished by the name Tantalid, which are probably of later date. Nearby, at the head of the Gulf of Smyrna, are the remains of towns and fortifications. Near Niobe are tombs of a distinctly Phrygian type. It seems probable from this evidence that there existed in this part of the world before the Ionian settlement an organised state dependent culturally, if not politically, upon Phrygia, and through Phrygia, and the Hittites who seem at an earlier date to have penetrated to the coast, deriving its ultimate inspiration from the Hittite Empire. The Hittite Empire itself owed much of its culture to Egypt and Mesopotamia; and with the growth of the Assyrian Empire was almost entirely absorbed into the Assyrian cultural sphere.

It was probably the existence of this power on the coast which made the settlement of Ionia later than that of the country to the north and south. In Homer Miletus is a Carian city; and tradition says that when the Ionians took the town they married Carian wives after slaying the Carian men. The Carians were by no means uncivilised, and seem to have shared the late Mycenaean or Aegean civilisation. Underneath the temple of Athena at Miletus, the only spot in the city which has been excavated to any depth, sherds of the "latest Minoan-Mycenaean ware" were found predominating. This is additional proof that the Aegean civilisation survived to some extent in Ionia; though we cannot say whether these sherds should be attributed to Ionians or Carians. There was also a tradition that Miletus was once a Cretan colony. There was a Milatos also in Crete, and the name Thales, uncommon in Greece as a whole, is found in Crete, so that it is probable that a late Minoan colony formed part of the population of Miletus, and became Ionicised.

Thus from their very foundation the Ionian cities were equipped with a cultural tradition derived through their Greek, and perhaps Carian, ancestors from Mycenae and Minoan Crete, with which was combined the Northern influence mentioned above, and an Oriental influence derived through the people of Mt. Sipylus from the Hittites, Assyrians and Sumerians. The Ionians were further exceptionally free from hampering social and religious traditions; their religion, or that side of it represented by Homer, was highly rationalised, and contained the germs of a sceptical philosophy; they developed a social system—the republican City-State—very favourable to progress; and lastly were from the outset a race of intrepid mariners.

From the beginning the Ionian cities were in close touch with the civilised peoples of Anatolia, although, fortunately for the growing colonies, there was at first no state strong enough to interfere with their development. Their chief cities were situated at the ends of the caravan routes which led through the central uplands of Asia Minor to Assyria and Babylonia, and they must early have begun to take part in the trade which passed along these routes. The chief nations of the interior were the Phrygians and Lydians, whose strongly Egyptian culture was mostly derived immediately from the Hittites and the Assyrians. Unfortunately our knowledge of the archaeology of Anatolia is at present very scanty. In the eighth century the Phrygians seem to have been the dominant power, and the Lydians, though they possessed their own line of kings, called the Heraclids, were probably subject to them. From Phrygia, according to Greek tradition, a particular type of music, in the "Phrygian mode," was derived. About the year 685 B.C. there was a revolution in Lydia which established the Mermnad dynasty on the throne. Gyges, the first king of this dynasty, won a powerful empire, independent of Phrygia, which seems to have been eventually absorbed into his kingdom. The rise of Lydia was sudden. Gyges entered Greek history with an attack on the Ionian cities; and appears in Assyrian history as Gugu, King of a nation hitherto unknown to the Assyrians, called Luddi. He applied to Ashurbanipal for aid against the Cimmerians, who were at that time invading Asia, and received aid which enabled him to defeat them in 663 B.C. In 660 Gyges is described by the Assyrians as a feudatory; but the supremacy of Assyria was probably only nominal, and we find him shortly afterwards joining Psammetichus I of Egypt against his overlord. He raided, as mentioned above, the cities of Ionia; but he did not conquer them permanently; and to Miletus he is said to have granted generous terms. From this time on contact between Ionia and Lydia was constant. Wars were frequent, and ended in the subjection of Ionia by Croesus, who came to the throne of Lydia soon after 560 B.C. But in spite of these wars trade between the two nations constantly increased, to the enrichment of both. The Lydians appear to have been a wealthy and civilised nation, in close contact with Assyria, and their influence on the character and civilisation of Ionia must necessarily have been immense.

Herodotus states that the Lydians were the earliest "retailers"; which may mean that the Ionians, who had formerly indulged only in piracy and occasional barter, learnt from early intercourse with Lydia to become regular merchants. The Lydians must at an early date have tried to trade with the Ionians who commanded the end of the trade route which ran through their capital of Sardis. Of greater importance is the invention of coinage, also attributed to the Lydians by Herodotus and Xenophanes. In the second millennium B.C. large ingots of copper, and more rarely of silver and gold, of definite weight (a talent or hundredweight), stamped or marked as a guarantee of purity and full weight had been used as a medium of exchange. These ingots were shaped roughly like an ox-hide, or like an axe. They were extremely clumsy, and trade was carried on for the most part by exchange of goods, or by means of gold and silver weighed in the scales. Coinage proper was developed from roughly bean-shaped lumps of electron, which is an alloy of gold and silver found in a natural state in Lydia. These pieces were struck by private merchants in Lydia and perhaps Ionia, and date from the seventh, or perhaps the eighth, century B.C. They were of definite weight, but the only mark upon them at first was a punch-mark. The side opposite to this was flattened against the anvil on which the piece was placed to be struck. The next step was to engrave a design on the anvil which would leave an impression on the coin and show by whom it had been struck.

About the same time, the beginning of the sixth century, the rulers of the Mermnad dynasty, who were merchant princes as well as kings, began to issue their own coins. The Greek cities did the same, Miletus and Samos being among the earliest. Minting was too powerful a weapon to leave in private hands, and became a state monopoly. Lastly a stamp with a second design upon it was substituted for the punch, and a circular, flattish coin, with a different design on each side, resulted. In this form the invention spread over Greece, and eventually over the rest of the world. If the invention of coinage is to be attributed to the Lydians, the Ionians must at least be credited with a considerable share in its development; and the Greeks took the greater part in the spreading of the invention.

In the year 547 or 546 B.C. the kingdom of Lydia fell before the arms of Cyrus the Persian, and within a few years all the Greek cities in Asia had been reduced. Ionia was thereby brought into still closer relations with the civilisations of the East. Persian culture was mainly of Babylonian origin; but Darius (521–485 B.C.) conquered the Punjab and Sind; cultural influences from India may then have reached Greece. By this time, however, the art and civilisation of Ionia were well developed; Persia was probably more influenced by Greece than Greece by Persia.

The influence which reached Ionia in early times from the East through Lydia was not confined to commercialism and coinage. Smyrna, Ephesus, Miletus and Colophon were all strongly affected by Oriental influence, and the other Greeks tended to regard them as semi-Oriental cities. Excavations at Ephesus have shown the strong influence of Asiatic decorative style in Ionia. In particular early Ionian ivory statuettes from the same site are very reminiscent of Assyrian and Babylonian work. They are not, however, mere copies of Eastern objects, still less imported works of art. Some of the dresses and other details are distinctively Greek, and some of the patterns on the dresses are definitely Ionian and not Oriental. Moreover the carving of ivory statuettes goes back in the Aegean to Minoan times. We have to do here with foreign influences affecting a native art, not with the introduction of a foreign art. But the Eastern features are indisputable.

The Ionian ivories have been dated to the end of the eighth century. We cannot be sure whether the Mesopotamian influence they show reached Ephesus through Lydia, or was due to the Phoenicians, whom we must consider next. It should be noted that the Oriental influence so strong in early Ionian works of art soon weakened and almost completely disappeared. It proved a stimulus to the native art, and was absorbed without leaving very much trace.

The Phoenicians, we know from Homer and Greek tradition, traded in the Aegean from an early date, and brought with them the artistic works of the East. They were credited with working mines in the Aegean, but it is doubtful if they ever made any settlements there, as has been supposed. In connection with Phoenician trade in the Aegean, it is interesting to notice that the Greek word "chiton" meaning a kind of shirt, the normal Greek garment for men and women, is of Phoenician origin. The wealth of Tyre and Sidon, and the extent of their trade was proverbial in the Ancient World; their great days of prosperity coincided with the Dark Ages of Greece. Originally the Phoenicians were the carriers of the goods of others, and seem to have had little art of their own that has survived. Homer praises the woven work of the women of Sidon, which implies that Phoenician cloth and tapestry were imported into Greece. The Ionian and Corinthian archaic vases, decorated in an ornamental rather than a pictorial style, with every available corner of the design filled with ornaments which have nothing to do with the main picture, are not unlike pieces of tapestry or Persian carpet, and are probably influenced by woven designs. Of the two styles, the Corinthian is distinctly more Oriental in appearance than the Ionian; which is exactly what is to be expected if, as we have seen to be probable, Aegean art survived more strongly in Ionia than in Greece proper. The Ionians had their own artistic tradition; the Corinthians, whose art was originally less developed, were content to copy Phoenician models. It must be remembered too that in Homer not only the Sidonians, but Penelope and other Achaean ladies, were skilled in weaving. Perhaps we see the influence of purely Aegean woven work in the archaic Ionian vases.

Cloths and tapestries have not survived the passing of three thousand years. We must judge of Phoenician art, such as it was, from more durable objects. In the ninth century the Phoenicians established a flourishing industry in the manufacture of artistic objects, which were more remarkable for their quantity than for their quality. Their distinctive style was imitative and eclectic, derived largely from Egypt, also from Assyria and the Hittites of Syria, with rare reminiscences of Minoan work, derived from the late extension of Aegean civilisation in Cyprus and Cilicia. The Phoenicians showed no originality, and their hybrid art remained an unpleasant mixture of borrowed elements. They also produced large quantities of clumsy copies of foreign objects, for the most part Egyptian, which suggest bad modern forgeries. This Phoenician art had little influence in Greece. The Greeks certainly produced in the archaic period (seventh century) somewhat similar reproductions of Egyptian work: but when they wished to copy they did so directly from the Egyptians, and did it better than the Phoenicians.

Another and quite different class of objects has also been attributed to the Phoenicians; these are certain small ivory statuettes and other objects of the same material. Their style is much better and more original than that of the true Phoenician objects, and Mr. D. G. Hogarth has attributed them to North Syria. This district was in touch with Egypt, Mesopotamia and Phoenicia, and inherited cultural traditions also from the Hittites of Syria, and the "Minoans" of Cyprus or Cilicia. The Mesopotamian influence in these ivories seems to be derived from the fine late Sumerian period of the Patesi

Judea, and they have little in common with Assyrian and late Babylonian work. Minoan influence is shown by the hawk-headed Minoan
gryphon which frequently appears upon them. It is perhaps these
objects, dated to the ninth century, which inspired the fine eighth
century Ionian ivories described above. In that case the influence
would have reached Ephesus by sea, in the ships of Phoenician or
Ionian traders. But we saw that the Ephesian ivories, which are certainly very similar to those of Syria, presented also definitely Assyrian characteristics. It seems probable that Assyrian objects also
reached Ionia, possibly through Lydia.

From this part of the world, Phoenicia and Syria, the Greeks also
derived their alphabet. It is generally assumed that the Phoenician
letters were introduced into Greece in the ninth century B.C.; but it
has been suggested that they were really introduced much earlier. It
is now known that the primitive Semitic alphabet was in use much
sooner than was formerly suspected, certainly by the middle of the
second millennium B.C. Marks on copper one-talent ingots found
in Crete in circumstances suggesting a date on the border line between Middle and Late Minoan (or about 1550 B.C.) have been
plausibly interpreted as derived from the Semitic alphabet: and the
Greek legend of the introduction of the Phoenician script by Cadmus the Phoenician points to a similarly early date. Cadmus, according to tradition, lived many generations before the Trojan War,
which can be dated with some probability to the twelfth century B.C.
It would be unwise to dismiss the Greek legend too lightly, particularly as on the point of the Phoenician origin of Greek letters it has
been proved substantially correct. A possible solution of the problem
—which must yet remain mere speculation—is that the Semitic letters
were introduced into Greece in Mycenaean times by "Cadmus" or
the Phoenicians represented by that name, and were used by the side
of the Minoan script. It would not be surprising that all trace of
their use has perished, if that use was not very widespread, and
chiefly confined to writing on perishable papyrus. We may then
suppose that with the decline of civilisation in the Dark Ages, when
the knowledge of letters became rarer, the Minoan script perished,
while the Cadmean was kept alive, or reintroduced, by Phoenician
merchants trading in the Aegean.

The Greeks did not merely adopt the Semitic alphabet: they im-

proved it by addition of five vowels. The Ionians further improved
it by adding two more vowels to represent the long *e* and *o* sounds,
which in Ionic differed in quality as well as quantity from the
corresponding short sounds. It was this improved Ionian alphabet
which became the common alphabet of Greece in Hellenistic times.
The Latin alphabet, now used in all Western European countries,
was derived from the West Greek letters, which lacked the Ionian
improvements. From the Greek alphabet are ultimately derived all
the alphabets of Europe; while the Asiatic alphabets are mostly derived directly from the various Semitic alphabets. All the alphabets
of the world have a common origin in Syria.

Egypt and Greece

The last, and most important, country whose influence on Greece
must be considered, is Egypt. We have already seen that the Achaeans of the Heroic Age were accustomed to make the voyage to the
Delta: we have no reason to suppose that knowledge of the route
was ever lost. The Greek ships probably sailed straight for the Delta,
or from Crete to the nearest point on the Libyan coast, whence
they followed the coast to Egypt: they would thus avoid the Phoenician coast of Syria, and their presence in the Western or Canopic
branch of the Nile rather than in the East of the Delta is explained.
We have good reason to believe that Ionians were trading in the
Delta in the days of Tefnakhte—circa 726–718 B. c.—and his successor
Bokenranef Uahkere (Boechoris)—circa 718–712—who ruled Saïs
and Memphis while the Ethiopians ruled the rest of Egypt, and are
known as the XXIVth Dynasty. These were the first Egyptian kings
of whom the Greeks had personal knowledge. Diodorus says that
Boechoris was fabulously wealthy, and amended the law of contract,
making all contracts void in his law-courts save where there was a
written agreement. Many tales were told by the Greeks to illustrate
his commercial wisdom and justice. These kings were, like the Merm-
nads in Lydia, very commercial princes, and probably owed much
of their wealth and power to the Greek trade. This was certainly the
case with their successors, the Saïte princes of the XXVIth Dynasty.
The trade consisted mostly in the importation of oil and wine from
Greece, and in the export of wheat, barley and Libyan wool from

Egypt. It was largely in the hands of the Milesians, who at an early date founded a trading station on the Canopic mouth of the Nile near Saïs, known as the "Milesians' Fort." This emporium of the Milesians was the predecessor of the Greek city of Naucratis. The date of its founding is not known for certain but it may have been even before the time of Tefnakhte. The numerous references to this matter by ancient writers are very contradictory.

The site of the city has been excavated by Sir Flinders Petrie and Professor Ernest Gardner, who claim they have proved that Naucratis was an important Greek town in the middle of the seventh century. These excavations show that Naucratis was an Egyptian town before the Greeks settled there. On the balance of the evidence it seems probable that the Milesians' Fort was founded in the middle of the eighth century; that from about 700 B.C. Greeks, mostly Milesians, were trading in the Egyptian city on the site of Naucratis; and that about 650 B.C. Psammetichus granted a concession to the Greeks in that town, and the Milesians moved there from their fort and were joined by other Greeks.

In the year 663 B.C. Psamatik, whom the Greeks called Psammetichus, succeeded his father Niku (Necho) to the dominion of Saïs and Memphis. At this time Egypt was subject to Assyria, and Psammetichus was invested with the government of all Egypt by Ashurbanipal, perhaps after he had conquered it himself. He claimed the royal titles, as his father may have done before him, and was acknowledged by all Egypt (presumably with the assent of the Assyrian King) as the lawful successor of the Pharaohs. The Assyrian power was weakening, and Psammetichus seems gradually to have reached a position of independence. When at length Ashurbanipal roused himself to reduce him to obedience, the Assyrian troops were met and defeated by "brazen men from the sea." These were Ionian, and perhaps Carian, mercenaries in heavy armour, who may have been sent by Gyges of Lydia. Henceforward Egypt was independent. Psammetichus was the first King of the Saïte or XXVIth Dynasty. His power was founded on the wealth which he derived from the Greek and Phoenician trade, and on the military strength of Greek hoplites—the "brazen men"—whom he employed in great numbers. These troops he stationed in two camps, one at Marea, near Canopus, and the other at Daphnae, on the Eastern side of the

Delta, where they could protect Egypt against invasion from Asia. Daphnae for a few years became an important Greek settlement. It was also probably Psammetichus, as we have seen, who granted land to the Greeks at Naucratis. This new city was an "International Concession," rather like Shanghai to-day. The separate Greek States which contributed to the colony all had a voice in the choosing of the magistrates. In the time of Amasis twelve Greek States, of which the chief was Miletus, shared in the concession: all of them, with the exception of Aegina, lay in Asia Minor or the neighbouring islands, and six were Ionian.

In the eighth century, in the dominion of Tafnekht and Boechoris, there had begun a revival of Egyptian art (which had long been degenerate) based on a conscious imitation of the works of the Old Kingdom, and, where that was not possible owing to the scantiness of the remains, of the XIIth Dynasty. With the rise of Psammetichus this movement spread all over Egypt, and, as the power and prosperity of Egypt increased under the Saïte Kings, produced a remarkable renaissance of Egyptian civilisation. It is interesting to notice that this revival coincided with the rise of the new Greek civilisation. The two events cannot be dissociated.

The connection of the Greeks with the Saïte Kings was close and continuous. They regarded the Egyptians as the wisest of men.

The history of the Saïte Dynasty demonstrates that during the formative period of Greek civilisation—the Archaic period of Greek art—that is, from the eighth to the end of the sixth century B. C., the Greeks, and in particular the Ionians, were in close and continuous touch with Egypt; at the same time Egypt underwent a remarkable economic and artistic revival, and began once more to produce works of art rivalling those of the Old and Middle Kingdoms from which they were copied. The Greeks held a remarkably high opinion of the wisdom and civilisation of the Egyptians; tales were told of Greek artists who went to Egypt in the seventh century to study the technique of their crafts; and almost every philosopher from Thales to Plato was said to have visited Egypt. In view of these facts it would be very surprising if the influence of Saïte Egypt on Greek civilisation was not profound and far-reaching.

It is nevertheless not easy to define the precise results of this influence. The reason is that the Saïte period was not the first time in which Egyptian influence reached the Aegean. Most of the elements of ancient civilisation originated, as we have seen in earlier chapters, in Egypt. Aegean civilisation seems to have been founded directly by a settlement of Egyptians in Crete. These people came from the Delta at the end of Predynastic times, perhaps driven out by the conquest of the Delta when the two kingdoms of Egypt were first united. Their culture was probably identical with that of the Egyptians in the Delta. The great cultural influence which Egypt exercised in the Aegean during the times of the Old Kingdom, XIIth Dynasty and New Empire has been demonstrated again and again by the discoveries of the archaeologists. The Greek legends even suggest that an Egyptian Dynasty (that founded by Danaus) ruled in the Peloponnese in early Mycenaean times. Such a supposition, though it is not, and perhaps could not be, proved by archaeological evidence, is in itself by no means improbable. Minoan and Mycenaean civilisation was thus full of elements of Egyptian origin, and Greek civilisation contained many Egyptian features inherited from the Aegean Age. Egyptian civilisation changed little, and the people of the XXVIth Dynasty consciously imitated their ancestors of much earlier times. It is consequently often impossible to distinguish elements borrowed from Egypt in the seventh or sixth centuries from those borrowed many centuries earlier. We cannot always rely on the negative evidence of "Aegean" archaeology —especially in questions of religion, custom, and work in perishable materials—to prove that a particular feature is a late introduction; nor does the occurrence of a feature in "Aegean" times prove that it was not reintroduced from Egypt in the Saïte period.

In Rhodes Egyptian influence is clearly shown in the early sites, and imitations of Egyptian objects, similar to those at Naucratis, have been found. According to Dr. H. R. Hall ". . . it is probable that the Greek picture of the soul as a human-headed bird is directly derived from Egypt"; and "The name of the witch goddess Hekate is probably Egyptian (hike, magic)." The same authority also writes: "In gem-cutting, always a Greek speciality, we note the taking over by the Greeks of the Egyptian scarab, which, shortly to disappear in its own home, was to obtain a new lease of life in a slightly altered form in Greece and Italy.

An Egyptian creation that struck the imagination of the Greeks at the time was the dancing figure of the god Bes. . . . Bes was very popular under the XXVIth Dynasty in small figures of faience and other materials, and he seems undoubtedly to have been the original of the Satyr or 'Silen' of the Greek vase painters."

There is thus a strong antecedent probability that Egyptian influence of Saïte times affected Greek civilisation in other directions also.

It is generally admitted that Archaic Greek sculpture shows striking resemblances to the sculpture of Egypt; but the debt of Greece to Egypt in this respect has often been unduly minimised. It would not be incorrect to say that Greek sculpture owes its origin wholly to Egypt. The people of the Aegean Age, though they could model exquisite small human figures in ivory, faience or marble—as the figure of the goddess in the FitzWilliam Museum at Cambridge bears witness—never made life-size statues. A comparison of Archaic Greek sculptures, whether ancient or Saïte, makes clear at once the debt of the one to the other, though the Greeks had not yet obtained the same skill as the Egyptians in the delineation of the human face. The figures stand in exactly the same position, with the arms hanging straight down, and the left foot slightly advanced. There is the same stiffness in their general pose. The resemblance is particularly striking in the case of the so-called "Apollos" of early Greek sculpture, which were really portraits of athletic prize-winners. There was a distinctly Egyptising school of sculpture in Cyprus in the sixth century; and some of the figures even have the round wig and conventional waist-cloth of the Egyptian statues. The Egyptian sculpture of the time was, like most Saïte art, archaistic, and derived directly from Old Kingdom and XIIth Dynasty sculpture. This was carried so far as to represent Saïte nobles clad, not in the fashions of the day, but in those of two thousand years before. At the same time the Egyptians returned to the ancient custom, long neglected, of making their statues accurate portraits; and succeeded in rivalling their ancestors in that art. Greek sculpture was thus similar, not only to Saïte, but also to the earliest Egyptian work.

Tradition said that many Greek artists went to Egypt to learn their craft; and it is true that the technique of stone-carving must have been learnt in Egypt, the home of its invention.

On the subject of Egyptian influence in the Aegean at this period Dr. H. R. Hall writes that "the revival of improved methods of casting bronze may have been due to Egypt." In the middle of the sixth century, in the reign of Amasis, the art of casting bronze on a core was brought to the highest pitch of perfection in Egypt.

It is thus practically certain that the original stimulus which started Greek sculpture and bronze casting came from Egypt. But the Greeks had a vigorous artistic tradition of their own, and were not afraid of originality. Once started, sculpture therefore developed characteristics of its own on Greek soil, and all trace of Egyptian influence soon disappeared.

The debt of Greece to Egypt in architecture at this period was also considerable, though it is not so generally admitted. The general form of the Greek temple was derived from the Late Mycenaean megaron, which combined the features of the dwelling-houses of Northern invaders with the pillared halls of the palace of Cnossus. It was also not unlike Egyptian temples; but several features which are peculiarly Aegean are found.

Much of the detail of the decoration was derived ultimately from Egypt, but through the Mycenaean civilisation. The gable is a peculiarly Greek feature; that is, it is not found in Egypt. The purpose of a gable is of course to turn the rain; and it was consequently unnecessary in the rainless land of Egypt, but required in Greece.

The earliest Greek temple of the normal type with a colonnade around it (a "peristyle" or "peripteral temple") of which any remains are known, is the Doric Heraeum at Olympia. Its foundation probably dates from the eleventh century. The ground plan shows clearly the derivation from the late Mycenaean megaron; but the outer colonnade is a new feature. Once the colonnade was developed, its aesthetic possibilities were realised, and it became the most striking feature of Greek temples. Though columns were used for structural reasons in 'Aegean' times, it is probable that the aesthetic use of a long row of well proportioned and well spaced pillars was learnt from the interior of Egyptian temples, such as that at Karnak. The colonnade of the Heraeum was originally of wood. Stone columns were substituted gradually, probably beginning in the seventh century.

It is clear then that much of the form of the Greek temple was native to Greek soil, but that in the seventh century the Greeks began to build their temples wholly of stone, instead of wood, rubble and brick, copying the old temples in the new material; and at the same time they introduced a stone column of very different form from the wooden column they had used before. These two changes were of fundamental importance and created, almost in a moment, the fully developed Doric architecture of Greece. Probably both were due to Egyptian influence.

It seems certain at any rate that the Doric column was derived ultimately from Egypt. In the enclosure of the step pyramid at Sakkara, built by King Zoser of the Third Dynasty (circa 3000 B.C.), among what are the earliest known stone buildings—probably among the first ever built in the world—there have been discovered by Mr. Cecil M. Firth columns extraordinarily suggestive of those of the Greek orders. These columns are of two kinds. The entrance colonnade consists of columns tapering gracefully to the top, and roughly resembling Doric columns in proportion, though slightly more slender. The proportion of their height to their diameter at the base is about 5 to 1. They have a square base, and apparently a square capital—that is, the Doric *abacus* without the *echinus*. They differ from the Greek columns in that the moulding of the shaft is convex; that is to say, they have pointed grooves and rounded ridges instead of vice-versa. The general effect is much the same. Secondly, on each of the facades of two chapels attached to the tombs of the wives or daughters of King Zoser are four columns without bases of very slender proportions (12 to 1 and 13 to 1) with the concave fluting of the Doric order. Their capitals are of a curious type, having "flaps" hanging down on either side of the pillar, probably derived from a conventional leaf decoration.

The convex moulding is clearly an imitation in stone of a bundle of reeds or of a coat of reeds tied to a pillar. It has been suggested that the concave fluting is derived from reeds split down the middle with their hollow interior facing outwards. This may be so, or it may be merely the result of a reversal of the convex type. It is certainly an improvement, giving sharper and clearer lines. The fluted column is not a natural form, like the smooth round column, or the simple square pillar which, given the idea of a pillar, might arise independently in any country, and any number of times. It is a highly special form, and all later fluted columns must be derived ultimately from these Third Dynasty types.

The examples at Sakkara are the earliest but not the only fluted columns known in Egypt. Others generally called "Protodoric" are known among the cliff tombs at Beni-Hasan and Thebes, and were in use until the XIXth Dynasty (circa 1300 B. C.). In these the proportion of height to diameter varies from 5½ to 1 to 6 to 1. There was sometimes a base, there was no *echinus,* and the *abacus* was the same breadth as the top of the column. There were sixteen grooves or flutes.

Messrs. Anderson and Spiers deny that the Doric column could have been derived from the "Protodoric." They claim that if the Greeks had copied the Protodoric columns, they would also have adopted other forms from Egypt. This argument is not of much consequence. In the transmission of art-forms the selection and special development of particular features to the neglect of others is a common phenomenon. The Greeks, above other nations, avoided the indiscriminate adoption of foreign forms, and were quite capable of choosing from the great variety of Egyptian columns the one which best suited their taste and purpose. As regards the differences between the Greek and Egyptian forms, they are mostly unimportant. There was a difference of proportions, the Doric columns having in early examples the proportion of height to diameter of 4 to 1. This ratio is already fixed in an early temple at Corinth, which, save for the Heraion of Olympia, is the oldest known to us. In the Heraion itself the columns, as we have seen, varied in diameter. The proportion is surely a small matter compared to the essential similarity of the fluting. The addition of an *echinus* to the capital, and the greater width of the *abacus* in the Doric are also minor points, which may go back to the old wooden temple. The curvature of the sides of the pillars does not seem to be derived from either Egypt or the Aegean civilisation. It is a very great improvement, due presumably to the Greeks themselves. But the fact that the Greeks greatly improved upon the Protodoric column is no proof that they did not copy from it the fluting of their own columns.

The argument from the original use of wooden columns is very curious; for the writers themselves suggest that the wooden column was of Minoan form, completely different from the Doric column. The Doric column may well have been substituted for Minoan columns: it could not conceivably have been derived from them. The difficulty of date remains; but fluted columns were visible in Egypt, and could have been copied by the Greeks, even if the Saïte never made them.

We cannot avoid the conclusion that the Doric column was derived ultimately from Egypt, and that the form goes back to the Third Dynasty. It is possible, however, that the Greeks derived it from Mycenaean ancestors, and not directly from Saïte Egypt.

That the fluted column was known in Mycenaean times is proved by the discovery in the second Tholos-tomb at Mycenae of the lower portion of a fluted half-column beside the door of the tomb, and by two tiny fragments of ivory showing the upper portions of fluted columns. But this form does not seem to have been common in Mycenaean Greece; its use of course must have been due to Egyptian influence. There is one reason why it seems more probable that the Doric column was derived directly from Egypt. The Egyptian form tapered upwards; the Mycenaean, like all Mycenaean and Minoan pillars, tapered downwards. This is clearly shown in the case of the half-column at Mycenae, which measured 48 cm. in diameter at the bottom, and 53 cm. a metre higher just below the place where it was broken off. The ivory fragments are too small for us easily to judge the form of the columns they represent.

The men of Cnossus and Mycenae seem always to have used a great deal of wood in their architecture, for entablatures, roofs and pillars. Even at Cnossus the only stone pillars are the square basement pillars, which were sacred, and supported wooden columns in the stories above. The great Tholos-tombs alone seem to have been roofed with stone and had columns of stone, but these half-columns were decorative only, and had no structural purpose. Even this limited use of stone died out at the end of the Mycenaean period. The men of the Dark Age built temples such as the Heraion, the walls of which were made of unburnt brick and rubble masonry enclosed on the outside by a stone dado, and which were for the rest constructed of wood. Then in the seventh century, five or six hundred years after the great period of Mycenae, the Greeks suddenly began to build stone temples with stone columns resembling indeed certain columns found at Mycenae, but still more closely a type found in Egypt. The simplest explanation is surely that the Greeks, who were then in close touch with Egypt, received from Egypt at the same time the form of their stone columns, the custom of building wholly in stone, and the artistic use of a rhythmic row of pillars.

This view is further strengthened by the consideration of the Ionic order of architecture. As in the Doric order, the general form of the temple and of the entablature is derived from the wooden originals, but the column is derived from Egypt. The Ionic shaft, with its deeper fluting, and the broad ridge left between the grooves (which is the necessary condition of deeper fluting) is manifestly only a variation of the Doric column. The Ionic capital, with its volutes, has been conclusively proved to be an adaptation of the Egyptian papyrus-lily capital. It was first introduced into stone architecture in the seventh century; an early example, dated circa 620 B.C., having been found at Naucratis in Egypt: but the form was originally developed in wood from an Egyptian wooden capital. Transitional forms in stone, which make this derivation quite clear, have been found in Asia Minor, Athens and Cyprus.

More important in the history of mankind than the origin of a particular style of architecture or sculpture are the beginnings of science and philosophy in Greece. Greek science was curiously limited, chiefly because the Greeks were interested in the study of perfect, unchangeable and highly reasonable laws, where these could be found in Nature, and of the theoretical and perfect world of mathematical conceptions; but not at all with the varied and imperfect phenomena of Nature. Nothing resembling the Baconian theory of science is found in Greece; and their discoveries in natural science were mostly unimportant and by-the-way. Much accurate observation in biology was undertaken and recorded by Aristotle (end of fourth century B.C.) and his pupil Theophrastus (beginning of third century). The same was done in the science of medicine by Hippocrates (end of fifth century B.C.) and his successors. Empedocles (circa 500 B.C.) discovered the material nature of air, and some mechanical discoveries were made by Archimedes, Hero and others of the Alexandrian Age; and a succession of ob-

servers made great advances in Astronomy. But the great glory
of the Greeks is that they founded and developed pure mathematics,
crated a rational philosophy, and in general started the spirit of
scientific enquiry.

The movement started in Ionia with the philosopher Thales,
whose dates were approximately 624–548 B.C. Like most of his successors he is said to have studied in Egypt, and also to have travelled
in the East. He is reputed to have started scientific geometry, which
is quite probable; and to have foretold an eclipse. But he is chiefly
famous for having put forward a theory of the origin and nature
of the universe. We know little about his theory, save that according to him water was the origin of all things, that the world
we know was a kind of hemispherical bubble in the water, and
that the earth was a flat cylinder or disk floating on the flat side of
the interior of the hemisphere. This system is fundamentally Egyptian. It is really only the ancient cosmogony stated in a more rational form. The idea that Oceanus was the father of all things
is found in the Greek traditional cosmogonies; a view very similar
to that of Thales was held by the Babylonians; and everyone is
familiar with the Hebrew conception of the waters which are
above the firmament, and the waters which are under the earth.
Thales' view that all things were formed from water is clearly
the Osirian doctrine of Egypt. A careful reading of the first few
verses of the first chapter of Genesis reveals that the water was
assumed to be already there before Jehovah began His six days'
labour of creation.

Such speculation as that of Thales was continued by his successors, Anaximenes and Anaximander, who were both Ionians.
They continued to be interested among other things in the stuff
out of which the world was made, and suggested alternatives to
Thales' water. In the hands of later philosophers—Pythagoras, an
Ionian of Samos who went to live at Crotona in Italy in the latter
part of the sixth century; Heraclitus, about 500 B.C.; Parmenides,
Empedocles, Zeno, Leucippus, Democritus and others in the fifth
century—the discussion developed into an enquiry into the nature of reality and the possibility of knowledge thereof. Thus
"Philosophy," in the usual modern sense, was born from the rather
crude speculations of Thales. It attained its finest development

in Greece in the works of Plato and Aristotle in the fourth century, B. C.

Greek mathematics was certainly founded on the mathematical knowledge of the Egyptians. In arithmetic the Greeks continued to treat fractions, as the Egyptians did before them, by reducing them to the sum of a number of fractions whose numerator was one. But they made considerable advances on the work of their teachers; Pythagoras at an early date, besides much useless speculation about the shapes and moral qualities of numbers, studied the arithmetical, geometrical and harmonic progressions. The Egyptians only used arithmetic for practical purposes, such as architectural calculations and commercial transactions: the Greeks studied it for its own sake as a pure science. This was in itself an advance, but the love of pure science was carried so far as to separate what the Greeks called "logistic" (the science of calculations concerning material things) from "arithmetic" (the abstract study of numbers). An undue contempt for the former greatly retarded progress.

The Greeks were also the inventors of geometry. Thales was said to have propounded the first geometrical propositions; but the main credit for the elaboration of elementary geometry seems to be due Pythagoras and his disciples. In this subject the Greeks built on the empirical knowledge which the Egyptians used in the building of pyramids and temples, and the measuring of land. But the Egyptians had no theoretical geometry. Thus they certainly knew that a right-angle could be constructed by making a triangle the sides of which were in the proportion 3:4:5; and they seem to have realised the relation of the areas of the squares constructed on the sides of a right-angled triangle. They could prove this relation in the case of the 3:4:5 triangle by dividing the squares into 9, 16, and 25 small equal squares respectively; and could show it to be approximately true in the case of other triangles by dividing them into very small equal squares and neglecting fractions. It was left to Pythagoras or his successors to devise a logical and perfect proof applicable to any right-angled triangle. That is merely one example of what is meant by saying that the Greeks "invented" geometry. From the Egyptians they learnt certain geometrical facts; but they had to start at the very beginning with the invention of a logical apparatus of definitions and axioms, and to construct their theoretical geometry theorem by theorem.

In astronomy the Greeks owed more to Mesopotamia than to Egypt. The Egyptians had made accurate observations of the movements of the sun for the purpose of making the calendar, the Babylonians had done the same of the planets for astrological purposes, had kept accurate records of eclipses from which the eclipse cycles were determined, and used certain instruments for observation and the measurement of time, such as the polos (a hollow half sphere with a style in the centre, used for observing the sun's movements by means of the shadow of the style on the interior of the sphere), and the clepsydra (water-clock). It was in Mesopotamia, too, that the division of the circle into 360 degrees originated; but the date of this is uncertain. From Babylonia the Greeks said they derived the signs of the zodiac. As in the case of mathematics, the astronomy of the ancient civilisation was limited by its practical applications. The Greeks, learning the accumulated knowledge of Egypt and Babylon, and bringing a more inquisitive and rational mind to the subject, developed astronomy further than either the Egyptians or Babylonians. It should be noticed, however, that Greek astronomy was limited by the desire to find that the heavenly bodies moved in perfect circles. When Aristarchus of Samos (310–250 B.C.) suggested that the earth moved round the sun, the notion was soon abandoned even by its author, because it could not be made to fit in with the theory of the circular orbits of all heavenly bodies. The foundation of Greek science, as of modern science, was the belief that the universe was rational; but to the Greeks, who had no conception of the law of gravitation, the movement of heavenly bodies in circles was rational, and required no further explanation; any other movement was irrational and inexplicable, and therefore impossible.

The history of the progress of mathematics and astronomy in Greece was very different from that of the arts and literature. The latter developed rapidly, culminated in the fifth and fourth centuries B.C., and thereafter slowly declined. The former shared in the rapid development of the great renaissance, but continued to develop for centuries afterwards. The best work was done in the

Alexandrian or Hellenistic Age; and progress at a slower rate continued during the Roman period.

An adequate discussion of the sources of Greek religion would in itself make a lengthy treatise. The utmost diversities of opinion are expressed by different scholars. The diffusion of religious ideas in the Eastern Mediterranean started so early, and was so free and prolonged, that obviously there were striking resemblances between the cults of all the nations in that region. As we have seen in earlier chapters, all religious ideas were probably propagated in the first place from Egypt. Consequently they all show a family resemblance. When, in addition, intercourse and the interchange of cults had been taking place for some two and a half thousand years it is not surprising that a fundamental unity can be detected. Moreover, religious ideas combine, and cults amalgamate with great ease, particularly when populations are mixed; and the evidence is necessarily much less tangible than the sherds and ornaments with which the archaeologist deals. Thus the cult of Dionysus has been said to have been derived from Thrace, Phrygia, Crete, Egypt and India, and also to have been indigenous in Attica, Boeotia and Delphi. Evidence can be found to support all these views, and several of them may be partly true without necessarily eliminating the rest, for the cult probably contained elements from different sources.

All that need be said here is that though Greek religion had its own peculiar features, and was not exactly like any other, yet it was formed from the same elements as the religions of the neighbouring countries, and that to these elements the Greeks added practically nothing. They showed no striking originality, and made no great progress, in religious matters, as, for instance, did the Jews and the Persians.

On the other hand the Greeks did create a very wonderful literature. We have already seen that the Epic was the particular creation of the early Greeks, and owed its existence to the Heroic Age. It was their earliest literary adventure and both stimulated the later Greeks to create other forms, and influenced those forms themselves.

Most, and perhaps all, of the other classes of poetry, including drama, had their origin in ritual songs and dances of a religious nature. This fact is generally admitted, although the question of the particular cults, from which arose the various forms, Tragedy, Comedy, Dithyramb, Paean, Hymn, Ode, and so forth, is much disputed, and cannot be answered with certainty. The transition from ritual to literature was the unaided work of the Greeks. Prose was developed, on the whole, at a later date than poetry, by the philosophers and chroniclers of Ionia in the sixth century B.C.; but for a long time many writers preferred the verse form. Solon (circa 590 B.C.) wrote political pamphlets in verse, and Empedocles, Parmenides and Xenophanes, among others, expressed their philosophies in poems. Prose only became a recognised artistic medium towards the end of the fifth century with the Histories of Herodotus and Thucydides, and the rhetoric of Gorgias of Leontini and his pupils, the Attic orators.

In most aspects of civilisation the lead was at first taken, as we have seen, by the cities of Ionia. But with the ruin of Ionia after the disastrous revolt of 499 B.C., and with the rise of Athens after the Persian Wars to be the centre of an empire which included all the Ionians, the leadership of Greek civilisation was transferred to Athens; and it was there that the height of Greek achievement in art, literature, and philosophy was reached in the fifth and fourth centuries.

It has been the aim of this chapter to give a picture of Greek civilisation, not as a miraculous creation from a state of barbarism, but as a natural growth from the high civilisations of the Aegean and Egypt with some help from Mesopotamia. Its rise was due to the stimulating effect in Ionia of intercourse with Egypt and the East, at a time when political, social and economic conditions particularly favoured progress in all aspects of national life.

CHAPTER XV

THE WORLD WIDE INFLUENCE OF GREECE

THE influence of Greece on Western Civilisation in mediaeval and modern times is so well known, and so universally admitted, that it is unnecessary to discuss the matter here in any detail. The main facts can be found in any history of Europe, and have recently been summarised in the collection of essays called "The Legacy of Greece" (Oxford) edited by Principal R. W. Livingstone. Our concluding chapter will be concerned chiefly with the study of the influence of Greece in the East, which is not so generally recognised. It is well, however, to keep in mind the admitted facts concerning Western Civilisation, because they provide an excellent illustration of the general theorem of the diffusion of culture, which none will dispute. It is also instructive to notice both the parallel and the contrast between the rôles of Greece and Egypt in the history of mankind. We have seen that most, if not all, the elements of the ancient civilisations were derived directly or indirectly from Egypt. It is equally true that Greece provided most, if not all, the elements which distinguish the higher culture of Western Civilisation, as well as those of Asia and Pre-Columbian America.

Our mathematics, our science, and our philosophy originated in Greece; almost the whole of European literature shows the influence of the Greeks, and with few exceptions every literary *genre* can be traced back to Greece. Even our alphabet is derived from the Greek alphabet. In the same way, though the plastic arts did not begin in Greece, the art of Europe has always been largely dependent on that of Greece. Lastly, according to the Dean of St. Paul's among other theologians, we owe the half of modern Christianity to the Greeks. In his essay "What the Modern World Owes to Ancient Greece," (*Harmsworth's Universal History of the World*) Mr. H.

A. L. Fisher gives an eloquent and illuminating appreciation of the magnitude of our debt to Greece.

The diffusion of the elements of Greek civilisation throughout Europe has taken place in many ways, and has extended over long ages. The main development of that civilisation took place before the conquests of Alexander in an area which included two large regions, the coasts and islands of the Aegean on the one hand, and the coasts of Southern Italy and Eastern Sicily on the other, and a number of scattered communities extending from Cyprus and the Caucasus to Cyrene in Africa and Marseilles in Gaul. From the beginning the Greeks were influencing their neighbours over a wide area. The Britons before the Roman conquests used coins stamped with apparently meaningless designs, which comparison with a series of Pre-Roman coins from Gaul has shown to be derived ultimately from the designs on the coins of Massilia. At a later date the heathen Germans received their mystic runes from Greece. But most important was the influence of the Greeks in Italy. The Etruscans, who were colonists from Anatolia, became half Hellenised, adopting the Greek alphabet, and copying Greek art. Rome no less was from the beginning under the influence of Greece. This is shown in the alphabet, and in many details of cult. According to tradition the first Tarquin, the Etruscan tyrant of Rome, was in reality the son of a Corinthian exile. But Greek influence in Rome was intensified after the conquest of the Greek cities of Italy and Sicily in the third, and of Greece itself in the second century B.C. The Romans themselves admitted that they owed all their higher civilisation to Greece, their literature, art and philosophy, as well as their luxuries. With the exception of the satire, all Latin literature is frankly an imitation of the Greek. The first Latin plays were but rough and very free translations of Greek originals. The first Latin authors were Greek slaves and freedmen; and for centuries the artists, schoolmasters, and professors of philosophy and rhetoric at Rome were almost all Greeks.

The next stage was the spread of this Graeco-Roman civilisation by the Roman Empire: the work was continued after the collapse of the Empire by the civilisation of the Germanic and Slavonic barbarians; in the West by Rome and the Latin Church, in the East by Byzantium and the Orthodox Church. In the hands of non-Christian peoples, Buddhists and Mohammedans, Greek influence was spread even more widely. Finally the revival of the direct influence of Greece in the Renaissance, which was largely due to the Arabic speaking people in Spain and elsewhere, created modern, as opposed to mediaeval, civilisation. It must not be supposed, however, that the direct influence of Greece was not active in Europe before the Renaissance. In a variety of ways it was continually affecting thought and action: but at the Renaissance it acquired a dominating supremacy.

Reference has already been made to the still earlier influence of the Aegean civilisation in impressing the seal of Mycenaean and Greek culture more and more widely on Europe, Africa and Asia. The effect of this upon Asia was profound and far-reaching. In the Chapter on Elam and Sumer attention was called to the diffusion of Elamite culture during the third millennium B. C., not merely to India (the Punjab and Sind), but also to Turkestan, thence into the heart of Siberia and China (Figure 59).

Some centuries later the discovery of the means of making the alloy bronze, which was probably made in Northern Persia (see Figure 61, BR) stimulated a very intimate intercourse between that region in Asia with Mesopotamia, Asia Minor, Crete and Egypt. Moreover the inauguration of the Age of Bronze produced intense activity throughout Europe and Western Asia. The frequent comings and goings of the peoples in these areas linked civilisation into a more closely interrelated whole. The intimacy of the connections between the Aegean, Scythia and India during the twenty centuries after the events just mentioned produced results which, hitherto, have been unduly minimised, if not wholly ignored.

Scythia and Siberia

Numerous discoveries by Russian archaeologists and others have revealed the existence of an artistic and impressively homogenous culture which once extended over a large area in Russia and Siberia. It flourished at the time when iron was coming into use. The fact that in some of the objects found the influence of both archaic and classical Greece and of Iranian art of the Achaemenian period is manifest, has led archaeologists to assign it roughly to a period from the eighth century B.C. onward until the Christian era. It extended from South Russia and the Caucasus to the Perm district in the North, and to Minusinsk, the Altai and Lake Baikal and Mongolia in the East. The three main regions of South Russia (Scythia proper, Permia and Siberia) show certain distinctions of style; but the similarities between the cultures of the three areas are so great, and the evidence of the transmission of types from one to another is so abundant, that we are justified in speaking of a single civilisation. This vast area was inhabited by many different peoples; and the homogeneity of their culture at this time must have been due to widespread and quick diffusion, the special reasons for which it is our aim to explain.

The most remarkable feature of the civilisation of the Scythians (if this name may be applied vaguely to all the peoples of the Steppe) was its great wealth in gold, derived presumably from the mines in the Urals, and to a greater extent, of the Altai, and the alluvial deposits of the rivers which attracted people to settle in Turkestan and neighbouring lands (Figure 61).

It cannot be doubted that the first impulse to the Scytho-Siberian civilisation came from the prospectors who had long before been searching Central Asia for gold and other substances to which they attached a superstitious value. As early as the first part of the third millennium B.C. civilised men, coming for the most part from Elam, had reached Anau near the Caspian Sea in Russian Turkestan in search of copper ore, turquoise and lapis lazuli; they found gold also in Turkestan, and a long chain of ancient irrigation works and stone monuments ranging from the Oxus to Bukhara, to Issyk-Kul and Kulja, and as far as Minusinsk on the Yenesei (Figure 36, Y) show the route by which their culture spread into Siberia. They determined the caravan routes (see Figure 36) that have been used ever since for about fifty centuries. Later waves of culture from Mesopotamia and Western lands passed into Central Asia by the same ways. The Scythians and Siberians, with whose culture we are now concerned, occupied the homes of these ancient miners, and, judging from their wealth in gold, must still have worked the old mines of the Altai range, and washed gold from the same rivers as their predecessors. The search for gold is a very insistent witness to the dominating influence of the Egyptians, who created the artificial value of the metal.

In the other section of their extensive area, in the Kuban district of the Caucasus, they occupied the homes of an older civilised people who had sought the gold of Colchis (Figure 61, CO); their culture, with its megalithic dolmens, and hafted axes, shows clear signs of the influence both of Egypt and Sumer. This early Kuban civilisation spread over the steppes of Southern Russia and was another source of the "Scythian" culture.

The character of Scythian art may be described as a curious blend of naturalism and conventionalism. It consists almost exclusively of animal subjects stylistically and decoratively treated. No attempt is made to reproduce Nature with photographic exactitude; indeed, animal figures are often treated as mere patterns, amplified by the addition of parts of other animals regardless of Nature. Thus the antlers of stags are greatly elaborated, and are frequently made to end in conventional birds' heads. The bird's head is also found worked into many other animal designs. Yet the better examples are extremely vivid and lifelike, and show a careful observation of nature. Paradoxical as it may sound, the Scythian craftsmen were able to combine a thorough-going conventionalism and the most unnatural and impossible features with a suggestion of vigorous life.

The source of artistic inspiration was probably Mesopotamia, the great breeding place of mythical monsters. The Ionian Greeks had settled all round the Black Sea, and their colonies in Scythian lands extended from the Danube to the Caucasus. The Tauric Chersonese (Crimea) and the Cimmerian Bosporus were in particular thoroughly Hellenised. Here arose a powerful Greek state, half kingdom, half republic, with its centre at Panticapaeum. Greeks and half-breeds spread far up the rivers as traders, and in time the Scythians of that area became half-barbarian. The process of the Hellenisation of Scythian art continued during the fifth and fourth centuries B.C., and was almost complete at the end of the latter century. At the same time Iranian influences were penetrating the Scythian area further east, and were manifested in the introduction of West Asiatic motives (such as the lion-headed gryphon) and in a tendency to cover metal objects with polychrome inlays of turquoise, coral and carnelian, which much obscured the original naturalism and vigour of the designs. This influence spread far to the east into Siberia.

Scythian and Siberian art bears a remarkable resemblance to the Minoan-Mycenean art. In his book *Scythian Art* (1928) Gregory Borovka writes: "the Scytho-Siberian animal style exhibits an inexplicable but far-reaching affinity with the Minoan-Mycenean. Nearly all its motives recur [it would have been more accurate to say "are foreshadowed"] in Minoan-Mycenean art."

Perhaps the most striking motive common to both is the so-called "flying-gallop"; animals portrayed in rapid movement with their fore-legs stretched forward, and their hind-legs stretched back, almost in a straight line with the body. The position is one which no galloping animal takes up, but it is a very effective method of suggesting swift motion. It is typical of Minoan-Mycenean style, but as M. Salomon Reinach has shown, it is foreign to the art of all other ancient and modern peoples, except in Scythia, Siberia and the Far East.

Other types common to the two cultures are animals with bodies twisted so that the forequarters are turned down, and the hindquarters turned up; animals with reverted heads; animals curled into almost complete circles; and others with legs hanging loosely down as if they were suspended in mid-air. The general style of some of the Scythian products often reminds one of the work of the ancient Cretans. The scroll-work of the conventionalised antlers in a bronze object (girdle plate or horse's frontlet from the Kuban district attributed to fourth century B. C.) is typical of Middle Minoan decoration—and resembles also the painted ceiling of the hypogeum in Malta, which Sir Arthur Evans holds to be derived from Crete. Some of the curious monsters which Borovka calls bears—though they do not in the least resemble bears—with narrow snouts are very suggestive of Minoan mythical animals, and among others of the libation-pouring Genii, which may have been derived from the Egyptian hippopotamus goddess Ta-urt.

Whether or not these facts are an indication of a real derivation of Scythian art from Crete is a problem which cannot at present be certainly solved. The main objection to such a view is that of date.

The Minoan-Mycenean art which the Scythian resembles flourished from about 1900 to 1400 B.C. After the end of the fifteenth century it degenerated, and could scarcely have inspired the Scythian art, unless it persisted for six centuries in or near Scythia.

The Scythian products are assigned to the period from the eighth century onwards, on the evidence of those examples which show Greek influence. The purely Scythian work is so similar to the latter that writers have assumed it to be not much earlier than the classical age. If that opinion were justified there would be a clear interval of 600 years between the best Minoan-Mycenean work and the earliest Scythian. Against this it is possible to argue that, apart from objects showing very definite Greek influence, the Russian and Siberian finds are undated, and many of them may be very much older than is supposed. It is possible under certain conditions for a particular artistic tradition to remain unchanged for centuries, and there is no valid reason for denying the possibility of such a survival in Scythia.

The other argument brought forward against the hypothesis of Minoan influence in this culture, is the spatial distance between Crete on the one hand, and Scythia and Siberia on the other. But we have definite evidence that Aegean influence did, in early times, reach South Russia and Turkestan.

In her important monograph on *Gournia,* Mrs. Harriet Boyd summarises the evidence for connection between Crete and Turkestan.

"When the Pumpelly expedition returned from Turkestan in 1904, one of the members brought potsherds indistinguishable at first sight from the brilliantly mottled ware found at Vasiliki (Crete) during the same season. . . . The strong likeness between the two fabrics . . . is more reasonably explained by intercourse than by accident. Moreover Dr. Hubert Schmidt . . . reports that a neighbouring tumulus (near the large one in which the pottery was found) gave him a three-sided seal-stone of Middle Minoan type, engraved with Minoan designs—man, lion, steer and griffin. How shall we explain these evidences of Aegean influence in Southern Turkestan? They must be brought into line with other proofs of contact. We see that at *circa* 2500–2000 B.C. [figures that need to be reduced by 500] Asia Minor shared with the Aegean the knowledge of bronze . . . we may suggest the probability that, long before tin was discovered in Europe, it was being brought overland through Asia Minor, and also by way of Transcaucasia and the Black Sea from distant Khorassan, Strabo's Drangiana. . . . Excavations at Elizabethpol in Transcaucasia have revealed a culture in early contact with the Aegean."

Strabo declared that tin was produced in Drangiana.

We have thus clear evidence of Cretan influence in Turkestan in Middle Minoan times (which lasted roughly 2100–1550 B.C.) We do not know how long this intercourse continued—it is unwise to argue from the lack of later finds that it did not continue into the period of greatest prosperity in Crete, the sixteenth and fifteenth centuries.

From South Russia and the Kuban comes evidence of intercourse with the Aegean, if not with Crete, in Early Aegean times, before 2100 B.C. In the *Dawn of European Civilization* Professor Gordon Childe writes: "In the Don-Donetz region the peculiarly Cycladic phallic beads of copper and the very form of the catacomb graves proves intercourse with the Aegean. The extension of that connection to the Kuban itself may be indicated by the alabaster idol from Ulski. The Caucasus is rich in metals and Early Aegean merchants may well have anticipated the Argonauts. Perhaps the introduction of the axe-adze into Crete was the reflex of such a voyage."

This Cycladic influence in itself will not of course explain the Minoan appearance of Scythian art; but it suggests the possibility of direct influence from Crete at a later date, or of Mycenean influence at the time when the whole Aegean world was absorbed in Mycenean culture. There is no contemporary proof of such influence at present, but its possibility cannot be denied.

There can be no doubt that the Aegean did at certain times exercise a considerable cultural influence in or near the lands where the Scytho-Siberian art subsequently flourished; and this influence may possibly have been stronger, and lasted later than the present evidence shows. The relatively late date of Scythian art is the only objection to the theory that it depended on Minoan inspiration. If that objection is not valid, there is no reason why we should not regard the derivation of Scythian art from the Minoan as the most reasonable hypothesis. The internal evidence of the art itself is surely conclusive proof of the genetic relationship.

Siberian art, and therefore probably other elements of culture, exercised a considerable influence in China, whether by trade or by invasions of barbarian nomads from the steppes. The Mongolians of the Chinese frontiers, whether they were of the same race as the people of the Yenesei or not, were within their cultural sphere. There seems to have been little difference culturally between the various nomads of Asia, Mongols or Turki-Alpine in race (with possibly some Nordics) and Indo-European or Turki in speech.

"From China, principally indeed, from the northern frontier provinces and Mongolia, come bronze and gold articles that agree so exactly with Siberian products that we must regard them as pure Siberian manufactures imported into China. . . . There are quite well attested finds of Siberian works on Chinese soil" (Borovka).

Further, other objects, partly in Chinese and partly in Siberian style, and evidently Chinese imitations of Siberian work, are found in China. They are attributed to the Han Dynasty (250 B.C. to 200 A.D.). Certain objects attributed to the Chou Dynasty (1122–250 B.C. — the first date is more or less mythical, so that 'Chou' may be taken to mean before 250 B.C.) also show the influence of the Siberian animal style.

The motive of the Tao-tieh—the symbol of the Storm God—is very common in the early art of China. It is a very conventionalised lion's mask. It seems to be derived, in part at least, from the Siberian art. The same is true of the Chinese art-type of the dragon. Certain weird animals in Siberian work resemble very closely the Chinese dragon—particularly early Chinese examples. The most striking of these Siberian "dragons" in their resemblance to Chinese (Borovka, Plate 52 B), are two beasts heraldically opposed from a gold girdle-clasp in the collection of Peter the Great in the Hermitage. They have long thin bodies; the hind-quarters are twisted upwards behind, so that while the fore-quarters are in profile, the hind-quarters are viewed as from above, with the legs splayed out at either side; their snouts are long and thin, their mouths gape widely, their chins are bearded; large horns rise from their brows; they have long tails, and appear to be provided with rudimentary wings. In their twisted bodies and the form of their snouts they are reminiscent of Minoan animals; which suggests the interesting possibility of the derivation of the Chinese art-type of dragon from Crete! Borovka suggests "the Iranian horned lion-griffin and the Scytho-Siberian 'bear,' probably not without the collaboration of Greek influences" as sources for this Siberian type.

Of the Han period Borovka writes, "As far as we can judge at present such indebtedness to Siberia can be detected in nearly all Chinese bronzes of this age, and also on other artistic products such as nephrite articles."

Borovka suggests that elements of the Scythian culture persisted in mediaeval Russia, and were brought into Central and Western Europe by the Goths and Slavs, who came from or passed through the ancient "Scythian" lands and "became a weighty element in the rise of West European civilisation in the early Middle Ages."

Buddhism

Attention has been directed to the widespread and intimate relationships between the Hellenic world and the heart of Asia to prepare us for the consideration of an event which was destined to influence the lives of innumerable millions of human beings and profoundly affect the course of Human History. Within fifteen years of the death of Thales in Ionia—exact figures are lacking, there may even have been an overlap—there was born to the ruler of the Sakyas at the town of Kapila-vastu, 100 miles Northeast of Benares in India, a boy to whom the name Gautama was given. When he reached man's estate and, like Thales, adopted a rationalistic attitude, he received the name Buddha, "The Enlightened One." To-day, twenty-four centuries after his death, nearly one-third of the population of the world enroll themselves as his followers.

When we consider the manifold ways in which information was being spread abroad in the sixth century B. C. was it merely a coincidence, as the late Professor Rhys Davids pretended (*Buddhist India*), that Thales and Gautama should both have repudiated the hieratic conventions at the same time and adopted a rational system of thought and behaviour?

The learned Pali scholar quotes with approval Sir Henry Maine's statement that "Nothing is more remarkable than the extreme fewness of progressive societies." The sole difficulty in accepting a causal relationship between these deeply significant events is the wide separation between Asia Minor and India. But as we have seen intercourse was free and uninterrupted. Moreover there are reasons which will be given later in this chapter, for believing that even before the birth of the Buddha Greek ideas were exercising an influence in India.

"Whatever the secret, above and beyond the influence of economic conditions, may have been, we know that civilization, of a kind at least, extended back in time, on the four great river basins of the Nile and Euphrates, the Ganges and the Yellow River, not merely through centuries, but through thousands of years, if reckoned from to-day. Yet in each of those places—though there was a real and progressive civilisation, and ideas and customs were no doubt constantly changing and growing—there was a certain dead level, if not a complete absence of what we should call philosophic thought. The animistic hypotheses, the soul-theories, of their savage ancestors seemed sufficient, even to the progressive races, to explain all that they saw or felt. Men varied, but never dreamed of rejecting, the soul-theories. They did not even build up on the basis of them any large and general views, either of ethics, or of philosophy, or of religion. Then suddenly, and almost simultaneously, and almost certainly independently, [the phrase that mars Professor Rhys Davids's teaching] there is evidence, about the sixth century B. C., in each of these widely separated centres of civilisation, of a leap forward in speculative thought, of a new birth in ethics, of a religion of conscience threatening to take the place of the old religion of custom and magic. In each of these countries similar causes, the same laws regulating the evolution of ideas, had taken just about the same number of centuries to evolve, out of similar conditions, a similar result. Is there a more stupendous marvel in the whole history of mankind? Does any more suggestive problem await the solution of the historian of human thought?

"The solution will not be possible till we have a more accurate knowledge of the circumstances which led up, in each country, to the awakening. And in India one important factor in the preceding circumstances seems to me to have been, hitherto, too much neglected. The intense interest, from the world-history point of view, of the sixth century B. C.—the best dividing line, if there ever was any, between ancient history and modern, between the old order and the new—would be sufficient excuse, if one were needed, for a somewhat detailed consideration of this particular point." (T. W. Rhys Davids, *Buddhist India.*)

In the light of our present knowledge the reasons Professor Rhys Davids has given for refusing to identify the Ionian and the Buddhist revolutions of thought as part of one movement are discredited and wholly unconvincing speculation.

While it would be rash at present to claim that Buddhism was one of the results of the new vision in Miletus, it would be even more reckless to deny an inference that seems so highly probable.

Indian Art and Architecture

If it is still uncertain what was the relationship between the emancipation of Greek and Indian thought and religion—if such rational philosophy as that of Thales and Gautama can be called religion—there is no room for doubt as to the source of the artistic and architectural ideas and motifs with which Buddhism expressed itself. They are frankly and unquestionably Greek.

It is important not to forget that apart from the rough stone monuments—the dolmens and other megalithic structures—which remain as abiding witnesses of the prospecting for gold in India on the part of immigrant colonies from the West, there was no architecture in India until the advent of Buddhism. The remains of ancient cities at Harappa and Mohenjo-Daro, to which reference was made in Chapter IX, show that the Punjab and Sind once enjoyed a high state of Elamite civilisation: but during the twenty centuries that intervened between them and the birth of Gautama this seems to have lapsed, in spite of the fact that during at least part of that time cultured people speaking an Aryan language were immigrating into the Punjab from Afghanistan, Persia and Turkestan. But apart from the mythology, which afterwards was put into writing as the Vedas, little remains of material contribution to the civilisation of India. It is, however, important not to forget the Mesopotamian and Persian background of Indian culture, which prepared the soil for the eventual cultivation of the seeds of Greek culture.

Western, and in particular Greek, influence in India in the period we are considering (roughly 500 B.C. to 500 A.D.) is most clearly marked in sculpture and architecture, which it will there-

fore be as well to consider first. For our purpose we may distinguish
two periods in which foreign influence was clearly displayed, and
one in which Indian culture, having thoroughly assimilated the
alien inspiration, developed on its own peculiar lines. The first
period of foreign influence may be roughly dated 300 B.C. to 450
A.D. This style of architecture and sculpture of this period developed
under the Maurya Dynasty (321–184 B.C.) and in particular under
Asoka (272–232 B.C.) from whose reign date the earliest remains;

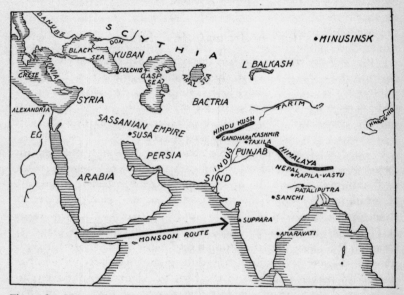

Figure 64—Map to show the relations between the Greek world, Scythia, and India.

and most of the monuments probably date from Maurya times.
Therefore, although the period extends considerably beyond the
limit of the Maurya Dynasty, it is convenient to call it the *Maurya*
Period (and the Maurya style) of art. The second phase, commonly
known as the *Gandhara* Period, extends from about 50 A.D. to 300
A.D. The most important remains are those found in Gandhara—
the district around and to the north of what we now know as
Peshawar, on the Northwest frontier of India. It was succeeded by
a phase of consolidation, called the *Gupta Period*, from the Gupta

Dynasty which ruled most of Northern India from 320–330 A. D. to about 480 A. D. But, like the Maurya, the Gupta style continued long after the dynasty which gave it its name had passed away.

The Maurya Period

Twenty centuries before the period which we are considering, India had enjoyed a civilisation which seems to have been inspired by Elam (Harappa and Mohenjo-Daro—the "Indus Culture"), and by maritime influences from the Mediterranean, which introduced the Megalithic culture in Southern India at an early but undetermined date. The influence of the West in India was probably never wholly absent. In particular Aryan-speaking people doubtless brought something more than their speech and folk-lore. About the time of the death of Guatama the Buddha (the first half of the fifth century B. C.) we know that the Indians were already skilled masons, accomplished stone cutters, and cunning makers of jewellery and workers in gold. The "stupa" of Piprahwa on the Nepal frontier, which is referred to the period about 450 B. C., is a solid cupola of brick; and it contained a stone coffer for relics of Buddha. The houses and palaces of the time were built of wood on brick or stone foundations. We may presume that the carving of wood was practised for the decoration of palaces and stupas, in the way that stone-carving was used later. Temples were at this time unknown. Apart from the Megaliths, Harappa and Mohendaro, we have no evidence of any stone architecture or stone sculpture before the reign of Asoka; no remains are known which can be dated earlier than about 260 B. C. It is of course probable that these arts were practised slightly before that date; but it is very unlikely that they began before the reign of the first Maurya, Chandragupta (321–297 B. C.). It is therefore particularly important to notice the relations of India with the West during the earlier Maurya reigns.

To start at a somewhat earlier date, the Indians had long been in communication with their kinsmen, the Persians; this communication became closer with the establishment of the Achaemenian Empire. Darius the Great (521–485 B. C.) had conquered the Punjab and at least part of Sind, which were ruled for some time by Persian satraps. In the years 327 to 325, B. C. Alexander the Great was in

India, conquering the same districts. After his death Chandragupta Maurya (Sandracottus), who was said to have met Alexander, drove the Greeks out, conquered all Northern India, and in 305 defeated Seleucus Nicator, who attempted to regain the lost provinces. Nevertheless some Greeks, perhaps married to Indian wives, probably continued to live in India. Alexander's foundation of Alexandria on Indus was long known as "Alasanda of the Yonas," that is of the Ionians or Greeks.

It is more important that when Chandragupta had defeated Seleucus, he made a treaty of alliance with him, and even married a Syrian princess. Megasthenes was sent by Seleucus (308 B. C.) as ambassador to the court of Chandragupta at Pataliputra (Patna); and Deimachus, about 296, as ambassador to Bindusara, whom the Greeks called Amitrochates (= Amitraghata), the second Maurya King (297-272). Shortly afterwards, in either Bindusara's or Asoka's reign, an ambassador called Dionysius came from Ptolemy Philadelphus of Egypt. Asoka evidently remained in friendship and communication with the Macedonian princes; and even boasted that he had sent missionaries to them, and converted them all to Buddhism.

Ptolemy Philadelphus (285-246 B. C.) built several ports on the Red Sea for the Indian trade: Arsinoe near Suez, where he hoped, but failed, to build a canal; and Berenice and Myos Hormos further south. The trade was, however, mostly indirect. Merchandise changed hands at Aden (Arabia Felix). Few made the voyage to India.

It is clear that during this period there must have been a number of Greeks living in India—remains of Alexander's troops, and the retinues of the Seleucid princess, and of the ambassadors; and that India was open to Hellenistic influence.

Maurya Art

In his zeal for Buddhism Asoka endowed monasteries richly, and built stupas, monasteries with chapels attached to them. The principal remains have been found (in Central India) at Barhut, where the actual buildings have been destroyed, though the sculptures were first removed and have been preserved; and at Sanchi. Other less notable remains have been found at Buddha Gaya, in Bihar, and at the Mauryan capital, Pataliputra (Patna). There are also the pillars that Asoka set up in various parts of his empire. Almost all the artistic work of the period seems to have been connected with Buddhism, though the Buddhists must have been in a minority. The sculptures from Sanchi and Barhut belong in part to Asoka's reign, mostly somewhat later; the latest were completed by 140 B.C.

The style of the most ancient Indian works of art in stone, those of this period, is described by Mr. Vincent A. Smith as "a compound of Hellenistic, Persian, and Indian elements."

The monolithic inscribed pillars of Asoka are of Persian form, with Hellenistic ornament. In the *Imperial Gazeteer of India* Mr. Vincent A. Smith says:—

"The principal member of the Asoka capital is reeded and bell-shaped in the Persepolitan style. The edge of the abacus is in some cases adorned by a row of wild geese pecking their food, a decoration probably suggested by the frequent introduction of the goose in Alexandrian sculpture. The abacus of the pillar at Allahabad is decorated with a graceful scroll of alternate lotus and honeysuckle, resting on a beaded atragalus of Hellenistic style. A fine capital found at Pataliputra exhibits the acanthus leaf ornament delicately carved in low relief. In general terms the Asoka pillars may be described as imitations of the Persian columns of the Achaemenian period with Hellenistic ornament."

Further emphasis is laid on the honeysuckle and cable ornament by Mr. J. Burgess, also in the *Imperial Gazeteer*:—"On the inscribed pillars or 'lats' set up by Asoka, besides the Persian form of capital, we find the honeysuckle with the bead and reel and the cable ornaments employed in earlier Assyrian and Persian sculpture. . . . These continued in use in Gandhara on the Northwest frontier for about four centuries, which seems to indicate that it was from Persia that these forms first came, along with the suggestion that led to the conversion in India of wooden architecture into stone."

The Persian form of capital gave rise to all the forms of capital since used in India—excluding the Greek capitals used at Gandhara—and is found all over India, among the Gandhara monasteries as elsewhere.

The principal sculptures of the period are reliefs, mostly executed on the railings and "toranas" (or gates) which surrounded the Buddhist Stupas. These railings and gates were evidently no more than stone copies of wooden structures. Could we discover what the wood-carving was like, we should be more certain of the history of early Indian art. As it is, we can only judge from the surviving stone reliefs.

"Although it certainly appears to be true" according to Mr. Vincent Smith (*The Early History of India*), "that Indian plastic and pictorial art, such as it was, drew its inspiration from Hellenistic Alexandrian models during the Maurya Period, the Greek influence merely touched the fringe of Hindu civilisation . . . and when Indians have condescended, as in the case of relief sculpture and the drama, to borrow ideas from European teachers, the thing borrowed has been so cleverly disguised in native trappings that the originality of the Indian imitators is stoutly maintained even by acute and learned critics.

"Although the details of real life in the sculptures of the early period are invariably purely Indian, the compositions as a whole, and the representations of mythical monsters, are certainly Hellenistic, and exhibit the distinctive characteristics of Hellenistic art. The practice of decorating buildings with "pictures in relief" might well have been borrowed from Persia; but the composition and style of the Indian work are so remote from the Persian, and so akin to the Alexandrian, that it is impossible to doubt that the Indian artists imitated European [really Alexandrian] rather than Iranian models. . . . The drawing and execution of the Indian 'pictures in relief' are, of course, much inferior to the Greek, but the general principles of the composition in both are identical."

Concerning the sculptures at Barhut (or Bharhut) Mr. Vincent Smith once more emphasised the importance of the evidence of the garland, previously mentioned:—

"The series of reliefs on the coping manifests the Alexandrian influence with special distinctness, the long garland being very cleverly used to divide the subject into compartments by its sinuosities. This garland was long a favourite motive in Hellenistic and Graeco-Roman sculpture, continuing in use up to Byzantine times, and even later. In the second period of Indian art it was largely employed by the artists of Gandhara."

The use of this garland as evidence of Graeco-Roman (and in particular Alexandrian) influence acquires special interest and importance when we examine the geographical distribution and details of the design, variously described by writers as "the graceful scroll of alternate lotus and honeysuckle," "the honeysuckle with bead and reel," "the cable ornament," and "old Indian scroll work." When Indian civilisation spread to the Far East the use of this floral scroll for architectural decoration became even more obtrusive. In Cambodia and Java, for example, from the eighth and ninth centuries A. D. onwards it appears upon innumerable temples, and in China it became one of the most distinctive characters of the art of the Tang period. In the same centuries it made its appearance in America and scrolls, which might have been carved by Coptic sculptors (Figure 50), are found on Maya monuments. Some years ago, in the course of a discussion of a series of drawings of the Maya buildings at Palenque made nearly a century ago by the French artist M. de Waldeck, drawings revealing unmistakable Indian elephants modelled in accordance with the conventions that held sway in Java in the ninth century A. D., the writer was vigorously criticised for refusing to ignore M. de Waldeck's sketches. Apart from the representation of the elephant, criticism was directed at the scrollwork, which if accurately portrayed would provide certain evidence of the date and Asiatic provenance of the design. It is not necessary, however, to argue only from M. de Waldeck's sketches. In Figure 50 one of the drawings made for Dr. A. P. Maudslay, the reliability of which no one questions, provides evidence which is much more valuable and decisive.

This criticism was responsible for directing the writer's attention to the widely recognised value of this very design in the Old World as evidence of influence emanating from the Egyptian city of Alexandria.

The influence of Greek art in India can be traced in various details of the sculptures. For instance the "nimbus" or halo placed behind the heads of gods and saints, and found at Sanchi, as well as among the later sculptures of Gandhara and Amaravati, is of

Greek origin; it was used in Greek paintings as an attribute of gods.

It is thus clear that while the architecture of this period was formed under influence partly Persian and partly Greek, the sculpture was influenced almost solely by Greek art—though both architecture and sculpture were assimilated and adapted to acquire a distinctively Indian facies. Some have supposed that the Persian forms were taken over in wood during the Achaemenian period, and that the Greek influence followed later. It is possible, however, that the Persian and Greek forms were introduced at the same time in the days of the Seleucid and Maurya empires. Naturally the Greek influence gradually became dominant, and is found in the sculpture and decoration which probably developed later, while the Persian columns were adopted early, and survived the Greek influence.

During the Maurya Period Taxila in the Northern Punjab or Gandhara, near the Persian frontier, was the centre of Indian learning, science and philosophy—especially medicine, such as it was.

Persian and Hellenistic influences were obtrusive—the Persian in the administration, in manners, and in the basic forms of stone architecture, the Hellenistic in the decoration of buildings, particularly in the reliefs. It is important not to forget, however, the intimate relationship of Persia with both Greece and Egypt. Much of the Persian influence in India was merely the diffusion of Mesopotamian, Egyptian and Greek culture under a Persian disguise.

The Egyptians invented the arts of shipbuilding and seamanship and, as we have seen, used this achievement to establish intimate relations with Syria and Crete, with East Africa, Arabia and Sumer, and, possibly by the middle of the third millenium B.C., with India. The culture of Southern India is obtrusively Egyptian in its essential features. There still survive in India, Burma and Indonesia, types of sea-going ships which were in use in Egypt as early as 2600 B.C. but soon afterwards were supplanted by later types.

Most of this maritime trafficking, which before the beginning of our era may have encircled the continental land masses of the whole world, was coastal, although as we have seen voyages to

Crete were undertaken before 3000 B.C. About 45 A.D., however, a Greek sailor called Hippalus is said to have discovered the "Etesian" wind (the south and west monsoon): but the Arabs (and no doubt still earlier sailors) had appreciated the use of this wind long before, and had guarded it as a secret. From this time Romans began to sail directly from the Red Sea to India, instead of coasting by way of Oman and Persia.

The direct trade with India rapidly increased in volume. An unknown Greek sailor has left a record (Periplus of the Erhtyraen Sea), which gives a detailed record of the maritime trafficking, which was surprisingly widespread and searching.

According to Mr. Vincent Smith "Colonies of Roman subjects engaged in trade were settled in Southern India during the first two centuries of our era. European soldiers, described as 'powerful Yavanas, dumb barbarians clad in complete armour' acted as body-guards to Tamil kings, while 'the beautiful large ships of the Yavanas' were laden with cargoes of pepper, which was paid for by Roman gold."

This reference to armour is of special interest because further east, and in particular in distant islands in Oceania, not long afterwards the people were wearing helmets and armour which are obviously crude imitations of the military uniforms of Imperial Rome.

The Gandhara Period

When Chandragupta drove the Greeks from India, they still remained in Bactria, the country around Balkh, north of the Hindu Kush. Here the Greek power was firmly established. About 247 B.C. the ruler of Bactria revolted from the Syrian (Seleucid) Empire, as did Arsaces the Parthian. The Greek Kingdom in Bactria lasted until about 130 B.C. when it was destroyed by the Saka (so-called Scythians). But before this Bactrian Greeks had established themselves in India. About 190 B.C. Demetrius conquered the Kabul Valley, the Punjab and Sind; shortly afterwards Eucratides raised a revolt against him in Bactria, and henceforward there were a number of warring Greek dynasties in Bactria and India, whose history cannot be clearly made out. About 155 B.C. another Greek, Menander, gained an extensive kingdom in Northwestern India.

He was apparently converted to Buddhism, and appears in Indian story as Milinda. After the conquest of Bactria by the Saka soon after Menander, the Greeks continued to hold out in the Punjab and the Kabul Valley amid neighbouring Parthian and Saka princes until they were conquered about 50 A.D. by another people from Central Asia, the Yueh-chi (see Figure 36) or Kustran, who followed the Saka. The Greek kings were partly Indianised, and worshipped both Greek and Indian gods. But the Greek language, and some degree of Greek civilisation were, to judge from the evidence of the coins, preserved.

An anticipation of the Gandhara period has been found at Taxila in the form of a temple with Ionic columns built about 80 B.C. The earliest examples of Indo-Greek sculpture belong to the same period.

The Yueh-chi or Kustran entered India about 60 A.D. and before 100 A.D. had conquered India as far as Benares. The greatest of their kings, Kanishka, who came to the throne about 123 A.D., extended his empire northwards, conquering Kashgar, Yarkand, and Khotan, and defeated the armies of the Chinese Empire, which had shortly before extended to the Pamirs and beyond. Kanishka became a Buddhist, and the Buddhist monasteries flourished in his reign. The best of the Gandhara sculptures date from the reign of Kanishka, and his immediate successors.

The barbarian Kustran seem soon to have adopted the mixture of Greek, Persian and Indian culture which they found in Bactria, Gandhara and the Punjab. Their coins show inscriptions in both Greek and Sanskrit. Their capital was Peshawar in Gandhara.

The establishment of peace over a wide area by these powerful kings, and the encouragement which Kanishka gave—probably with liberal endowments—to the Buddhists, gave a new impetus to architecture and art; and the Gandhara period began.

The Gandhara Sculptures

The Gandhara period may be roughly dated 50 A.D. to 300 A.D., but the period of greatest development was between 120–185 A.D.

Mr. Vincent Smith says: "The florid Corinthian capitals and many other characteristic features of the style prove that the Gandhara school was merely a branch of the cosmopolitan Graeco-Roman art of the Early Empire. The most competent critics are now generally agreed that the school reached its highest point of development in the second century of the Christian era."

The Gandhara sculptors were Greeks imported from Syria or Egypt. When bidden to portray Gautama they used the convention of the Graeco-Roman Apollo (either identifying Gautama as a "god" of enlightenment with Apollo, or simply because they were asked to produce a type of youthful beauty), only modifying it so far as to comply with some of the traditional marks of a Buddha— e. g. the spot between the eyebrows.

The Greek influence in Gandhara was not a survival of the earlier Hellenisation of the Punjab. The latter seems to have left little trace. Further, the closest approach to the Gandhara style is found in the art of the Roman Empire in the second century A. D., i. e. Gandhara was influenced by the contemporary art of the Roman world.

The similarities are so close and striking that the artists must have been imported from the West to execute the works.

In this period sculptures showing Greek influence were made, not only in the remote and foreign-ruled frontier province of Gandhara, but in India proper under native kings. The fact is of importance with regard to the influence of this Indo-Hellenic art on later Indian art. Many authorities assert that it had none. This might seem a priori probable if the Indo-Hellenic art was confined to Gandhara. But it was not.

At Amaravati, in the Kistna district of the Madras presidency, was a Buddhist monastery and stupa, the design of the outer railing of which can be studied in the cast alongside the main staircase of the Britist Museum. To quote Mr. Vincent Smith again:

"The features of the decoration, *especially the wavy roll* [the Graeco-Roman or Alexandrian garland discussed on a previous page], enable us to determine the age and affinities of the monument." The general style may be defined as an Indianised adaptation of an Antonine development of Alexandrian art. This proposition, which might be deduced from considerations of style alone, is confirmed by a few inscriptions and other items of internal evidence. The work, of course, took many years to execute, and no single date can express the chronology with accuracy. It is, however, safe to say that the outer railing should be referred to the second half of the second century A. D.

"Although the resemblances between the works of the Gandhara school and the Amaravati marbles are to some extent obscured by differences of material and treatment, the close relationship of the two schools cannot be denied. Both are essentially Indianised adaptations of Graeco-Roman art; but the sculptors of Amaravati seem to have drawn their inspiration chiefly from Alexandrian models, whereas the artists of Gandhara were more indebted to the Hellenistic schools of Asia."

The Gupta Period

About 226 A. D. a revolution in Persia established the powerful Sassanian Monarchy. Indian Empires were disrupted: the Kushan kings continued to rule only in the Kabul Valley. Intercourse between Rome and India by land was broken by the Sassanian power. The history of India for a century is obscure. But intercourse with Alexandria by sea continued to flourish, chiefly with Southern India.

About 480 A. D. the Gupta Dynasty was overthrown by the Huns. The "Golden Age" of the Guptas—the period of great power and prosperity—lasted from 330 to 455 A. D. In the latter year the Gupta king (Kumaragupta) was defeated by the White Huns, who later overthrew the Empire altogether.

The Gupta period, roughly 300–500 A. D., was marked by the development of a distinctly Indian art; by the creation of classical Sanskrit literature, secular and to be clearly distinguished from earlier literature, the Vedic and Brahmanic sacred books of the Brahmins, or the Pali books of Buddhists; and finally by the establishment of Brahmin ascendancy, and the slow decay of Buddhism.

It is often claimed that the art of the Gandhara Period had no influence on that of the Gupta Period. Before the Gandhara (or at any rate its predecessor the Maurya) India had no art that is known to us. Is it at all conceivable that a people who previously had displayed no artistic impulse, but for five centuries had become familiarised with the practice of an alien art and architecture, should, as soon as the Sassanians cut their land communications with their art masters, have set to work, to create an art of their own? Such a suggestion is altogether incredible. The Gupta art provides evidence of unquestionable significance that it was due to the assimilation of the knowledge and skill which the centuries of training during the Maurya and Gandhara Periods had taught. It was the development of an art which was Indian only in the sense that the important ideas and methods had now been adapted by Indian artists to express in a distinctively national manner the motives which an alien influence had originally suggested. The influence of Greece on Indian science, philosophy and literature is not so generally recognised as is that of architecture and art, although it is difficult to believe the latter could have been so freely adopted without the other elements of culture.

It is certain that the Indians learned astronomy from the Greeks. This is admitted even by Indian writers, usually so reluctant to admit any alien influence.

"The Yavanas are barbarians," writes the author of the *Garge Samhita,* "yet the science of astronomy originated with them, and for this they must be reverenced as gods," an interesting commentary when we recall that astronomical knowledge was in large measure responsible for conferring divinity on the first god, Osiris.

Indian astronomy was derived directly from Alexandria. Of the mediaeval treatises, one was called *Romaka,* which indicates the source of its foreign origin. The word also means Alexandria. Another was known as the *Paulisa Siddhanta,* after Paul of Alexandria (circa 378 A. D.) on whose works it was based.

The astronomical writers called the signs of the zodiac by their Greek names, more or less corrupted, instead of by their Sanskrit names. They also used Greek technical terms.

The evidence is not so definite in the case of mathematics. But it is difficult to imagine that the Indians could have imported astronomy from Alexandria without mathematics. Yet the earliest evidence of the use of the cipher o seems to be Indian. If the Indians really invented the cipher and the place-value decimal system of writing numbers they have the right to be regarded as the pioneers of a great development of science.

Additional interest attaches to this question because for several

Figure 65—Bas-relief from a stone altar at Copan (after Maudslay) illustrating the obvious influence of Indian civilisation in America. This distinctive type of turban is still worn in Sumba (Malay Archipelago) right on the route to America. The grotesque face on the chest is also found in the Prambauau Sculptures in Java (ninth century A. D.).

years the surprising claim has been repeatedly advanced by certain
archaeologists that the Maya people of Central America invented
the cipher. They make the even more astounding pretense that
this imaginary achievement affords decisive evidence of the indigenous origin of American civilisation.

In view of the considerations, first that the people of India had
the cipher long before the Maya people, and, secondly, that the earliest civilisation of India displays the most obtrusive evidence of
Hindu inspiration, the emphasis laid on the zero acquires a special
significance as further corroboration of America's debt to India.

Figure 66—A sculptured representation of an Indian Elephant at Copan in Central
America.

In the writer's book *Elephants and Ethnologists* (1924) the evidence has been set out fully in substantiation of the view that the

sculpture represented (after Dr. A. P. Maudslay) in Figure 66 is an Indian elephant with Indian embellishments and additions of symbolic motive. The spiral ornament is of peculiar interest, as it was originally adopted in India after Alexander the Great used as the symbols of his two great expeditions (to India and Egypt respectively) the head of an Indian elephant in conjunction with the spiral horn of the Amen (Ammon) ram. With the diffusion of culture to Indo-China, China and Indonesia, the spiral became a common embellishment of the elephant's head in sculpture and pictures, The fact that this irrelevant spiral is found in the representation of the elephant in America completes the proof of its Indian origin.

Diffusion from India

The Gandhara style was the basis of the art of Central and Eastern Asia. In the time of Asoka, Buddhism spread to Kashmir and Turkestan and thence to China along the caravan route (see Figure 36), which was established by the early searchers for gold and jade about 2500 B.C., and has been in use ever since. In spite of her early acquisition of Elamite culture and the continuous, if somewhat attenuated, connections with the West ever afterward, China was content to cultivate her original cultural capital with a persistence and a slavish conservatism which are unique in Human History. Then when India felt the stimulus of Greek culture she began to transmit the effects to China, at first by way of Turkestan and Central Asia, but later also through Nepal and Tibet. This put the Northeastern lands into close touch with the Buddhist (Mahayana) monasteries of Gandhara.

The Chinese Buddhists kept up communications with India. About 65 A.D. the Han Emperor of China, Ming-ti, had Buddhist books brought from India. In the succeeding centuries Buddhism made gigantic strides in East and Central Asia and became a factor of fundamental importance in the Human History of that part of the world.

During the century when Thales in the West was "liberating thought from the bondage of religious ritual" and "applying to the fundamental problems of existence the free, unfettered activity of the human intellect" (to quote the words of Mr. H. A. L. Fisher),

Gautama in India and Confucius (following up the pioneer work of Lao-tze) in China were attempting much the same task in their own way. But in the placid story of China the teaching of her two philosophers meant little more than giving concrete and unemotional form to what most of the people were thinking. The Indian philosophy of the first century exerted a more potent influence, which affected art and architecture.

One illustration was the adoption in Eastern Asia of the "torana" or ceremonial gateway, which India had previously adopted from the earlier civilisations of the West, where the pylon or gateway was the obtrusive feature of the temple. At the Sanchi stupa in India the whole surface of the toranas is carved in a most complex and elaborate manner. The P'ai-lu or P'ai-fang in China, and in Japan the Tori-i, generally made of wood, were definitely inspired by the torana of India.

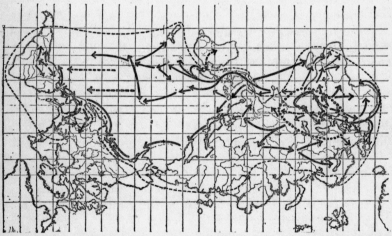

Figure 67—Map compiled by Dr. W. J. Perry and the writer to illustrate the diffusion of culture. Starting in Egypt during the fourth millennium it extended as far as the inner (dotted) oval by 2500 B.C. at the latest. By the time of the European expansion (1500 A.D.) it had reached the outer (broken) line, beyond which Food-Gatherers were left undisturbed.

Reference has already been made to the influence of India upon Indo-China and Indonesia. China also came under its sway during the T'ang period (602–907 A.D.). According to Dr. Cohn, although the earliest monuments of Indian art go back to the time of Asoka, about the middle of the third century B.C., the five centuries from the fourth to the ninth A.D. include the time of the zenith of Indian art. It left its mark on Chinese Buddhistic art, and probably also upon Japanese art of the Nara period. But this does not represent the limit of its sphere of influence. The same phase of Indian culture was impressed unmistakably upon Central America and Mexico and played an obtrusive part in shaping the earliest civilisation that grew up in the New World. It is rightly regarded as distinctively American, though most of its ingredients came across the Pacific from the Old World. To the question; "Who created the art of Java and Indo-China?" Dr. Cohn answers: "Here we stand suddenly facing a full-grown art, which is certainly dependent on India, and yet has much that is its own." The same reply is applicable to the Maya civilisation of Central America.

Everyone who has seriously investigated the history of Cambodia recognises the predominant influence of Indian culture there. Its architecture sprang into existence quite abruptly, revealing from the beginning a certain mastery of design and technique which rapidly attained the summit of their expression. The analogy with the known facts relating to the Maya stonework is so close that one can confidently interpret the meaning of the American evidence in the light of the established history of Cambodia. The Maya architecture began suddenly because immigrants brought the knowledge and the technical skill to inaugurate the new practice. But there is something more than an analogy between the cases of Cambodia and Central America. Not merely was the mechanism of cultural diffusion identical and its results similar, but the American culture was actually derived in large measure from Indo-China, and bears to it the same relationship as Cambodia does to India. Their history was closely analogous. Both rapidly attained the highest expression of their art; in both cases the initial inspiration soon became exhausted and a process of degradation set in. In both cases there were centuries of cultural penetration before the great architectural achievements were effected. Having assimilated the art of architecture for two centuries, the Cambodians erected their great stone monuments mainly between the sixth and the thirteenth centuries A.D.; but it is generally admitted that Hindu influence upon the customs and beliefs of Indo-China was being exerted some centuries earlier. The same statements can confidently be made, both as regards the historical sequence and the approximate dates, as the only credible interpretation of the facts of Maya archaeology in America.

In his memoir entitled, "Some General Observations on the Temples of Angkor," (*Rupam,* 1922), M. H. Marchal questions whether one is justified in claiming Cambodian art simply as an expression of Indian inspiration, even if one recognises the predominant influence of Indian culture and many of its decorative motives. The nearest analogy to some of the representations of foliage and interlacing designs is to be found in Western mediaeval art. Winged figures, human and animal, reveal their Chaldean origin. He says the capitals of the galleries and vestibules of Angkor Vat remind him of the Doric order of classical Graeco-Roman architecture; and he suggests that the influences of Europe and Western Asia might have reached as far as Indo-China by way of Syria and Persia to India. As we have already seen, Greek influence had been impressed upon Buddhist culture before its easterly diffusion, if indeed it was not itself Hellenic in origin.

The solution of the problem defined by these quotations from M. Marchal's essay is a matter of fundamental importance. But due recognition has not been accorded by the majority of anthropologists to the fact that elements of early culture often survive in distant places long after they are lost or profoundly modified nearer the home of their invention. For example, the practice of mummification has been extinct in the home of its invention for more than twelve centuries. Only very slight traces of it can be discovered in India. In Indonesia and Indo-China it is still practised, but with profound modifications of the original technique. Yet in the islands of Torres Strait, in Melanesia and Polynesia, in Peru and elsewhere in America, the ancient Egyptian methods were more completely preserved than at any of the intermediate places. The late Dr. W. H. R. Rivers repeatedly called attention to this phenomenon, which for so many writers has been a cause of difficulty and confusion of thought rather than the revelation of a common historical fact. But its significance is plain enough. When the germs of an alien culture are planted in a new territory it takes a long time after they have taken root before the growth assumes a distinctive character peculiar to the new focus.

There is no doubt that India derived a great deal of its earliest (pre-Hellenic) culture from Babylon and Egypt, and gradually assimilated these adopted customs and beliefs until there developed a new cultural compound distinct from Babylonian and Egyptian civilisations and characteristic enough to receive the name "Indian." But during the centuries it took to effect this process, India was handing on to Indo-China the torch of Western knowledge before it had assumed its distinctively Indian form. Hence the Far Eastern civilisation preserves more definite traces of its original Egyptian and Babylonian inspiration, such, for example as Egyptian standards and Babylonian Liver-divination, than Indian civilisation itself, because the vigorous and prolonged development of the latter effected a much more profound transformation. This principle can be applied not only to early streams of culture but also to all the subsequent waves. Moreover it can be used to explain not only Cambodian problems, but also those of Indonesia, Oceania, and especially America, in the primitive civilisation of which can be recognised contributions from India, Indonesia, Indo-China, China, Melanesia and Polynesia, but also not a few ingredients of much earlier but quite unmistakable Mesopotamian, Mediterranean and Egyptian influence.

The most obtrusive factor in the customs and beliefs of the Maya civilisation is unquestionably Indian.

Theological Syncretism

In the cosmopolitan kingdoms of the Greeks, Sakas, and Parthians in Gandhara and the Punjab, and of their successors, a remarkable syncretism of religious ideas was effected. King Kanishka himself worshipped both Greek and Hindu gods, although he considered himself a Buddhist—a religion which in its original form was a philosophy without gods. But at his time Buddhism had recently undergone a profound transformation and developed into what was called the Mahayana (Great Vehicle). According to Mr. Vincent Smith this was "the result of a complex interaction of Indian, Zoroastrian (Persian), Christian, Gnostic and Hellenic elements, which had been made possible by the conquests of Alexander; the formation of the Maurya Empire in India, and above all by the unification of the Roman world under the sway of the earlier emperors." One of the reasons for the astounding success of such a colourless belief as the original Buddhism was its tolerance and complaisance. In the course of their wanderings the Buddhists seem to have been free to accept any other beliefs and rituals, any gods and forms of worship without any restriction. So that in different countries—and at different times in the same country—Buddhism presents the most profound contrasts. Buddha was made a god and the idea of a Messiah or Bodhisattva crept into the Mahayana. King Kasyapa was believed to lie uncorrupted in his stupa, as though mummified. Then as Maitreya Bodhisattva he was believed to be resurrected, to work miracles and to disappear in flames. This legend is obviously the outcome of Persian and perhaps Christian influence and later survived in Mohammedan stories.

It is possible that in addition to being the recipient of Western culture India may have influenced the West. Some scholars claim that the Gnostic heresy and Neo-Platonism reveal the influence of India, that Plotinus and his disciple Porphyry display an acquaintance with Indian doctrines.

There can be no doubt of the knowledge of Indian affairs by the Christian writer Clement of Alexandria, who died about 220 A. D., for he gives us exact information derived from one of the earliest Christian missionaries to India. His account found much favour with the Neo-Platonists. Thus Porphyry tells us the Brahmins take no wine and abstain from flesh and women. They despise death and set no value on life because they believe in transmigration. It was such a belief that almost destroyed civilisation in Europe between the fifth and the tenth centuries A. D.

The earliest reference in Western literature to the stupa, a unique feature of Buddhism, is contained in the same work in these terms:—"The Sramana (Buddhists) worship a kind of pyramid beneath which they imagine the bones of a divinity of some kind lie buried."

Going West

We have been discussing the influence of Greek civilisation in India and the profound influence with which the mixture of Buddhism and Sivaism, permeated with Hellenic ideas and practices, overran the Far East and then overflowed into the island world of the Pacific to reach America where amidst the jumble of distorted Buddhistic symbolism not a few elements of Greek civilisation crop out to excite our wonder. Witness for example the wonderful geometrical pattern in the interior of the ruin at Mitla (oaxaca), the Amen-horn of Alexander the Great as the spiral on the Copan elephant, the thunderbolts of the Rain-God depicted in the Maya and Aztec codices, among scores of other items.

But if the influence of Greece was carried far and wide in the East as part of the baggage of Buddhist missionaries, it also had another kind of diffusion in the West as part of Christianity. The Dean of St. Paul's refers back to Plato the religion and the political philosophy of the Christian Church and the Christian type of mysticism. Mr. H. A. L. Fisher says "the doctrine of the immortality of the soul was Greek, not Jewish," and further "that there was a close connection between Early Christianity and the Greek mystery religions is now generally acknowledged." Some critics have even described Christianity as "a decaying form of Hellenism."

It is clear that the diffusion of Christianity involved also the spread of the influence of the Greek philosophy of life.

But Hellenism also found another outlet in Islam. Summing up the argument of his book *Arabic Thought and its Place in History* (1922) Dr. De Lacy O'Leary describes Mohammedanism as "the most romantic history of culture drift which is known to us in detail." He traces the transmission of a particular type of Hellenic culture through the Syrian Church, the Zoroastrians of Persia, and the pagans of Harran to the Islamic community. It left a very distinct and enduring impression on Muslim theology and on popular beliefs. After a chequered career in the East it passed over to the Western Muslim community in Spain, where it had a very specialised development, which finally made a deeper impression on Christian and Jewish thought than on that of the Muslims themselves. It attained its final evolution in Northeast Italy, where, by virtue of its reputation as an anti-ecclesiastical influence, it prepared the way for the Renaissance. But when the Renaissance began to bear fruit the Church pinned its faith to Aristotle, Ptolemy and Galen, so that it became almost heresy to question their teaching. Thus the Christian Church, like the Buddhist religion, became a vehicle for the diffusion of Hellenism. Islam was an even more active agent in rescuing and spreading the learning of the Greeks.

Dr. O'Leary says with reference to this: "The real work of Islam in art and architecture lay in connecting the various portions of the Muslim world in one common life, so that Syria, Persia, Iraq, North Africa and Spain shared the same influences, which were ultimately Greek or Graeco-Persian, the Indian element of quite secondary importance, entering directly through Persia." As Professor Nicholson expresses the idea in his *Mystics of Islam* (1914): "Muslim theology, philosophy, and science put forth their first luxurious shoots in a soil which was saturated with Hellenic culture."

Intimately interwoven as Buddhism, Christianity and Islam were with Greek thought, which they helped to diffuse in their varied fashions throughout the world, the Arabic-speaking and Christian peoples took a strangely contrasted, or perhaps complementary, part in the further development of Hellenism.

The Greeks attained their distinctive influence in the world because the Ionians "liberated thought from the bondage of religious ritual" (Fisher). But a world of people habituated by thirty centuries of tradition to the soothing influence of religious ritual and seductive superstition was not likely to permit a small band of men of clear vision to dominate the world. It was not long before the mystics and the ritualists began to press in upon the rational thinkers and try to reintroduce their nostrums. The same thing happened in India where the philosophy and the way of life introduced by Buddha soon became a religion and assimilated the very extravagances against which the Enlightened One had revolted.

At its birth Christianity had at its service the wealth of Hellenic thought. But in the course of the first four or five centuries it concentrated its hopes and aspirations with increasing intensity and absorption on the prospect of a future life. Hence Christians despised learning and the cultivation of intellect. As the inevitable result of the neglect of reason they fell into superstition, and for the five centuries or more before the revival of learning gave a lamentable demonstration of the degradation of mind and morals which such neglect entails.

During the centuries in which the Greek leaven had ceased to work in Europe and, in the hands of the followers of Buddha and Siva, was inspiring marvellous achievements in Eastern Asia and America, it was being carefully treasured by the Arabic-speaking peoples, who thus became the instrument of saving Europe from the fate its own foolishness had almost precipitated—the relapse into almost complete barbarism. But the Arabic-speaking people did more than merely keep the torch of culture burning for Europe eventually to seize and make the bright illumination of modern civilisation. They handed to the modern world not only the heritage of Greece, but also the knowledge that for the cultivation of true science the laborious collection of evidence was at least as essential as theories of knowledge. True science was in fact created in Europe by the combination of the two legacies. The accumulation of facts is obviously essential before theories in attempted interpretation of them can be truly formulated and tested.

European civilisation is the achievement of men who have woven the heritage of the world into a new fabric.

EPILOGUE

It took Man hundreds of thousands of years to realise the vast possibilities conferred upon him by human powers of vision and skill.

When Man began to devise civilisation he became entangled in the meshes of the theory of the State, which he himself had spun. It remained for the Greeks to cut the Gordian knot and restore to human reason the freedom it had lost.

Ever since then Human History has been a conflict between the rationalism of Hellas and the superstition of Egypt.

It depends upon the human population of the world themselves which will win. For thought and courage can decide the issue.

BIBLIOGRAPHICAL NOTE

Instead of attempting to provide an elaborate bibliography, a short list is here provided of references to works which supply evidence to supplement the information and corroborate the arguments of this book.

The first eight references cover the general scope of the whole book. The rest deal with special topics.

The Cambridge Modern History
   Vol. I, The Renaissance, 1902.

The Cambridge Mediaeval History
   Vol. II, The Foundations of the Western Empire, 1913.

The Cambridge Ancient History, 1923 *passim.*

The Legacy of Greece, Oxford, 1921.

J. B. Bury, *The Idea of Progress,* London, 1920.

W. J. Perry, *The Children of the Sun,* 2nd Edition, London, 1926.

G. Elliot Smith, *The Evolution of Man,* 2nd Edition, London, 1927: *The Ancient Egyptians and the Origin of Civilization,* 2nd Edition, London, 1923: *The Migrations of Early Culture.*

W. H. R. Rivers, *Psychology and Ethnology,* London, 1926.

SPECIAL TOPICS

F. W. Knocker, "The Aborigines of Sungei Usong," *Journal of Anthropological Institute,* 1927.

C. G. and B. Seligman, *The Veddas,* London, 1911.

C. Christy, *Big Game and Pygmies,* London, 1924.

L. J. van den Bergh, *On the Trail of the Pygmies,* 1922.

S. S. Dornan, *Pygmies and Bushmen of the Kalahari,* 1925.

P. Schebesta, *Ben den Uzwaldzwergen von Malaya,* 1927.

Charles Hose, *Natural Man,* London, 1926.

These six memoirs are typical of many hundreds of reports on the true character of Primitive Man.

A. M. Hocart, *Kingship*, Oxford, 1927.

Sidney Smith, *Early History of Assyria*, London, 1928.
For evidence relating to the early history of Mesopotamia and its cultural links with Egypt, Syria, Anatolia, Turkestan and India.

Gregory Borovka, *Scythian Art*, London, 1928.
For the connections between Mycenaean culture and the heart of Asia.

V. Gordon Childe, *Dawn of European Civilization*, London, 1928.
For the influence of the Ancient East in Europe.

P. N. Ure, *The Origin of Tyranny*, Cambridge, 1922.
For the influence of coinage in the rebirth of civilisation.

Vincent A. Smith, "Graeco-Roman Influence on the Civilization of Ancient India," *Journal of the Asiatic Society of Bengal*, 1889: *The Early History of India*, 2nd Edition, Oxford, 1902.

Joseph Hell, *Arab Civilization*, Cambridge, 1926.
For the influence of Greek civilisation on the Arabic-speaking peoples and on Islam.

C. Daryll Forde, *Ancient Mariners*, London, 1927.
For the part played by ships of Egyptian design in the worldwide diffusion of culture.

Otto Sittig, "Compulsory Migration in the Pacific Ocean," *Annual Report of the Smithsonian Institution*, 1896.

W. Baldwin Spencer and F. J. Gillen, *The Arunta*, London, 1927.
For evidence of the ritual of mummification-initiation in Australia.

Publication d'hommage offerte au P. W. Schmidt, Vienna, 1928.
For a series of memoirs by different writers to establish the reality of the cultural link between the Old World and the New.

Jessie L. Weston, *From Ritual to Romance*, London, 1920.
For evidence of the Life Quest in the story of the Holy Grail.

Ivor Brown, *First Player*, London, 1927.
On drama as a life-giving ritual.

Havelock Ellis, *The Dance of Life*, London, 1923.

Evelyn Sharp, *Here We Go Round*, London, 1927.
On the origin of dancing.

S. H. Hooke, *New Year's Day,* London, 1927.
The relation of the calendar to life-giving ceremonies.

H. S. Harrison, *Pots and Pans,* London, 1928.
The origin of pottery.

W. J. Perry, *Gods and Men,* London, 1927.

H. J. Massingham, *The Heritage of Man,* London, 1929.

Donald A. Mackenzie, *Myths of Pre-Columbian America,* London, 1923.
Especially Chapter XI on the influence of the belief in milk as an elixir of life, even in America, before cow's milk was used as human food.

Curt Sachs, *Geist und Werden der Musikinstrumente,* Berlin, 1929.

J. Kunst en C. J. A. Kunst-v. Wely, *De Toonkunst van Bali,* Batavia, 1925.
For the evidence of musical instruments and musical scales for the diffusion of culture from the Ancient East to Eastern Asia, Oceania and America.

INDEX